VMware ESX and ESXi in the Enterprise

VMware ESX and ESXi in the Enterprise

Planning Deployment of Virtualization Servers

Edward L. Haletky

PRENTICE
HALL

Upper Saddle River, NJ • Boston • Indianapolis • San Francisco
New York • Toronto • Montreal • London • Munich • Paris • Madrid
Cape Town • Sydney • Tokyo • Singapore • Mexico City

Many of the designations used by manufacturers and sellers to distinguish their products are claimed as trademarks. Where those designations appear in this book, and the publisher was aware of a trademark claim, the designations have been printed with initial capital letters or in all capitals.

The author and publisher have taken care in the preparation of this book, but make no expressed or implied warranty of any kind and assume no responsibility for errors or omissions. No liability is assumed for incidental or consequential damages in connection with or arising out of the use of the information or programs contained herein.

The publisher offers excellent discounts on this book when ordered in quantity for bulk purchases or special sales, which may include electronic versions and/or custom covers and content particular to your business, training goals, marketing focus, and branding interests. For more information, please contact:

U.S. Corporate and Government Sales
(800) 382-3419
corpsales@pearsontechgroup.com

For sales outside the United States, please contact:

International Sales
international@pearson.com

Visit us on the Web: informit.com/aw

Library of Congress Cataloging-in-Publication Data:

Haletky, Edward.

   Vmware ESX and ESXI in the enterprise : planning deployment of virtualization servers / Edward Haletky. -- 2nd ed.

      p. cm.

   ISBN 978-0-13-705897-6 (pbk. : alk. paper) 1. Virtual computer systems. 2. Virtual computer systems--Security measures. 3. VMware. 4. Operating systems (Computers) I. Title.

   QA76.9.V5H35 2010

   006.8--dc22

                                    2010042916

Pearson Education, Inc.
Rights and Contracts Department
501 Boylston Street, Suite 900
Boston, MA 02116
Fax (617) 671-3447

ISBN-13: 978-0-137-05897-6
ISBN-10: 0-137-05897-7

Text printed in the United States on recycled paper at Edwards Brothers in Ann Arbor, Michigan.

First printing January 2011

Editor-in-Chief
Mark Taub

Executive Editor
Chris Guzikowski

Senior Development Editor
Chris Zahn

Managing Editor
Kristy Hart

Project Editor
Jovana San Nicolas-Shirley

Copy Editor
Barbara Hacha

Indexer
Tim Wright

Proofreaders
Michael Henry
Sheri Cain

Publishing Coordinator
Raina Chrobak

Cover Designer
Chuti Prasertsith

Compositor
Gloria Schurick

To my mother, who always told me to read to my walls.

Contents

Preface

How often have you heard this kind of marketing hype around the use of VMware vSphere 4?

The latest version of ESX does everything for you!

Virtualize Everything!

It is cloud ready!

VMware ESX and ESXi, specifically the latest incarnation, VMware vSphere 4, does offer amazing functionality with virtualization: fault tolerance, dynamic resource load balancing, better virtual machine hardware, virtual networking, and failover. However, you still need to hire a consultant to share the mysteries of choosing hardware, good candidates for virtualization, choosing installation methods, installing, configuring, using, and even migrating machines. It is time for a reference that goes over all this information in simple language and in detail so that readers with different backgrounds can begin to use this extremely powerful tool.

Therefore, this book explains and comments on VMware ESX and ESXi versions 3.5.x and 4.x. I have endeavored to put together a "soup to nuts" description of the best practices for ESX and ESXi that can also be applied in general to the other tools available in the Virtual Infrastructure family inside and outside of VMware. To this end, I use real-world examples wherever possible and do not limit the discussions to only those products developed by VMware, but instead expand the discussion to virtualization tools developed by Quest, Veeam, HyTrust, and other third parties. I have endeavored to present all the methods available to achieve best practices, including the use of graphical and command-line tools.

> **Important Note**
>
> Although VMware has stated that the command-line is disappearing, the commands we will discuss exist in their VMware Management Appliance (vMA), which provides similar functionality of the service console. In essence, most of the command-line tools are still useful and are generally necessary when you have to debug an ESX or ESXi host. Required knowledge of these tools does not disappear with the service console.

As you read, keep in mind the big picture that virtualization provides: better utilization of hardware and resource sharing. In many ways, virtualization takes us back to the days of yore when developers had to do more with a lot less than we have available now. Remember the Commodore 64 and its predecessors, where we thought 64KB of memory was huge? Now we are back in a realm where we have to make do with fewer resources than perhaps desired. By keeping the big picture in mind, we can make the necessary choices that create a strong and viable virtual environment. Because we are doing more with less, this thought must be in the back of our mind as we move forward; it helps to explain many of the concerns raised within this tome.

As you will discover, I believe that you need to acquire quite a bit of knowledge and make numerous decisions before you even insert a CD-ROM to begin the installation. How these questions are answered will guide the installation, because you need to first understand the capabilities and limitations of the ESX or ESXi environment and the application mix to be placed in the environment. Keeping in mind the big picture and your application mix is a good idea as you read through each chapter of this book. Throughout this book we will refer to ESX as the combination of VMware ESX and VMware ESXi products.

Who Should Read This Book?

This book delves into many aspects of virtualization and is designed for the beginning administrator as well as the advanced administrator.

How Is This Book Organized?

Here is a listing, in brief, of what each chapter brings to the table.

Chapter 1: System Considerations

By endeavoring to bring you "soup to nuts" coverage, we start at the beginning of all projects: the requirements. These requirements will quickly move into discussions of hardware and capabilities of hardware required by ESX, as is often the case when I talk to customers. This section is critical, because understanding your hardware limitations and capabilities will point you in a direction that you can take to design your virtual datacenter and infrastructure. As a simple example, consider whether you will need to run 23 or 123 virtual machines on a set of blades. Understanding hardware capabilities will let you pick and choose the appropriate blades for your use and how many blades should make up the set. In addition, understanding your storage and virtual machine (VM) requirements can lead you down different paths for management, configuration, and installation. Checklists that lead to each chapter come out of this discussion. In particular, look for discussions on cache capabilities, the best practice for networking, mutual exclusiveness when dealing with storage area networks (SANs), hardware requirements for backup and disaster recovery, and a checklist when comparing hardware. This chapter is a good place to start when you need to find out where else in the book to go look for concept coverage.

Chapter 2: Version Comparison

Before we proceed down the installation paths and into further discussion, best practices, and explorations into ESX, we need to discuss the differences between ESX version 3.5.x and ESX version 4.x. This chapter opens with a broad stroke of the brush and clearly states that they *are* different. Okay, everyone knows that, but the chapter then delves into the major and minor differences that are highlighted in further chapters of the book. This chapter creates another guide to the book similar to the hardware guide that will lead you down different paths as you review the differences. The chapter covers hypervisor, driver, installation, VM, licensing, and management differences. After these are clearly laid out and explained, the details are left to the individual chapters that follow. Why is this not before the hardware chapter? Because hardware may not change, but the software running on it has, with a possible upgrade to ESX or ESXi 4, so this chapter treats the hardware as relatively static when compared to the major differences between ESX/ESXi 4 and ESX/ESXi 3.5.

Chapter 3: Installation

After delving into hardware considerations and ESX version differences, we head down the installation path, but before this happens, another checklist helps us to best plan the installation. Just doing an install will get ESX running for perhaps a test environment, but the best practices will fall out from planning your installation. You would not take off in a plane without running down the preflight checklist. ESX is very similar, and it is easy to get into trouble. For example, I had one customer who decided on an installation without first understanding the functionality required for clustering VMs together. This need to cluster the machines led to a major change and resulted in the reinstallation of all ESX servers in many locations. A little planning would have alleviated all the rework. The goal is to make the readers aware of these gotchas before they bite. After a review of planning, the chapter moves on to various installations of ESX and ESXi with a discussion on where paths diverge and why they would. For example, installing boot from SAN is quite different from a simple installation, at least in the setup, and because of this there is a discussion of the setup of the hardware prior to installation for each installation path. When the installations are completed, there are post-configuration and special considerations when using different SANs or multiple SANs. Limitations on VMFS with respect to sizing a LUN, spanning a LUN, and even the choice of a standard disk size could be a major concern. This chapter even delves into possible vendor and Linux software that could be added after ESX is fully installed. Also, this chapter suggests noting the divergent paths so that you can better install and configure ESX. We even discuss any additional software requirements for your virtual environment.

This chapter is about planning your installation, providing the 20 or so steps required for installation, with only one of these steps being the actual installation procedure. There is more to planning your installation than the actual installation process.

Chapter 4: Auditing and Monitoring

Because the preceding chapter discussed additional software, it is now time to discuss even more software to install that aids in the auditing and monitoring of ESX. There is nothing like having to read through several thousands of lines of errors just to determine when a problem started. Using good monitoring tools will simplify this task and even enable better software support. That is indeed a bonus! Yet knowing when a problem occurred is only part of monitoring and auditing; you also need to know who did the deed and where they did it, and hopefully why. This leads to auditing. More and more government intervention (Sarbanes-Oxley) requires better auditing of what is happening and when. This chapter launches into automating this as much as possible. Why would I need to sit and read log files when the simple application can e-mail me when there is a problem? How do I get these tools to page me or even self-repair? I suggest you take special note of how these concepts, tools, and implementations fit with your overall auditing and monitoring requirements.

Chapter 5: Storage with ESX

There are many issues dealing with storage within ESX. Some are simple, such as "Is my storage device supported?" and "Why not?" Others are more complex, such as "Will this storage device, switch, or Fibre Channel host bus adapter provide the functionality and performance I desire?" Because SAN and NAS devices are generally required to share VMs between ESX hosts, we discuss them in depth. This chapter lets you in on the not-so-good and the good things about each SAN and NAS, as well as the best practices for use, support, and configuration. With storage devices, there is good, bad, and the downright ugly. For example, if you do not have the proper firmware version on some storage devices, things can get ugly very quickly! Although the chapter does not discuss the configuration of your SAN or NAS for use outside of ESX, it does discuss presentation in general terms and how to get the most out of hardware and, to a certain extent, software multipath capabilities. This chapter suggests you pay close attention to how SAN and NAS devices interoperate with ESX. We will also look at some real-world customer issues with storage, such as growing virtual machine file systems, changing storage settings for best performance, load balancing, aggregation, and failover.

Chapter 6: Effects on Operations

Before proceeding to the other aspects of ESX, including the creation of a VM, it is important to review some operational constraints associated with the management of ESX and the running of VMs. Operation issues directly affect VMs. These issues are as basic as maintaining lists of IPs and netmasks, when to schedule services to run through the complexities imposed when using remote storage devices, and its impact on how and when certain virtualization tasks can take place.

Chapter 7: Networking

This chapter discusses the networking possibilities within ESX and the requirements placed on the external environment if any. A good example is mentioned under the hardware discussion, where we discuss hardware redundancy with respect to networking. In ESX terms, this discussion is all about network interface card (NIC) teaming, or in more general terms, the bonding of multiple NICs into one bigger pipe for the purpose of increasing bandwidth and failover. However, the checklist is not limited to the hardware but also includes the application of best practices for the creation of various virtual switches (vSwitches) within ESX, such as the Distributed Virtual Switch, the standard virtual switch, and the Cisco Nexus 1000V. In addition we will look at best practices for what network interfaces are virtualized, and when to use one over the other. The flexibility of networking inside ESX implies that the system and network administrators also have to be flexible, because the best practices dictated by a network switch company may lead to major performance problems when applied to ESX. The possible exception is the usage of the Cisco 1000V virtual switch. Out of this chapter comes a list of changes that may need to be applied to the networking infrastructure, with the necessary data to back up these practices so that discussions with network administrators do not lead toward one-sided conversations. Using real-world examples, this chapter runs through a series of procedures that can be applied to common problems that occur when networking within ESX.

This chapter also outlines the latest thoughts on virtual network security and concepts that include converged network adapters, other higher bandwidth solutions, and their use within the virtual environment. As such, we deep dive into the virtual networking stack within an ESX host.

Chapters 8 and 9: Configuring ESX from a Host Connection and Configuring ESX from a Virtual Center or Host

These chapters tie it all together; we have installed, configured, and attached storage to ESX. Now what? We need to manage ESX. There are five ways to manage ESX: the use of the web-based webAccess; the use of vCenter (VC), with its .NET client; the use of the remote CLI, which is mostly a collection of VI SDK applications; the use of the VI SDK; and the use of the command-line interface (CLI). These chapters delve into configuration and use of these interfaces. Out of these chapters will come tools that can be used as part of a scripted installation of ESX.

Chapter 10: Virtual Machines

This chapter goes into the creation, modification, and management of your virtual machines. In essence, the chapter discusses everything you need to know before you start installing VMs, specifically what makes up a VM. Then it is possible to launch into installation of VMs using all the standard interfaces. We install Windows, Linux, and NetWare VMs, pointing out where things diverge on the creation of a VM and what has to be done post install. This chapter looks at specific solutions to VM problems posed to me by customers: the use of eDirectory, private labs, firewalls, clusters, growing Virtual Machine Disks, and other customer issues. This chapter is an opportunity to see how VMs are created and how VMs differ from one another and why. Also, the solutions shown are those from real-world customers; they should guide you down your installation paths.

Chapter 11: Dynamic Resource Load Balancing

With vSphere, Dynamic Resource Load Balancing (DRLB) is very close to being here now. As we have seen in Chapter 10, virtual machines now contain capabilities to hot add/remove memory and CPUs, as well as the capability to affect the performance of egress and ingress network and storage traffic. ESX v4.1 introduces even newer concepts of Storage IO Control and Network IO Control. Tie these new functions with Dynamic Resource Scheduling, Fault-Tolerance, and Resource management and we now have a working model for DRLB that is more than just Dynamic Resource Scheduling. This chapter shows you the best practices for the application of all the ESX clustering techniques technologies and how they enhance your virtual environment. We also discuss how to apply alarms to various monitoring tools to give you a heads up when something needs to happen either by hand or has happened dynamically. I suggest paying close attention to the makeup of DLRB to understand the limitations of all the tools.

Chapter 12: Disaster Recovery, Business Continuity, and Backup

A subset of DLRB can apply to Disaster Recovery (DR). DR is a huge subject, so it is limited to just ESX and its environment that lends itself well to redundancy, and in so doing aids in DR planning. But, before you plan, you need to understand the limitations of the technology and tools. DR planning on ESX is not more difficult than a plan for a single physical machine. The use of a VM actually makes things easier if the VM is set up properly. A key component of DR is the making of safe, secure, and proper backups of the VMs and system. What to back up and when is a critical concern that fits into your current backup directives, which may not apply directly to ESX and which could be made faster. The chapter presents several real-world examples around backup and DR, including the use of redundant systems, how this is affected by ESX and VM clusters, the use of locally attached tape, the use of network storage, and some helpful scripts to make it all work. In addition, this chapter discusses some third-party tools to make your backup and restoration tasks simpler. The key to DR is a good plan, and the checklist in this chapter will aid in developing a plan that encompasses ESX and can be applied to all the vSphere and virtual infrastructure products. Some solutions require more hardware (spare disks, perhaps other SANs), more software (Veeam Backup, Quest's vRanger, Power Management, and so on).

Epilogue: The Future of the Virtual Environment

After all this, the book concludes with a discussion of the future of virtualization.

References

This element suggests possible further reading.

Reading

Please sit down in your favorite comfy chair, with a cup of your favorite hot drink, and prepare to enjoy the chapters in this book. Read it from cover to cover, or use as it a reference. The best practices of ESX sprinkled throughout the book will entice and enlighten, and spark further conversation and possibly well-considered changes to your current environments.

Acknowledgments

I would like to acknowledge my reviewers: Pat and Ken; they provided great feedback. I would like to also thank Bob, once a manager, who was the person who started me on this journey by asking one day, "Have you ever heard of this VMware stuff?" I had. I would also like to acknowledge my editors for putting up with my writing style.

This book is the result of many a discussion I had with customers and those within the virtualization community who have given me a technical home within the ever changing world of virtualization.

This edition of the book would not have happened without the support of my wife and family, who understood my need to work long hours writing.

Thank you one and all.

About the Author

Edward L. Haletky is the author of *VMware vSphere and Virtual Infrastructure Security: Securing the Virtual Environment* as well as the first edition of this book, *VMware ESX Server in the Enterprise: Planning and Securing Virtualization Servers*. Edward owns AstroArch Consulting, Inc., providing virtualization, security, network consulting, and development, and The Virtualization Practice, where he is also an analyst. Edward is the moderator and host of the Virtualization Security Podcast, as well as a guru and moderator for the VMware Communities Forums, providing answers to security and configuration questions. Edward is working on new books on virtualization.

Chapter 1

System Considerations

At VMworld 2009 in San Francisco, VMware presented to the world the VMworld Data Center (see Figure 1.1). There existed within this conference data center close to 40,000 virtual machines (VMs) running within 512 Cisco Unified Computing System (UCS) blades within 64 USC chassis. Included in this data center were eight racks of disks, as well as several racks of HP blades and Dell 1U servers, all connected to a Cisco Nexus 7000 switch. Granted, this design was clearly to show off UCS, but it showed that with only 32 racks of servers that it is possible to run up to 40,000 VMs.

Figure 1.1 *Where the Virtual Infrastructure touches the physical world*

The massive example at VMworld 2009 showed us all what is possible, but how do you get there? The first consideration is the design and architecture of the VMware vSphere™ environment. This depends on quite a few things, ranging from the types of applications and operating systems to virtualize, to how many physical machines are desired to virtualize, to determining on what hardware to place the virtual environments. Quite quickly, any discussion about the virtual infrastructure soon evolves to a discussion of the hardware to use in the environment. Experience shows that before designing a virtual datacenter, it's important to understand what makes a good virtual machine host and the limitations of current hardware platforms. In this chapter, customer examples illustrate various architectures based on limitations and desired results. These examples are not exhaustive, just a good introduction to understanding the impact of various hardware choices on the design of the virtual infrastructure. An understanding of potential hardware use will increase the chance of virtualization success. The architecture potentially derived from this understanding will benefit not just a single VMware vSphere™ ESX host, but also the tens to thousands that may be deployed throughout a single or multiple datacenters. Therefore, the goal here is to develop a basis for enterprisewide VMware vSphere™ ESX host deployment. The first step is to understand the hardware involved.

For example, a customer wanted a 40:1 compression ratio for virtualization of their physical machines. However, they also had networking goals to compress their network requirements. At the same time, the customer was limited by what hardware they could use. Going just by the hardware specifications and the limits within VMware vSphere™, the customer's hardware could do what was required, so the customer proceeded down that path. However, what the specification and limits state is not necessarily the best practice for VMware vSphere™, which led to quite a bit of hardship as the customer worked through the issues with its chosen environment. The customer could have alleviated certain hardships early on with a better understanding of the impact of VMware vSphere™ on the various pieces of hardware and that hardware's impact on VMware vSphere™ ESX v4 (ESXi v4) or VMware Virtual Infrastructure ESX v3 (ESXi v3). (Whereas most, if not all, of the diagrams and notes use Hewlett-Packard hardware, these are just examples; similar hardware is available from Dell, IBM, Sun, Cisco, and many other vendors.)

Basic Hardware Considerations

An understanding of basic hardware aspects and their impact on ESX v4 can greatly increase your chances of virtualization success. To begin, let's look at the components that make up modern systems.

When designing for the enterprise, one of the key considerations is the processor to use: specifically the type, cache available, and memory configurations. All these factors affect how ESX works in major ways. The wrong choices may make the system seem sluggish and will reduce the number of virtual machines that can run, so it is best to pay close attention to the processor and system architecture when designing the virtual environment.

Before picking any hardware, always refer to the VMware Hardware Compatibility Lists (HCLs), which you can find as a searchable database from which you can export PDFs for your specific hardware. This is located at www. vmware.com/support/pubs/vi_pubs.html.

> **Best Practice**
>
> Never purchase or reuse hardware unless you have first verified it exists on the VMware Hardware Compatibility Lists.

Although it is always possible to try to use commodity hardware that is not within the VMware hardware compatibility database, this could lead to a critical system that may not be in a supportable form. VMware support will do the best it can, but may end up pointing to the HCL and providing only advisory support and no real troubleshooting. To ensure this is never an issue, it is best to purchase only equipment VMware has blessed via the HCL database. Some claim that commodity hardware is fine for a lab or test environment; however, I am a firm believer that the best way to test something is 12 inches to 1 foot; in other words, use exactly what you have in production and not something you do not have—otherwise, your test could be faulty. Therefore, always stick to the hardware listed within the HCL.

Before we look at all the components of modern systems, we need to examine the current features of the ESX or ESXi systems. Without an understanding of these features at a high level, you will not be able to properly understand the impact the hardware has on the features and the impact the features have on choosing hardware.

Feature Considerations

Several features that constitute VMware vSphere have an impact on the hardware you will use. In later chapters, we will look at these in detail, but they are mentioned here so you have some basis for understanding the rest of the discussions within this chapter.

High Availability (HA)

VMware HA detects when a host or individual VM fails. Failed individual VMs are restarted on the same host. Yet if a host fails, VMware HA will by default boot the failed host's VMs on another running host. This is the most common use of a VMware Cluster, and it protects against unexpected node failures. No major hardware considerations exist for the use of HA, except that there should be enough CPU and memory to start the virtual machines. Finally, to have network connectivity, there needs to be the proper number of portgroups with the appropriate labels.

vMotion

vMotion enables the movement of a running VM from host to host by using a specialized network connection. vMotion creates a second running VM on the target host, hooks this VM up to the existing disks, and finally momentarily freezes a VM while it copies the memory and register footprint of the VM from host to host. Afterward, the VM on the old host is shut down cleanly, and the new one will start where the newly copied registers say to start. This often requires that the CPUs between hosts be of the same family at the very least.

Storage vMotion

Storage vMotion enables the movement of a running VM from datastore to datastore that is accessible via the VMware vSphere management appliance (ESXi) or service console (ESX). The datastore can be any NFS Server or local disk, disk array, remote Fibre Channel SAN, iSCSI Server, or remote disk array employing a SAN-style controller on which there exists the virtual machine file system (VMFS) developed by VMware.

Dynamic Resource Scheduling (DRS)

VMware DRS is another part of a VMware Cluster that will alleviate CPU and memory contention on your hosts by automatically vMotioning VMs between nodes within a cluster. If there is contention for CPU and memory resources on one node, any VM can automatically be moved to another underutilized node using vMotion. This often requires that the CPUs between hosts be of the same family at the very least.

Distributed Power Management (DPM)

VMware DPM will enable nodes within a VMware Cluster to evacuate their VMs (using vMotion) to other hosts and power down the evacuated host during off hours. Then during peak hours, the standby hosts can be powered on and again become active members of the VMware cluster when they are needed. DPM requires Wake on LAN (WoL) or IMPI functionality on the VMware ESX service console pNIC (VMware ESXi management pNIC) in order to be used; or it requires the use of IPMI or an HP ILO device within the host. WoL is the least desirable method to implement DPM. DPM is a feature of DRS.

Enhanced vMotion Capability (EVC)

VMware EVC ties into the Intel FlexMigration and AMD-V Extended Migration capabilities to present to the VMware Cluster members a common CPU feature set. Each CPU in use on a system contains a set of enhanced features; Intel-VT is one of these. In addition, there are instructions available to one chipset that may be interpreted differently on another chipset. For vMotion to work, these feature sets must match. To do this, there is a per VM set of CPU masks that can be set to match up feature sets between disparate CPUs and chipsets. EVC does this at the host level, instead of the per VM level. Unfortunately, EVC will work only between Intel CPUs that support Intel Flex Migration or between

AMD CPUs that support Extended Migration. You cannot use EVC to move VMs between the AMD and Intel families of processors. EVC requires either the No eXecute (NX) or eXecute Disable (XD) flags to be set within the CPU, as well as Intel-VT or AMD RVI to be enabled.

Virtual SMP (vSMP)
VMware vSMP enables a VM to have more than one virtual CPU so as to make it possible to run Symmetric Multiprocessing (SMP) applications that are either threaded or have many processes (if the OS involved supports SMP).

Fault Tolerance (FT)
VMware Fault Tolerance creates a shadow copy of a VM in which the virtual CPUs are kept in lockstep with the master CPU employing the VMware vLock-Step functionality. VMware FT depends on the VM residing on storage that VMware ESX or ESXi hosts can access, as well as other restrictions on the type and components of the VM (for example, there is only support for one vCPU VM). When FT is in use, vMotion is not available.

Multipath Plug-In (MPP)
The VMware Multipath Plug-in enables a third-party storage company such as EMC, HP, Hitachi, and the like to add their own multipath driver into the VMware hypervisor kernel.

VMDirectPath
VMDirectPath bypasses the hypervisor and connects a VM directly to a physical NIC card, not a specific port on a physical NIC card. This implies that VMDirectPath takes ownership of an entire PCIe or mezzanine adapter regardless of port count.

Virtual Distributed Switch (vDS)
The VMware vDS provides a mechanism to manage virtual switches across all VMware vSphere hosts. vDS switches also have the capability to set up private VLANs using their built-in dvFilter capability. This is a limited capability port security mechanism. The implementation of vDS enabled the capability to add in third-party virtual switches, such as the Cisco Nexus 1000V. The enabling technology does not require the vDS to use third-party virtual switches.

Host Profiles
Host Profiles provide a single way to maintain a common profile or configuration across all VMware vSphere hosts within the virtual environment. In the case of the VMworld 2009 conference data center, host profiles enable one configuration to be used across all 512 UCS blades within the VMworld 2009 Data

Center. Host Profiles eliminate small spelling differences that could cause networking and other items to not work properly across all hosts.

Storage IO Control

Storage IO Control allows for storage QoS on block level storage request exiting the host using cluster-wide storage latency values.

Network IO Control

Network IO Control allows for QoS on egress from the ESX host instead of on entry to the VMs.

Load-Based Teaming

When VMs boot, they are associated with a physical NIC attached to a vSwitch. Load-Based Teaming allows for this association to be modified based on network latency.

Processor Considerations

Processor family, which is not a huge consideration in the scheme of things, is a consideration when picking multiple machines for the enterprise because the different types of processor architectures impact the availability of vSphere features. Specifically, mismatched processor types will prevent the use of vMotion DRS, EVC, and Fault Tolerance (FT). If everything works appropriately when vMotion is used or FT enabled, the VM does not notice anything but a slight hiccup that can be absorbed with no issues. However, because vMotion and FT copy the register and memory footprint from host to host, the processor architecture and chipset in use need to match. It is not possible without proper masking of processor features to vMotion from a Xeon to an AMD processor or from a dual-core processor to a single-core processor, but it is possible to go from a single-core to a dual-core processor. Nor is it possible to enable FT between Xeon and AMD processors for the same reason. If the VM to be moved is a 64-bit VM, the processors must match exactly because no method is available to mask processor features. Therefore, the processor architecture and chipset (or the instruction set) are extremely important, and because this can change from generation to generation of the machines, it is best to introduce two machines into the virtual enterprise at the same time to ensure that vMotion and FT actually work. When introducing new hardware into the mix of ESX hosts, test to confirm that vMotion and FT will work. VMware EVC has gone a long way to alleviate much of the needs of vMotion so that exact processor matches may no longer be required, but testing is still the best practice going forward.

VMware FT, however, adds a new monkey wrench into the selection of processors for each virtualization host because there is a strict limitation on which processors can be used with FT, and in general all machines should share the same processors and chipsets across all participating hosts. The availability of VMware FT can be determined by using the VMware SiteSurvey tool (www. vmware.com/download/shared_utilities.html). VMware SiteSurvey connects to your VMware vCenter Server and generates a report based on all nodes registered within a specific cluster. The SiteSurvey Tool, however, could give errors and not work if the build levels on your hosts within your cluster are different. In that case, use the VMware CPU Host Info Tool from www.run-virtual.com to retrieve the same information, as shown in Figure 1.2. Within this tool, the important features are FT Support, VT Enabled, VT Capable, and NX/XD status. All these should have an X in them. If they do not exist, you need to refer to VMware technical resources on Fault Tolerance (www.vmware.com/resources/ techresources/1094). The best practices refer to all hosts within a given VMware cluster.

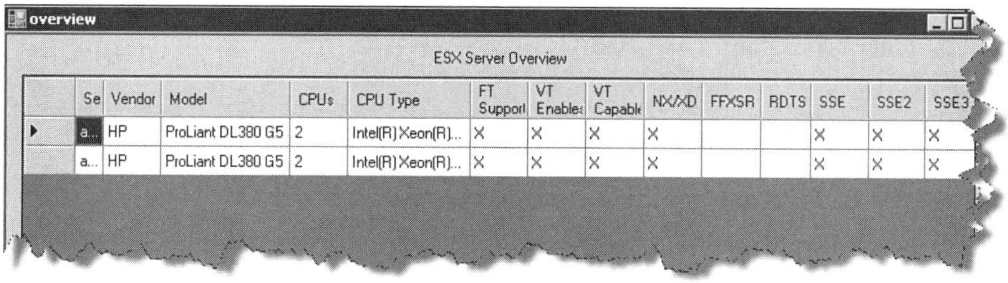

Figure 1.2 *Output of Run-Virtual's CPU Host Info tool*

Best Practice

Standardize on a single processor and chipset architecture. If this is not possible because of the age of existing machines, test to ensure vMotion still works, or introduce hosts in pairs to guarantee successful vMotion and FT. Different firmware revisions can also affect vMotion and FT functionality.

Ensure that all processors support VMware FT capability.

Ensure that all the processor speed or stepping parameters in a system match, too.

Note that many companies support mismatched processor speeds or stepping in a system. ESX would really rather have all the processors at the same speed and stepping. In the case where the stepping for a processor is different, each vendor provides different instructions for processor placement. For example,

Hewlett-Packard (HP) requires that the slowest processor be in the first processor slot and all the others in any remaining slots. To alleviate any type of issue, it is a best practice that the processor speeds or stepping match within the system.

Before proceeding to the next phase, a brief comment on eight-core (8C), six-core (6C), quad-core (QC), dual-core (DC), and single-core (SC) processors is warranted. ESX Server does not differentiate in its licensing scheme between 6C, QC, DC, and SC processors, so the difference between them becomes a matter of cost versus performance gain of the processors. However, with 8C and above you may need to change your ESX license level. The 8C processor will handle more VMs than a 6C, which can handle more VMs than a QC, which can handle more than a DC, which can handle more than an SC processor. If performance is the issue, 6C or QC is the way to go. Nevertheless, for now, the choice is a balance of cost versus performance. It is not recommended that any DC or SC processors be used for virtualization. These CPUs do not support the density of VMs required by today's datacenters. Granted, if that is all you have, it is still better than nothing. Even SMBs should stick to using quad-core CPUs if running more than two VMs.

Cache Considerations

Like matching processor architectures and chipsets, it is also important to match the L2 Cache between multiple hosts if you are going to use FT. A mismatch will not prevent vMotion from working. However, L2 Cache is most likely to be more important when it comes to performance because it controls how often main memory is accessed. The larger the L2 Cache, the better ESX host will run. Consider Figure 1.3 in terms of VMs being a complete process and the access path of memory. Although ESX tries to limit memory usage as much as possible through content-based page sharing and other techniques discussed later, even so the amount of L2 Cache plays a significant part in how VMs perform.

As more VMs are added to a host of similar operating system (OS) type and version, ESX will start to share memory pages between VMs; this is referred to as Transparent Page Sharing (TPS) or Content Based Page Sharing (CBPS). During idle moments, ESX will collapse identical 4KB (but not 8KB) pages of memory (as determined by a hash lookup then a bit by bit comparison) and leave pointers to original memory location within each VM's memory image. This method of overcommitting memory does not have any special processor requirements; during a vMotion or FT the VM has no idea this is taking place because it happens outside the VM and does not impact the guest OS directly. Let's look at Figure 1.3 again. When a processor needs to ask the system for memory, it first goes to the L1 Cache (up to a megabyte usually) and sees whether the memory region requested is already on the processor die. This action is extremely fast, and although different for most processors, we can assume it is an instruction or two (measured in nanoseconds). However, if the memory region is not in the L1 Cache, the next step is to go to the L2 Cache. L2 Cache is generally off the die, over an extremely fast channel (light arrow) usually running at processor speeds. Even so, accessing L2 Cache takes more time and instructions than L1 Cache access. If the memory region you desire is not in L2 Cache, it is possibly in L3 Cache (if one exists, dotted arrow) or in main memory (dashed arrow). L3 Cache or main memory takes an order of magnitude above processor speeds to access. Usually, a cache line is copied from main memory, which is the desired memory region and some of the adjacent data, to speed up future memory access. When we are dealing with nonuniform memory access (NUMA) architecture, which is the case with Intel Nahelem and AMD processors, there is yet another step to memory access. The memory necessary could be sitting on a processor board elsewhere in the system. The farther away it is, the slower the access time (darker lines), and this access over the CPU interconnect will add another order of magnitude to the memory access time.

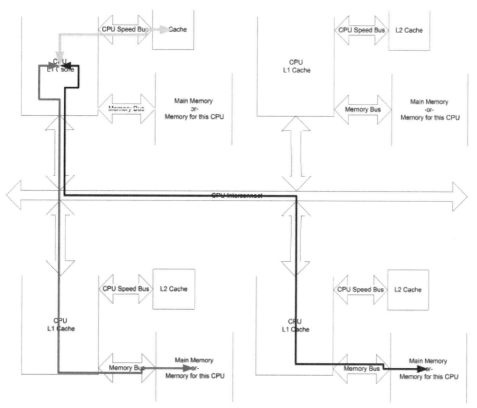

Figure 1.3 *Memory access paths*

What does this mean in real times? Assuming that we are using a 3.06GHz processor without L3 Cache, the times could be as follows:

- L1 Cache, one cycle (~0.33ns).

- L2 Cache, two cycles, the first one to get a cache miss from L1 Cache and another to access L2 Cache (~0.66ns), which runs at CPU speeds (light arrow).

- Main memory is running at 333MHz, which is an order of magnitude slower than L2 Cache (~3.0ns access time) (dashed arrow).

- Access to main memory on another processor board (NUMA) is an order of magnitude slower than accessing main memory on the same processor board (~30–45ns access time, depending on distance) (darker lines).

Now let's take the same calculation using L3 Cache:

- L1 Cache, one cycle (~0.33ns).

- L2 Cache, two cycles, the first one to get a cache miss from L1 Cache and another to access L2 Cache (~0.66ns), which runs at CPU speeds (light arrow).

- L3 Cache, two cycles, the first one to get a cache miss from L2 Cache and another to access L3 Cache (~0.66ns), which runs at CPU speeds (light arrow).

- Main memory is running at 333MHz, which is an order of magnitude slower than L3 Cache (~3.0ns access time) (dashed arrow).

- Access to main memory on another processor board (NUMA) is an order of magnitude slower than accessing main memory on the same processor board (~30–45ns access time, depending on distance) (darker lines).

This implies that large L2 and L3 Cache sizes will benefit the system more than small L2 and L3 Cache sizes: the larger the better. If the processor has access to larger chunks of contiguous memory, because the memory to be swapped in will be on the larger size, this will benefit the performance of the VMs. This discussion does not state that NUMA-based architectures are inherently slower than regular-style architectures, because most NUMA-based architectures running ESX host do not need to go out to other processor boards very often to gain access to memory. However, when using VMs making use of vSMP, it is possible that one CPU could be on an entirely different processor board within a NUMA architecture, and this could cause serious performance issues depending on whether quite a bit of data is being shared between the multiple threads and processes within the application. We will discuss this more in Chapter 11, "Dynamic Resource Load Balancing." One solution to this problem is to use CPU affinity settings to ensure that the vCPUs run on the same processor board. The other is to limit the number of vCPUs to what will fit within a single processor. In other words, for quad-core processors, you would use at most four vCPUs per VM.

Best Practice

Invest in the largest amount of L2 and L3 Cache available for your chosen architecture.

If using NUMA architectures, ensure that you do not use more vCPUs than there are cores per processor.

Memory Considerations

After L2 and L3 Cache comes the speed of the memory, as the preceding bulleted list suggests. Higher-speed memory is suggested, and lots of it! The amount of memory and the number of processors govern how many VMs can run simultaneously without overcommitting this vital resource. Obviously, there are trade-offs in the number of VMs and how you populate memory, but generally the best practice is high speed and a high quantity. Consider that the maximum number of vCPUs per core is 20 when using vSphere™. On a 4-QC processor box, that could be 320 single vCPU VMs. If each of these VMs is 1GB, we need 339GB of memory to run the VMs. Why 339GB? Because 339GB gives both the service console (SC) and the hypervisor up to 2GB of memory to run the VMs and accounts for the ~55MBs per GB of memory management overhead. Because 339GB of memory is a weird number for most computers these days, we would need to overcommit memory. When we start overcommitting memory in this way, the performance of ESX can degrade. In this case, it might be better to move to 348GB of memory instead. However, that same box with 8C processors can, theoretically, run up to 640 VMs, which implies that we take the VM load to the logical conclusion, and we are once more overcommitting memory.

Important Note

vSphere™ can only run 320 VMs per host regardless of theoretical limits and only supports 512 vCPUs per host.

Even so, 20 VMs per processor is a theoretical limit, and it's hard to achieve. (It is not possible to run VMs with more vCPUs than available physical cores, but there is still a theoretical limit of 20 vCPUs per core.) Although 20 is the theoretical limit, 512 vCPUs is the maximum allowed per host, which implies that 16 vCPUs per core on an 8C four-processor box is not unreasonable. Remember that the vmkernel and SC (management appliance within ESXi) also use memory and need to be considered as part of any memory analysis.

Note that VMware ESX hosts have quite a few features to enable the amount of memory overcommit that will occur. The primary feature is Transparent Page Sharing or Content Based Page Sharing (CBPS). This mechanism collapses identical pages of memory used by any number of VMs down to just one memory page as an idle time process. If your ESX host runs VMs that use the same operating system and patch level, the gain from CBPS can be quite large—large enough to run at least one or maybe even two more VMs. The other prominent memory overcommit prevention tool is the virtual machine balloon driver. We will discuss both of these further in Chapter 11.

Best Practice

High-speed memory and lots of it! However, be aware of the possible trade-offs involved in choosing the highest-speed memory. More VMs may necessitate the use of slightly slower memory, depending on server manufacturer.

What is the recommended memory configuration? The proper choice for a size of a system depends on a balancing act of the four major elements—CPU, memory, disk, and network—of a virtualization host. This subject is covered when we cover VMs in detail, because it really pertains to this question; but the strong recommendation is to put in the maximum memory the hardware will support that is not above the memory limit set by ESX as one of the ways the system overcommits memory is to swap to disk, which can be helped by moving to SSD style disks, but this is still 100 times slower than memory. When swapping occurs, the entire system's performance will be impacted. However, redundancy needs to be considered with any implementation of ESX; it is therefore beneficial to cut down on the per-machine memory requirements to afford redundant systems. Although we theoretically could run 320 VMs (maximum allowed by VMware vSphere™) on a four-processor 8C box, other aspects of the server come into play that will limit the number of VMs. These aspects are disk and network IO, as well as VM CPU loads. It also depends on the need for local and remote redundancy for disaster recovery and business continuity, which are covered in Chapter 12, "Disaster Recovery, Business Continuity, and Backup."

I/O Card Considerations

The next consideration when selecting your virtualization hosts is which I/O cards are supported. Unlike other operating systems, ESX has a finite list of supported I/O cards. There are limitations on the redundant array of inexpensive drives (RAID) controllers; Small Computer System Interface (SCSI) adapters for external devices including tape libraries; network interface cards (NICs); and Fibre Channel host bus adapters. Although the list changes frequently, it boils down to a few types of supported devices limited by the set of device drivers that are a part of ESX. Table 1.1 covers the devices and the associated drivers.

Table 1.1   *Devices and Drivers*

Device Type	Device Driver Vendor	Device Driver Name	Notes
Network	Broadcom	bnx2	NetXtreme II Gigabit
	Broadcom	bnx2x	NetXtreme II 5771x 10Gigabit
	Broadcom	tg3	
	3Com	3c90x	ESX v3 Only
	Intel	e1000e	PRO/1000
	Intel	e1000	PRO/1000
	Intel	e100	ESX v3 Only
	Intel	igb	Gigabit
	Intel	ixgbe	10 Gigabit PCIe
	Cisco	enic	10G/ESX v4 Only
	Qlogic	nx_nic	10G/ESX v4 Only
	Nvidia	forcedeth	
Fibre Channel	Emulex	lpfc820	Dual/Single ports
	Cisco	fnic	FCoE/ESX v4 Only
	Qlogic	qla2xxx	Dual/Single ports

continues

Table 1.1   *(Continued)*

Device Type	Device Driver Vendor	Device Driver Name	Notes
SCSI/SAS/SATA	Adaptec	aic79xx	Supported for External Devices
	Adaptec	adp94xx	Supported for External Devices
	Adaptec	aic7xxx	ESX v3 Only
	Intel	ata_piix	PATA/SATA
	Silicon Image	sata_sil	SATA
	Promise	sata_promise	SATA TX2/TX4
	ServerWorks	sata_svw	Frodo/Apple K2 SATA
	NVidia	sata_nv	SATA
	Vitesse	sata_vsc	SATA ESX v3 Only
	LSI Logic	megaraid_sas	SAS
	LSI Logic	mptscsi_2xx	ESX v3 Only
	LSI Logic	mptsas	SAS/ESX v4 Only
	LSI Logic	mptspi	LSI53C*/ESX v4 Only
Raid Array	HP	cciss	External SCSI is for Disk Arrays only
	Dell	aacraid	
	Dell	megaraid	
	IBM/Adaptec	ips	
	IBM/Adaptec	aacraid	
	Mylex	DAC960	ESX v3 Only
	LSI	megaraid	
iSCSI	Qlogic	qla4xxx	

If the driver in question supports a device, in most cases it will work in ESX. However, if the device requires a modern device driver, do not expect it to be part of ESX, because ESX by its very nature does not support the most current devices. ESX is designed to be stable, and that often precludes modern devices. For example, not all Serial Advanced Technology Attachment (SATA) devices are a part of ESX, and many drivers are dropped from support when you move to ESX v4, as shown in Table 1.1. Also noted in Table 1.1, various SCSI adapters have limitations. A key limitation is that an Adaptec non-RAID card is required for external tape drives or libraries, whereas any SCSI or RAID card is usable with external disk arrays.

Table 1.1 refers particularly to those devices that the vmkernel can access, and not necessarily the devices that the SC installs. There are quite a few devices for which the SC has a driver, but the host cannot use them. Two examples of this come to mind. The first are NICs (not listed in Table 1.1) that actually have a SC driver; Kingston or old Digital NICs fall into this category. For ESX to run, it needs at a minimum two NICs (yes, it is possible to use one NIC, but this is never a recommendation for production servers) and one supported storage device. One NIC is for the service console (management appliance for ESXi) and the other for the VMs. Although it is possible to share these so that only one NIC is required, VMware does not recommend this except in extreme cases (and it leads to possible performance and security issues). The best practice for ESX is to provide redundancy for everything so that all your VMs stay running even if network or a Fibre Channel path is lost. To do this, there needs to be some considerations around network and Fibre configurations and perhaps more I/O devices.

Best Practice Regarding I/O Cards

If the card you desire to use is *not* on the HCL, do not use it. The HCL is definitive from a support perspective. Although a vendor may produce a card and self-check it, if it is not on the HCL, VMware will not support the configuration.

Best Practice

The best practice is to have redundant NICs for each network trust zone in use for performance, security, and redundancy.

If adding more networks for use by the VMs, either use 802.1q VLAN tagging to run over the existing pair of NICs associated with the VMs or add a new pair of NICs for the VMs.

When using iSCSI with ESX or ESXi v3, the service console or management appliance must participate in the iSCSI network for CHAP authentication. For ESX or ESXi v4 this limitation no longer exists.

When using iSCSI, add at least another pair of NIC ports to provide performance and redundancy.

When using Network File System (NFS) via network-attached storage (NAS) with ESX or ESXi, add another pair of NIC ports to give performance and redundancy.

If you are using locally attached tape drives or libraries, use an Adaptec non-RAID SCSI adapter. No other adapter will work properly. However, the best practice for tape drives or libraries is to use a remote archive server.

With ESX v4, there is now support for Single Root I/O Virtualization (SR-IOV) devices (generally 10G Ethernet adapters) that make use of VMDirect-Path. VMDirectPath requires Intel VT-d or AMD IOMMU support within the hardware. VMDirectPath may grant greater IO capability within a VM, but because it bypasses the hypervisor there is no built-in redundancy or security. The VM would need to provide this functionality, much like a normal physical server using 802.3ad.

iSCSI and NAS support is available, and iSCSI support differs distinctly from ESX v3 to ESX v4 because the need for the service console or management appliance to participate within the iSCSI network has been removed. iSCSI and NFS-based NAS are accessed using their own network connection assigned to the vmkernel, similar to the way vMotion and FT work or how a standard VMFS-3 is accessed via Fibre. Although NAS and iSCSI access can share bandwidth with other networks, keeping them separate could be better for performance. For ESX v3.x the iSCSI vmkernel device must share the subnet as the SC for authentication reasons, regardless of whether Challenge Handshake Authentication Protocol (CHAP) is enabled, although an NFS-based NAS would be on its own network. Chapter 8, "Configuring ESX from a Host Connection," discusses this new networking possibility in detail.

10Gb Ethernet

10Gb Ethernet is sweeping through data centers and ESX has kept up to date with this wave by supporting various 10Gb network adapters. Use of 10Gb has increased the use of VLANs within the virtual environment and is in the midst of redefining the standard trust zones associated with networking. We cover this in Chapter 7, "Networking." Use of 10Gb should be considered for high-performance networking requirements such as storage or virtual machine networks. It can also be used to combine networks; however, this depends on whether VLANs are used to segregate networks or if physical separation is required.

Converged Network Adapters

Converged Network Adapters (CNAs) are a set of networking adapters that combine FC SAN and networking features onto one device, thereby eliminating the need for excessive cabling within the virtual environment.

Disk Drive Space Considerations

The next item to discuss is what is required for drive space. In essence, the disk subsystem assigned to the system needs to be big enough to contain the SC for

ESX, the swap file for the SC, storage space for the per VM virtual swap files (used to overcommit memory in ESX), VM disk files, local ISO images, and backups of the Virtual Machine Disk Format (VMDK) files for Disaster Recovery reasons. If Fibre Channel, NFS, or iSCSI is available, you should offload the VM disk files to these systems. Putting temporary storage (SC swap) onto expensive SAN or iSCSI storage is not a best practice; the recommendation is that there be some form of local disk space to host the OS and the SC swap files. It is a requirement for vMotion, FT, and HA that the VM configuration and VMDK files live on the remote storage device. For FT and HA, the per VM vmkernel swap file should live on the remote storage device. However, for vMotion the per VM vmkernel swap file could live on local storage because vMotion copies the non-zero pages over to the target host during a vMotion. The minimal recommendation is roughly 12GB of available space in a RAID 1 or RAID 10 configuration for the operating system (ESX) and minimally 2GBs for ESXi and its necessary file systems. Use NFS for ISO files and other items as necessary, while using FC or iSCSI SAN storage for all VMDKs.

The most common recommendation for any VMFS that contains VMs is to use a RAID 5 configuration over as many spindles as possible for the best protection of data, while using RAID 1 for all high disk performance virtual machines. For the highest performance, you may want to consider solid state drives as well. For archival and low disk performance VMs, RAID 5 or Advanced Data Guard (ADG/RAID-6) should be used. Chapter 12, covers the disk configuration in much more detail as it investigates the needs of the local disk from a Disaster Recovery (DR) point of view. The general DR point of view is to have enough local space to run critical VMs from the host without the need for a SAN or iSCSI device.

Best Practice for Disk

Use RAID-1 on FC or iSCSI SAN Storage for those VMs with high disk IO requirements.

Use RAID-5 for average use VMs.

Use anything you want for low disk IO or archived VMs.

Use NFS for storage of ISO Images.

Have as much local disk necessary to hold the OS, local backups of critical VMs, and perhaps some local VMs.

Basic Hardware Considerations Summary

Table 1.2 conveniently summarizes the hardware considerations discussed in this section.

Table 1.2 *Best Practices for Hardware*

Item	ESX v3	ESX v4	Chapter to Visit for More Information
CPU	4C Intel VT/AMD RVI No eXecute/eX-ecute Disable	4C or greater Intel VT/AMD RVI No eXecute/eX-ecute Disable Intel VT-d for SRIOV	
Fibre Ports	Minimally Two 4Gbps	Minimally Two 4Gbps	Chapter 5
Network Ports	Two per Trust Zone depending on physical network from 4–10 ports	Two per Trust Zone depending on physical network from 4–12 ports	Chapter 8
Local disks	SCSI/SAS/SATA RAID Enough to keep a copy of the most important VMs Consider SSD	SCSI/SAS/SATA RAID Enough to keep a copy of the most important VMs Consider SSD	
iSCSI	Two 1GB network ports via vmkernel or iSCSI HBA	Two 1GB network ports via vmkernel or iSCSI HBA	Chapter 8
SAN	Enterprise class	Enterprise class	Chapter 5
Tape	Remote	Remote	Chapter 11
NFS-based NAS	Two 1GB network ports via vmkernel	Two 1GB network ports via vmkernel	Chapter 8
Memory	Up to max allowed	Up to max allowed	
Networks	Four to five Admin/iSCSI net-work VM network vMotion network NFS network iSCSI network	Five to six Admin network VM network vMotion network NFS network iSCSI network FT network	Chapter 8

Specific Hardware Considerations

Now we need to look at the hardware currently available and decide how to use it to meet the best practices listed previously. All hardware will have some issues to consider, and applying the comments from the first section of this chapter will help show the good, bad, and ugly about the possible hardware currently used as a virtual infrastructure node. The primary goal is to help the reader understand the necessary design choices when choosing various forms of hardware for an enterprise-level ESX host farm. Note that the number of VMs mentioned is based on an average machine that does not do very much network, disk, or other I/O and has average processor utilization. This number varies too much based on the utilization of the current infrastructure, and these numbers are a measure of what each server is capable of and are not intended as maximums or minimums. A proper analysis will yield the best use of your ESX hosts and is part of the design for any virtual infrastructure.

With modern systems that support quad-core and greater processors as well as increased memory density, memory and CPU are no longer limiting factors in virtualization. We are in the phase of hardware development where IO becomes an issue. However, this is fairly cyclic and as workloads increase once more, CPU may become an issue again. Therefore it is best to consider all aspects of your hardware and not just concentrate on any specific issue. Well-rounded systems that provide security, redundancy, and performance are the necessities.

Blade Server Systems

Because blade systems (see Figure 1.4) virtualize hardware, it is a logical choice for ESX, which further virtualizes a blade investment by running more servers on each blade. Although blades generally lack the capability to add in PCIe cards, they do support several mezzanine structures. Most modern blades can handle the port density necessary for high performance, redundant, and secure networking and storage connectivity. Even so, a limit exists to how many ports can be placed within a blade and how these are handled within the enclosure itself. The solution from some vendors' enclosures is to aggregate all networking to several 1G or 10G links to limit the number of cables in use. HP's Flex10 and Cisco Unified Computing System are two examples of this type of networking.

In addition to possible port density issues and issues with aggregation, issues could exist with local disk requirements. Whether you need local disk depends entirely on your current design; however, many companies use local disk as a mechanism to back up their most important virtual machines (see Chapter 12 for details regarding backup and Disaster Recovery) in case their remote iSCSI,

NAS, or SAN devices fail. Some vendors, HP for example, have created storage blades that can be used with any number of compute blades within an enclosure.

Blades generally have several issues; port density issues are solved by the use of CNAs and other blade class aggregators (HP Flex10 and so on) as they provide a way to combine network and Fibre Channel into one adapter. However, given that blades have a dearth of expansion slots, these systems have some distinct limitations if you do not or cannot use CNAs. Other issues include a limited number of expansion ports, shared backplanes, which increase density but limit full redundancy, and limited PCI device support (usually to vendor-specific riser cards).

Figure 1.4 *Front and back of blade enclosure*

Best Practice with Blades

Pick blades that offer full NIC, Fibre redundancy, and sufficient local disk space.

1U Server Systems

The next device of interest is the 1U server (see Figure 1.5), which offers in most cases two onboard NICs and sometimes four, generally no onboard Fibre, perhaps two PCI slots, and perhaps two to four SCSI/SAS disks. This is perfect for adding a quad-port NIC and a dual-port Fibre controller; but if you need a SCSI card for a local tape device, which is sometimes necessary but never recommended, there is no chance to put one in unless there is a way to get more onboard NIC or Fibre ports. In addition to the need to add more hardware into these units, there is a chance that PCI card redundancy would be lost, too. Consider the HP DL360 G6 as a possible ESX host, which is a 1U device with up to eight SAS or SATA drives, two onboard NICs, and two PCIe expansion slots. In this case, we would want to add at least a quad-port NIC card to get to the six NICs that make up the best practice and gain more redundancy for ESX. In some cases, there is a SCSI port on the back of the device, so access to a disk array will increase space dramatically, yet often driver deficiencies affect its usage with tape devices.

1U servers can have up to two sockets with many cores and up to 128GBs of memory.

Figure 1.5 *1U server front and back*

In the case of SAN redundancy, if there were no mezzanine Fibre Channel adapter, the second PCI slot would host a dual- or quad-port Fibre Channel adapter, which would round out and fill all available slots. With the advent of quad-port NIC support, adding an additional pair of NIC ports for another network requires the replacement of the additional dual-port NIC with the new PCI card. There are some trade-offs when choosing this platform, just as there are for blades. The small number of available expansion slots limits the quantity of ports and adapters available for security, redundancy, and performance.

> **Best Practice for 1U Boxes**
>
> Pick a box that has on-board Fibre Channel adapters so that there are free slots for more network and any other necessary I/O cards. Also, choose large disk drives when possible. There should be at least two on-board network ports. Add quad-port network or dual-port 10Gbe and dual-port Fibre Channel cards as necessary to get port density.

2U Server Systems

The next server considered is the 2U server (see Figure 1.6), similar to the HP DL380. This type of server usually has two or four onboard Ethernet ports, perhaps two onboard Fibre Channel ports, and usually an external SCSI port for use with external drive arrays. In addition to all this, there are up to five PCIe slots, up to eight SAS or SATA disks, and possibly twice as much memory as a 1U machine. The extra PCIe slots add quite a bit of functionality; they can either host an Adaptec SCSI card to support a local tape drive or library, which is sometimes necessary but never recommended, or it can host more network (10Gbe) or storage capability. At the bare minimum, two to four more NIC ports are required and perhaps a dual- or quad-port Fibre Channel adapter if a pair of ports is not already in the server. Because this class of server can host eight SAS or SATA disks, they can be loaded up with more than 2TB of storage, which makes the 2U server an excellent stand-alone ESX host. Introduce six-core processors and this box has the power to run many VMs. This class of server makes an excellent virtualization host and generally provides the most for your dollar.

Figure 1.6 *Front and back of 2U server*

2U servers generally have up to two sockets with many cores but a limited amount of memory sockets. 128GBs of memory is not an uncommon maximum for 2U servers.

Pairing a 2U server with a small tape library to become an office in a box, which ships to a remote location, does not require a SAN or another form of remote storage because it has plenty of local disk space and the capability to connect to a disk array to provide even more storage.

Best Practice for 2U Servers

Pick a server that has at least two on-board NIC ports, two on-board Fibre Channel ports, plenty of disk, and as much memory as possible. Add a quad-port network card to gain port density and, if necessary, two single-port Fibre Channel adapters to add more redundancy.

Large Server-Class Systems

The next discussion combines multiple classes of servers (see Figure 1.7). The class combines the 4-, 8-, and 16-processor machines. Independent of the processor count, all these servers have many of the same hardware features. Generally, they have at least four SCSI/SAS/SATA drives and sometimes up to eight or sixteen for 8TBs of internal storage, at least six PCI slots, two onboard NICs, RAID memory, and very large memory footprints ranging from 32GB to 512GB. Some of these servers can even include 1TB of memory. The RAID memory is just one technology that allows for the replacement of various components while the machine is still running, which can alleviate hardware-based downtime unless it's one of the critical components. RAID memory is extremely nice to have, but it is just a fraction of the total memory in the server and does not count as available memory to the server. For example, it is possible to put a full 512GB of memory into an HP DL785, but the OS will see only 256GB of memory in mirrored mode, 504GB using an online spare, or the full 512GBs. The mirrored memory or online space, which comes into use only if there is a bad memory stick discovered by the hardware, alleviates crashes when DIMMs go bad. Historically, the larger machines have fewer disks than the 2U servers do, but it makes up for that by having an abundance of PCI buses and slots enabling multiple Fibre Channel adapters and dual-port NICs for the highest level of redundancy. Many of the larger system now can house more drives than the 2U servers offering up to 16TBs of disk. In these servers, the multiple Fibre Channel ports suggested by the general best practice would each be placed on different PCI buses, as would the NIC cards to get better performance and redundancy in PCI cards, SAN fabric, and networking. These types of servers can host a huge number of VMs, usually up to the maximum supported by ESX itself.

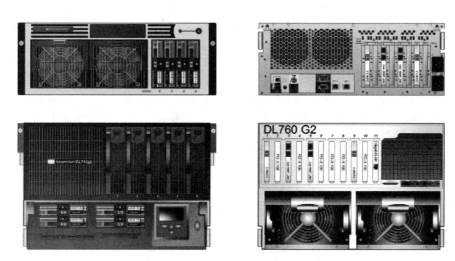

Figure 1.7 *Back and front of large server-class machines*

The Effects of External Storage

There are many different external storage devices, ranging from simple external drives, to disk arrays, shared disk arrays, active/passive SAN, active/active SAN, SCSI tape drives, to libraries and Fibre-attached tape libraries. The list is extensive, but we will be looking at the most common devices in use today and those most likely to be used in the future. We'll start with the simplest device and move on to the more complex devices. As we did with servers, this discussion points out the limitations or benefits in the technology so that all the facts are available when starting or modifying virtual infrastructure architecture.

For local disks, it is strongly recommended that you use SCSI/SAS RAID devices; although IDE is supported for running ESX, it does not have the capability to host a VMFS, so some form of external storage is required. Since ESX v3, there has been support for local SATA devices, but they share the same limitations as IDE. In some servers you can hand SATA drives off a SAS controller to gain SCSI-like functionality, but not the performance. In addition, if you are running any form of shared disk cluster, such as Microsoft Cluster servers across hosts, a local VMFS is required for the boot drives, yet remote storage is required for all shared volumes using raw disk maps. If remote storage is not available, the shared disk cluster will fail with major locking issues. We cover clusters in detail in Chapter 10, "Virtual Machines."

> **Best Practice for Local Disks**
>
> Use SCSI or SAS disks.

Outside of local disks, the external disk tray or disk array (see Figure 1.8) is a common attachment and usually does not require more hardware outside of the disk array and the proper SCSI cable. However, like standalone servers, the local disk array does not enable the use of vMotion to hot migrate a VM. However, when vMotion is not required, this is a simple way to get more storage attached to a server. If the disk array is using a SATA controller, it is probably better to go to a SAS controller instead, because you gain all the supported benefits of using SCSI/SAS controllers. Unfortunately, you do not gain the performance of SCSI/SAS when using SATA drives.

Figure 1.8 *Front and back of an external disk array*

The next type of device is the shared disk array (see Figure 1.9), which has its own controllers and can be attached to a set of servers instead of only one. The onboard controller allows logical unit numbers (LUNs) to be carved out and to be presented to the appropriate server or shared among the servers. It is possible to use this type of device to share only VMFS-formatted LUNs between at most four ESX hosts, because that is generally the limit on how many SCSI interfaces are available on each shared disk array. It is a very inexpensive way to create multimachine redundancy. However, using this method limits the cluster of ESX Servers to exactly the number of SCSI ports that are available, and limits the methods for accessing raw LUNs from within VMs. With ESX v3 it is possible to use local raw LUNs directly within a VM but with ESX v4, this is no longer possible and all local virtual disks must live on a VMFS. We cover this in more detail in Chapter 10.

This type of device should not be confused with a standard disk array; the differentiation is that the shared disk array has its own built in controllers.

Figure 1.9 *Front and back of a shared SCSI array*

A SAN is one of the devices that will allow vMotion to be used; it generally comes in entry-level (see Figure 1.10) and enterprise-level (see Figure 1.11) styles. Each has its uses with ESX and all allow the sharing of data between multiple ESX hosts, which is the prime ingredient for the use of vMotion. SAN information is covered in detail in Chapter 5, "Storage with ESX."

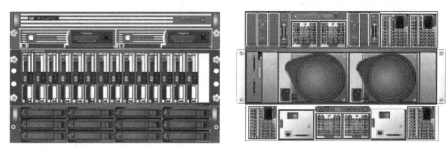

Figure 1.10 *Front and back of an entry-level SAN with SATA drives*

Although SATA controllers are supported directly by ESX or within a SAN, they are generally slower than using SCSI or SAS controllers. Because of poor performance numbers, SATA may not be a good choice for primary VMDK storage, but would make a good temporary backup location. The best solution is to avoid non-SCSI, SAS controllers as much as possible. Although the entry-level SAN is very good for small installations, enterprise-class installations really require an enterprise-level SAN (refer to Figure 1.11). The enterprise-level SAN provides a higher degree of redundancy, storage, and flexibility for ESX than an entry-level version. Both have their place in possible architectures. For example, if you are deploying ESX to a small office with a pair of servers, it is less expensive to deploy using an entry-level SAN than a full-sized enterprise-class SAN.

Best Practice for SAN Storage

Use SCSI- or SAS-based SAN storage systems. For two to four hosts, entry-level systems may be best. However, for anything else, it is best to use enterprise SAN systems for improved availability, performance, and redundancy.

Figure 1.11 *Front and back of an enterprise-level SAN*

The last physical entry in the storage realm is that of NAS devices (see Figure 1.12), which present file systems using various protocols, including Network File System (NFS), Internet SCSI (iSCSI), and Common Internet File System (CIFS). VMware ESX does not support CIFS as a data store but does support NFS, iSCSI, and FC SAN. iSCSI and NFS have a throughput similar to that of FC SAN on ESX v4 now that you can use jumbo frames with each of these protocols. Granted, to achieve this level of performance, you must either use iSCSI HBAs, CNAs, or 10G ethernet adapters. With NAS, there is no need for Fibre Channel adapters, only more NICs to support the iSCSI and NFS protocols while providing redundancy.

Figure 1.12 *NAS device*

There is a new class of storage devices called virtual storage appliances (VSAs) that should be considered. These devices make use of locally available disk space and make it available to a cluster of ESX or ESXi hosts. Some VSAs serve up only NFS and others serve up NFS and iSCSI. VSAs can replicate data from host to host for redundancy and work with multiple LUNs, or only one LUN. In either of these cases, VSAs could be a viable option for small-scale deployments that have lots of local disk space available that now need cluster functionality such as vMotion and shared disk clusters between multiple hosts.

Examples

Now it is time to review what customers have done in relation to the comments in the previous sections. The following six examples are from real customers, not from our imagination. The solutions proposed use the best practices previously discussed and a little imagination.

Example 1: Using Motherboard X and ESXi Will Not Install

This is a very common issue because many think that ESXi, being free, will run on nearly all hardware. Unlike VMware Workstation, which requires a host operating system, ESXi is a bare metal install. Like ESX, ESXi has a fairly large official and unofficial hardware compatibility list (HCL). In general, the reasons for ESXi not installing relate to the hardware involved, or the firmware for said hardware. It is best to first peruse the HCLs and look for the hardware that composes your system, if you do not find your hardware or anything similar, there is a good chance ESXi will not install nor work properly. When using existing hardware, it is best to look at the HCL for the storage and networking devices that may be onboard your motherboard. You may need to disable the onboard hardware and add in supported IO devices.

In addition to hardware issues, you need to be cognizant of the BIOS used on the motherboard. To run vSphere ESX or ESXi 4, you must be able to enable Intel-VT or AMD-V and enable the No eXecute (NX) or eXecute Disabled (XD) bits. Without these BIOS settings, vSphere ESX or ESXi 4 will not run properly and perhaps at all. These settings only affect EVC within VMware Virtual Infrastructure ESX or ESXi 3.x.

Example 2: Installing ESX and Expecting a Graphical Console

Another interesting issue that comes up within the VMware Communities Forums (http://communities.vmware.com) is installing ESX or ESXi on a laptop. Although this is possible, and in some cases could be useful for demos and development, in general it will not install. On modern laptops with at least Intel Nahalem or similar AMD support, it may be possible to install ESXi even though this is not listed on the HCL, which limits your support options. Even more interesting is that no GUI or method exists to access the VMs within the ESX or ESXi host directly from the ESX or ESXi host. A command line has limited functionality to manage and create VMs, but there is no self-contained method to access a VM after it is running.

This is by design. VMware wants ESX and ESXi to be treated as appliances; therefore, management tools require at least one external system in order to access the VMs.

Example 3: Existing Datacenter

A customer was in the midst of a hardware-upgrade cycle and decided to pursue alternatives to purchasing quite a bit of hardware. The customer wanted to avoid buying 300+ systems at a high cost and decided to pursue ESX host. Furthermore, the customer conducted an exhaustive internal process to determine the need to upgrade the 300+ systems and believes all of them could be migrated to ESX, because they meet or exceed the documented constraints. The existing machine mix includes several newer machines from the last machine refresh (around 20), but is primarily made up of machines that are at least two to three generations old, running on processors no faster than 900MHz. The new ones range from 1.4GHz to 3.06GHz 2U machines (see Figure 1.6). The customer would also like to either make use of existing hardware or purchase very few machines to make up the necessary difference, because the price for ESX to run 300+ machines approaches the customer's complete hardware budget. In addition, a last bit of information was also provided, and it really throws a monkey wrench into a good solution: The customer has five datacenters, each with its own SAN infrastructure.

Following best practices, we could immediately state that we could use the 3.06GHz hosts. Then we could determine whether there were enough to run everything. However, this example shows the need for something even more fundamental than just hardware to run 300+ virtual machines. It shows the need for an appropriate analysis of the running environment to first determine whether the 300+ servers are good candidates for migration, followed by a determination of which servers are best fit to be the hosts of the 300+ VMs. The tool used most often to perform this analysis is the VMware Capacity Planner. This tool will gather up various utilization and performance numbers for each server over a one- to two-month period. This information is then used to determine which servers make good candidates to run as VMs.

Instead of VMware Capacity Planner, which is available only to VMware Authorized Consultants (VAC), you can use the lighter-weight guided consolidation tool built in to VMware vCenter Server to determine what systems would be good candidates for virtualization. The reporting is lighter weight and the tests are not as exhaustive, but it does not require anything more than an evaluation license of VMware vCenter Server.

> **Best Practice**
>
> Use a capacity planner or something similar to get utilization and performance information about servers.

When the assessment is finished, you can better judge which machines could be migrated and which could not. Luckily, the customer had a strict "one application per machine" rule, which was enforced, and which removes possible application conflicts and migration concerns. With the details released about their current infrastructure, it was possible to determine that the necessary hardware was already in use and could be reused with minor hardware upgrades. Each machine would require an additional quad-port NIC and Fibre Channel cards, as well as an increase in memory and local disk space. To run the number of VMs required and to enable the use of vMotion, all hosts were paired up at each site at the very least, with a further recommendation to purchase another host machine per site (because there were no more hosts to reuse) at the earliest convenience so that they could alleviate possible host failures in the future. To perform the first migrations, some seed units would be borrowed from the manufacturer and LUNs carved from their own SANs, allowing migration from physical to virtual using the seed units. Then the physical host would be converted to a ESX and the just-migrated VM vMotioned off the borrowed seed host. This host would be sent to the other sites as their seed unit when the time came to migrate their hosts. This initial plan would be revised after the capacity planner was run and analyzed.

Example 4: Office in a Box

One of the author's earliest questions was from a company that wanted to use ESX to condense hundreds of remote locations into one easy-to-use and administer package of a single host running ESX with the remote office servers running as VMs. Because the remote offices currently used outdated hardware, this customer also felt that ESX would provide better remote management capability. The customer also believed that the hardware should be upgraded at these remote offices all over the world. The goal was to ship a box to the remote location, have it plugged in, powered up, and then remotely manage the server. If there were a machine failure of some sort, the customer would ship out a new box. The concern the customer had was the initial configuration of the box and how to perform backups appropriately.

They set up their eight-drive dual-quad core processor hosts with a full complement of memory and disks, an extra quad-port Ethernet card, an external tape device via an Adaptec card (see Figure 1.13), and enough file system space for a possible shared virtual machine disk file, which should be on its on virtual machine file system, due to locking concerns. We discussed a SAN and the use of vMotion, but the customer thought that this would be overkill for the remote offices. For the datacenter, this was a necessity, but not for a remote office.

Figure 1.13 *Office in a box server with tape library*
Visio templates for image courtesy of Hewlett-Packard.

However, the best-laid plan was implemented incorrectly, and a year after the initial confirmation of the design, the customer needed to implement Microsoft Clustering as a cluster in a box. Because of this oversight, the customer had to reinstall all the ESX host to allocate a small VMFS for a shared virtual machine disk file. The customer chose to reinstall the machines, but first set up the operating system disk as a RAID 1, making using of hardware mirroring between disks 1 and 2, leaving four disks to make a RAID 5 + 1 spare configuration of 146GB disks. Then another LUN was carved from the remaining two disks of RAID 1 just for the shared VMDK for a cluster of VMs.

One other solution was to initially build the units with only six drives, leaving the last two slots for drives to be added if there was a need to add more VMFS space, or special use VMFS space such as for a cluster. Although for a Cluster in a Box the clustered VMDK can use the same VMFS as the general use drives, separating out the cluster VMDKs allows for ESX to handle the locking more efficiently.

Best Practice

When using clusters of machines, place the cluster virtual disk volumes on separate LUNs.

Example 5: The Latest and Greatest

One of our opportunities dealt with the need for the customer to use the latest and greatest hardware with ESX, and in doing so to plan for the next release of the OS at the same time. The customer decided to go with a full blade enclosure using dual CPU quad-core blades with no disk, and iSCSI TOE cards in order to boot the ESX host via iSCSI from a NAS (see Figure 1.12). The customer also required an easier and automated way to deploy the ESX hosts.

This presented several challenges up front. The first challenge was that the next release of the OS was not ready at the time, and the HCL for the current release *and* the first release of the next version of ESX showed that some of the customer's desired options would *not* be available. So, to use ESX, the hardware mix needed to be modified to support the common set of devices between ESX v3.5 and v4.0. The customer therefore traded in the iSCSI TOE cards for supported 10G cards.

The main concern here is that the customer wanting the latest and greatest instead got a mixed bag of goodies that were not compatible with the current release, and the prelist of the HCL for the next release did not list the customer's desired hardware either. In essence, if it is not on the HCL now, most likely it will not be on the list in the future; if you can get a prerelease HCL, this can be verified. In essence, this customer had to change plans based on the release schedules, and it made for quite a few headaches for the customer and required a redesign to get started, including the use of 10G mezzanine cards and 10G network switches. In essence, always check the HCL on the VMware website before purchasing anything.

As for the deployment of ESX, the onboard remote management cards and the multiple methods to deploy ESX made life much easier. Because these concepts are covered elsewhere, we will not go into a lot of detail. ESX provides its own method for scripted installations just for blades. Many vendors also provide mechanisms to script the installations of operating systems onto their blades. It should be noted that with vSphere ESX v4, host profiles make installations simpler. The key to scripted installations is adding in all the extra bits often required that are outside of ESX, such as hardware agents.

Example 6: The SAN

Our sixth example is a customer who brought in consulting to do a bake-off between competing products using vendor-supplied small SANs. The customer made a choice and implemented the results of the bake-off in a production environment that used a completely different SAN and SAN layout than used in the bake-off. Although this information was available during the bake-off, it was pretty much a footnote. This, in turn, led to issues with how the customer was implementing ESX in production that had to be reengineered.

The customer wanted fully compatible multipath features, such as load balancing, failover, and path aggregation (which is not available by default) in order to place within their hosts more than two Fibre ports to increase overall SAN throughput. Unfortunately, the customer's existing licensing did not consider this option and the SAN provider chosen did not have the proper capability at the time of the bake-off.

The solution is to increase the customer's license level to Enterprise Plus, as well as look into using a vendor supplied Multi-Path Plug-in for vSphere ESX v4. Unfortunately, very few vendors have multipath drivers for vSphere ESX v4.

It is crucial to look at all aspects of your hardware needs during any bake-offs and testing and to measure everything 12 inches to the foot, or exactly what you will use in production.

Example 7: Secure Environment

It is increasingly common for ESX to be placed into secure environments as long as the security specialist understands how ESX works and why it is safe to do so. However, in this case, the security specialist assumed that because the VMs share the same air within the host, they are therefore at risk. Although we could prove this was not the case, the design of the secure environment had to work within this scope. The initial hardware was two-socket quad-core CPU machines and a small SAN that would later be removed when they proved everything worked and their large corporate SANs took over. The customer also wanted secure data not to be visible to anyone but the people in the teams using the information.

This presented several concerns. The first is that the administrators of the ESX box must also be part of the secure teams, have the proper corporate clearances, or be given an exception, because anyone with administrator access to an ESX host also has access to all the VMDKs available on the ESX Server. Chapter 4, "Auditing and Monitoring," goes into auditing your ESX environment in detail. Because the customer wanted to secure the data completely, it is important to keep the service console, vMotion, iSCSI, NFS, FT Logging, and the VM networks all on their own secure networks. Why should we secure vMotion and everything? Because vMotion will pass the memory footprint of the server across an Ethernet cable and, combined with access to the service console, will give a hacker everything a VM is doing. If not properly secured, this is quite a frightening situation.

Whereas the company had a rule governing use of SANs to present secure data LUNs, it had no such policy concerning ESX. In essence, it was important to create an architecture that kept all the secure VMs to their own set of ESX hosts and place on another set of ESX hosts those things not belonging to the secure environment. This kept all the networking separated by external firewalls and kept the data from being accessed by those not part of the secure team. If a new secure environment were necessary, another pair of ESX hosts (so we can vMotion VMs) would be added with their own firewall.

The preceding could have easily been performed on a single ESX cluster, yet require the administrators to have the proper corporate clearances to be allowed to manipulate secured files. Given this and the appropriate network configuration inside ESX, it is possible to create many different secure environments within a single ESX cluster, including access to other secure machines external to ESX. However, this customer did not choose this option.

Example 8: Disaster Recovery

We were asked to do a Disaster Recovery (DR) plan for a customer that had two datacenters in close proximity to each other. The customer wanted a duplicate set of everything at each site so that they could run remotely if necessary. This is not an uncommon desire, because they in effect wanted a hot site implementation. The current ESX Server load was many dual quad core CPU hosts at each location, two distinctly different SANs, and some slightly different operational procedures.

Because of the disparate SAN environments, it was impossible to create a SAN copy of the data, because the SANs spoke different languages. Therefore, a hardware solution to the problem was out of the question. This, in turn, led to political issues that had to be ironed out. Finally, the decision was made to create backups using some other mechanism and physically copy the VMs from site to site using some form of automated script. Although plenty of tools already do this, ESX comes equipped with the necessary tools to make backups of VMs while they are still running, so in essence a hot copy can be made by ESX with a bit of scripting. Tie this to an existing tape subsystem (which the customer also wanted to place into the mix), and a powerful local and remote backup solution emerges.

Various other approaches were discussed, but unfortunately, they would not work. A key idea was to use vMotion, but this requires each site to access shared storage. Although long-distance vMotion was demonstrated at VMworld 2009 and EMCworld 2010, it requires specialized hardware on each side, which this customer did not have and which was not available at that time. This is the EMC VPLEX technology covered in Chapter 5. Another possibility was the use of an offsite backup repository, but that would make restoration slower. Last, there is a host of third-party tools to make backups and replicate as well.

A plan was devised that made the best use of the resources, including remote backups, backup to tape, and storage of tapes offsite. In essence, everything was thought about, including the requirement for a third site in case the impossible regional disaster hit. Little did we know that a major natural disaster would hit the region within months.

The DR plan that was implemented made restoration much easier when the natural disaster hit. What could have taken weeks to restore took just days because the customer had DR backups of the virtual disk files for every VM on the system. These types of backups should be considered as part of any deployment of ESX. A backup through the VMs, which is the traditional method to back up servers, requires other data-restoration techniques that take much longer than a backup and restore of a single file.

Hardware Checklist

Now that we have been through a few of the concepts related to the hardware and the individual limitations of various machines types, we can devise a simple hardware checklist (see Table 1.3) that, if followed, will create a system that follows best practices.

Table 1.3 *Hardware Checklist*

Hardware	Best Practice	Comments
Network adapters (discussed further in Chapter 8)	Two gigabit ports for service console	Or ESXi Management console
	Two gigabit ports for vMotion or use a CNA	
	Two gigabit ports per network available to the VMs or use a CNA	
NFS	Two or more gigabit ports for NAS or use a CNA	NFS is the only supported NAS protocol. CIFS is not supported.
iSCSI	Two gigabit ports for iSCSI either in the form of gigabit NICs, an iSCSI HBA, or use a CNA	Support for boot from iSCSI required an iSCSI HBA. An iSCSI HBA is a specialized TCP Offload Engine NIC.
FT Logging	Two gigabit ports for Fault Tolerance logging between two, more ESX v4 hosts, or use a CNA	vSphere ESX v4 only.
Fibre Channel adapters (discussed further in Chapter 5)	Two 8Gb FC ports	This will provide failover and some multipath functionality with active-active style of SANs (4Gb FC can also be used).
	Two 12Gb FC ports	In the future, 12Gb FC Fibre Channel ports will be supported.

Hardware	Best Practice	Comments
Tape drives or libraries	Adaptec SCSI card	Internal and external tape drives or libraries require an Adaptec SCSI card to be of use. This is not a best practice because it pins VMs to hosts, and when the tape has issues, requires the host to be rebooted.
CPU	Match CPUs within a host	
	Match CPUs between hosts within a cluster	Required for vMotion
Disk (discussed further in Chapter 12)	Minimum a 72GB RAID 1 for OS	
	RAID 1 for local VMFS	Only necessary if using Cluster in a Box
	RAID 5 for local VMFS	This is mainly for DR purposes, or if you do not have SAN or iSCSI storage available.

Conclusion

There is quite a bit to consider from the hardware perspective when considering a virtualization server farm. Although we touch on networking, storage, and disaster recovery in this chapter, it should be noted that how the hardware plays out depends on the load, utilization goals, consolidation ratios desired, and the performance gains of new hardware (which were not discussed). The recommendations in this chapter are suggestions of places to start the hardware design of a virtualization server farm. Chapter 2, "Version Comparison," delves into the details of and differences between ESX version 3.5 and ESX version 4, to help you better understand the impact of hardware on ESX. Understanding these differences will aid you in coming up with a successful design of a virtual environment.

Chapter 2

Version Comparison

Virtualization as a technology has been around for a very long time. VMware was founded by a group out of Stanford and was one of the early companies that brought virtualization to the x86 platform. Their initial product was a "please try this, it is cool, and tell us what to fix" version of VMware Workstation. Soon after that, VMware Workstation version 2 came out, and the world of computing changed. When version 4 of VMware Workstation came out, more and more people started to use the product, and soon after came the server versions GSX and ESX. With ESX, another change to computing took place; *virtualization* has become the buzzword and driving force behind many datacenter choices.

VMware produces four major products with varying capabilities and functionality. The products form a triangle in which VMware Workstation, Player, and Fusion are at the bottom with the broadest ranges of functionality and capability. Here VMware tries out new ideas and concepts, making it the leading edge of virtualization technology. The second tier is VMware ACE that adds to VMware Workstation the Assured Computing Environment that allows more control over the virtual machines in use. The third tier of the triangle is VMware Server (formerly GSX Server), which could be said to be VMware ESX-light because it is a middle ground between VMware Workstation and ESX, providing VM Workstation-style functionality while running on another operating system: Windows or Linux. VMware Server is a collection of programs that includes a management interface that has its own SDK, and other programs to launch VMs in the background. The pinnacle tier is ESX and ESXi, which are their own operating systems and the version comparison covered within this chapter.

ESX v3 and ESX v4 differ in many small ways, but both differ greatly from ESX v2. These differences revolve around how the system boots and how the functionality of the earlier version was implemented inside the new version. Between ESX v3 and ESX v4 there are changes in just about every subsystem, and all for the better. This is the release of ESX that brings many of the VMware Workstation cutting-edge technologies into the server environment, including the new virtual hardware and disk file format and functionality (including thin provisioning).

Because so many subsystems have had modifications and enhancements, they need to be broken out in more detail. It is easy to say it is a new operating system, but in essence ESX v4 is an enhancement to ESX v3 that simplifies administration, increases functionality and performance, and incorporates common customer-requested improvements.

The version comparison of ESX in this chapter looks at the following:

- The vmkernel (the nuts and bolts of the virtualization hypervisor)
- The boot process and tools of the console operating system or service console (SC)
- The changes to virtual networking (vNetwork)
- VMFS datastores
- Availability
- Backup methods
- Licensing methods
- Virtual hardware functionality
- VM management
- Server and VM security
- Installation differences
- VMware Certified Professional changes

Although the text of these sections will discuss the differences between ESX v3 and ESX v4, the author has left in the tables the data referring to ESX v2 so that the reader can see the growth of the product. In addition, the tables also included VMware ESXi where necessary. In many ways, ESXi is identical to ESX. The major differences are in how ESXi boots and the lack of a full-blown service console. Unless stated in the table or discussion, the differences also refer to ESXi as well as ESX.

VMware ESX/ESXi Architecture Overview

VMware ESX and ESXi is a multilayer architecture comprising multiple types of software. In Figure 2.1, we see that the top of the software stack is the application that runs within each guest operating system, which in turn runs within the virtual machine. The virtual machine is composed of the stack that contains the Application (APP) and the Guest Operating System (OS). Below the Guest OS is the virtual machine manager (VMM). Each VM talks to its own VMM, which is composed, among other things, with the virtual hardware in use by the VM.

The VMM is a software layer that provides interaction between the Guest OS and the kernel layer. The kernel layer is referred to as the vmkernel, which provides a layer that coordinates VMM interactions with the physical hardware and schedules the VMs to run on their associated physical CPUs. The vmkernel is the guts of the VMware ESX and ESXi. The vmkernel coordination includes the virtual network components, such as virtual switches that can connect the virtual machines to each other as well as to physical NICs. The vmkernel provides VMs access to the physical resources of the host. The vmkernel breaks down all resources into CPU, memory, network, and disk and provides these to the VMM layer for use by the VMs.

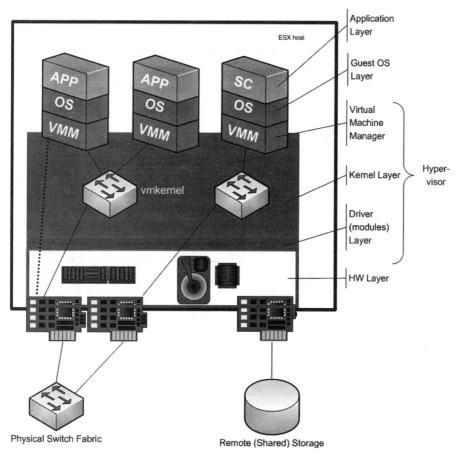

Figure 2.1 *ESX/ESXi architecture in a nutshell*

The vmkernel manages the physical devices within its core code but talks to them using drivers or modules that speak the language of the physical devices. Even though this is the case, each VM could possibly talk to one of the devices directly using a pass through mode supported by the vmkernel, which literally maps the device directly to the VM, bypassing many of the vmkernel layers (dashed line in Figure 2.1). The VMM, Kernel, and Driver or Modules layer compose what is referred to as a hypervisor.

VMs run within the hypervisor that coordinates and schedules access to the physical hardware required by the VMs. Hosts can be combined into clusters of hypervisors. Hypervisors can also communicate directly with each other via management and other networks that have physical and virtual components. VMs can communicate with each other and physical machines via virtual and physical networks.

In short, a hypervisor runs VMs and interacts with hardware.

vmkernel Differences

The heart of ESX is the vmkernel, and future enhancements all stem from improvements to this all-important subsystem. The new vmkernel supports new and different guest operating systems and upgrades to support the latest service console version and driver interactions. The vmkernel looks similar to a Linux kernel, but it is not a Linux kernel. The most interesting similarity is the way modules are loaded, and the list of supported modules has changed. Table 2.1 shows the standard modules loaded by each version of ESX.

Table 2.1 *Module Version Differences (Proliant DL380; Found Using vmkload –b Command)*

ESX v4	ESX v3.5	ESX v3.0	ESX 2.5.x	Comments
vmklinux	vmklinux	vmklinux	vmklinux	Linux interface
random				Random numbers
ehci-hcd				USB support
usb-uhci				
usb-storage				
pclassify				
cbt				
hid				Human interface devices

ESX v4	ESX v3.5	ESX v3.0	ESX 2.5.x	Comments
ipmi_msghandler				IPMI drivers
ipmi_sr_drv				
ipmi_devintf				
dm				
cosShadow	cosShadow			
vmci				VMCI (VM to VM Communication Interface)
vmkstatelogger				vmkernel state logging
libata	ata_piix	ata_piix	IDE CDROM	IDE CDROM
ata_piix				
aic79xx	aic7xxx	aic7xxx	aic7xxx	Adaptec SCSI HBA for local tape device
	aic79xx			
bnx2	e1000	e1000	e 1000	Intel and Broadcom pNIC drivers
e1000e	e100	e100	e100	
e1000*	tg3	tg3e	bcm5700	
tg3*	forcedeth*			
forcedeth*	bnx2*			
cdp	tcpip	bond	bond	Cisco Discovery Protocol, vSwitch drivers, and network drivers
etherswitch	etherswitch			
hub	netflow			
tcpip2				
tcpip2v6*				
dvsdev				Distributed
dvfilter				Virtual Switch
deltadisk	deltadisk	deltadisk		Snapshots

continues

Table 2.1   *(Continued)*

ESX v4	ESX v3.5	ESX v3.0	ESX 2.5.x	Comments
lpfc820*	lpfc_740*	lpfcdd_7xx	lpfcdd_2xx	Emulex and Qlogic FC-HBA
qla2xxx	qla2300_707	qla2300_7xx*	qla2[23]00_xxx*	
ccisslvmw_satp_local	cciss	cciss	cpqarray*	RAID HBA
vmw_satp_default_aa	ips*	ips*	cciss	
vmw_satp_alua	aic...*	aic...*	ips*	
vmw_satp_cx	mptscsi_2xx*	aic...*		
vmw_satp_default_ap	sata_nv*			
vmw_satp_eva	sata_promise*			
vmw_satp_lsi	sata_svw*			
vmw_satp_symm	sata_vsc*			
vmw_satp_inv				
vmw_satp_eql				
vmw_satp_msa				
vmw_satp_svc				
vmw_satp_alua_cx				
vmw_psp_rr				
vmw_psp_mru				
nmp				Native multi-path driver
		vmkapimod		vmkernel API module
vmfs2	vmfs2	vmfs2		VMFS-2
vmfs3	vmfs3	vmfs3		VMFS-3 and VMFS LVM-Driver
lvmdriver				
multiextent				extents
nfsclient	nfsclient	nfsclient		vmkernel NFS client

ESX v4	ESX v3.5	ESX v3.0	ESX 2.5.x	Comments
iscsi_trans	iscsi_mod	iscsi_mod		vmkernel iSCSI support
iscsi_linux	qla4010	qla4010*		
iscsi_vmk*	qla4022			
qla4xxx*				
shaper	shaper	shaper	nfshaper	vSwitch traffic shaper
migrate	migration	migration	migration	vmkernel vMotion
filedriver	filedriver			
vmkibft*				Fault Tolerance
tpm_tis*				Trusted Platform Module
fsaux*	fsaux*	fsaux		VMFS filesystem utilities

*Not loaded by default

In ESX v3, the split between the service console and the vmkernel was physical, but there was quite a bit of bleed-through nonetheless. As of ESX v3.5, this bleed-through had been nearly eliminated. This bleed-through was in the need for third-party management agents to properly control some aspects of the hardware; however, with ESX v4 VMware has pretty much done away with the need for third-party management agents by including new drivers to handle these needs. Such agents include the Dell Openmanage and HP Insight Management agents, which are now handled by the improved IPMI support.

With the introduction of ESX v4, VMware deprecated some modules that were present in earlier versions of ESX. If the devices that these modules support are a requirement for your ESX installation, you will not be able to upgrade to ESX v4. Table 2.2 lists the devices in ESX v3 that are missing from ESX v4, whereas Table 2.3 includes the differences between ESX 2.5 and ESX v3 for historical purposes. The developers of ESX v4 preferred to settle on modern hardware, and much of the older PCI or PCI-X hardware is obsolete. From a stability point of view, this is a very good thing. Minimizing the number and type of devices that must be supported enables the development team to focus their attention on building quality support for the devices that are supported.

Table 2.2   *ESX v3 Devices Obsolete in ESX v4*

Driver	Device
3c90x	3Com Etherlink 10/100 PCI NIC
e100	Intel 10/100 NIC
aic7xxx	Superseded by the aic79xx driver
sata_vsc	Vitesse VSC7174 4 port DPA SATA
mptscsi_2xx	Superseded by mptspi driver
DAC960	Mylex DAC960 RAID

Table 2.3   *ESX 2.5 Devices Obsolete in ESX v3*

Driver	Device
cpqarray	Compaq SmartArray devices earlier than the SmartArray 5300
gdth	GDT SCSI disk array controller
3c990	3Com EtherLink 10/100 PCI NIC with 3XP Processor
acenic	AceNIC/3C985/GA620 Gigabit Ethernet
ncr53c8xx	NCR53C SCSI
sym53c8xx	SYM53C SCSI
dpt_i20	Adaptec I20 RAID Driver
nfshaper	Traffic Shaper

Several other vmkernel features should be noted that are different between ESX v3 and ESX v4. The first and foremost change is the exposure of internal vmkernel constructs via well-defined APIs that allow third parties to add elements into the vmkernel. These APIs are vNetwork, vStorage, vCompute, and VMsafe, which are discussed throughout the rest of this book.

vStorage is a new marketing name for the virtual disk development kit (vDDK) that was available for ESX v3. The other APIs are all brand new and add major functionality.

In addition to these changes, with ESX v4, the vmkernel is now 64-bit and supports up to 1TB of memory and 320 VMs utilizing up to 512 virtual CPUs.

ESX Boot Differences

Simply put, the service console has been upgraded from being based on a variant of 32-bit Red Hat Enterprise Linux Enterprise Server 3 Update 8 to being based on a variant of 64-bit Red Hat Enterprise Linux Enterprise Server 5.1. ESX is in no way a complete distribution of GNU/Linux. Technically, it is not Linux at all, because the vmkernel is what is interacting with the hardware, and the service console (SC) is running within a VM. Legally, the vmkernel is not Linux either, because it is proprietary. Although the SC is a variant of GNU/Linux, it is a management appliance and not the operating system of ESX.

Even with the change in SC version, the rule that "no Red Hat updates should be used" has *not* been changed. All updates to the SC should come only from VMware. This is crucial. Consider the following: ESX consists of a single CD-ROM, whereas the official version of RHEL5 takes up five CD-ROMs. Therefore, they are not the same and should never be considered the same. For RHEL5, the method to configure any part of the system is to use the supplied system-config- scripts. These are not a part of ESX. Instead, there are a series of esxcfg- scripts that do not map one-to-one to the original Red Hat scripts.

The esxcfg- scripts, however, outlined in a later chapter, do map pretty well to the new management tool: vSphere Client (vSC). This allows for either the client to be used to configure an ESX host directly or through the use of a VMware vCenter server. Although there continues to be a web-based interface, it does not present a method to configure the ESX host or a way to create VMs.

ESX v4 has a kernel that is proprietary, the vmkernel, as well as a modified from the stock RHEL5 kernel that runs within the service console and therefore cannot be Linux. ESXi v4 has a kernel that is proprietary, the vmkernel, only. The modifications to the stock kernel enable the SC to manage the ESX hypervisor. The SC in ESX v4 sees only devices presented or passed through from the vmkernel and does not interact directly with the hardware unless using a pass-through device. Granted, the modifications for ESX are limited in scope to controlling the addition and removal of device drivers to the vmkernel and the ability to control virtual machine and virtual switch objects running within the vmkernel.

In ESX versions earlier than version 3, the vmkernel would load after the SC had fully booted, and the vmkernel would usurp all the PCI devices set to be controlled by the kernel options. In ESX version 3, this changed. The vmkernel loads first, and then the SC, which runs within a specialized VM with more privileges than a standard VM. In ESX v3 the SC was installed onto a local disk, and the VM accessed the local disk through a RAW pass-through SCSI device. In ESX v4, this has changed so that the RAW pass-through SCSI device is no longer used. Instead, the GNU/Linux environment lives within a virtual machine disk file (VMDK). This change further punctuates the difference between the hypervisor and GNU/Linux. So to repeat: The hypervisor is *not* Linux.

Table 2.4 lists the boot steps for ESX versions 4, 3.x, and 2.5.x, as well as the boot steps for ESXi. This documents the changes in the boot sequences for each version. Note that other than a few changes to the daemons used, such as sfbc instead of Pegasus for CIM, and the order of some startups (wsman), there are not many changes between ESX v3.5 and ESX v4. The most significant change is that IPMI has been moved to a vmkernel driver and is no longer part of the service console.

Table 2.4 *ESX Server Boot Steps*

ESX v4	ESX v3.x	ESXi	ESX 2.5.x	Comments
GRUB	GRUB	GRUB	LILO	Boot Loader (Boot strap process that loads the kernel).
N/A	N/A	N/A	kernel-2.4-9vmnix	Loaded by the boot loader.
vmkernel	vmkernel	vmkernel	N/A	vmkernel is loaded from the RAM disk associated with the kernel during the first phase of the kernel boot.
vmkernel devices	vmkernel devices	vmkernel devices	Linux devices	Devices loaded from the RAM disk associated with the kernel during the first phase of the kernel boot.
VM Booted	VM Booted	Start BusyBox	N/A	Boot the VM that runs the service console.
2nd phase kernel loaded	2nd phase kernel loaded	N/A	2nd phase kernel load	The second phase of the kernel is loaded into the administrative VM created when the vmkernel was loaded and becomes the kernel for the COS.
init	init	init	init	Process that loads all other processes and that is started by the second phase of the kernel boot.
S00vmkstart	S00vmkstart	N/A	S00vmkstart	S00 represents the first set of usermode programs to run. S00vmstart ensures that there is no other vmkernel process running; if there is, the vmkernel process is halted.

ESX v4	ESX v3.x	ESXi	ESX 2.5.x	Comments
S01vmware	S01vmware	hostd	N/A	S01 represents the second level of user mode programs to run on boot. In this case, the vmkernel network and storage modules are started.
S09firewall	S09firewall	N/A	N/A	S09 represents the tenth level of user mode programs to run on boot. In this case, the ESX firewall is started using esxcfg-firewall.
S10network	S10network	N/A	S10network	S10 represents the eleventh level of user mode programs to run on boot. In this case, the COS network is started.
S12syslog	S12syslog	N/A	S12syslog	S12 represents the thirteenth level of user mode programs to run on boot. In this case, the logging daemon syslog is started.
Moved to vmkernel driver	S14ipmi	N/A	N/A	S14 represents the fourteenth level of user mode programs to run on boot. In this case, the IPMI service is loaded.
S19slpd	N/A	N/A	N/A	S19 represents the twentieth level of user mode programs to run on boot. In this case, the Service Locator process loaded.
S21wsman	N/A	N/A	N/A	S21 represents the twenty-second level of user mode programs to run on boot. In this case, the VMware Web Services are started.

continues

Table 2.4   *(Continued)*

ESX v4	ESX v3.x	ESXi	ESX 2.5.x	Comments
N/A	S32vmware-aam	N/A	N/A	S32 represents the thirty-second level of user mode programs to run on boot. In this case, the Legato AAM service is loaded to support VMware HA and DRS.
N/A	S55vmware-late	N/A	N/A	S55 represents the fifty-sixth level of user mode programs to run on boot. In this case, the NAS and iSCSI vmkernel devices are initialized using esxcfg-nas and esxcfg-swiscsi tools.
S56xinetd	S56xinetd	N/A	S56xinetd	S56 represents the fifty-seventh level of user mode programs to run on boot. In this case, the Internet super-daemon xinetd is started. The vmware-authd server is now running inside the COS.
N/A	N/A	hostd	N/A	Starting Hostd on ESXi only.
S58ntpd	S58ntpd	ntpd	N/A	S58 represents the fifty-ninth level of user mode programs to run on boot. In this case, the Network Time Protocol Daemon is started.
S62vmware-late	N/A	N/A	N/A	S62 represents the sixty-third level of user mode programs to run on boot. In this case, the NAS and iSCSI vmkernel devices are initialized using esxcfg-nas and esxcfg-swiscsi tools.

ESX v4	ESX v3.x	ESXi	ESX 2.5.x	Comments
N/A	S85vmware-webAccess	N/A	N/A	S85 represents the eighty-sixth level of user mode programs to run on boot. In this case, the Web Based MUI is started.
N/A	S90pegasus (ESX v3.0 Only)	N/A	N/A	S90 is the ninety-first level of user mode programs to run on boot. The OpenPegasus Common Interface Model/ Web Based Enterprise Management server used for managing the ESX server.
N/A	N/A	N/A	S90vmware	S90 is the ninety-first level of user mode programs to run on boot. The vmkernel starts here and vmkernel devices are loaded after the vmkernel usurps PCI devices; in addition the vmware-serverd, and vmware-authd processes start.
N/A	N/A	N/A	S91httpd.vmware	S91 represents the ninety-second level of user mode program to run on boot. The MUI is now running.
S97vmware-vmkauthd	S97vmware-vmkauthd	N/A	N/A	S97 represents the ninety-eighth level of user mode programs to run on boot. The vmkernel authorization server is initialized inside the vmkernel.
S98mgmt-vmware	S98mgmt-vmware	N/A	N/A	S98 represents the ninety-ninth level of user mode programs to run on boot. The vmware host agent is now running. The host agent replaces the vmware-serverd server.

continues

Table 2.4   *(Continued)*

ESX v4	ESX v3.x	ESXi	ESX 2.5.x	Comments
N/A	N/A	sfcbd	N/A	Start Small Footprint CIM Broker Daemon
S98sfcbd-watchdog	N/A	sfcbd-watch-dog	N/A	S99 represents the hundredth level of user mode programs run on boot. The Small Footprint CIM Broker Daemon is launched.
N/A	N/A	slpd	N/A	Launch Service Location Protocol ESXi
N/A	N/A	vobd	N/A	Launch vobd service
N/A	S99pegasus (ESX v3.5 Only)	N/A	N/A	S99 is the one-hundredth level of user mode programs to run on boot. The OpenPegasus Common Interface Model/ Web Based Enterprise Management server used for managing the ESX server.
S99vmware-autostart	S99vmware-autostart	N/A	N/A	S99 represents the one-hundredth level of user mode programs run on boot. The VMs that need to be autostarted are at this time.
S99vmware-vpxa	S99vmware-vpxa	N/A	N/A	S99 represents the one-hundredth level of user mode programs run on boot. The vCenter Agents are started if vCenter manages this node.
N/A	S99wsman	wsman	N/A	S99 represents the one-hundredth level of user mode programs to run on boot. The Web Services Management is started.
Login enabled	Login enabled	Login enabled	Login enabled	After the startup processes are run, the system is fully operational and login is enabled on the console.

In Table 2.4, we can also see the boot process for ESXi. ESXi boots entirely differently than ESX does. Specifically, ESXi does not launch a VM; instead it launches a Posix environment called BusyBox. BusyBox then launches very few user mode processes: just enough to support the necessary management daemons.

This is a significant change, because the BusyBox processes are running within the context of the vmkernel. This implies the vmkernel can run arbitrary code. In ESX, a clear distinction exists between the management console and the vmkernel. In ESXi this distinction is blurred.

Tool Differences

In addition to all the boot changes and OS changes, the ESX-specific commands have changed, forcing many custom scripts to need some form of rewriting. Table 2.5 shows the ESX v4 specific commands and what has been deprecated. Many information tools have been replaced; even so, more information is now available within ESX v4 using the new tools.

Table 2.5 *New and Deprecated ESX Commands*

ESX Command	Status	Functionality
esxcfg-addons	New	List all add-ons within the vmkernel, such as VMsafe drivers.
esxcfg-linuxnet	Deprecated	
esxcfg-vmhbadevs	Deprecated	Replaced by esxcfg-scsidevs
esxcfg-volume	New	Interact with SAN snapshot/replica volumes
esxnet-support	Deprecated	
esxcli	New	Tool to configure/query specific devices like corestorage, Native Multipath Plug-in, and iSCSI
vmfsqhtool, vmfsqueuetool	Deprecated	
vmkiscsi-device, vmkiscsi-ls, vmkiscsi-util	Deprecated	Replaced by vmkiscsiadm, vmkiscsi-tool
vmkperf	New	Command to look at performance information by event type (which is really clock-related data)
vmkvsitools	New	Command to interact with the vmkernel to grab useful information about processes, kernel options, and so on

continues

Table 2.5   *(Continued)*

ESX Command	Status	Functionality
vmsnap.pl, vmsnap_all, vmres.pl	Deprecated	ESX v2 style REDO mode. Removed from ESX v4.
vm-support	Changed	Different output
vmkload_mod		This command has not changed.

Virtual Networking

There are six major changes to virtual networking between ESX v4 and ESX v3.x:

- Introduction of the vNetwork Distributed Switch (vDS)

- Capability to add in third-party virtual switches, such as the Cisco Nexus 1000V

- Introduction of another vmkernel network for Fault Tolerance Logging

- Support for Jumbo Frames for NFS and iSCSI

- IPV6 implementation

- Introduction of Network IO Control (NetIOC) within the vNetwork Distributed Switch (ESX v4.1)

- Introduction of PVLANs when using vDS

- Introduction of Network vMotion when using vDS, in essence the ability to allow the network state to also move when a VM is vMotioned

- Introduction of Load Based Teaming (LBT), which allows the assignment of VM to pNIC to be changed based on the outbound load requirements within the vDS. (ESX 4.1)

- A subtle change in how iSCSI now works within the vNetwork

One other change will be discussed later, and that is the introduction of the VMsafe-net API that allows third-party security tools to work from within the hypervisor.

vNetwork Distributed Switch

The vNetwork Distributed Switch (vDS), available when you have an Enterprise Plus license, allows you to manage per ESX host virtual networks from the cluster level as well allowing for more switch functionality. The vDS is a datacenter or cluster construct seen within VMware vCenter but not necessarily at each host. With previous versions of ESX, you were required to maintain identical virtual network labels across all your hosts. vDS takes care of this for you (as do host profiles, which we will talk about later).

The vDS also supports the concept of Private VLANs (PVLAN), which are Access Control List (ACL) protected VLANs. PVLANs can span more than one ESX v4 host. PVLANs are implemented using the internal functionality called dvFilter. At this time, however, dvFilter has not been exposed to an API for use.

vDS adds the concept of Network vMotion to allow vMotion to also include the network state of a VM as it moves around the virtual network controlled by vDS. This state information is required to allow dvFilter to be used after a vMotion occurs.

vDS works for every type of virtual switch port, including vmkernel ports, which includes the ability to create PVLANs for the vMotion network and other interesting enhanced controls of the virtual networks within the virtual environment.

As of ESX v4.1, vDS now includes Network IO Control (NetIOC) which is a form of traffic shaping where you can split the pNICs connected to a vDS by shares for all outbound traffic. In addition, you can set limits for all outbound connectivity. While traffic shaping does exist for ports attached to VMs, this is the only traffic shaping that exists for outbound traffic on given pNICs. NetIOC is by pNIC on each host. The other new feature is Load Based Teaming, which allows for the mapping of VM to pNIC to be modified based on outbound load congestion but no more often than every 30 seconds.

Third-Party Virtual Switches

ESX v4 exposes the vNetwork API, which allows third parties to create virtual switches. One such virtual switch is the Cisco Nexus 1000V, which you can add into the system if you have the Enterprise Plus licensing level. The Cisco Nexus 1000V works quite a bit differently than normal VMware virtual switches. Specifically, there is only a single Cisco Nexus 1000V allowed per host. In essence, the Cisco Nexus 1000V becomes a new edge switch sitting before the virtual machines.

Even if the Cisco 1000V is in use, it is possible to use normal VMware vSwitches for vmkernel devices and other virtual network needs.

Fault Tolerance (FT) Logging

There is another vmkernel network available when you add virtual portgroups within ESX v4—the Fault Tolerance Logging (FT Logging) network. Like vMotion, the FT Logging network passes critical information between two hosts participating in FT. This information is critical to keeping the virtual machine in lockstep, so it must utilize a high-speed network.

iSCSI Participation

In ESX v3, the service console was required to participate in all forms of iSCSI networking. The service console was used for authentication, whether you were using CHAP or not. In ESX v4, the service console is no longer required to participate in the iSCSI network and therefore will lead to better isolation.

IPv6 Support

IPv6 support now exists for the service console and vmkernel devices within an ESX v4 host. This allows ESX to be used within IPv6 only and mixed IPv6/IPv4 networks. However, iSCSI support using IPv6 is experimental.

VMsafe-Net

VMware has exposed another set of APIs to allow third parties to manage security within the vmkernel which can be authoritative about what is connected to the ESX host. VMsafe-net is one of these APIs. VMsafe-net sits just before the vNIC attached to a VM and not within any virtual switches. This functionality does not exist within ESX v3 and is entirely new for vSphere.

Summary

Table 2.6 summarizes the virtual network functional differences between ESX v4, 3, and 2.5.x.

Table 2.6   *Virtual Network Functional Comparison*

vNetwork Functionality	ESX v4	ESX v3	ESX 2.5.x
Logical ports	Settable to 8, 24, 56, 120, 248, 504, or 1016 ports	Settable to 8, 24, 56, 120, 248, 504, or 1016 ports	Fixed 32 Ports
Portgroups	Many per vSwitch	Many per vSwitch	Many per vSwitch
802.1q	Supported	Supported	Supported

vNetwork Functionality	ESX v4	ESX v3	ESX 2.5.x
802.3ad	Supported	Supported	Supported
NIC Teaming	Supported	Supported	Supported
Source Port ID Load Balancing	Supported	Supported	N/A
Source MAC Address Load Balancing	Supported	Supported	Supported
Source IP Address Load Balancing	Supported	Supported	Supported
GUI Settable standby pNICs	Supported	Supported	N/A
Rolling mode for standby pNICs	Supported	Supported	N/A
vMotion through router/gateway	Supported	Supported	N/A
SC required to participate in iSCSI network	No	Yes	N/A
VMCI	Supported	Supported (ESX v3.5 only)	N/A
IPv6	Supported	N/A	N/A
Virtual Distributed Switch	Supported	N/A	N/A
Network vMotion	Supported with vDS	N/A	N/A
Network IO Control (NetIOC)	Supported with vDS and ESX 4.1	N/A	N/A
Load-Based Teaming	Supported with vDS and ESX 4.1	N/A	N/A
Third-Party vSwitch	Cisco Nexus 1000V	N/A	N/A
Private VLAN	Supported within vDS & Cisco Nexus 1000v	N/A	N/A
Jumbo Frames Support	Supported for iSCSI and NFS	Supported but NOT for iSCSI or NFS	N/A
VMsafe NET	Supported	N/A	N/A
iSCSI vmkernel	Supported	Supported	N/A

continues

Table 2.6   *(Continued)*

vNetwork Functionality	ESX v4	ESX v3	ESX 2.5.x
vMotion vmkernel	Supported	Supported	Supported
NFS vmkernel	Supported	Supported	N/A
Service Console vSwif	Supported	Supported	N/A
Management Console vmkernel (ESXi only)	Supported	Supported	N/A
FT vmkernel	Supported	N/A	N/A
Multilayer vSwitch	Only with VM between each vSwitch	Only with VM between each vSwitch	Only with VM between each vSwitch
Beacon Monitoring	Supported	Supported	Supported

Storage

The biggest change from ESX v3 to ESX v4 occurred within the storage sub-system. Although the VMFS-3 major version number did not change, there are many changes to storage for the better, which included a minor version number change from VMFS 3.31 to VMFS 3.32. However one item has already bitten some people performing upgrades to vSphere; the VMFS-3 file system supports up to 2TB LUNs whereas ESX v4 supports up to (2TB minus 512 bytes) of space. This small change of not supporting a full 2TBs will create a little havoc for those doing upgrades that have LUNs sized exactly 2TBs.They will have to find a way to re-create the LUNs.

> **Important Note**
>
> ESX v4 supports LUNs up to 2TB – 512bytes only.
>
> Migration to ESX v4 from v3 with LUN sizes exactly 2TBs will require LUN modifications.

Other changes to storage introduced with ESX v4 include the capability to grow a VMFS volume, Multipath Plug-in support, extension of virtual disks on-the-fly, storage path load balancing, Jumbo Frames support for iSCSI and NFS (as well as other improvements), FCoE support, and the capability to better use storage device LUN snapshots.

In addition to all these other changes, ESX v4 has simplified the creation of thin provisioned VMs. Although not a new concept, thin provisioning support has been improved within all the management tools.

Grow a VMFS Volume

One of the most significant changes to ESX v4 is the long-awaited capability to manage the size of a VMFS by growing the LUN underneath the VMFS, and then being able to grow the VMFS on top of the LUN. This capability alleviates the need to use extents for smaller VMFS to gain more space or the need to destroy and re-create LUNs bigger than originally planned. Even though you can grow a LUN, the LUN size limits still apply, which are 2TBs – 512 bytes.

Storage IO Control (SIOC)

ESX v4.1 introduces the concept of per virtual disk SIOC for Fibre Channel and iSCSI connectivity. SIOC allows you to set how to split up the storage controller outbound traffic per virtual disk. In other words, SIOC provides Fibre Channel and iSCSI traffic shaping based on a number of shares assigned to each virtual disk on a given LUN presented over Fibre Channel and iSCSI.

Multipath Plug-in (MPP)

The standard multipath capability for ESX has now been modularized within the kernel. ESX has had support for multipath failover since ESX 2.x days. In ESX v3.5, VMware added experimental support for multipath load balancing. These two features exist within the Native Multipath Plug-in (NMP).

Multipath in the storage world has always implied failover, link aggregation, and link load balancing. Multipath makes it possible to improve overall throughput within a server by adding more links (FC-HBAs or Ethernet) to the SAN through multiple controllers.

Now a third party can create its own multipath plug-in and add link aggregation and improvements to load balancing and failover into an ESX v4 host. One such MPP available as of this writing is EMC's PowerPath module written specifically for ESX v4. To use MPP, however, you need to have an Enterprise Plus license.

iSCSI and NFS Improvements

ESX v4 improves overall iSCSI and NFS performance by introducing the capability to use Jumbo Frames with these storage protocols. Jumbo Frames allow more data to be transferred per Ethernet frame (packet) than the default size.

This one change improves overall performance because fewer packets will be transferred, which implies less TCP overhead.

Furthermore, with iSCSI, there has been one other major change mentioned previously. This change is the removal of the requirement that the management console participate within the iSCSI network for authentication reasons. This improves the overall security of using iSCSI within the virtual environment.

FCoE

Fibre Channel over Ethernet (FCoE) using Converged Network adapters was experimentally supported in ESX v3.5. It is fully now supported in ESX v4 using several different 10GB FCoE converged network adapters. FCoE is really a networking solution, but because the vast majority of all bandwidth belongs to the storage channel, it is often considered a storage protocol.

FCoE can reduce the overall cabling required by an ESX host, yet could impact the overall security of the virtual environment. It is best to consider all options when using FCoE. In many cases, the reduction in cabling without loss of functionality is the way to go.

Storage Summary

The ESX Storage subsystem has seen many improvements in ESX v4. The key enhancements include the capability to grow VMFS volumes and the introduction of the modularized multipath capabilities, which allow third parties to add multipath drivers into ESX v4. Table 2.7 presents a summary of the datastore options by ESX version.

Table 2.7 *Datastore Functional Comparison*

Datastore Functionality	ESX v4	ESX v3	ESX v2.5.x
VMFS on SAN	Supported	Supported	Supported
VMFS on SCSI	Supported	Supported	Supported
VMFS on IDE	N/A	N/A	N/A
VMFS on iSCSI	Supported	Supported using iSCSI Initiator within COS. Requires vmkernel device be attached as a port to the COS vSwitch.	N/A

Datastore Functionality	ESX v4	ESX v3	ESX v2.5.x
VMFS on SAS	Supported	Supported	N/A
VMFS on SATA	Supported	Supported (ESX v3.5 only)	N/A
NFS	Supported	Supported for 2GB sparse files only, which is the old style Workstation, GSX, or template file formats	N/A
VMFS-1	R/O	R/O	R/O
VMFS-2	R/O	R/O	R/W
VMFS-3	R/W	R/W	N/A
LUN Size	2TB – 512 bytes	2TB	2TB
LUN Count	256 (but only 128 at a time)	256 (but only 128 at a time)	128
Thin Provisioning	Supported (through Management tools)	Supported	N/A
vStorage API	Supported	Supported as VDDK	N/A
FCoE	Supported	Supported (ESX v3.5 only)	N/A
Load Balancing	Supported	Experimental	N/A
Multipath Plug-in	Supported	N/A	N/A
VMFS Volume Grow	Supported	N/A	N/A
LUN Resignature	Supported	Supported	Supported
Storage IO Control (SIOC)	Supported w/ESX or ESXi v4.1 only	N/A	N/A
Default Disk. MaxLUN Setting	128	128	8
Access to COS File Systems	None	Limited to JUST / vmimages	Full Access
COS Access to Datastores	Supported	Supported	Supported

Availability

ESX version 4 does not introduce any new virtual resources into ESX. The basic four still exist: CPU, memory, network, and storage. However, ESX version 4 adds new availability constructs. The new constructs are Host Profiles, Fault Tolerance, Dynamic Power Management, VMware High Availability improvements, and official support for Storage vMotion.

Host Profiles

Host Profiles does not sound much like an availability component of the service because it enables you to manage the configurations of your ESX hosts from within vCenter. However, it is an availability control mechanism because it will alleviate the common issues of misnamed or misconfigured networking controls that currently plague large installations with respect to virtual networking. As we will see in a later chapter, virtual networking requires that the vSwitch and Portgroup names be identical (case sensitive) across all hosts in order for vMotion, High Availability, and other migrations to be seamless. Host Profiles can maintain these configurations across a multitude of ESX hosts and even apply an existing configuration to newly installed systems.

With ESX v3, this was achieved by the use of scripts written by the administrators. These scripts would configure virtual networking, storage, high availability, and other ESX specific options. Host Profiles moves toward eliminating the need for such scripts, other than one to apply a chosen host profile with the appropriate networking options (vmkernel IP addresses for example).

Host Profiles is available only with an Enterprise Plus license of VMware ESX and, as we will see in Chapter 3, "Installation," can be used in evaluation mode to aid in the upgrade from ESX v3 to ESX v4 for more than one ESX host. Given the license level availability of Host Profiles, there will still be a need for scripts to achieve the same features and configure many more. Host Profiles can only modify those things within ESX exposed by the vSphere Software Development Kit (SDK). Scripts that perform security hardening, for example, will still be necessary.

Host Profiles enables the quick deployment and recovery of an ESX v4 host, which improves the overall availability.

Fault Tolerance

Fault Tolerance (FT) provides a mechanism to keep a VM alive even if the host on which it is running fails. Unlike VMware HA, which will reboot a VM on a new host, with FT the VM keeps running with no interruption. FT does this by keeping a shadow copy of a single vCPU virtual machine using VMDKs and/or virtual RDMs on shared storage in lockstep with the running virtual machine. The shadow copy would run on another ESX v4 host that shares the same storage used by the ESX v4 host where the VM is already running (primary VM). VMware achieves this using its vLockStep technology, which uses a private fault tolerance logging network to keep the primary and shadow copy VMs in sync. In the case of a host or VM failure the FT shadow copy VM would be promoted to the primary VM as soon as such a failure is detected (almost immediately).

When FT is enabled, the shadow copy of a VM is created on a new host by first performing some parts of a vMotion, namely starting a VM linked to the same datastore on the new host, performing a memory copy, and then copying the CPU state. After that is achieved, the vLockStep technology kicks in and the FT logging network is used to communicate nondeterministic events (keystrokes, mouse movements, I/O events, and so on) from the primary VM to the shadow copy. Each VM will process the events independently; however, everything between the nondeterministic events is deterministic, so you know that the vCPUs are in a consistent state between the VMs. This technology builds on the shadow copy VM created normally during a vMotion.

So why is FT for multiple vCPUs a difficult problem to solve?

Keeping one vCPU in vLockStep with another just requires the transfer of nondeterministic events from one VM to its shadow copy. However, when you deal with more than one vCPU, you also deal with timing issues between the vCPUs, which implies that the previously understood deterministic events between nondeterministic events are no longer deterministic. These timing issues deal with when instructions on each of the vCPUs are issued. If even one instruction in one vCPU is issued before the appropriate one within another vCPU, the operation could manipulate the wrong chunk of memory, producing incorrect results. which implies the VM's applications would behave poorly on the shadow copy and at best case keep running but at worst case crash the application as well as the VM with some sort of random violation. This is actually the classic multithreaded application race condition. If you consider each vCPU as its own thread (which most likely they are) you can see that locking and timing information is all important when discussing FT over multiple vCPUs. This has yet to be solved by the world's threads developers. Thread debuggers solve this problem by almost serializing threaded programs, which greatly impacts performance. Although useful for debuggers, this approach does not work for virtual machines.

Because FT has a limit of currently supporting only a single vCPU, the utilization of this capability is limited in scope. For example, a vCenter Server running within a VM often requires two vCPUs; given this, it is not usually a candidate for FT, however much we would like it to be. Unfortunately, FT for multiple vCPUs is a very difficult problem to solve. Eventually it will be, and FT will get widespread use as one more availability tool.

Dynamic Power Management

Dynamic Power Management (DPM) was experimental within ESX v3. DPM allowed vCenter Server to move VMs off an ESX host to other hosts using vMotion, then would power off the ESX host to save on electricity use. For significantly underutilized ESX clusters, this feature allows lull times to use fewer hosts. An ESX host would be powered on using wake-on-lan (WoL), IPMI, or HP ILO technology when the lull times were over, and VMs would automatically be vMotioned back to the waiting host using Dynamic Resource Scheduling. WoL is the least reliable method to wake a host.

ESX v4 moves DPM from experimental to fully supported and adds other mechanisms to use instead of WoL. These additions are use of IPMI and the HP ILO cards to power on and power off hosts. These other technologies are much more specific and directed than WoL, which is still supported. These technologies alleviate false WoL starts due to existing network traffic such as AD broadcasts and other directed requests.

High Availability (HA) Improvements

HA has been improved so that it is now aware of hosts in maintenance mode. There are also improvements in the admission control of nodes within the cluster with many more controllable options. In ESX v3, there were many HA-related problems because of nodes suddenly dropping out of an HA cluster or HA failing for relatively unknown reasons. Many of these issues have now been fixed.

vMotion

vMotion is an availability tool that allows you to move VMs from one host to another host without downtime, as long as the VM used shared storage and both hosts (target and source) could see the storage). ESX v4 introduces some new capability into vMotion as well. Whereas vMotion is used to move VMs from host to host when combined with a vDS, it can also move the network state from host to host (Network vMotion). With ESX v4.1, EVC has also been improved to add another EVC mode. Currently there are EVC modes for AMD CPUs and one for Intel CPUs. ESX v4.1 changes the AMD mode to be a mode with 3Dnow! support and one without 3Dnow! support, because AMD has dropped 3Dnow! from some of its processors.

Storage vMotion

Storage vMotion allows the virtual disk of a VM to be moved from datastore to datastore within a single ESX or ESXi host with no downtime to the VM.

Storage vMotion has moved from the experimental state in ESX v3 to fully supported, with its own vSphere Client integrations. You no longer need to use a third-party plug-in to gain this level of integration. In addition, Storage vMotion is no longer bundled with vMotion, which implies you need at least an Advanced license to use this technology.

Availability Summary

VMware ESX and ESXi are all about redundancy and availability. Many of the major features added to each version of ESX are to improve overall availability and redundancy. When planning ESX, nearly all plans will include many, if not all, of the availability tools and functions.

Table 2.8 provides a comparison of the how the versions support virtual resources.

Table 2.8 *Virtual Resource Functional Comparison*

Functionality	ESX v4	ESX v3	ESX v2.5.x
CPU	Supported	Supported	Supported
Memory	Supported	Supported	Supported
Disk	Supported	Supported	Supported
Network	Supported	Supported	Supported
Resource Pools	Based on CPU/ Memory Resources Utilization Only	Based on CPU/ Memory Resources Utilization Only	N/A
Clusters	Supported	Supported	N/A
Distributed Re-source Scheduling	Based on CPU/ Memory Resource Utilization Only, requiring an ESX Cluster	Based on CPU/ Memory Resource Utilization Only, requiring an ESX Cluster	Extremely limited via HPSIM Virtual Machine Manager plug-in
Dynamic Power Management	Based on CPU/ Memory Resource Utilization Only, requiring an ESX Cluster	Based on CPU/ Memory Resource Utilization Only, requiring an ESX Cluster (experi-mental)	N/A
Fault Tolerance	Requiring an ESX Cluster	N/A	N/A
Host Profiles	Requiring an ESX Cluster	N/A	N/A

continues

Table 2.8   *(Continued)*

Functionality	ESX v4	ESX v3	ESX v2.5.x
Storage vMotion	Supported	Experimental but widely used	N/A
High Availability	Full Support via Legato Automated Availability Management requiring an ESX Cluster	Full Support via Legato Automated Availability Management requiring an ESX Cluster	By hand/poor man's cluster

Disaster Recovery and Business Continuity Differences

VMware ESX and ESXi implementations are all about redundancy, but what is redundancy without the capability to improve uptime via Business Continuity (BC) or disaster avoidance mechanisms? Hand in hand with BC is Disaster Recovery (DR). DR has also been improved within the environment, either by improving backup capabilities or data replication. With ESX or ESXi v3, the only VMware backup mechanism was to use VMware Consolidated Backup and for data replication was the Site Recover Manager (SRM). These tools worked quite differently from each other.

VMware Consolidated Backup made use of a backup server that mounted the VM datastores directly from the SAN, NAS, or iSCSI Server. The backup server is used to offload backups from the actual ESX or ESXi hosts, using the backup server would, working with VMware vCenter, copy the virtual disk blocks direct from SAN after a snapshot was created through vCenter. This resulted in faster backups.

Site Recovery Manager, on the other hand, would aid in LUN to LUN duplication by allowing the storage device to communicate with vCenter to create snapshots and quiesce disks in order to allow the data for the VMs to be copied with great accuracy.

The idea behind both VCB and SRM was to end up with non-crash-consistent backups or replication of VMs. A crash-consistent backup leads to the possibility of quite a bit of testing and repair when problems exist. If the resultant VM is not crash consistent, the recovery time is shortened, and there is less overall risk of failure when there is a critical recovery required. VMware achieves this by having the quiesce scripts tie directly into VSS on Windows machines and use of the sync command to ensure all disk writes have completed before backup or replication can continue.

VMware Consolidated Backup is still supported within ESX v4 but is basically replaced by VMware Data Recovery (VDR) to centralize the management of backups. VDR makes use of the vStorage API to make backups of VMs using a virtual appliance. Similar to VCB, VDR supports using SAN as well as network transfers. Unlike VCB, VDR performs data de-duplication to save on disk space. Many of the third-party backup tools, such as PhD Virtual Backup for VMware ESX, Veeam Backup, and Vizioncore vRanger DPP, make use of the vStorage change block tracking (CBT) functionality. CBT makes use of the block map made when a snapshot is created to know exactly which blocks of a virtual disk have changed since the last time a snapshot has been made. This block map represents every block within a VMDK or a virtual RDM. Every time a block has changed, the block map gets updated that the corresponding block of data has changed. If a backup tool tracks the block map, it can be used to reduce the overall amount of data to be backed up on incremental backups. It also implies you do not need to rely on the Guest OS within the VM, but on the vStorage API only. When you have terabytes of data, backup times need to be reduced and CBT allows this to happen.

SRM allows the SAN, NAS, or iSCSI servers to make use of the vStorage API as well to increase their overall replication throughput. SRM is the glue between the virtual environment management and the hardware LUN replication mechanisms.

Table 2.9 summarizes the backup functions by ESX version.

Table 2.9 *Backup Functional Comparison*

Functionality	ESX v4	ESXi	ESX v3	ESX v2.5.x
vmsnap.pl	N/A	N/A	Deprecated	Supported
Snapshots	Supported	Supported	Supported	N/A
VMware Consolidated Backup	Supported	Supported (paid version only)	Supported	N/A
VMware Data Recovery	Supported	Supported (ESXi v4 and paid version only)	N/A	N/A
VDR De-Duplication	Supported w/VDR only	Supported (ESXi v4 and paid version only)	N/A	N/A
Site Recovery Manager	Supported	Supported (paid version only)	Supported	N/A

continues

Table 2.9 *(Continued)*

Functionality	ESX v4	ESXi	ESX v3	ESX v2.5.x
Third-Party Backup	vRanger, Veeam, PhD Virtual Backup	Paid version only	vRanger, Veeam, PhD Virtual Backup	vRanger, esXpress
LUN Mirroring	Supported only by datastore appliance	Supported only by datastore appliance	Supported only by datastore appliance	Supported only by SAN appliance

Virtual Hardware

ESX v4 has some interesting improvements to the virtual hardware presented to a VM as compared to ESX v3. There is now support for Paravirtualized SCSI (PVSCSI) to improve overall disk IO; an improved third-generation paravirtualized network driver (VMXNET 3); the capability to hot add memory and vCPUs for specific guest operating systems; the capability to implement eight-way vSMP VMs, which requires an Advanced or Enterprise Plus license; support for 255GBs of memory per VM; additional VMDK disk types (SAS and IDE); and the capability to use VMDirectPath to bypass the ESX v4 virtual network layer completely or to directly access any PCI device if the host has Intel VT-d or AMD IOMMU support and the PCI device supports Single Root IO Virtualization.

Guest OS customization continues to support sysprep, so it now includes Windows 2008. The open source customization tools now support more Linux operating systems, such as Debian and Debian-based distributions such as Ubuntu.

All this new functionality requires the use of the virtual hardware version 7, yet virtual hardware version 4 is still supported. This enables the migration of VMs from ESX v3 to ESX v4 without requiring any changes, which improves upgradeability from ESX v3 to ESX v4. Virtual hardware version 7 is also the same virtual hardware used by the new VMware Workstation 7.

With ESX v3.5, VMware added VIX, VMCI, and vProbe functionality to virtual machines. This functionality has not significantly changed with ESX v4. VIX enables the administrator to run commands within a VM from a remote location, and VMCI is an inter-VM communication channel that bypasses the virtual network layer. vProbe enables better debugging of virtual machines and to determine exactly what the VM is doing.

Table 2.10 summarizes the virtual hardware comparison between ESX v4 and ESX v3.

Table 2.10 *Virtual Hardware Functional Comparison*

Functionality	ESX v4	ESX v3	ESX 2.5.x
vCPU (vSMP)	1-8 including odd numbers	1, 2, or 4	1 or 2
USB	Yes (with Update 1)	No	No
MSCS	Up to 8 nodes	Up to 8 nodes	2 node
Configuration File Location	With VMDK	With VMDK	In /home
Memory	255GB	64 GB	3.6 GB
SCSI HBA	PVSCSI/SAS/ LSI|BUSLogic	LSI|BUSLogic	LSI|BUSLogic
IDE VMDK	Supported	N/A	N/A
SAS VMDK	Supported	N/A	N/A
vNIC	Flexible	Flexible	Selectable pcnet32
VMXNET	Version 1,2 or 3	Version 1 or 2	Version 1
PVSCSI	Supported for non-boot and boot in ESX v4.1	N/A	N/A
Hot Add Disk	Supported[1]	Supported[1]	N/A
Hot Add CPU	Supported[1]	N/A	N/A
Functionality	**ESX v4**	**ESX v3**	**ESX 2.5.x**
Hot Add Memory	Supported[1]	N/A	N/A
NPIV	Supported (disk only)	Supported (disk only)	N/A
VMDirectPath	Supported[1]	Supported[1]	N/A
64-Bit Guests	Only on 64-bit hardware	Only on 64-bit hardware	N/A
vHardware Level	> Workstation 5.5	> Workstation 5.5 < 7.0	<Workstation 5.5
Snapshots	Supported	Supported	N/A
vProbes	Supported	N/A	N/A
VIX	Supported	Supported (ESX v3.5)	N/A
VMCI	Supported	Supported (ESX v3.5)	N/A

continues

Table 2.10   *(Continued)*

Functionality	ESX v4	ESX v3	ESX 2.5.x
vSWP	With VMDK	With VMDK	Global

[1]With proper support within guest operating system

Virtual Machine and Server Management

There are only a few changes to the way VMs are managed when moving to ESX v4. VMware has rewritten the Virtual Infrastructure Client user interface and named it the vSphere Client. The look and feel is quite a bit different, but the most important things are the same, such as editing VM settings and moving around the different host and VM views.

In addition to the changes to the management client, which are numerous, VMware has improved the vSphere SDK to expose even more capability. There is also a new version of the vSphere SDK in Beta named Onyx. Onyx exposes even more of the functionality via powershell cmdlets to interact with the virtual distributed switch and other new features. The vSphere SDK has language bindings for nearly every language available, most notably PowerShell, Perl, .NET, and Java.

At the time of ESX v3, an appliance was introduced named Virtual Infrastructure Management Appliance (VIMA). VIMA has been replaced by the Virtual Management Appliance (vMA), which is a Just Enough Operating System (JeOS) version of Linux with the Perl vSphere SDK language bindings installed and scripts written to make use of them. Also included in this is the Remote CLI commands. The goal of the vSphere SDK, vMA, and Remote CLI is to alleviate the need to ever log in to the management console to perform any work.

All the improvements imply that ESX v4 is highly automatable.

Table 2.11 summarizes the virtual management differences across versions.

Table 2.11   *Virtual Management Functional Comparison*

Functionality	ESX v4	ESXi	ESX v3	ESX 2.5.x
webAccess	Supported for access to VMs ONLY	Supported for access to VMs ONLY	Supported for access to VMs ONLY	Supported, independent of MUI or CLI
vSphere Client	**Supported**	**Supported**	**Supported**	R/O
Virtual Infrastructure Client	N/A	Supported (ESXi v3 Only)	Supported	R/O

Functionality	ESX v4	ESXi	ESX v3	ESX 2.5.x
Remote CLI	Supported	Supported	Supported	N/A
vSphere (VI) SDK	Supported	Supported	Supported	N/A
vMA	Supported	Supported	Supported	N/A
Command Line (CLI)	Supported, Integrated with vSphere Client	Available in unsupported mode	Supported, Integrated with VIC	Supported, independent of VC
vCenter	Supported, integrated with CLI and webAccess	Supported, integrated with CLI and webAccess	Supported, integrated with CLI and webAccess	Supported, independent of MUI and CLI
VM Creation	No special requirements for 2.6 Kernels; in addition, Virtual Floppy image for Windows XP SCSI driver now a part of ESX Install	No special requirements for 2.6 Kernels; in addition, Virtual Floppy image for Windows XP SCSI driver now a part of ESX Install	No special requirements for 2.6 Kernels; in addition, Virtual Floppy image for Windows XP SCSI driver now a part of ESX Install	2.6 Kernel Versions of Linux require Custom VM creation modes

Security Differences

There are a few security differences between ESX v4 and ESX v3.

The first is the availability of VMware vShield Zones. vShield Zones implements an inline firewall appliance that sits between two virtual switches within your virtual network. vShield Zones requires an Advanced or higher license to use. In addition, vShield Zones is a Zone firewall based on iptables without NAT or port redirection support as such is not designed for edge firewall use. After v4.1, there is a new suite of VMware vShield security tools, of which Zones is one such tool. There is now vShield Edge (Edge Firewall), vShield App (VMsafe Firewall), and vShield Endpoint (used by Antivirus vendors).

The second is VMware VMsafe. VMsafe is a set of APIs that splits functionality between slowpath and fastpath. The fastpath implies the use of a third-party driver within your hypervisor, whereas the slowpath uses a virtual appliance that the fastpath driver talks to for management purposes. With VMsafe a certain amount of intelligence can live within the fastpath driver, but any heavy lifting must be performed within the slowpath appliance. The first use of VMsafe is the VMsafe-net APIs, which allow third-party vendors to implement firewalls.

Antivirus vendors are looking at using VMsafe-memory APIs to do per ESX v4 host virus checking instead of per VM.

Another security difference is the capability to use a trusted platform module (TPM) to do disk integrity checks to ensure that the vmkernel has not been modified. This does require a TPM device within your server to enable. In addition, for ESX v4.1, the TXT extensions for TPM are supported.

With the introduction of the Cisco Nexus 1000V and Virtual Distributed Switch, there is also now the concept of Private VLAN support or VLANs that have an access control list to control who can use these VLANs.

The security differences between versions are summarized in Table 2.12.

Table 2.12 *Security Functional Comparison*

Functionality	ESX v4	ESXi	ESX v3	ESX v2.5.x
iptables/Firewall	Installed and configured	N/A	Installed and configured	On media not installed by default
vShield tools	Supported	Supported (ESXi v4)	N/A	N/A
Third-Party Inline Firewalls	Supported	Supported	Supported	Supported
VMsafe	Supported	Supported (ESXi v4)	N/A	N/A
TPM	Supported	Supported (ESXi v4)	N/A	N/A
Private VLANS	Supported with Virtual Distributed Switch or Cisco Nexus 1000V	Supported with Virtual Distributed Switch or Cisco Nexus 1000V (ESXi v4)	N/A	N/A
Data-Link Layer Security	On vSwitch and Portgroup and Port with dVSwitch	On vSwitch and Portgroup	On vSwitch and Portgroup	With VM

Installation Differences

Minor differences exist between ESX v4 and ESX v3 in the installation or upgrade routines. Although the install can work on unsupported SCSI or RAID hardware, the boot of ESX will generally fail. So it is important to use a supported SCSI or RAID adapter. It is possible to upgrade various versions of ESX earlier than version 3, and that list is fully available in Chapter 3. Not all versions of ESX support this upgrade, however.

Three noticeable differences exist between the upgrade routine for ESX v4 and ESX v3. In ESX v2.x, you were requested to add a license key during install. With ESX v3 this requirement was dropped; with ESX v4, you are again requested to enter a license key. However, this can be delayed until you use the vSphere Client for the first time, whether through vCenter or direct access. The second is the automated disk layout during upgrades. During upgrades the VMware default disk layout is assumed to be overriding your existing settings. Another significant improvement in the ESX v4 install routine is that you can now choose your initial service console NIC rather than the installer automatically choosing whatever NIC shows up first.

ESX versions earlier than version 3 install on and run from any disk media supported by Red Hat Linux version 7.2. With ESX v3, although it is possible to install onto disk media supported by RHEL3-ES, is it not possible to run from anything but one of the supported SCSI/RAID devices. With ESX v4, you can install onto media supported only by ESX now because the Red Hat based service console version no longer matters. If the drivers do not exist inside ESX for your installation device, there is no way to install onto that media. ESX v4 now installs everything onto a VMFS with a small boot volume, which is how ESXi has always been installed.

In ESX v3, there was always confusion about what was supported, because the installer ran RHEL3, yet you ran ESX. VMware rewrote the installer for ESXi so that *only* the supported devices could be installed upon. This new installer is the one used by ESX v4.

Licensing Differences

There have been major changes in licensing within ESX v4; the most important change is that there is now no need for a License Manager (except when managing ESX v3 systems from vSphere vCenter 4). Instead there is now a single license key that you either input via VMware vCenter Server or directly into the host using the vSphere Client. This single license key contains all the necessary information to enable or disable the features you have purchased.

The other major change is that VMware no longer sells features a la carte; instead they sell in bundles of functionality. If you previously purchased items a la carte and you still have service and support when you upgrade to vSphere, you can retrieve your license keys, and your a la carte functionality should still exist. If you do not have service and support, when you go to retrieve your vSphere licenses, you will not be able to do so until you purchase service and support for your older ESX v3 licenses.

All VMware vSphere licensing is done per individual socket (ESX v3 was licensed per TWO sockets), not per core. However, now there are limits based on license level for the number of cores of which you can make use. The split is at six cores. So when you upgrade CPUs to eight cores, you may also need to upgrade your license to make use of the two extra cores.

Although not exactly a licensing change, it is a cost change, VMware vSphere ESX v4 is now licensed by socket; in the past, VMware was licensed by a pair of sockets.

The license levels have also changed:

- Essentials—Equivalent to Starter

- Essentials Plus—Equivalent to Foundation

- Standard—No change

- Advanced—New, adding some new features to Standard

- Enterprise—No change

- Enterprise Plus—New, adding all new features to Enterprise

Table 2.13 provides a rundown of the licensing differences between ESX versions 2.5.x and 3.

Table 2.13 *Virtual Resource Functional Comparison*

Functionality	ESX4	ESX v3	ESX v2.5.x
ESX	Essentials, Essentials Plus, Standard, Advanced, Enterprise, Enterprise Plus	Starter, Foundation, Standard, Enterprise	Separate, VI Bundle
vCenter Server	Bundled	Separate or with a Bundle	Separate
VCB	Bundled	Bundled	N/A
Host Based Licenses	Supported	Supported	Supported
Server Based Licenses	N/A	Supported	N/A

Functionality	ESX4	ESX v3	ESX v2.5.x
Virtual SMP Support	Supported Four-way Eight-way (Enterprise Plus only)	Supported Four-way (Separate or Enterprise)	Supported Two-way (Separate)
Multiple Cores per Processor	Supported Up to 6 Up to 12 (Advanced or Enterprise Plus only)	Supported Unlimited	Supported Unlimited
Memory/Physical Server	256GB Unlimited (Enterprise Plus only)	128GB	64GB
Thin Provisioning	Supported	Supported	Supported
Update Manager	Supported	Supported	N/A
VMsafe	Supported	N/A	N/A
vStorage API	Supported	Via VDDK	N/A
Resource Pools	Based on CPU/Memory Resources Utilization only. Requires vCenter.	Based on CPU/Memory Resources Utilization only. Requires vCenter.	N/A
Clusters	Supported	Supported	N/A
High Availability	Full Support via Legato Automated Availability Management requiring at least Essentials Plus	Full Support via Legato Automated Availability Management separately purchasable or Enterprise	By hand/poor man's cluster
Data Recovery VDR	Not available for Essentials or Standard	N/A	N/A
Hot Add Memory	Requires at least Advanced and a Guest OS that supports functionality	N/A	N/A
Fault Tolerance	Requires at least Advanced Limited to one vCPU and requiring an ESX Cluster	N/A	N/A

continues

Table 2.13   *(Continued)*

Functionality	ESX4	ESX v3	ESX v2.5.x
vShield	Zones is free with at least Advanced. Other vShield tools are licensed separately.	N/A	N/A
vMotion	Requires at least Advanced	Separately purchasable, Standard or Enterprise	Separately purchasable
Storage vMotion	Requires at least Enterprise	Comes with vMotion	N/A
Distributed Resource Scheduling	Based on CPU/ Memory Resource Utilization only, requiring an ESX Cluster. Requires at least Enterprise.	Based on CPU/ Memory Resource Utilization only, requiring an ESX Cluster. Separate or Enterprise.	Extremely limited via HPSIM Virtual Machine Manager plug-in
Dynamic Power Management	Comes with DRS	Experimental	N/A
Enhanced vMotion Capability	Comes with DRS	Supported	N/A
Storage IO Control	Requires Enterprise Plus	N/A	N/A
Network IO Control	Requires Enterprise Plus	N/A	N/A
Load Based Teaming	Requires Enterprise Plus	N/A	N/A
Virtual Distributed Switch	Requires Enterprise Plus	N/A	N/A
Host Profiles	Requires Enterprise Plus	N/A	N/A
Multipath Plug-in	Requires Enterprise Plus	N/A	N/A

VMware Certification

The VMware Certified Professional (VCP) exam has been updated for ESX v4. Any previous VCP will still exist, *but* will not apply to ESX v4. Any ESX v3 VCP could have taken the VCP for version 4 without first having to sit a class until January 30, 2010. After this date, all VCPs are required to sit a class. Scoring of the exam has also changed—it is no longer just a percentage but a score that is a count of the questions answered correctly.

If you fail the VCP for ESX v4 exam, to retake the exam you must first take the full four-day VMware ESX v4 course. The passing grade for the VCP is 70%; to be eligible to become a VMware Certified Instructor, the passing grade is 85%.

VMware has also introduced the VMware Certified Design Expert (VCDX), which is one of the more difficult certifications to achieve; you need to take at least two more exams and defend a design you created, much like you would for a master's or PhD thesis. The steps to gain this certification are these: have a VCP3/VCP4, complete the Qualification Review, pass the Enterprise Exam, pass the Design Exam, apply for the VCDX Defense, and pass the defense of your design as judged by those who sit on the defense panel, which mainly consists of those who already have their VCDX and work for VMware.

Last, VMware has introduced the VMware Certified Advanced Professional (VCAP). VCAP has two tracks: Datacenter Administrator (DCA) and Datacenter Design (DCD). To gain either of these certifications, you are required to have a VCP4 (for vSphere 4) and pass the appropriate exams. After you have your VCP4, you are not required to sit any classes.

Conclusion

This chapter provided a review of the major differences between VMware ESX v4 and ESX v3, as well as the key differences between ESXi and ESX. As you can see, not that many differences exist between ESX and ESXi. This chapter serves as a starting point from which to plan an upgrade. Major differences were pointed out in each of the sections. The chapters following this one go into ESX and ESXi v4 in detail.

Chapter 3

━━━━━━━━━━

Installation

Installing or upgrading ESX and ESXi host software can take about 20 minutes depending on the hardware involved. However, it takes a lot longer to plan the steps we need to take before we start installing. With proper planning, we can avoid the costly mistake of finding out much later we did not really want to boot from the SAN or that the file system size for root or for log messages is too small and end up reinstalling and starting over again. See the section "Example 4: Office in a Box," in Chapter 1, "System Considerations," for a case where changes were necessary that could equate to needing to start over. We also do not want to find out after the fact that the hardware we have on hand is not compatible with the software and is unsupported. In this chapter, we go through a checklist of all the information you need to make the right decisions for installing the ESX host software in your environment. For information about ESX hardware issues, see Chapter 1.

When you install or upgrade an ESX or ESXi host, you can quickly install more ESX or ESX hosts that share similar configurations using Host Profiles and judicious scripting during install. The kickstart capabilities of ESX have changed only slightly and have been introduced into ESXi. See the end of this chapter for detailed information about how to perform a scripted installation.

This chapter presents more than the installation of ESX or ESXi; that is just one of the steps we discuss. There is more to planning an install than there is to the actual installation. We start with a preinstallation checklist and then work through the actual steps. In the following paragraphs, ESX is mentioned and this implies ESXi as well unless explicitly stated that it is not related to ESXi.

Preinstallation Checklist

Table 3.1 lists the general information necessary before the installation or upgrade of an ESX host takes place. Most of these items are mere reminders of tasks that may be completed by others in an organization, but they are still very important to gather nonetheless. The checklist also refers you to other chapters that cover the details of the item of the checklist.

Table 3.1 *Installation Checklist*

Step #	Additional Decision or Step Short Description	Information Needed	Dependency
1	Read the release notes.		
2	Read all relevant documentation.	This includes the Installation Guide.	
3	Is the hardware configuration supported?		See Chapter 2
4	Is the hardware functioning correctly?		Vendor diagnostics
5	Is the firmware at least at minimum supported levels?		Vendor information
6	Is the system BIOS correctly set?		Vendor information
7	Boot disk location	Local SAN iSCSI	
8	VMware ESX/ESXi host licenses		
9	VM License and installation materials		
10	Service console/Management Appliance network information	Static IP address Hostname (FQDN) Network mask Gateway address DNS information NTP information	

Step #	Additional Decision or Step Short Description	Information Needed	Dependency
11	vmkernel network information (iSCSI, vMotion, Fault Tolerance, and possible NFS [NAS] vSwitches)	Static IP address Hostname (FQDN) Network mask Gateway address DNS information	Chapter 10
12	Memory allocated to service console		ESX specific
13	Number of virtual network switches		Chapter 10
14	Virtual network switch label name(s)		Chapter 10
15	File system layout		ESX specific
16	Configure the server and the FC-HBA to boot from the SAN	Or disconnect if not using boot from SAN.	Chapter 6
17	ESX/ESXi host installation		
18	Connecting to ESX/ESXi for the first time		
19	Third-party tools to install	Cisco Nexus 1000V PowerPath MPP VMsafe	
20	Additional software packages to install		ESX specific
21	Patch ESX or ESXi		
22	Guest operating system software		
23	Guest operating system licenses		

continues

Table 3.1   *(Continued)*

Step #	Additional Decision or Step Short Description	Information Needed	Dependency
24	Network information for each guest operating system	IP address	Chapter 10
		Hostname (FQDN)	
		Network mask	
		Gateway address	
		DNS information	
25	Guest upgrades	Virtual hardware 7	Chapter 10
		New VMware Tools	

Preinstallation/Upgrade Steps

In an upgrade of ESX 4 from ESX 3, you have some additional up-front considerations as well as a slightly extended process in order to keep your existing configuration settings intact. Review Chapter 2, "Version Comparison," in detail and pay close attention to the unsupported hardware. If you must upgrade hardware to move to ESX 4, a reinstallation is recommended, yet you can still maintain your existing configurations using Host Profiles outlined in the general process previously.

It is very important to fully understand one of the major differences between ESX 4 and ESX 3: the fact that instead of using a RAW disk within the service console virtual machine, in ESX 4 the service console VM is built from a VMDK. A RAW disk, as we will discuss in Chapter 10, "Virtual Machines," is a direct link from the virtual machine to a LUN on local disk. This one change implies that in order to create the service console VMDK, there must be a VMFS of at least 10GBs available on which the VMDK can be created.

This space requirement on a local disk is often the cause for switching gears and going the route of reinstallation instead of the upgrade path as most local disks within an ESX host are fully utilized. If you boot from SAN instead of from a local disk, it is easy to solve this by presenting another unused 10GB LUN to the ESX host. However, it is not necessarily the wisest move to place this VM with your other VMs on your everyday use VMFS. You can, but it is not recommended. If you are short on local disk space for the 10GB VMFS, go the reinstallation route.

If you are also moving from ESX to ESXi you will need to reinstall because no upgrade path exists for this type of installation.

However, before you upgrade anything, this is one important question to ask: *Are you satisfied with your backup?*

This is such a simple question, but often it is overlooked. Although upgrades are possible, it is not recommended that you perform an upgrade, as explained later in this chapter. An upgrade to ESX 4 would override your current disk layouts. However, the upgrade is supported if the proper version of ESX 3 is in use. The full list will be part of the ESX upgrade documentation from VMware. Here is a short list of upgradeable versions of ESX:

- ESX version 3.0.0

- ESX version 3.0.1

- ESX version 3.0.2

- ESX version 3.0.3

- ESX version 3.0.4

- ESX version 3.5.x

- ESXi version 3.5.x

The steps for an upgrade are similar to the steps for an install, with some minor differences. For example, the original RAW disk file system placements and allocations will not be changed; however, new file systems will be created within the VMDK. If the system is a "boot from SAN" configuration, be sure that the only LUNs mounted are the boot volume and necessary VMFS volumes. All other LUNs should not be seen by ESX—specifically, ext3 type file systems other than the boot LUN.

If the desired path is to reinstall, it is strongly recommended that the complete ESX host be backed up to a remote location on either tape or disk. At the very least, back up all ESX host configuration files and data, located in /etc and /etc/vmware, or any other configuration file locations for your third-party applications. In addition, disable all remote SAN connections so that the installation has no chance to affect the SAN VMFS LUNs. The specific pre-upgrade steps are covered in the following sections.

Step 1: Back Up ESX

Be sure to answer the following question: Are you satisfied with your backup? Are all the specialized system changes in the service console saved somewhere? Is everything you added into /vmimages saved? What about copies of all the VMs? In effect, you are asking this question: "Are all the little changes made to

ESX stored somewhere safe?" Consider backing up the contents of the /etc and /home directories at the very least for all configuration changes. Such a backup could easily be screenshots of all the configuration windows from the VMware Infrastructure Client connected either to vCenter or the ESX host. Note that any configuration changes made for security purposes that are service console specific will need to be remade with the latest version of the service console in mind. Even so, it is best to make a backup of the necessary configuration files for security purposes. At the very least make a copy of /etc/pam.d/system-auth, /etc/security/access.conf, /etc/hosts.allow, /etc/hosts.deny, and /etc/security/login.defs.

Step 2: Read the Release Notes

Read the release notes to find out whether any features or special instructions match your desired installation and hardware. The release notes will mention newly added features, resolved and known issues, bug fixes, security alerts, and necessary workarounds for various installation issues. Release notes are available for each version of ESX at the VMware website: www.vmware.com/support/pubs/vi_pubs.html.

Step 3: Perform a Pre-Upgrade Test

The pre-upgrade test for ESX 4 is not provided directly by VMware. You need to run a few tools to determine if your system will support ESX 4 as well as determine whether you need to modify your BIOS to add this support. The other item this test will perform is to determine what feature set of vSphere is supported, such as being able to use fault tolerance. The tools useful for this are the VMware SiteSurvey tool (www.vmware.com/download/shared_utilities.html) and the VMware CPU Host Info tool from www.run-virtual.com. VMware SiteSurvey connects to your VMware vCenter Server and generates a report (see Figure 3.1) based on all nodes registered within a specific cluster. The SiteSurvey tool, however, could yield errors and not work if the build levels of ESX or ESXi within your cluster are different. In that case, use the VMware CPU Host Info tool from www.run-virtual.com to retrieve CPU information, as shown in Figure 3.2.

If these tools show that you do not have at least 64-bit CPU support, you cannot upgrade to vSphere ESX 4 until you upgrade your hardware. If the Intel-VT or AMD-V bit and NX or XD bit are not enabled, this implies that you need to upgrade your server BIOS to enable these features. In some cases, you cannot change your BIOS to enable these settings, and this implies you need to upgrade your hardware as well.

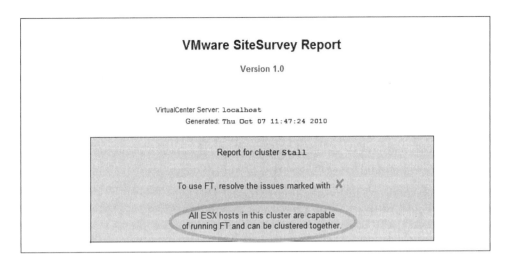

Figure 3.1 *Output of VMware SiteSurvey*

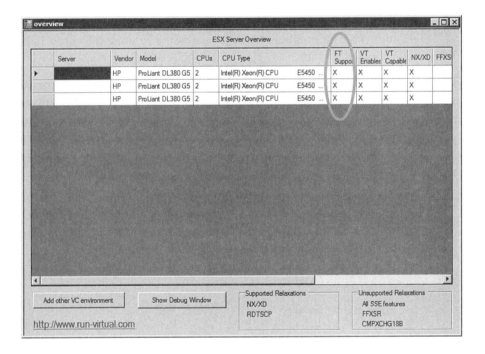

Figure 3.2 *Output of Run-Virtual's CPU Host Info tool*

Step 4: Prepare Your ESX Host

Follow these steps to prepare your ESX host for upgrade, assuming the pre-upgrade test has been passed and you have vMotioned all the VMs you can from the existing host (if vMotion is licensed):

1. Once more, are you satisfied with your VM backups?

2. Are there any VMs in suspended state? Resume the guest OS, shut it down, and power off the VM.

3. Are there any disks in undoable mode? Shut down the guest OS, commit or discard the changes, and power down the VM.

4. Did the shutdown of the guest OS and powering down of the VMs go cleanly? If not, debug the shutdown until they are cleanly powered down.

5. Are all .vmdk and .vmx files backed up? If not, back up all VMs.

6. Write down the virtual network configuration, or capture the list from the VMware Infrastructure Client (VIC) via some form of graphical capture tool. This information is also available by running the commands `esxcfg-vswitch -l`, `esxcfg-route -l`, and `esxcfg-vswif -l`.

7. Write down existing storage configuration information, or capture this information from the Storage Management pages of the VIC. This information is also available in the output of the `esxcfg-vmhbadevs` and `esxcfg-mpath` commands.

8. ESX only: What third-party applications are running on your current ESX host? Specifically, any hardware or backup agents should be reviewed. In most cases, these agents or tools will need to be de-installed prior to the upgrade. You will definitely have to de-install the HP Insight Manager and other hardware agents. At this time, it is a good idea to make sure that any agent configurations are recorded or saved to a remote location. If you are moving to ESXi, these agents cannot be used and you may need to find alternatives.

9. ESX only: Back up any security settings for your host, specifically `/etc/pam.d/system-auth`, `/etc/security/access.conf`, `/etc/hosts.allow`, `/etc/hosts.deny`, and `/etc/security/login.defs`.

10. Make a copy of the password file and any other user-specific information.

    Remember the upgrade process is irreversible!

    So, are you comfortable with your backup?

Most if not all of this information is also gathered by the running of a vm-support script, which can be done for both ESX and ESXi.

Installation/Upgrade Steps

The installation and upgrade steps are just a little more involved than the back-up steps. However, they begin simply enough.

At step 14, we also have a change to how we progress. Specifically we will be using either the VMware Update Manager or VMware Host Update Utility to perform the upgrade instead of performing an installation. Although this step itself covers quite a bit of process, that is covered in other books and material well enough. The important aspect of this chapter is all the planning elements to any installation or upgrade.

Step 1: Read the Release Notes

Read the Release Notes to find out whether any features or special instructions match your desired installation and hardware. The Release Notes will mention newly added features, resolved and known issues, bug fixes, security alerts, and necessary workarounds for various installation issues. Release Notes are available for each version of ESX at the VMware website: www.vmware.com/support/pubs/vi_pubs.html.

Step 2: Read All Relevant Documentation

Read the relevant installation documentation for ESX. Although it is extremely easy to install ESX, reading through the procedure once will prepare you for all the possible contingencies for the chosen installation path.

Step 3: Is Support Available for the Hardware Configuration?

Verify and understand your hardware configuration per Chapter 2.

Step 4: Verify the Hardware

Verify the hardware on which ESX will be installed. Specifically, run any hardware diagnostic tools available from the hardware vendor to test all subsystems for failures and deficiencies. Because ESX will stress any hardware past any normal operational point, be sure that all components are in working order. For example, normally a Windows-based operating system installation barely uses resources, whereas ESX makes use of *all* available resources. Use the memtest86 program to stress test memory before ESX is put into production. Memtest86, from www.memtest86.org, will run multiple types of memory tests in a repetitive fashion to determine whether there are bad sticks somewhere in the system. Use of hardware diagnostics such as the SmartStart tools from HP, or similar tools for other hardware types, will determine whether there are also any failures in memory or other subsystems. This step can save time and frustration later. However, if you do run vendor diagnostics, be sure to skip any disk-timeout tests because these will extend the test period by days instead of just hours. For both memtest86 and for vendor diagnostics, you want minimally a good solid 10 runs during your test period, which could take at least 72 hours. More is often better because some issues do not occur until there is sufficient time elapsed or stress on the system. CPU overheat issues often take a long time to show up.

It is also very important to physically inspect the inside of any chassis. This step seems fairly obvious but is the one overlooked the most. A physical inspection of a machine made by the author found that a heat sink was not properly fastened and that the loop to which it fastened was missing. No wonder the system had trouble running the vendor-provided diagnostics and had unexplained crashes during production runs.

The "Best Practice for Hardware" steps are also great to follow if the host fails during production, and they are not just for installation or upgrade processes.

Best Practice for Hardware

1. Inspect the inside of any server chassis looking for obvious issues. At this time, also reseat any memory and boards.

2. Run memory tests for at least 48 hours, or at least 10 runs, which could take 72 hours.

3. Verify that memory is balanced across CPU sockets for AMD and Intel (Nehalem) based NUMA machines.

4. Be sure the system has been verified; ESX taxes hardware more than any other OS and will find hardware issues other operating systems will not.

Step 5: Are the Firmware Levels at Least Minimally Supported?

Verify that the firmware versions on each ESX host are at the appropriate levels; in most cases, this implies the latest level of firmware, but in some cases this could be a not-so-recent level. While verifying the firmware versions on each ESX host, take the extra time to also verify the firmware versions on all switches, Fibre, or network (and on SANs or other attached storage devices). This is the most important step and an often ignored step of the installation, and it can cause the most dramatic of failures. For example, a customer had a periodic ESX failure related to a SAN rebooting, which in effect knocked the ESX host offline while the storage processor rebooted. The firmware revision of the SAN was several iterations below the minimum required level for a SAN connected to an ESX host. After this item was fixed, the problems went away. In some cases, the minimum required firmware for your storage, systems, switches, and I/O cards will not be listed in the ESX installation guide or HCLs; in this case, contact the hardware vendor for the information.

> ### Best Practice for Hardware Firmware Versions
>
> Ensure the firmware versions for all hardware connected to or associated with ESX are at the proper levels.

Step 6: Is the System and Peripheral BIOS Correctly Set?

Verify that the BIOS settings are correct for the systems and peripherals to be used. This is another often-overlooked installation step. Some system hardware requires that various BIOS settings be set properly for ESX to run properly. If the BIOS is not set properly, the ESX host will crash or experience mysterious problems. For example, on some HP Xeon-based hardware, the BIOS needs to have the MPS Table Mode set to Full Table APIC. If BIOS setting is not configured correctly, when the systems are fully loaded with PCI cards, IRQs are not assigned properly, and either PCI cards do not get registered or the devices show up with unexpected and quite incorrect settings. Cases in point are NICs, which often show up in unchangeable half-duplex modes.

It is very important to ensure that the Intel-VT or AMD-V bit is enabled in the BIOS and that the No eXecute (NX) or eXecute Disable (XD) bit is enabled in the BIOS. These two settings are required to run vSphere ESX 4 properly.

Ensure the "Best Practice for System BIOS" is followed. This step, like the hardware verification step, should be reverified if there are also production failures.

> ### Best Practice for System BIOS
>
> For multicore systems, node Interleaving should be disabled (this enables NUMA) for significant performance gains.
>
> Be sure the add-in (Fibre Channel, SCSI, network, and so on) hardware BIOS settings are set properly.
>
> Be sure the system BIOS settings are set properly, per vendor specifications, so that ESX runs properly and does not mysteriously crash.

Be sure that Intel-VT or AMD-V is enabled in the BIOS.
Be sure that the No eXecute (NX) or eXecute Disable (XD) bits are enabled in the BIOS.

Step 7: Where Do You Want the Boot Disk Located?

Decide how to boot your server. A typical installation is to install the OS on a server's internal disk or on a disk directly attached to the server, yet some FC HBAs have an enhanced configurable BIOS that supports booting from a storage device attached to a SAN, or even from iSCSI. Booting from SAN or iSCSI has some limitations and unique benefits over a traditional installation.

Installing to boot from SAN or iSCSI should be considered when the ESX host system is diskless or has no usable local storage devices. In these cases, the system could be a diskless blade or some other server that has multiple paths to a SAN. Installing to boot from SAN or iSCSI will allow the cloning of an ESX host by copying the system LUN to another LUN on a SAN or iSCSI server. This form of ESX host deployment in conjunction with Host Profiles could save time over other forms of ESX host deployments. In addition, booting from SAN or iSCSI creates the capability to make an ESX host independent of the server hardware. If the hardware goes bad, just point the new ESX host, which matches the original host closely, to the existing LUNs and reboot from an already installed LUN, thereby increasing possible DR capabilities. Yet now the ESX host in question depends entirely on the Fibre or network fabric. So, part of the decision needs to be based on what part of the ESX host has the lowest mean time to failure: SAN, iSCSI, or local disks.

In ESX 3, there was a limitation based on using shared disk clusters. This limitation has been removed in ESX 4. In ESX 3, installing to boot from SAN or iSCSI should not occur if shared disk clusters, such as Microsoft Clustering and Red Hat clusters, would be in use, raw disk maps are required, or when there is a need for a raw SCSI device mapped from the ESX host to a VM.

Booting from SAN or iSCSI can also increase the complexity of an ESX host configuration, because now the replacement server needs the FC or iSCSI HBAs properly configured, SAN connections to a machine must be via switch fabric and not an arbitrated loop connection, any IDE or non-SCSI local drives may need to be disabled to perform the installation, and each ESX host must only see its respective boot LUN at installation time by masking, zoning, or presentation. In some cases, use of a SAN or iSCSI server is slightly more expensive than one based on a local disk, but that depends on the type of SAN or iSCSI server and drives used.

Step 8: VMware ESX Host License

Register the vSphere registration keys to receive the individual licenses for the ESX host(s) for the license level you purchased. Without the ESX host license, you will not be able to complete the configuration of the ESX host or create and launch VMs. For ESX 4, there are new licenses and license management tools. The differences between ESX 4 and ESX 3 regarding licensing are documented in Chapter 2. Be sure to have the appropriate license keys available as part of the post installation process for ESX 4.

VMware ships out a code that is used to retrieve your licenses. To retrieve your licenses, you must have a login on the VMware site. Select the Account link and then Manage Product Licenses; from there you can access the appropriate license keys.

It is not necessary to have the license applied during or prior to installation, just prior to running your VMs. Actually, use of evaluation mode components such as Host Profiles will improve an upgrade or fresh install post-process configuration.

Step 9: Guest OS License and Installation Materials

Determine the location of any license and installation materials necessary to install the actual VMs. Although not particularly a part of an ESX host install, these will be necessary to install any VMs. In some cases, the delay in finding the necessary license and installation materials for the VMs has delayed the implementation of ESX.

Step 10: Service Console Network Information

Acquire all network information required to install ESX properly. In general, No ESX host should boot from DHCP in an enterprise environment without redundancy within the DHCP environment. If a DHCP server disappears for too long, and a lease expires, the ESX host will suddenly lose access from its service console, which implies the ESX host can no longer be managed remotely, VMware High Availability may kick in, and Dynamic Power Management may fail. It is best to have ready the network addresses, netmasks, gateways, and DNS servers for the installation. Also, include addresses for the service console, the vmkernel ports to support VMotion, Fault Tolerance, and access to various NFS or iSCSI data stores.

Step 11: Memory Allocated to the Service Console

Determine how many VMs will run on this ESX host. A VM has access to the physical host's hardware resources, such as CPU, memory, disk, and network, and there is a little bit of a VM within the SC to handle the management of the Virtual Machine. Therefore, it is important to pick the proper size of memory for the service console before installation. Note that each ESX host can host up to 512 vCPUs and up to 320 registered VMs.

Because changing the service console memory configuration requires a reboot, it is best to determine the appropriate value ahead of time. Unfortunately, the only way to set the memory configuration for the service console VM is after installation. The maximum service console memory setting is 800MB. The author generally runs agents and increases the amount to this limit.

> **Best Practice for Service Console Memory Allocation**
>
> For ESX, increase the service console memory to 800MBs.

Step 12: vmkernel Network Information

At this time, it is important to determine the VLANs and network requirements for the various vmkernel networks to be used within the ESX host. Each vmkernel network must be on at least a different subnet, but more than likely different VLANs or distinctly different network segments. You need at least the IP and netmask for each vmkernel network. This is covered in depth in Chapter 7, "Networking." The vmkernel networks are

- vMotion

- iSCSI

- NFS

- Fault Tolerance

- Management Console (ESXi only)

Step 13: Number of Virtual Network Switches

At this time, you should have some idea of how your virtual network will be laid out. If not, take the time to properly plan your virtual network using the available virtual network components of virtual switches, virtual distributed switches, or the Cisco Nexus 1000V. It is very important to work with your networking team when designing your virtual network. This is also covered in Chapter 7.

Step 14: Virtual Network Switch Label Name(s)

It is very important to pick a virtual switch naming convention that is easy to use and does not give away too much information to attackers. In other words, do not use a virtual network label that gives away the IP range or what is running on each of the VMs. A label like DMZ or 192.168.230.0/24 will give an attacker a great deal of information and further attack points. Some would claim that if an attacker can see the labels, the attacker has already gotten an incredible amount of access. But consider the case where support data is intercepted and an attacker does not yet have access; you have handed over useful information.

Naming conventions are incredibly important because the virtual switch labels need to be identical across all hosts within a cluster and something your administrator will understand. Host Profiles will ensure you have consistent labels across all hosts within a cluster, but it can also be achieved with judicious scripting.

Step 15: File System Layouts

Determine the file system layout to use for the ESX host, where the file systems will live, and how much space to allocate for each. Often, customers have created ESX hosts without paying too much attention to the file system layout and have had to reinstall ESX when they find out later that there is not enough room to create a local VMFS, a VM images directory in which to store ISO images, or backups of the VMs. They also may experience full file systems that crash the service console.

The automatic partition option creates five partitions: `root`, `boot`, `swap`, `/var/log`, `vmkcore`, and `VMFS`. Within these partitions will be created file systems into which the bits of ESX will be installed. Because the `/var` partition is where the per process core or dump files get stored when a process crashes, and because the `/var/log` file system already exists, there is a chance that these core files might grow to fill up the `root` partition. If the `root` partition gets full, it often results in unpredictable behavior such as the inability to connect to the service console, connect to the management tools, create, or manipulate a VM. If the `root` partition gets full, critical files can be corrupted. With ESXi there is a set file system layout that cannot be modified. This implies that there needs to be an increase in disk usage auditing when using ESXi to watch for the issues discussed. We cover auditing methods in Chapter 4, "Auditing and Monitoring," within the section.

To avoid such issues, Table 3.2 defines a disk partition and file system layouts for ESX.

Table 3.2 *File System Layout Recommendations for ESX*

LUN	Mount Point	Partition Size	Partition Type	Use
OS RAID 1 (minimum 146GB*) 2GB)	/boot	100MB 1GB	ext3 swap	Store Linux and VMware kernal images Service console swap (2x desired service) service console memory up to 2GB
	/	4GB	ext3	Root
	/home	4GB	ext3	Home Directories, required by some security scanners
	/var/log	4GB	ext3	Log files
	/tmp	4GB	ext3	Store temporary files
	/var	4GB	ext3	Core files and other variable files, system files, system initialization images for scripted install
VMFS RAID 5	100MB	vmkcore Grow to fill LUN	VMFS-3	Core dump (vmkernel) VM directories VM templates Used for MSCS drive C: virtual disks or for disaster recovery of failed remote storage
Up to 256 VMFS RAID LUNs off SAN/iSCSI/ NFS		# of VMs per LUN[1] size of VMs	VMFS-3	VM directories VMFS templates Installation ISOs

* For ESX v4, this is minimally a 10GB partition.

[1] This assumes the local disks are 146GB disks. Smaller is possible. You need enough local disk space to store the most important VMs for business continuity reasons.

More about LUN sizes for business continuity/disaster recovery can be found in Chapter 12, "Disaster Recovery, Business Continuity, and Backup."

> ### Best Practice for File System Layout
>
> Do not let the root system get full! Keep the location the `/var`, `/tmp`, `/home`, and `/var/log` file systems on separate partitions.

The major difference between ESX 4 and ESX 3 is that ESX 4 places these partitions within a VMDK and does not use a RAW disk within the service console VM.

Step 16: Configure the Server and the FC HBA to Boot from SAN or Boot from iSCSI

This is a decision point. All of step 16 reviews how to set up booting from SAN or iSCSI for all versions of ESX. If booting from SAN or iSCSI is desired, continue through this step. However, if a traditional installation is desired, skip to the next step.

If booting from SAN or iSCSI is the desired boot method for the ESX host, configure the server and FC HBA appropriately. To configure a server to boot from SAN, a few adjustments are necessary to the system BIOS to specify the boot order so that the SAN or iSCSI device is seen first in the boot order for the server. In addition to boot order adjustments, any IDE controllers may need to be disabled.

For example, to configure an HP blade server for boot from SAN, enter the server BIOS by pressing F9 at the appropriate prompt to start the ROM-based Setup Utility (RBSU), resulting in what is shown in Figure 3.3. After entering the RBSU, the first step in setting up boot from SAN is to change the boot order, making the Fibre Channel HBA (FC HBA) the first boot controller by selecting the Boot Controller Order menu option. From the Boot Controller Order screen, select the appropriate line to move the primary FC HBA to be the first controller, as shown in Figure 3.4.

The next step is to return to the main RBSU screen (refer to Figure 3.1) and head down a new path to disable any IDE controller for an IDE non-SCSI disk-based system. On a ProLiant Blade BLxxx Server, this can be found under Advanced Options, which has an IDE Controller item (see Figure 3.5). Select the IDE Controller item and change its state to Disabled (see Figure 3.6). If the blade or server in question does not have an IDE disk controller, skip this step.

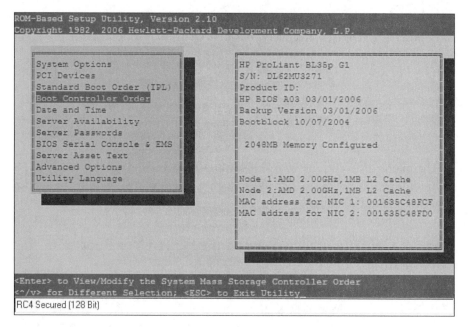

Figure 3.3 *BIOS*

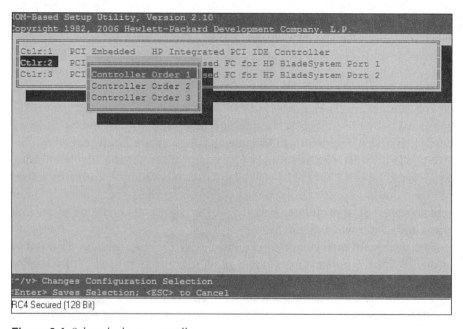

Figure 3.4 *Select the boot controller*

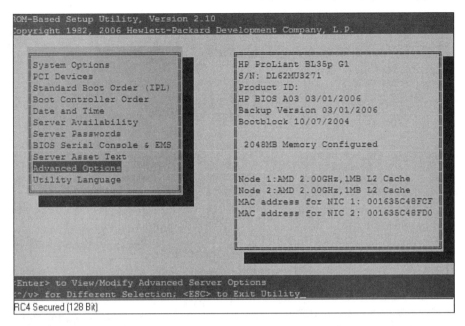

Figure 3.5 *Advanced options*

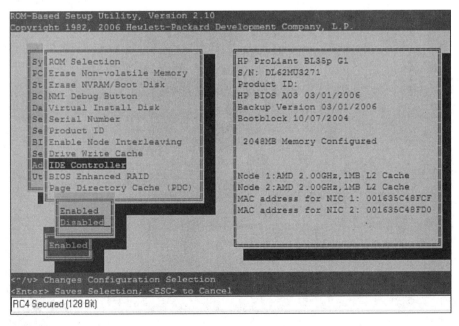

Figure 3.6 *Disable the IDE controller*

Exit the RBSU and reboot the system and the FC HBA BIOS is now accessible and configured for boot from SAN or iSCSI.

The next major step in the process for boot from SAN, or even iSCSI, is to enable the FC HBA device BIOS that allows the FC HBA to see boot disks hanging off the SAN or NAS. If the FC HBA BIOS is disabled, the SAN disks are not accessible as boot devices.

The FC HBA has its own configuration for boot from SAN that depends on the controller being used. The main goal of these BIOS changes is to configure the HBA to recognize the SAN or NAS LUN presented as the boot LUN for the ESX host. There are multiple types of FC HBA hardware, and we will cover Emulex and QLogic brands.

Setting Up the Emulex HBAs

After configuring the system BIOS to change the boot order, reboot the server and monitor the POST power-on messages for the following phrase:

```
Press <Alt E> to GO TO Emulex BIOS Utility
```

Just prior to this message, there is a list of the World Wide Numbers (WWNs) for all the FC HBA ports installed in the system. Record the WWN to perform the proper SAN zoning and presentation. When the message appears, press the Alt and E keys simultaneously to enter the Emulex BIOS Utility, as shown in Figure 3.7.

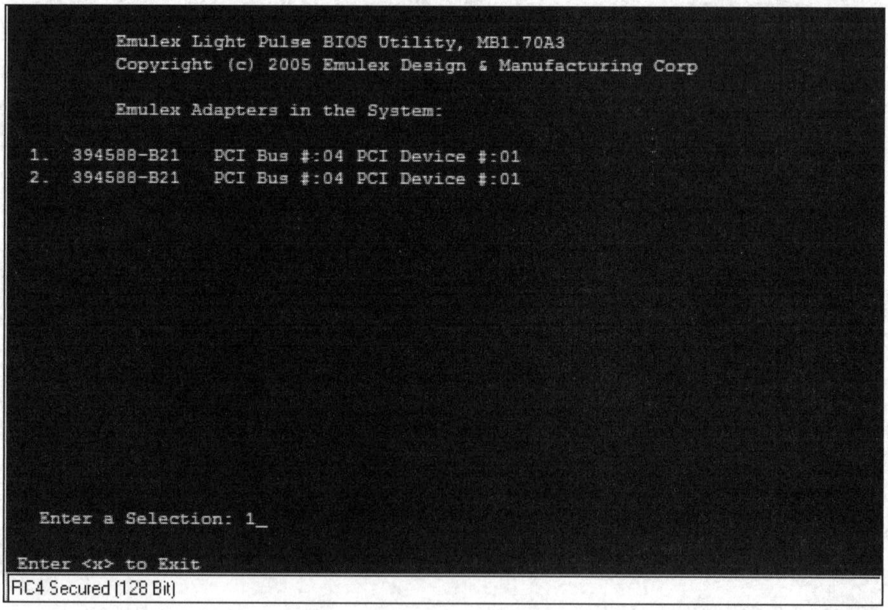

```
        Emulex Light Pulse BIOS Utility, MB1.70A3
        Copyright (c) 2005 Emulex Design & Manufacturing Corp

        Emulex Adapters in the System:

   1.  394588-B21    PCI Bus #:04 PCI Device #:01
   2.  394588-B21    PCI Bus #:04 PCI Device #:01




















   Enter a Selection: 1_

  Enter <x> to Exit
  RC4 Secured (128 Bit)
```

Figure 3.7 *Emulex BIOS Utility*

At the Enter a Selection prompt, select the first FC HBA, which is the primary FC HBA port or card, then proceed to Option 2, Configure This Adapter's Parameters, with the results shown by Figure 3.8.

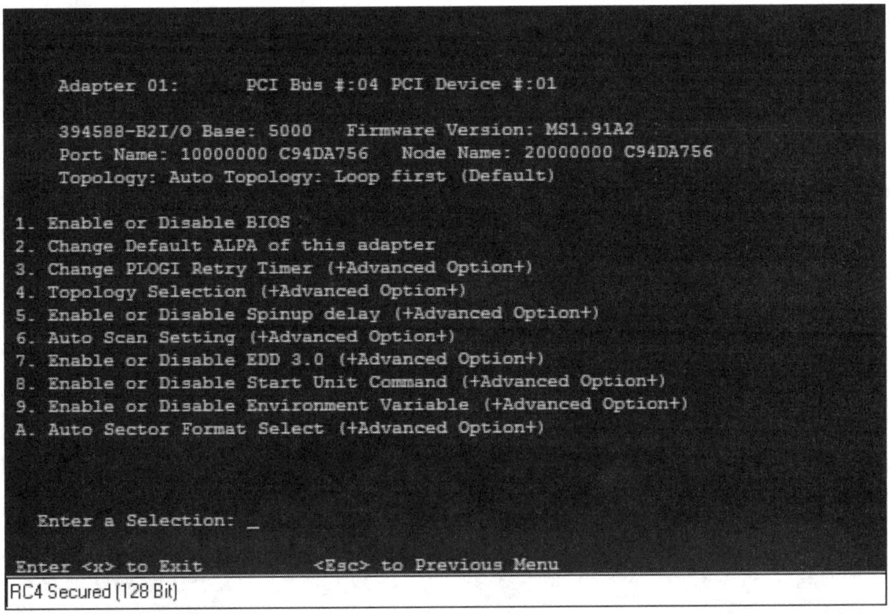

```
     Adapter 01:        PCI Bus #:04 PCI Device #:01

     394588-B2I/O Base: 5000    Firmware Version: MS1.91A2
     Port Name: 10000000 C94DA756    Node Name: 20000000 C94DA756
     Topology: Auto Topology: Loop first (Default)

1. Enable or Disable BIOS
2. Change Default ALPA of this adapter
3. Change PLOGI Retry Timer (+Advanced Option+)
4. Topology Selection (+Advanced Option+)
5. Enable or Disable Spinup delay (+Advanced Option+)
6. Auto Scan Setting (+Advanced Option+)
7. Enable or Disable EDD 3.0 (+Advanced Option+)
8. Enable or Disable Start Unit Command (+Advanced Option+)
9. Enable or Disable Environment Variable (+Advanced Option+)
A. Auto Sector Format Select (+Advanced Option+)



     Enter a Selection: _

Enter <x> to Exit          <Esc> to Previous Menu
RC4 Secured (128 Bit)
```

Figure 3.8 *Emulex Configure This Adapter*

As stated, you need to set up the BIOS for the FC HBA to allow it to see drives as bootable volumes. You do that by selecting Option 1, Enable or Disable BIOS and then pressing 1 to enable the BIOS. After enabling the BIOS, the next step is to set the topology of the Fibre network to be point to point. The topology tells the FC HBA how to view the Fibre network, and because there is a one-to-one mapping between the FC HBA port and the boot LUN, the topology is set to point to point. To do this, choose Option 4, Topology Selection, (+Advanced Option+), and select Point to Point. After you have made these selections, the BIOS can be exited and the server rebooted.

The system is still not fully configured, because the boot devices have not been defined. The boot device will be presented by the SAN and zoned by the switches to the primary FC HBAs WWN recorded earlier. After the presentation and zoning are completed, the device must be chosen as a boot device. So once more, enter the Emulex BIOS Utility and select the first FC HBA, which is the primary FC HBA to which everything has been presented and zoned. Now select Option 1, Enable or Disable BIOS, and modify the list of saved boot devices. As shown in Figure 3.9, set up the primary and secondary boot paths for the listed devices. Each FC HBA has at least one port listed. Each port has an associated

World Wide Port Number (WWPN). Because it is recommended to have two FC HBA ports per ESX host, there will be two WWPNs, whose last two digits are unique. The unique last two digits are used to pick which port is to be used as the primary and secondary boot path. Choose 1 to pick the primary boot path, and when prompted, enter the hexadecimal LUN ID of the LUN defined as the boot disk. Of all LUNs associated with the ESX host, the lowest-valued LUN is the boot disk, with the exception of LUN ID 0, which is often the controlling LUN. If LUN ID 0 is present, do not select it as a boot LUN.

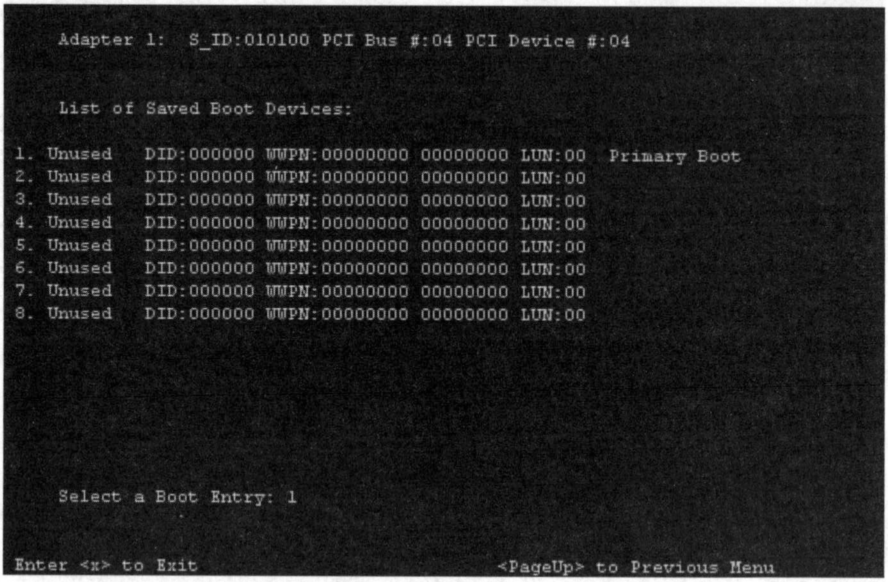

```
     Adapter 1:   S_ID:010100 PCI Bus #:04 PCI Device #:04


     List of Saved Boot Devices:

1.  Unused   DID:000000 WWPN:00000000 00000000 LUN:00   Primary Boot
2.  Unused   DID:000000 WWPN:00000000 00000000 LUN:00
3.  Unused   DID:000000 WWPN:00000000 00000000 LUN:00
4.  Unused   DID:000000 WWPN:00000000 00000000 LUN:00
5.  Unused   DID:000000 WWPN:00000000 00000000 LUN:00
6.  Unused   DID:000000 WWPN:00000000 00000000 LUN:00
7.  Unused   DID:000000 WWPN:00000000 00000000 LUN:00
8.  Unused   DID:000000 WWPN:00000000 00000000 LUN:00




     Select a Boot Entry: 1


Enter <x> to Exit                        <PageUp> to Previous Menu
```

Figure 3.9 *Emulex saved boot devices*

After the saved boot devices have been set up, select option 01 representing the WWPN that is the boot device, as shown in Figure 3.10, to tell the system which WWPN is to be booted. Once more, exit the Emulex BIOS and reboot the server. Now the Emulex FC HBA is ready to boot from the SAN, and ESX or ESXi can be installed.

Setting Up QLogic FC HBAs

Similar to Emulex FC HBAs, QLogic FC HBAs need to have their BIOS enabled and the boot LUN specified. Unlike Emulex, however, the topology does not need to be set to boot from the SAN, nor is there a reboot in the middle of the configuration. After configuring the system BIOS to change the boot order, reboot the server and monitor the POST power-on messages for the following phrase:

```
Press <CTRL-Q> for Fast!UTIL
```

```
    Adapter 1:   S_ID:010100 PCI Bus #:04 PCI Device #:04

00. Clear selected boot entry!!
01. DID:010000 WWPN:500805F3 000014D1 LUN:01COMPAQ  MSA1000 VOLUME  2.38




                                                        ¢
    Select The Two Digit Number of The Desired Boot Device:01

Enter <x> to Exit   <PageUp> to Previous Menu   <PageDn> to Next Page
```

Figure 3.10 *Emulex select boot device*

When the phrase appears, press Ctrl+Q to enter the QLogic BIOS to configure it for boot from SAN. When you are in the BIOS, the Select Host Adapter menu will appear, listing all available QLogic FC HBAs. The first in the list is the primary FC HBA port. Select it as the device from which to boot per Figure 3.11.

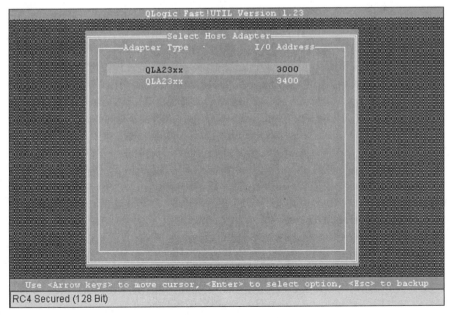

```
                   QLogic Fast!UTIL Version 1.23

                  ===Select Host Adapter===
            ─Adapter Type      ·      I/O Address─
                QLA23xx                3000
                QLA23xx                3400
```

```
    Use <Arrow keys> to move cursor, <Enter> to select option, <Esc> to backup
RC4 Secured (128 Bit)
```

Figure 3.11 *QLogic Select Host Adapter*

After selecting the host adapter to manipulate with the Fast!UTIL, options will be displayed with an opportunity to select the Configuration Settings option. Under the Host Adapter Configuration Settings menu, select the Host Adapter Settings Menu item to enable the BIOS per Figure 3.12.

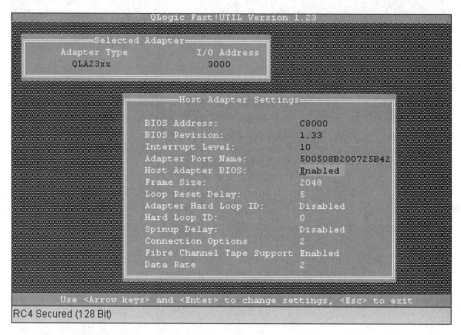

Figure 3.12 *QLogic Select Host Adapter Settings*

After returning to the Configuration Settings menu, select the Selectable Boot Settings menu option to set the enabled primary boot LUN, as shown in Figure 3.13. The display will show the primary boot port name and LUN. Be sure to select the proper LUN. The proper LUN is the zoned and presented LUN to be used as the boot volume. During a boot from SAN configuration, only those LUNs necessary for installation should be zoned and presented. Some installations require more than one LUN, such as the controlling LUN or at least one data LUN. Do not select the controlling LUN, which is usually either LUN 0 or 31; ensure you get the LUN number of the controlling LUN from your storage administrator. If more than one data LUN is required for installation, work with the storage administrators to ensure the data LUN has a well-known ID so that you can disregard it and choose the other LUN.

Select the primary boot port name and LUN, and a new menu appears, enabling you to select the Fibre Channel device associated with the SAN from which to boot and then the specific LUN, which will become the boot LUN, as shown in Figure 3.14.

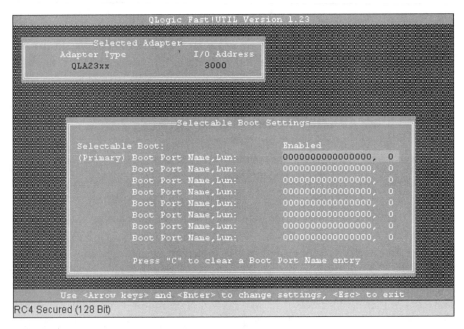

Figure 3.13 *QLogic Selectable Boot Settings*

Save all the changes to configure the QLogic device for boot from SAN and reboot the server to complete the installation.

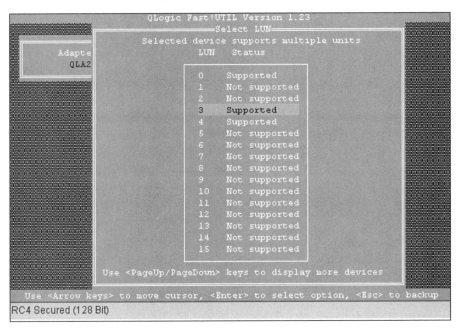

Figure 3.14 *QLogic Select LUN*

Set Up Boot from iSCSI

Currently, only the QLA4xxx QLogic iSCSI HBA cards are supported for Boot from iSCSI. The configuration is similar to that of a QLogic FC HBA. The major difference is the selection of an iSCSI target and not a SAN LUN.

Step 17: Start ESX/ESXi Host Installations

ESX/ESXi Preinstallation

If you are not planning to boot from SAN, disconnect the system from the SAN or iSCSI server. A disconnect from remote storage is accomplished by taking the ESX host out of the zoning or presentation of LUNs; alternatively, if you have the access, you can unplug the cables from the host in question. Having VMFS LUNs containing VMs connected during installation can adversely affect the boot of the ESX host when the installation is completed, because you may have accidentally installed onto a remote storage LUN and boot would fail if your system is not set up for boot from SAN. Another common issue is the possibility of overwriting the wrong LUN with a VMFS, because, in many cases, the SAN or iSCSI LUNs are nearly the same as local LUNs in naming convention. SAN or iSCSI LUNs appear to the installer as /dev/sd? devices and usually show up first in the list instead of last. Many hosts' local disks also show up to the installer as /dev/sd? devices. One notable exception is HP hardware, whose local disks often show up as /dev/cciss/c?d? devices.

De-presenting, de-zoning, or disconnecting the Fibre cables will prevent accidental erasure of the SAN or iSCSI LUNs during installation or upgrade. Although it is not necessary to disconnect the SAN from the server, be aware that the installation will show all presented disks, and even a slight slip-up could destroy existing SAN VMFS volume data.

ESX/ESXi Installation

This step is the starting point for any installation. However, the goal here is not to repeat every other ESX and vSphere book that runs through an installation in painful detail. As such, unless otherwise specified, the steps taken are for both products so we will call out only what is important to consider during any installation.

Start the system installation by either using a remote console device with virtual CD-ROM capability similar to the HP ILO device, or insert the ESX host CD-ROM into the disk tray of the ESX host. During the installation, you will use the values you've entered into your checklist based on the decisions you've made in steps 1 through 13. At this point, the ESX host will boot, and two types of installations can be performed: If the installation is over the HP ILO or similar type of virtual media device, it is recommended to use the text-based installation; otherwise, installations should use the graphical install. In addition to choosing between graphical and text-based installation, there is a need to apply the boot from SAN decision and either choose the Boot from SAN option or not when performing an install.

When the installation begins, you must address certain critical sections. Although an installation can occur by accepting all the defaults and typing a few items such as the root password, such an installation is not necessarily one that will stand up to long use. Granted, for a test environment, or to get your feet wet, this might be the best approach, but for production environments, follow the planning steps we have already been through.

The first decision point (see Figure 3.15) of an installation is whether to use different drivers than those provided on the installation media. A few non-standard devices are supported by VMware ESX 4 and as such you need to add more drivers to the default installation disk using a different CD-ROM or ISO image. These devices are listed at http://downloads.vmware.com/d/info/datacenter_downloads/vmware_vsphere_4/4#drivers_tools when you expand the Driver CDs option. You do this by following these steps:

1. Clicking *Yes*, you want to install custom drivers.

2. Click the *Add...* button to get a dialog that allows you to find the customer drivers.

3. Select the customer driver.

4. Repeat for all drivers.

5. Click *Next* to proceed with the rest of the installation.

The next decision point for ESX 4 is whether to enter the license keys during installation or to wait until after installation (see Figure 3.16). If you do not have Enterprise Plus license keys, the recommendation is to enter the keys after installation so that you can make use of Host Profiles to ensure you have a common configuration across all hosts within your cluster.

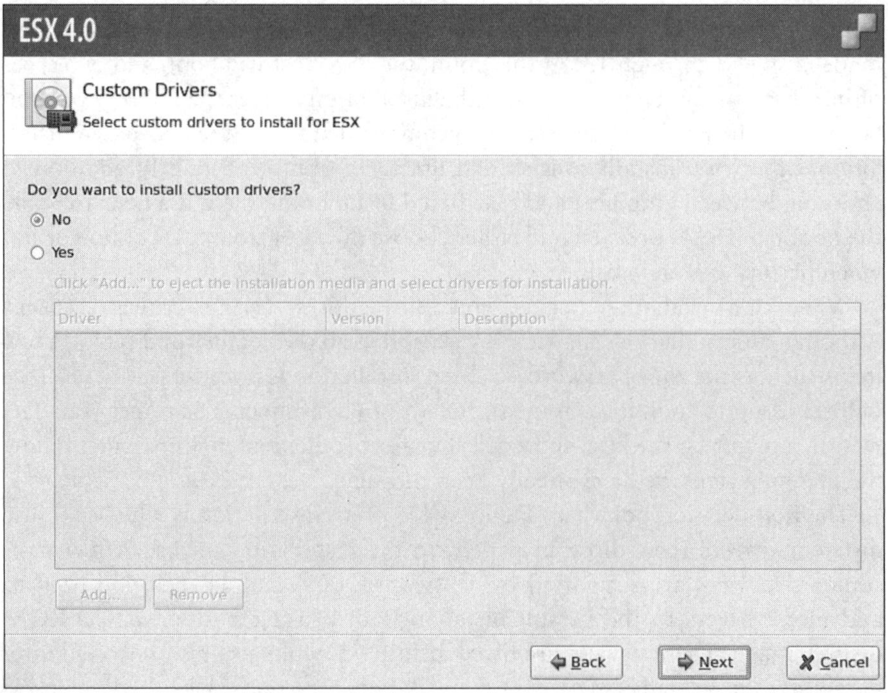

Figure 3.15 *Add custom drivers*

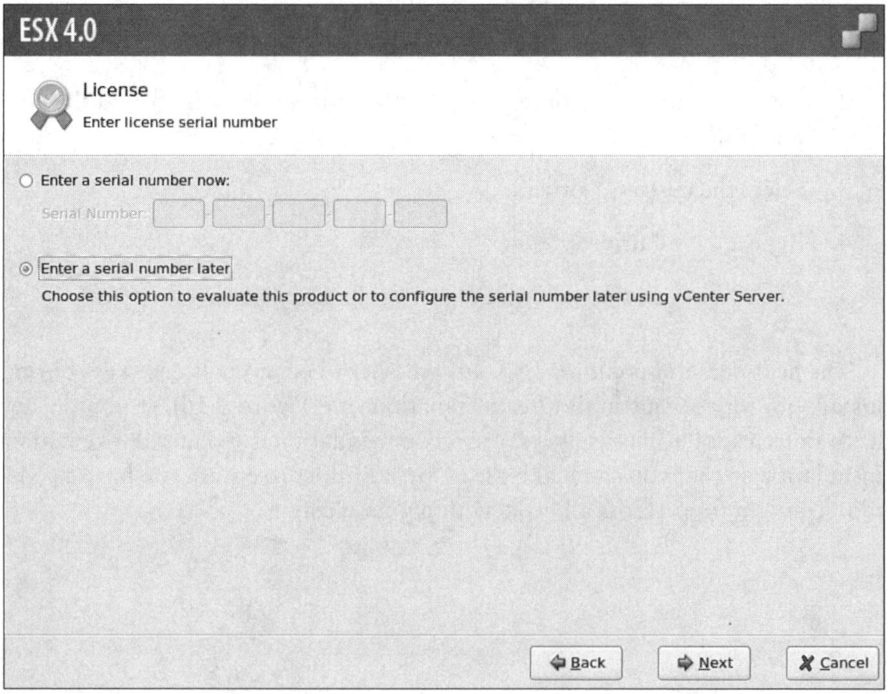

Figure 3.16 *Enter the license key*

Next is another series of taking the defaults (unless you happen to require a keyboard layout or language that is not US English), and then you are at the screens used to define the file systems for ESX and the service console. We previously defined the best practice file system layouts for ESX in Table 3.2; this is the point at which these get applied. If there is an existing VMFS on the disks, and it is desirable to keep the VMFS intact, this is definitely the time to make that selection, too. The default disk setup will wipe out all partitions, including any VMFS that may exist. Figures 3.17 through 3.19 depict how the file system layouts are changed.

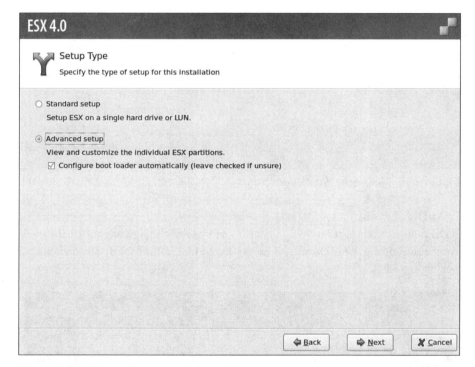

Figure 3.17 *Choose the setup type*

The first step of this process, shown in Figure 3.17, is to choose whether to use a standard setup type or advanced. You want to choose advanced.

This is the section of the installation that almost always requires the LUNs not be presented from a SAN or iSCSI server. However, read carefully and choose the proper option to preserve any VMFS on the system. What you see in the list shown in Figure 3.18 are only supported devices. Note that you need at least 9.5GB of space to create a VMFS on which the service console VMDK will be created.

Figure 3.18 *Choose the installation location*

ESXi Disk Layout

ESXi does not contain any way to set up or change the disk layout of the environment. You can only choose where to install ESXi, not modify the disk layout per Figure 3.19.

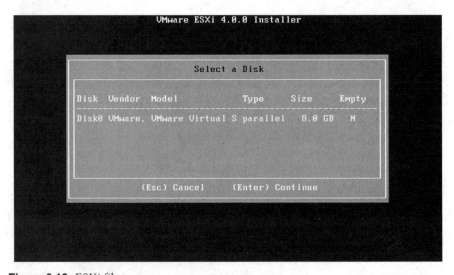

Figure 3.19 *ESXi file systems*

ESX Disk Layout

For ESX only, it is best to choose the recommended setting and then proceed to the next step. As shown in Figure 3.20, it is possible to save existing VMFS LUNs instead of re-creating or deleting everything. Even so, create your own file system partitions per Table 3.2 and that previous decision.

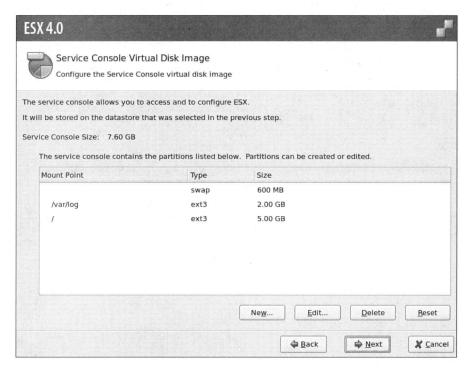

Figure 3.20 *Default file systems*

For ESX only, there are five changes to the standard file system layout that the author recommends to make for an ESX installation. The first is to expand the /var/log partition to something larger: 4GB is recommended. The second is to add at least a 2GB /tmp partition. The third is to create a 4GB /var partition. The fourth is to create a 4GB /home partition. The last is to increase the swap size to a 1600MB; although swap can go to a maximum of 2000MB, this is not necessary because swap should be 2x memory. To modify a partition, use the down-arrow key on the text installation or the mouse to select the partition to modify, and then press Return for text installation or click Edit to display the dialog pictured in Figure 3.20. Make the appropriate changes—for example, expanding the maximum size of the file system—and then use the Tab key to reach the OK button, and then press Enter on the OK.

For ESX only, when adding a new partition, use Tab to reach the New button and select using the Enter button, and then modify the dialog shown in Figure

3.21 to set the appropriate fields once more for the new /tmp file system. Follow these same steps to create any other file system.

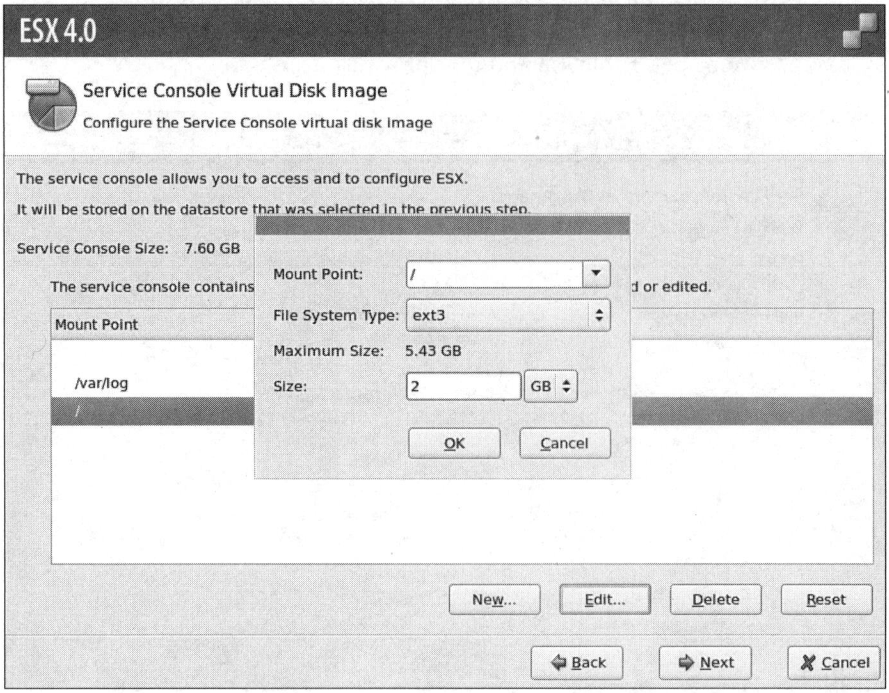

Figure 3.21 *Adding a partition*

Finishing Install

The next step is to enter the appropriate network time protocol (NTP) information and to verify that the NTP server entered is available.

The last data entry before the installation starts loading packages onto your ESX host is to add an administrative user. You will use this administrative user to log in to the service console or perform actions instead of using root. This will be discussed in more detail in Chapter 4, "Auditing and Monitoring."

After the install has completed, click Finish, and the server will reboot. Now ESX is running and ready for post-installation configuration.

ESXi Installation Conclusion

An ESXi installation is quite a bit different from an ESX one. The only major decision point is which disk to select for installation. Again, it is wiser to de-present, de-zone, or disconnect all FC or iSCSI HBA cards from your storage fabric before proceeding. Compared to the 36 graphical installation steps for ESX 4, there are only 14 for ESXi 4.

General Upgrade/Installation Process

When upgrading from ESX 3 to ESX 4, there is a process to follow that could lead to many other seemingly unrelated upgrades. This process is as follows:

1. Upgrade VMware vCenter from 2.5 to version 4 (if you are using vCenter).

2. Point vCenter 4 at the existing License Manager used for ESX 3.

3. Using vMotion, migrate any VMs from the target host to other hosts within the cluster. If vMotion is not available, cold migrate the VMs from the node.

4. Place the host into Maintenance mode (could be used to replace step 3, but I personally like to do my own vMotions instead of letting DRS perform this task).

5. De-present or un-zone any existing VMFS SAN LUNs.

6. Upgrade any BIOS and firmware for the host.

7. Reboot the node and reconfigure the host BIOS settings to ensure Intel-VT or AMD-V are enabled and the No eXecute (NX) or eXecute Disabled (XD) bit are also enabled. This is also a good time to change out or add any necessary hardware.

8. Upgrade your first VMware host of a cluster using VMware Update Manager or the VMware Host Update Utility.

9. Re-zone and re-present any existing VMFS SAN LUNs to the host.

10. Join the host to vCenter 4 Server if using vCenter.

11. Capture the Host Profile of the first host upgraded (this can be done even if you do not have an Enterprise Plus license using evaluation mode for your vCenter Server).

12. For each remaining host within the cluster, repeat steps 3 through 10 but instead of upgrading, do a fresh installation in step 8. A fresh installation allows you to clean up your local disks and make better use of existing disk space if using ESX. If using ESXi, an upgrade is acceptable. For each remaining host, apply the captured Host Profile to each newly installed host.

13. For ESX only: Using another node, capture a new Host Profile (this can be done even if you do not have an Enterprise Plus license using evaluation mode for your vCenter Server).

14. For ESX only: As the last step, reinstall the first node upgraded to a clean install, and then perform steps 9 and 10 once more.

15. Shut down any ESX/ESXi v3– and vCenter 2.5–specific processes and servers, such as the License Manager and VMware vCenter 2.5, VMware Update Manager, and so on. These could be running on your newly upgraded vCenter Server or another server that contains those processes.

This general process will enable you to fix anything that is currently out of compliance with VMware or your company policies, as well as ensure a solid upgrade of your hosts. Note that with ESX 4 in many cases, hardware agents are no longer required, but we will cover them later in this chapter.

Also as stated at the beginning of this section, one upgrade could lead to others; specifically, you may need to upgrade your SQL Server because VMware vCenter 4.0 does not support Microsoft SQL Server 2000. If you currently use Microsoft SQL Server 2000, you will have to upgrade to at least Microsoft SQL Server 2005. In addition, vCenter 4.1 requires a 64-bit operating system, so if you plan to upgrade to vSphere v4.1, you need to plan this as part of your upgrade of vCenter.

For the author, an upgrade from Microsoft SQL 2000 led to going to Microsoft SQL 2008 on Windows Server 2008 Enterprise, which in turn led to an upgrade of the company domain controller from Samba 3.0.x to Samba 3.4.1, which is the latest version that supported Windows Server 2008. Although many companies use Microsoft domain controllers, these other upgrades may still be necessary.

Always plan your upgrades and double-check that all the versions of critical software components support your upgrades.

ESX/ESXi Upgrade

If upgrading, remove any hardware agents before performing the upgrade, because different versions of ESX often require different versions of hardware agents. The vmkernel exposes different aspects of the hardware to the service console depending on the ESX version.

ESX-Only Decision Point

When upgrading to ESX 4, the first options to consider are whether to upgrade, whether there is an existing installation, or whether to reinstall per the initial discussion in this chapter. Many people opt to use the supported upgrade option. However, most Linux gurus perform reinstalls instead of upgrading. Upgrading the service console to use a new version is the same for ESX as it is for any other variant of the Linux operating system or any technology derived from the Linux operating system. ESX 3's service console is a variant of RHEL 3.0

ES, whereas ESX 4's service console is a variant of RHEL 5.1. The difference in versions is rather extreme, yet there is no chance that the configuration from ESX 3 will stick around within critical file locations as there is with Linux upgrades. The reason for this is that ESX 4 creates brand-new file systems within a VMDK and does not overwrite any existing ESX 3 file systems. It does provide links to the older data to aid in upgrades of configuration data, but it is a complete replacement with migration of the necessary ESX specific configuration to ESX 4. This implies that an upgrade could keep lots of data hanging around that is not of much use to ESX 4. Reinstallation makes it possible to clean up the file systems and to create a new plan for the new version of ESX.

Satisfied with Backup

However, prior to reinstallation or upgrade, ask this question:

Are you happy with your current backup?

If not, do not proceed with an upgrade until you are comfortable.

Perform Upgrade

When performing an upgrade there are no major decision points, just a very different process to follow: specifically, whether to use the VMware Update Manager or Host Update Utility. Choose the Host Update Utility only if you are upgrading single machines or if you do not have vCenter. If you upgrade multiple machines, using VMware Update Manager is recommended.

The process for either is the same for all methods of upgrade:

1. Load the installation media into the Update Manager or Host Update Utility.
2. Connect to the target host.
3. Apply the upgrade.

With ESX only, the major concern when performing an upgrade, however, is that the upgrade does not duplicate your existing file systems, but will provide a link to them so that you can complete any necessary configurations using the older file systems as reference. The older file systems grant RAW access from within the VM to the original file systems while maintaining the `root`, `swap`, and `/var/log` partitions within a VMDK. This access is via a mount point within the service console so that you can copy things between the old install and the new install as needed. However, this ends up being a waste of space, and to clean up requires you to repartition your physical disk. I find that this space could be better used for local data stores.

An ESX or ESXi upgrade maintains all ESX and ESXi specific configurations, such as virtual switch naming and configuration, data store names, and so on.

Step 18: Connecting to the Management User Interface for the First Time

After the ESX host reboots, it is time to log in to ESX using the vSphere Client. Although the post installation steps do not differ much from ESX 3 to ESX 4, we list them here for completeness. There is more about configuration in Chapter 8, "Configuring ESX from a Host Connection." Table 3.3 includes ESX 2.5 so that you can see the changes across all versions. Table 3.3 also lists out the process by which you connect to the management user interface for the first time.

Table 3.3 *Post-Install Configuration*

ESX 4	ESX 3.0	ESX 2.5
Access MUI (webAccess)	Access MUI (webAccess)	Access MUI (webAcess)
The MUI for ESX version 4.0 will allow the download of the VIC. Access the MUI using http://machinename/.	The MUI for ESX version 3.0 will allow the download of the VIC. Access the MUI using http://machinename/.	The MUI for prior versions of ESX requires a login as the root user, using the password specified during installation.
Download vSphere Client	Download VIC	Download Remote Console
Download and install the vSphere Client (vSC) to a machine installed with a form of the Windows OS.	Download and install the VIC to a machine installed with a form of the Windows OS.	After a login to the MUI is made, the remote console can be downloaded to a machine installed with either Linux or Windows.
Start the vSC and select the ESX host, and log in using the root username and the password specified during ESX Installation, or select the Virtual Center Server.	Start the VIC and select the ESX host, and log in using the root username and the password specified during ESX Installation, or select the Virtual Center Server.	

ESX 4	ESX 3.0	ESX 2.5
Apply Appropriate Licenses	Apply Appropriate Licenses	Apply Appropriate Licenses
License keys are distributed in a file for use either by the VMware License Server or to be loaded into the host.	License keys are distributed in a file for use either by the VMware License Server or to be loaded into the host.	If a license key was not entered during the installation phase, a license key will be required to progress. Enter the appropriate keys and the host will reboot.
Network Management	Network Management	Network Management
The installation of ESX 4 will result in a pre-created vSwitch for the service console.	The installation of ESX version 3 will result in a pre-created vSwitch for the service console.	Create virtual switches that the VMs will use to talk to an external network. Each virtual machine can have a maximum of four virtual NICs (vNICs). Each vNIC connects to a port on the virtual switch for communicating with other virtual machines and servers that are on the network. Be sure to give each vSwitch a descriptive name. Most customers use either network names such as Production, Backup, or Test, or they use actual IP addresses of the networks involved.
Create new vSwitches for the vmkernel NFS, iSCSI, Fault Tolerance, and vMotion networks. Then create a VM network as necessary. The network configurations are covered in Chapter 7.	Create new vSwitches for the vmkernel NFS and vMotion networks as well as a vmkernel portgroup off the service console vSwitch for an iSCSI network. Then create a VM network as necessary. The network configurations are covered in Chapter 7.	

continues

Table 3.3 *(Continued)*

ESX 4	ESX 3.0	ESX 2.5
N/A	N/A	Create the Virtual Swapfile
		The first virtual swapfile for vmkernel use must be created and activated from the management tool.
		If you need to add additional swap space for vmkernel use, you would do that from the Service Console. Each ESX host may have up to 8 virtual swap files, with a maximum file size of 64GB per virtual swap file.
		Here is one way of creating a secondary 1GB swap file:
		`# vmkfstools -k 1024M vmhba):):):6vmhba0:0:0`
		`:6:addswap.vswp` To activate swap:
		`# vmkfstools -w 1024M vmhba0:0:0:6:addswap.`
		`vswp` ESX host starts using the additional swap file immediately. You can check this by using esxtop.
		To make sure all the swap gets activated upon reboot, add the following line to `/etc/rc.local`:
		`vmkfstools -w 1024M vmhba0:0:0:6:addswap.` `vswp`

ESX 4	ESX 3.0	ESX 2.5
Storage Management	Storage Management	Storage Management
ESX 4 pre-labels any VMFS created during installation. However, it is possible and recommended to change the local storage label using the vSC or from the service console command line. The symbolic link command can be used to change the local storage label, which is discussed further in Chapter 13. Without a proper label the only way to access the VMFS is to know the UUID number assigned to the VMFS, or to know the vmhba name. Tools like vmkfstools use the vmhba name, while the rest of ESX 3 uses the UUID associated with the datastore.	ESX version 3 pre-labels any VMFS created during installation. However, it is possible and recommended to change the local storage label using the VIC or from the COS command line. The symbolic link command can be used to change the local storage label, which is discussed further in Chapter 13. Without a proper label the only way to access the VMFS is to know the UUID number assigned to the VMFS, or to know the vmhba name. Tools like vmkfstools use the vmhba name, while the rest of ESX version 3 uses the UUID associated with the datastore.	Use the MUI to label the VMFS volume created by the default installation. In addition, it is now possible to create new VMFS volumes. Before accessing a SAN, consider the contents of Chapter 5.
Before accessing a SAN consider the contents of Chapter 5.	Before accessing a SAN consider the contents of Chapter 5.	After creating a VMFS volume or after accessing the VMFS volume automatically created upon install, give the volume a label and use that label when specifying VMFS files on that volume. For example if you created a VMFS partition, vmhba0:0:0:10, to hold all test VMs, you may label this TESTVMFS. You can then refer to the testvm1.vmdk as TESTVMFS:testvm1.vmdk instead of vmhba0:0:0:10:testvm1.vmdk in a virtual machine configuration file, which makes for easy reference when manipulating the VMDKs from the command line. If there is no persistent connection, it is possible that when a new LUN is presented the LUNs will be renumbered. Good labels are therefore important.

continues

Table 3.3 *(Continued)*

ESX 4	ESX 3.0	ESX 2.5
Create a Login User	Create a Login User	Create a Login User
Done as a part of the installation. If skipped, create a new user using the vSC connected directly to the ESX host, not via vCenter.	It is impossible to initially log in to the ESX host as the root user remotely. In case it is necessary to log in to manage the system by hand, it is best to create an administrative user. To further secure the system, this login is also required.	This step is necessary only if the security recipe in Chapter 4 is to be followed, because root access should be limited.
Storage Upgrade (If Performing Upgrade)	Storage Upgrade (If Performing Upgrade)	N/A

Using either the vSC or the command line upgrade the appropriate VMFS-3.2 to VMFS-3.3.1. This may require re-creating any data store after using SVMotion or migration to move all VMs off the data store.	Using either the VIC or the command line upgrade the appropriate VMFS-2 to VMFS-3.2.
	
	`vmkfstools -T /vmfs/`
	`volumes/<VMFSName>`
	
	`vmkload_mod -u vmfs2;`
	`vmkload_mod vmfs2`
	
	`vmkload_mod -u vmfs3;`
	`vmkload_mod vmfs3`
	
	`vmkfstools -u /vmfs/`
	`volumes/<VMFSName>`	

ESX host is now ready for further configuration and use. However, now is the time to install optional third-party agents and other software that is necessary for the day-to-day use of ESX.

Step 19: Third-Party Tools to Install

Now is the time to install those third-party add-on tools, such as the Cisco Nexus 1000V, Multipath Plug-in (MPP), and VMsafe appliances. Each of these tools requires drivers to be added to your ESX 4 host, which will require a reboot in order to use it. As of the writing of this chapter, there exists an MPP from EMC and VMsafe appliances from Altor Networks, Reflex Systems, IBM, TrendMicro, and so on.

Step 20: Additional Software Packages to Install

Log in to the service console to install any additional packages. If you downloaded any of the RPM packages you plan to install on your ESX host to your Windows workstation first, remember to FTP them over to your ESX host in *binary* mode.

Note that it is never recommended to install third-party software within your service console for ESX 4. In some rare cases you may be required to install third-party agents to monitor your hardware or other aspects of your ESX host. In these cases, be sure you use software specifically designed for ESX and not for Linux. Remember ESX is not Linux. Furthermore, always pick up patches directly from VMware and *not* from Red Hat.

With ESXi, it is possible to install third-party packages, but they will be removed on an update of ESXi because an ESXi update is, in effect, a complete reinstall. It is possible to install such packages on local datastores unrelated to the boot datastore of the ESXi host, which would require the tools to be written to make use of the new location. All in all, it is best not to install third-party tools into ESXi unless they are specifically designed for ESXi.

This is also the right time to look into any vendor-specific diagnostic and monitoring packages that should be installed on the server. For example, on Dell servers, you may want to install the open manage packages that help you monitor the system hardware.

Step 21: Patch ESX or ESXi

One of the more important steps to take after an install or upgrade to ESX or ESXi is to apply any patches available for the products. This step is easily done using the VMware Update Manager and applying patches, not upgrades.

Step 22: Guest Operating System Software

If you want to install guest operating systems within virtual machines you will need to locate any installation media to use. If you have the media in ISO format, you can copy it to any ESX datastore or anywhere else that the vSphere Client can reach. In this way you could easily access it from all ESX hosts attached to the same datastore. Often an NFS datastore would be used for ISO storage.

Step 23: Guest Operating System Licenses

It is also important to have any licenses available in order to install guest operating systems. If these licenses are unavailable, guest deployment will be delayed.

Step 24: Network Information for Each Guest Operating System

It is also important to have any network information available in order to install guest operating systems.

Step 25: Guest Upgrades

Now that you've upgraded your hosts to ESX(i) 4, you need to update the virtual hardware to gain access to new functionality. When upgrading your guests, you should first upgrade VMware Tools, and then upgrade the virtual hardware from version 4 to version 7. This process often requires many reboots and may lead to other issues. Given this, it is best to test version 7 virtual hardware before using it within production. To upgrade your virtual hardware, follow these steps:

1. Back up your VM, including all configuration files.

2. Using the vSphere Client Upgrade VMware Tools of a selected VM to the level shipped with your version of ESX or ESXi.

3. Reboot the VM after the VMware Tools is updated if a reboot does not happen automatically.

4. Using the vSphere Client Upgrade the Virtual Hardware of the VM you just upgraded to the latest VMware Tools.

Automating Installation

The key to the scripted installation is the creation of a kickstart file. Linux installers use the kickstart file to configure servers and to create installs that do not require human intervention.

EXi 4.1

With ESXi v4.1, it is possible to kickstart an installation of ESXi. This is the same as the kickstart for ESX v4 outlined next.

ESX 4

For ESX 4, there is no longer a web-based scripted installation kickstart file creator as there is for ESX 3. Instead, two sample kickstart scripts are available on the installation media: ks-first-safe.cfg and ks-first.cfg. Both of these scripts install on the first disk found, and the safe version will preserve any existing

VMFS files. The first disk found is referenced as `/dev/sda`, which on HP hardware most likely points to a SAN or iSCSI LUN and not the `/dev/cciss` devices it should. So some care must be taken to alleviate confusion. These configuration scripts will need to be edited.

Kickstart scripts should be placed on the CD-ROM used to do the installation, a USB flash drive, NFS server, web server, or the local hard disk.

Kickstart Directives

VMware has added some functionality to the kick-start file that should be explained. The functionality outside what is normally expected for a kickstart file is in Table 3.4. You can find information about a normal kickstart file within the VMware ESX-VC Installation Guide starting on page 46.

Table 3.4 *VMware Kick-Start Options*

VMware Kickstart Option	Definition	Comments
accepteula	Accepts the VMware License Agreement	ESX 3 uses vmaccepteula

vmlicense	Sets up licensing in the form of:
	
	`vmlicense -mode=server`
	`-server=<server>`
	`--features=<features>`
	`--edition=<edition>`
	-or-
	`vmlicense -mode=file -`
	`features=<features>`
	`--edition=<edition>`
	Features can be backup and edition could be one of esxFull or esxStartup
		ESX 3 only

firewall	Configure the ESX 4 firewall	ESX 4 only
firewallport	Configure specific ports within the service console firewall	ESX 4 only
network	Used to configure the default virtual switch used by the service console	
auth or authconfig	Enable various authentication options not available with the standard `esxcfg-auth` command	Configure only Hesiod, smbauth, and caching
%vmlicense_text section	Contains the host based license file contents	ESX 3 only

continues

Table 3.4   *(Continued)*

VMware Kickstart Option	Definition	Comments

virtualdisk cos	The location and size of the service console virtual disk; for example:
	
	`virtualdisk cos`
	`--size=15000 --onvmfs`
	`storage1`
	`  part / --fstype=ext3`
	`  --size=0 -grow`
	`  --onvirtualdisk=cos`
	
	. . .
		ESX 4 only

serialnum	ESX serial number (license key); that is,
	
	`serialnum --esx=XXXXX-`
	`XXXXX-XXXXX-XXXXX-XXXXX`
		ESX 4 only

%post	Discussed below	

Of special note is the `%post` section of a kickstart file. This section contains a script of commands to run after the installation to configure the host, but before the first reboot of the server. The specialized configuration commands are covered in Chapters 8 through 10, and so are not covered here. However, to hook them in so that the configuration is automated, it is first required that the vmkernel be running. All the ESX-specific commands require the vmkernel to be running, and during the installation phase this is not the case. The following `%post` section creates a first boot script that will then configure the machine after the installation tool has rebooted the server:

```
%post
/bin/cat >> /etc/rc.d/rc.firstboot << EOF
#!/bin/bash
if [ -e /.firstboot ]
then

    # Place Configuration commands here

    /bin/rm -f /.firstboot
fi
EOF
/bin/touch /.firstboot
/bin/chmod 500 /etc/rc.d/rc.firstboot /.firstboot
/bin/echo ". /etc/rc.d/rc.firstboot" >> /etc/rc.d/rc.local
```

The code can be used anytime just by creating the file `/.firstboot` on the system, too. If the file does not exist, the firstboot script will not run. Also note that the firstboot script has restricted permissions, so other users cannot see the configuration changes made during boot.

Another sticky point with kickstart-based installations is that many people want to install from a VLAN. This is possible, but the capability to use virtual switch tagging is not yet available, because the vmkernel is not loaded, so any ESX host using a VLAN needs to be plugged directly into the VLAN in question. Installations support only external switch-tagging networks. Chapter 7 goes into networking in detail and covers these concepts.

Conclusion

Before installing, be sure to have all the pertinent data at hand and all the decisions made. Although redoing one installation is simple, if there are 300 to perform, a change to the plan could take many more hours to fix. Now that the installation is complete and customized, we should make sure this server is properly audited and monitored. The next chapter discusses in detail various ways of auditing and monitoring the newly built ESX host.

Chapter 4

Auditing and Monitoring

In the previous chapters, we discussed the differences between versions of ESX and ESXi, hardware on which the OS can be installed and installation, and upgrades. But a large part of your planning should be around auditing and monitoring not just a single ESX host but the entire virtual environment. Auditing and monitoring of the entire virtual environment is becoming much more important as more and more workloads are transferred to virtual machines across multiple clusters. However, what does auditing and monitoring actually mean? When I ask people what they want to audit or monitor, there are varied and distinct answers. The most common answers are that a customer wants to monitor the following:

- State of a virtual machine

- State of an ESX host

- Performance

- Hardware

- Security

- Compliance

- Applications running within VMs

This list, however, is fairly endless. For some people, the list is extremely specific, but for others it is wide open. In many cases, a customer will want end-to-end monitoring but cannot define what this means for the virtual environment. For auditing, however, the consensus is that they are aiming to meet some compliance regulation such as FDIC, SOX, HIPPA, or PCI. Auditing for regulatory compliance is very well defined, yet strangely, the compliance guidance for the regulation does not yet include virtualization. FDIC and PCI are working on some guidance, but many others do not have such guidance and often leave it up to the auditor. PCI now has some guidance on Virtualization but it is not yet complete.

In this chapter, we present an auditing recipe and a method to get end-to-end monitoring. This is not a chapter on securing the virtual environment, because that is covered in the book *VMware vSphereTM and Virtual Infrastructure Security: Securing the Virtual Environment* (Haletky, Edward. Boston, MA: Addison-Wesley, 2009).

Auditing Recipe

Auditing has one goal and only one goal, to determine who did what, when, where, how, and, hopefully, why. However, the why is often extremely difficult to ascertain, so our auditing recipe will look at trying to determine who did what, when, where, and how. But what does this mean? Is this required for regulatory compliance or is it just a good practice?

Regulatory compliance requires heightened auditing in order to know who did what, when, where, and how, as required by the compliance guidance. We also must admit early on that many methods exist to authorize users within the virtual environment, which implies that knowing who did what, when, where, and how could be a difficult task. There is not just one entry point for management of the virtual environment. So we will decrease the scope of the task and look at each individual ESX and ESXi host and the primary management tool, which is VMware vCenter.

We have our goals and scope, so now what is our recipe?

ESX and ESXi

A handful of tools apply both to ESX and ESXi for auditing purposes, and some interact directly with the vSphere Software Development Kit (SDK) to either access ESX and ESXi or to talk to the hosts via VMware vCenter. These include configuration management and authentication tools as well as remote log file monitoring tools.

Configuration Management

Configuration management has many definitions, but the one used in this section is about maintaining a common configuration across all your hosts and ensuring that files on those hosts have not changed, or if they have changed, gaining the knowledge of what, when, where, and how. As such, it is extremely important to implement some form of configuration management tool for your VMware ESX and ESXi systems. Although many configuration management tools exist for normal servers, you should choose one that interacts with the virtualization host directly. Two of the more popular ones are Tripwire Enterprise and ConfigureSoft, which looks like it will be pulled into the EMC Ionix product that is now a VMware tool named VMware vCenter Configuration Manager.

In the next section on ESX, I present a free tool that can also provide the same functionality for an ESX host, but not for ESXi because it installs into the service console. VMware has stated that the service console will soon disappear, but for VMware ESX 4 and ESX 3 it still exists and can be extremely useful.

Patch Management

A fairly major component of configuration management is patch management. By this, we mean whether your ESX or ESXi hosts are at the proper patch level. This is handled using the VMware Update Manager (VUM) and in some ways Host Profiles (if you have an Enterprise Plus license). With VUM the patches to ESX and ESXi are downloaded to a patch server that can be a separate server from vCenter, but in many cases they are the same server. If you want to be more secure, make it a separate server. Patching using VUM is covered in Chapter 8, "Configuring ESX from a Host Connection."

Compliance (Host Profiles)

Host Profiles provides a minimal amount of configuration management by continually monitoring your hosts for compliance with a baseline configuration. This configuration is quite limited, however, to network settings, labels, and other items that may be unrelated to the actual files installed on your system. To verify the integrity of your files, you need other tools. Host Profiles compliance should not be confused with regulatory compliance.

Authentication and Authorization

Authentication is the act of using a password to log in to the system, whereas authorization is what you have a right to access after you log in. Because of the myriad ways ESX and ESXi can be managed, there is a major issue with both ESX and ESXi: split brain authentication and authorization can exist. In essence, there is no clear master authentication and authorization database, but instead there are multiple ones. Within our defined scope, there are two: the ESX or ESXi host and VMware vCenter. These have yet to be unified using a tool from VMware. However, this has been addressed by a third party.

The HyTrust Appliance (www.hytrust.com) addresses this exact issue by providing an inline proxy that sits between the users and vCenter, as well as between the users and ESX or ESXi. Eventually, I expect this will also sit between ESX and vCenter. The appliance provides a single authentication and authorization database for use within the environment. By tying into a directory service, the HyTrust Appliance provides that single database of authentication and authorization information that is desperately missing from the virtual environment. In addition, all actions by a user are logged so that we can answer the question who did what, when, where, and how?

Even so, the current versions of the HyTrust appliance can be bypassed. It is not a mandatory access control tool, but still a discretionary access control tool.

Root Has Access to Everything

Within ESX and ESXi, the root user, otherwise known as the Administrator, Super Admin, or Super User (only the root user exists on a host, however), has access to everything within the virtual environment. VMware vCenter communicates to ESX and ESXi using a user named vpxuser, which actually runs all its commands with root privileges.

Given that this root user has access to everything, and therefore can destroy everything, extreme care should be taken with who has access to this account. Perhaps place some auditable compensating control on the user, such that the account can be used only for a specific amount of time or requires at least two people to gain access to the password, and so forth. We can use many options to protect the root user, but when we design an auditing recipe, compensating controls must be considered as part of it. Several tools and options exist to manage root users now, often referred to as *password vaulting until use*. Such controls could be literally placing the passwords within a vault, having another organization control the password and who can access it, or use such tools from HyTrust and Reflex Systems to achieve the same functionality.

Remote Logging

Within ESX and ESXi, you can set up remote logging of all important log files created by the two hypervisors. There are several reasons to do this from an auditing perspective. First, the logs contain any errors that occurred as well as when they occurred. These errors are what has happened and could have been triggered by how something happened, which, if we have proper auditing, could also give us who and when. Second, remote log files make it harder for attackers to cover their tracks. If they can break your virtualization host security, they can certainly doctor a few local log files to cover their tracks. Remote log files are more difficult to doctor. Last, and perhaps most important for the virtualization administrator, these remote log files can be fed into a number of tools that can warn you that something needs to be fixed, or even fix the problem for you, so you can continue to sleep in the wee hours of the morning.

Several tools can be used with the remote logs to get this information to the virtualization administrators and are invaluable to your auditing capability. Even without these tools, there are log servers that will store the data for later automated or by-hand analysis.

Because of the split-brained authentication and authorization, it is very important to use off-system logging mechanisms to store the logs for later perusal. This is achieved by using a syslog server such as RSA Envision, Splunk, Tri-Geo, and standard syslog daemons for the OS of choice such as Linux syslogd, Kiwi Syslog Daemon, Winsyslog, and so on. In the enterprise, such a log server most likely already exists. Not only should you set up ESX and ESXi to send logs to your log server (covered in Chapter 8), but you should also set up vCenter Server, and the other management tools such as Lab Manager, HyTrust Appliance, Lifecycle Manager, and others to send logs to a log server. This way you have all the data necessary to reconstruct who did what, when, where, and how. It may not be easy to do, but the data exists.

When an incident happens, having a common time source for all your hosts and management servers within your virtual environment will be critical; otherwise, you will spend most of your time doing time transformations instead of solving the problem.

> ### Best Practice
> Always have a common time source for all hosts and management servers within the virtual environment.

Capacity Management

Capacity management is a major component of auditing because you are trying to predict when your environment will need more resources, but it is also a good method to use to determine if any issues exist within the environment. There are several tools to manage capacity, such as Vizioncore's vFoglight, vKernel's tools, and Hyper9. Simply running these tools will point out where you have bottlenecks and other issues that could lead to finding even further issues. Case in point: I recently had an issue with vKernel showing me orphaned VMDKs. Tracking back the timestamp of this led me to an issue with Storage vMotion not correctly hooking the disks' backup. So now we have a policy in place to ensure that Storage vMotions occur properly.

Wasting storage resources could be very expensive as you increase your capacity. This is a simple example of how these tools can aid your environment.

Automated Dashboard Search Queries

Another important auditing tool is software that will enable you to easily search the voluminous data available through the vSphere SDK. Some of these search tools can also search remote logs, but in general they all provide a set number of queries that can be displayed in a dashboard format to make auditing and monitoring of your ESX and ESXi hosts easier. The search tools cover both auditing and monitoring, and how they are used depends entirely on the queries performed.

Queries that try to detect changes in your environment and determine when, how, or what has happened belong to the auditing category. Such search tools include Hyper9, Reflex Systems VMC with VQL, vKernel's SearchMyVM, as well as specific purpose-built tools using PowerShell, such as vCheck from Alan Renouf.

Common Auditing Conclusion

Auditing is a complex yet important aspect of your virtual environment. You audit for security as well as other issues. The key component of auditing is to determine who did what, when, where, and how. That is the only goal of auditing. To that end, we need to do the following:

- Restrict access to the root user via password vaulting techniques.

- Restrict access to the vpxuser.

- Provide remote log analysis.

- Ensure a common time source across the hosts and management servers of the virtual environment.

- Verify that authentication and authorization controls are in place and the same across all management tools (either via a tool such as HyTrust or by hand).

- Ensure your virtual environment's configuration is managed.

ESX

Auditing recipes that apply only to ESX are a bit more involved than those that apply to ESXi. They add some new tools to the toolbox to avoid items such as root kits, to monitor actions, and to help interpret results. Because we will be adding more functionality into ESX, we should install most of these tools onto read-only media such as a CD-ROM, floppy, or some other file system that can only be mounted read-only. In most cases, I recommend a CD-ROM. Most of these tools, when run in a cluster of ESX hosts, should have staggered start times so that the cluster does not get overloaded or cause unnecessary LUN locking; unfortunately, this will need to be done by hand because ESX has no cooperative tasking between hosts. (See Chapter 6, "Effects on Operations," for more details.) The recipe for adding the additional auditing capabilities involves the following steps:

1. Force all users to use the sudo command instead of directly accessing root when doing administration via the service console. This functionality does not exist for ESXi, which we covered previously with the HyTrust Appliance (which is also recommended for use with ESX hosts). For every administrator, create a local account and do not allow a direct login as root by restricting its password; if someone needs root access to the system, require use of sudo. sudo will log in as root using the user's password and run a set of predefined commands. This set of commands can be wide open or restricted by group and user. One thing you absolutely do not want to allow is shell access, because after the shell access is granted, sudo's capability to log actions disappears completely. A shell is the environment in which you run commands, but granting shell access as root is dangerous. sudo has its own log file, and it records *when* a command was run, *what* the command was that was run, and by *whom* the command was run. The most simplistic /etc/sudoers file is to allow access to everything but the shells by adding the following line to the file. In addition, we do not want nonadministrative users to edit the /etc/sudoers file directly or anyone to access the su command to bypass our requirement to use sudo.

   The following is a sample /etc/sudoers file that could work in your environment preventing the necessary access discussed and also including an idmgmt role that could be a secondary organization that can manage passwords and users if you are not using a directory service.

```
Defaults syslog=auth
Cmnd_Alias
SHELLCMD=!/bin/sh,!/bin/bash,!/bin/csh,!/bin/ksh,!/sbin/nash,!
/bin/tcsh,!/usr/bin/ksh
Cmnd_Alias                    SUDOERS=!/usr/sbin/visudo,!/bin/vi
/etc/sudoers,!/bin/ed  /etc/sudoers /etc/sudoers,!/usr/bin/nano
/etc/sudoers,!/bin/sed /etc/sudoers,!/bin/awk /etc/sudoers
Cmnd_Alias SUCMD=!/bin/su,!/bin/cp /bin/su*
Cmnd_Alias
USERCMD=/usr/sbin/useradd,/usr/sbin/userdel,/usr/sbin/usermod
Cmnd_Alias
NOUSERCMD=!/usr/sbin/useradd,!/usr/sbin/userdel,!/usr/sbin/use
rmod
%wheel ALL=/*bin/*,/usr/*bin/*,SHELLCMD,SUDOERS,SUCMD,NOUSERCMD
idmgmt ALL=USERCMD
```

   Note, that the preceding sudoers entries work, but if you add too many wild cards ("*") to the lines, then sudo may cause a segmentation fault as it runs out of memory. Editing sudo should always be performed using visudo.

2. Run a periodic check for root kits. Root kits are malicious code that will be placed on a system when a system is hacked, to make logging in once more as root easier. That enables someone to launch further attacks on the internal systems, whether VM or a physical machine. It is a good idea to keep this tool on read-only media and to keep it up-to-date from time to time by checking (www.chkrootkit.org). chkrootkit will spit out a large amount of detail about the checks it has made. The key is to check this output for *any* positives. Any positive requires investigation and could imply, at the very least, that something has failed on the system on which it occurred. Earlier versions of chkrootkit did have some false positives, so run it and investigate often.

3. Periodically run a security assessment so that you know whether your security stance has changed. At the very least, run the tools after applying any patches. The idea here is to ensure that your score is either at least what it was or higher. Tools such HyTrust, VMinformer, and others are built around each of the available security guidances available from VMware, DISA, CIS, and NIST. Some tools report, whereas the DISA SRR actually implements its settings.

4. Install and configure tripwire or a similar tool. Tripwire and its primary database should be on read-only media so that modification is impossible, such as a CD-ROM that can be written using any other Linux system. Tripwire creates a database of checksums for critical files and will enable you to check whether these files have changed. This free and for fee auditing tool will catch changes to critical files nightly when the audit normally runs. Like most tools, tripwire needs adjustments for ESX, so we should make some changes to the configuration files to include ESX configuration directories, VM configuration files, and any nonpersistent VMDK files. The following is a list of changes suggested for tripwire to work best on ESX. Even so, the default tripwire configuration file is extremely useful without modification. Generating the list of files to check is fairly straightforward and can be achieved using the following script:

```
cat >> twpol.txt << EOF
  ###############
 #            ##
############### #
#             # #
# VMware dirs # #
#             ##
###############
(
  rulename = "VMware dir",
  severity = $(SIG_MED)
)
```

```
{
  /usr/lib/vmware                          -> $(SEC_BIN) ;
  /var/lib/vmware                          -> $(SEC_BIN) ;
  # Following is only if scripted install in use
  /var/vmware                              -> $(SEC_BIN) ;
}

    ##################################
 #                              ##
################################# #
#                              # #
# VMware Administration Programs # #
#                              ##
#################################

(
  rulename = "VMware Administration Programs",
  severity = $(SIG_HI)
)
{
EOF
for x in `rpm -qa|grep vmware-esx`; do rpm -ql $x|awk
 '{printf("%s -> \$(SEC_CRIT) ;\n",$1);}' >> twpol.txt ; done

echo "}" >> twpol.txt
```

There are two configuration files for tripwire: twcfg.txt and twpol.txt. The suggested changes are for twpol.txt and can be added to the end of the file. To make use of these changes, run the following commands, which will initialize and sign the files and databases, and run a baseline scan of the system for the sake of comparison. Quite a few errors will be reported, and they can either be ignored if running on a clean system that has not touched a network, or the twpol.txt file can be edited to comment out the offending lines. However, if your system is on the network, you will want to investigate any issues. If you do comment out the offending lines, rerun the following commands to re-sign and recompile the database. To sign and encrypt the files against change, several pass phrases will be required and will need to be repeated to re-create the policy and database files.

```
twinstall.sh
tripwire —init
```

Anytime you patch the system, the database for tripwire should be re-created. Use the second of the preceding commands (tripwire —init) to do this. For ESX 4 and ESX 3, adding the VMX files is a great addition. If a VMDK is in nonpersistent mode, including that in a tripwire database would ensure notification in case it changes. This last one implies that only one host that accesses the SAN should have the VMDK in its tripwire database (ensure this by auditing configuration files when changes are made). Having it on more than one host would be a duplication of effort. The contents would look similar to the following:

```
##############################
 #                          ##
################################## #
#                          # #
# VMware VMX/VMDK           # #
#                          ##
##################################

(
  rulename = "VMware VMX/VMDK",
  severity = $(SIG_HI)
)
{
  /vmfs/VMFS-SAN-1/vMachine/vMachine.vmx        ->
$(SEC_CRIT) ;
}
```

5. Enable process accounting on ESX so that you can tell when a process is started or stopped, or to gather other information. Although not incredibly important, an increase in processing time could imply someone is running something that should *not* be running, the server is experiencing a DoS-style attack, or the system is generally not behaving well. For ESX 3, you would install the laus RPM. ESX 4 already includes the auditd tool. Configure auditing using the following script:

```
NEWFILES=/tmp/$$
mkdir $NEWFILES
if [ `/sbin/chkconfig --list audit | /bin/grep -c :on` = 0 ];
then
   /sbin/chkconfig audit on
fi
if [ `/sbin/service audit status | /bin/grep -c stopped` = 1
];
then
   /sbin/service audit start
fi
for x in priv mount system
do
  if [ `/bin/grep "@${x}-ops" $NEWFILES/filter.conf|
/bin/egrep -c -v "^\#|^[:space:]\#"` = 0 ]; then
    if [ `/bin/grep PROC_$x $NEWFILES/filter.conf| /bin/egrep
-c -v "^\#|^[:space:]\#"` = 0 ]; then
      echo "tag \"PROC_$x\"" >> $NEWFILES/filter.conf
    fi
    echo "syscall @${x}-ops = always;" >>
$NEWFILES/filter.conf
  fi
```

```
done
/bin/cp -f $NEWFILES/filter.conf /etc/audit
/bin/chmod 640 /etc/audit/filter.conf
```

6. From a remote system, or a special VM you run only when this test is to be performed, periodically run tools such as Nessus (www.nessus.org) or NMAP to scan your service console's and management appliance's network connectivity for vulnerabilities. The output of Nessus can be extremely verbose. Investigate any negative result. After your initial configuration is completed, run this tool to get a baseline, and if a difference exists between the baseline and your new run, you should investigate, because some part of the defense in depth we are trying to establish has failed.

7. Enable remote logging by modifying the `/etc/syslog.conf` file on ESX 3 and the `/etc/rsyslog.conf` file on ESX 4 by adding the following line to the end of the file where hostname is either the hostname or IP address of your remote log server.

```
*.*          @hostname
```

8. The last general auditing tool to install is not really a part of ESX or anything else; log the console to a file using a script that can talk to the DRAC, ILO, or similar remote console access card if available. This script may be available from your hardware vendor; otherwise, it is something that will have to be written, usually involving the `expect` tool. This script has a two-fold effect. The first is to gather any console text that appears for later forensic analysis or for support analysis, because it will capture any crash or "purple screens of death" data that is necessary for the support specialist. The drawback to this is that many times a text-based access to the console for logging will *not* allow access by any other means, including sitting at the console when necessary. Any such script needs to be a control mechanism to interrupt the script to allow other users to log in remotely. If all you want to get is the PSOD information that is available within the dump file, you can extract it from an ESX or ESXi host with help from your VMware support specialist.

9. Although the previous item was the last general tool, two other tools could be used. The first is the Coroner's Toolkit, which will take a checksum of *all* files on the system, which will produce gigabytes of data. Do this once just after the machine is fully configured to get baseline data. Without this baseline data, forensic analysis can fail quickly, so gathering a baseline initially and anytime the system is patched will be a great benefit for when forensic analysis is required. Because it is gigabytes of data *and* it is important for forensics, this data should be stored on some form of removable

media (tape, DVD-ROM, USB disk [mounted remotely], and so on). The other tool, named Tara, is yet another assessment tool that can add some value and reams of data just like the Coroner's toolkit. Tara is another means of getting a baseline of the system that is slightly different. Having both of these baselines will be useful for future analysis. These two tools should be run *only* after the system is initially configured and then when it is patched. Do not overwrite old data; keep it around and safe, preferably in a vault. Forensic analysis will piece together what should be there from this data and compare it to what is there now. It could be that the root cause is back several revisions, which makes each baseline valuable data.

ESXi

You cannot do much from an auditing perspective with VMware ESXi of any version, just like you cannot do much to secure ESXi. The most important action is to enable remote logging using the following command using the Remote CLI for ESXi v3 or via vMA for ESXi v4. This can also be performed from the tech support mode (ESXi v3), login shell (ESXi v4), and via PowerShell. The following command does not work from PowerShell but via the command line mechanisms mentioned:

```
vicfg-syslog --server ESXiServerName --username root --password
password --setserver remotehost --port remotehostport
```

Auditing Conclusion

The most important aspect of any auditing recipe is to have a clear understanding of what information you need to collect for any regulatory compliance, forensics, or security needs. If you leave this question open ended, you may need petabytes of space to store everything, and some sort of data-mining tool just to assimilate it all. This is clearly a case of when too much information may be just that: too much. Be sure you gather what you need, or think you may need, and have the tools in place to properly analyze the output.

For auditing, nothing beats a good design.

Auditing Best Practice

Know exactly what auditing information you are required to gather.

Monitoring Recipe

Now that the recipe for setting up auditing is complete, it is time to turn our hand to the issues of monitoring your ESX host in a more automated fashion and for security and support issues. ESX has quite a few methods to monitor the system, including, but not limited to, the vSphere Client connected to ESXi and ESX, by manually looking at log files, vCenter and its various reports and alarms, various third-party tools, and open source tools such as Nagios that can monitor various subsystems for VMs or hosts. For end-to-end monitoring, we need to monitor not only the ESX and ESXi host, the hardware, but also the VMs and vCenter. To that end, we will break up monitoring into different subcategories. You may have noticed that there is quite a bit of overlap with auditing. Whereas auditing is trying to determine who did what, when, where, and how, monitoring is trying to determine that something has happened and whether to tell the virtualization administrator about it so that it can be fixed, repaired, or ignored.

Host Hardware Monitoring

Host hardware monitoring is of crucial importance because you have or are planning to consolidate multiple hosts into one or more. The consolidation ratios I have seen average about 20 VMs to one host, with the lowest number being 2 VMs to a single host and the highest number being 120 VMs to a single host. This implies that the health of this host is very important to assure as well as monitor. Predictive hardware monitoring is best.

Many vendors have monitoring suites for their hardware, and in general, these should be used unless you have some other tool. All these tools should speak IPMI or SNMP in order to assess hardware monitoring without the need to install agents within the ESX hosts. Because it is generally not suggested that you install agents within ESXi, if ESXi is in use then IPMI and SNMP are the only true agentless avenues to assess hardware functionality.

If you do use agents, predictive solutions are possible. For HP hardware, the agents can perform predictive failure analysis for disk and memory. In addition, some modern hardware has the capability to self-heal by using RAID-based RAM, RAID arrays with local storage, and entire RAID blade type configurations. The more redundant your hardware, the better the recovery, yet all this should also be monitored using hardware monitoring components. VMware vCenter has its own mechanisms, as does Dell OpenManage, IBM Director, and HP SIM. All these will talk to the hardware using SNMP and IPMI.

Virtual Machine State Monitoring

Virtual machine state monitoring is more than just the up/down state of the VM, but the health of the virtual machine as well. In general, you want to know as much about your VMs as possible. You will want to monitor the following:

- Up/down/suspended state

- Whether CPU is over/under allocated

- Whether memory is over/under allocated

- Whether network is over/under allocated

- Whether disk is over/under allocated

Many of these can be seen within the performance graphs of VMware vCenter, but there are specific tools that will help you with doing the heavy lifting and making the proper recommendations, such as vKernel and search type tools such as Hyper9. These tools will be predictive and allow you to look at trends of usage throughout the lifecycle of your VMs.

Network Monitoring

Network monitoring is always important and boils down to existing monitoring systems that you have in play and whether they have a virtual component. Although the existing physical mechanism can see the physical network, they may not be able to see the virtual network; as such you may need a virtual component. Network monitoring should look at the following elements:

- Traffic flow

- Network statistics

- Network state of Physical NICs (pNICS), Physical Virtual NICs (pvNICs such as the Palo Adapters within UCS), and Virtual NICS (vNICs) attached to each VM

- Intrusion Detection and Protection Systems (IDS/IPS)

The first three should give you trends of network usage and can be seen using SNMP and other techniques to query the VM or by querying ESX, ESXi, and vCenter directly. If the Cisco Nexus 1000V is in use, this information can be directly queried from the vSwitch itself using standard Nexus mechanisms.

The last element (IDS/IPS) is more of a security element and will require a tool that knows about the virtual network, such as Altor Networks via Juniper, Catbird Security via Sourcefire, IBM, or Reflex Systems via Tipping Point. These tools provide many more security capabilities with respect to network security, but this discussion is about using these tools to produce trends that can be applied to networking to determine whether you need more networking or whether traffic shaping should be employed to limit network bandwidth for certain VMs.

Performance Monitoring

Performance monitoring is similar to virtual machine and network monitoring but encompass the entire virtual environment instead of just VMs and networks. Performance monitoring tools need to look at disk, CPU, network, and memory across entire clusters of ESX or ESXi hosts, as well as look at behavior on storage and other arrays. When people say they need monitoring, this is the type that they are really asking about. There are many tools that can fit this need, such as Akorri Balance Point, vKernel, eG Innovations, and so on. The list is very large and all the tools should be investigated with an eye to continual monitoring, not just toward spot troubleshooting. Both capabilities, however, should be present in whichever tool you choose.

Application Monitoring

Application monitoring is the process of tracking what happens within the VM and specifically with the application being hosted. A great number of traditional tools will work within the virtual environment, but there are also a small number of tools that will work with the application and the virtual environment to allow tuning of both for the virtual environment. VMware AppSpeed is one such tool that works with a subset of applications. Tuning could be in the nature of throttling down resources when not in use or adding extra capacity (such as another VM) when required.

Security Monitoring

Security monitoring is nearly the same as monitoring your system for problems because the smallest of "problems" could be a security issue. In essence, any monitoring you do for all other aspects of virtualization can be used by the security team to determine whether there are other issues such as Denial of Service (DoS), illegal use of resources, and the like. However, there are a set of tools specifically designed to monitor your systems for vulnerabilities; one of these is Nesuss, as we discussed previously.

Running Nessus against your system to produce an external security report to determine what external vulnerabilities exist is just one part of the overall security monitoring tools suite. Nessus should be run from a machine on the administrative network.

Now that the log files and security are being monitored better, we should turn our thoughts to what services to monitor, too. Monitoring services will let you know whether for some reason they are not available. Various monitoring programs go about this in different ways. For example, vCenter monitors port 902 with its alarm system. If suddenly the ESX host were no longer available, first alarms will go off, and then eventually the ESX host would be automatically disconnected, telling you that there was an issue.

From a security perspective, a failure to access a service could imply that a DoS attack has been launched against that service and perhaps the host. However, from a support perspective, knowing when a system or service is unreachable proves extremely useful to debug problems.

Monitoring, security, and support concerns go hand in hand.

ESX-Specific Auditing and Monitoring Concerns

The previous sections of this chapter deal with ways to audit and monitor the service console, which is a variant of Linux. The recipe presented is a pretty standard recipe for generic Linux that accounts for the ESX peculiarities. Now it is time to delve into the ESX-specific issues related to the virtualization of machines into ESX guests and the various modes of networking available: specifically, the split between the networks for the service console, VMs, storage, fault tolerance, and vMotion. Ideally, neither network should overlap. From a security point of view, if a break-in occurs on the service console, the service console should *not* be able to sniff the packets coming from the VMs and absolutely should *not* be able to sniff the packets for the vMotion network. The vMotion network transmits a memory footprint, and access to this will allow a hacker to see what is currently in memory, which should be prevented at all costs. Allowing someone to not only grab your data, but to see what is currently in running memory is a recipe for security disaster, so be sure that the service console network is not shared with the VMs or the vMotion networks. There should be other vSwitches for the VMs and vMotion. Let the service console have a vSwitch just for itself, thereby not allowing the service console to gain access to the VM or vMotion networks.

vmkernel Considerations

vmkernel security should be addressed differently from vMotion security because as of ESX v3 it is possible to have multiple vmkernel connections. The vmkernel connections require physical security because there is no packet-filtering firewall for the vmkernel yet and because it is possible to use this connection for iSCSI or NAS, which contain information about VMDKs and possibly the VMs in use. It is important to realize that access to this network could imply access to the VMDKs, so access to the vmkernel NAS and iSCSI directories should be on their own private network and audited for access.

vMotion and Fault Tolerance Considerations

vMotion security should be addressed separately. As stated earlier, the vMotion network transmits a current running clear-text memory image from one ESX host to another while the Fault Tolerance network transfers data in clear text from one ESX host to another. The only way to prevent this data transfer is to not use vMotion or Fault Tolerance, which is not desirable. Not even the administrative network should be able to access the vMotion and Fault Tolerance networks, because a break in on the admin network could allow the sniffing of the clear-text memory image as well as CPU instructions. A little simple decoding makes it possible to see all your data for the running VM, which could include credit card and other personal identification information as well as giving anyone on the administrative network the capability to decrypt encrypted data. The only way to prevent packet sniffing is to place the vMotion and Fault Tolerance networks on their own physical switch or VLAN segmented and detached from any other network. This physical security will keep any other computer from being able to sniff vMotion and Fault Tolerance packets as they happen. This includes making sure no VM is attached to the vMotion and Fault Tolerance vSwitch. This requires a heightened sense of auditing to ensure these two networks are properly maintained.

Other ESX Considerations

In addition to the vSwitch layout, we need to consider the VMs themselves. Because many VMs will share the same physical NIC, it is best to lay some ground rules for both the VMs and the service console:

1. VM deployments happen over the administrative network or locally within the service console, so the administrative network needs to have some form of physical security.

2. Do not configure any network card in promiscuous mode, and disallow the VMs from doing so. There is no way to prevent the service console from running its network interfaces in promiscuous mode prior to ESX version 3, but by not having any VM or vMotion networks on the same network as the service console promiscuous settings will not grab private data not already belonging to the service console. For ESX and ESXi, these settings are attached to vSwitches and portgroups rather than to the individual VM. It is possible to also make these changes for each network, instead of directly on the virtual network, by selecting the appropriate network configuration and not the virtual switch. See Chapter 9, "Configuring ESX from a Virtual Center or Host," for how to set these settings.

3. Do not allow the VMs to spoof MAC addresses. It is very easy and extremely common for hackers to spoof MAC addresses to attack another host or gain access to protected networks. Prevent your VMs from being able to do this and prevent crackers from using the VMs as a base to hack other computers using this method.

   For ESX and ESXi, this setting is part of the vSwitches and portgroups rather than the individual VM. To make these changes, use the vSwitch security properties Because it is possible to have multiple networks on each vSwitch, these changes apply to the vNetwork, the vSwitch, or both. See Chapter 9 for how to set these settings.

4. Do not allow forged retransmits. Forged transmits are a cracker's way of trying to get around IP-based security settings by modifying a packet to have a different source address. Because it is possible to have multiple networks on each vSwitch, these changes apply to the vNetwork, the vSwitch, or both. See Chapter 9 for how to set these settings.

5. Disable copy and paste into and out of a VM when using the remote console, thereby requiring users of a VM to use existing secure mechanisms to transfer data. Adding the following options to the VM configuration file will force users to use normal and secured data transfer methods to move data from machine to machine, whether virtual or otherwise:

```
isolation.tools.copy = FALSE
isolation.tools.paste = FALSE
```

   Or set these options using VM advanced options, which allows the addition of new VM configuration settings via a graphical interface, using the same options as earlier versions.

These are some basic policies that could be enforced, and as a policy they need to be audited in an agile environment. It becomes even more important to audit your system on a continual basis to make sure that the basic security stance and policies you have defined are maintained. Some tools prevent you from making changes but as we already determined, it is possible to bypass many of these tools and as such you need to have a more active continual auditing tool in place to catch these lapses.

What to Do If There Is a Break-In

In the beginning of this chapter, we mentioned that one of our goals was to be prepared to know who did what, when, where, how, and hopefully why (or forensic analysis) within ESX or ESXi, not necessarily the VM, which is covered within the book mentioned at the beginning of the chapter, because we will assume that even our most rigid security recipe can eventually be cracked. To allow for forensic analysis, we have implemented additional auditing that will result in more logs to keep so we can determine who did what, when, from where, and how. Although it looks good in words, the where and the how are often the hardest things for forensic analysis to determine, and with the advent of antiforensic cracking tools, forensic analysis for computing systems is a difficult task. We need to make this easier for the experts. Here is a list of tasks to perform after a break-in has been determined to have occurred. Note that these steps are suggestions, and the corporate security policy should be consulted. If such a policy does not exist, the following list makes a good starting point for any digital forensics:

1. Notify corporate security of a break-in or any attempt at a break-in.

2. Because we mirrored the OS drive, break the mirror and place the tainted disk into an antistatic bag and seal it. Tag the bag with the date, time, and from where it was removed, and lock it away in a safe until needed.

3. In another bag, place a copy of your original baseline data for the system in question, plus any additional baseline data created. Ensure this bag is sealed and tagged with the appropriate date, time, and hostname.

4. vMotion all live VMs off the system in question and cold migrate any VMs powered down.

5. Reinstall the host from original media, patch, and secure using an appropriate script. At this time, we start to wonder whether the backup was also tainted, so original media is best.

6. Get a fresh baseline! This is extremely important.

7. Bring the host back into service by using vMotion to move VMs to the host in question.

As you can see from the previous discussion, a break-in does not have to be catastrophic with ESX, but it should be taken seriously and dealt with. Step 5 says to reinstall from original media, and this advice is offered mostly from experience: In an analysis of a break-in, it was determined that the break-in was noticed only recently because the cracker covered his tracks exceedingly well, and that the original break-in happened some time ago. This meant all recent backups were tainted. In this case, a restore from backup would have had to been done from a backup made three or so years earlier. Even if you regularly upgrade ESX, the attacker could have placed a rootkit on the system, which the patches may not alleviate. This is much more difficult with ESXi because updates, in effect, reinstall the OS; even so, reinstallation from original media is strongly suggested.

Conclusion

Securing any machine is generally a task for those who understand the OS in question in great detail, but the judicious use of preformed scripts from trusted sources, additional logging, and quite a bit of common sense will lead to a secure system, one that can monitor itself for possible security, performance, and support issues. In addition, if you follow the advice in this chapter, you will be prepared for the eventuality of a break-in, and you will audit and monitor your system so that you do not rest on your laurels. Keeping a secure system is an active task, and the system should be audited and monitored closely.

In Chapter 5, "Storage with ESX," we delve into the SAN and NAS fabric as it relates to ESX, and we can be thankful that this fabric currently just needs physical security.

Chapter 5

Storage with ESX

The need for fast, dependable, highly available, and easily managed storage is certainly a design component vital to ensuring a virtual infrastructure implementation is successful in all aspects. Successful in this situation means the implementation meets the organization's expectations moving into this new virtualization world of computing. Up to this point, we have discussed planning your server hardware and implementing the best server configuration requirements. Now let's consider doing the same decisive planning for our virtual datastores.

When implementing and planning new or using existing storage in an ESX or ESXi host, it is essential to have a thorough understanding of the VM requirements in the present, and far into the future, to get the most out of storage. After selecting the optimal storage hardware based on a design (see Chapter 1, "System Considerations"), it is essential to understand the best practices when managing the storage environment from the ESX perspective. As the virtual environment grows, you will deal with increasing amounts of data that may grow at an unexpected pace. With the high cost of storage products, an organization may consider cutting corners, which might come back later to hit you where it hurts: in the wallet. Take the time to purchase the correct storage hardware components and verify that your existing or new SAN, NAS, iSCSI, or locally attached storage configuration is acceptable to use with the virtual environment and the anticipated capacity. This preliminary step will save you time, money, and anguish. After selecting the storage hardware best for meeting the design goal, it is essential to understand how to connect this storage to your ESX Server, and then understand how to manage this storage using the provided tools.

Because many organizations have separate groups that manage servers and storage, it is best to provide a view from how the remote storage sees the vSphere host, and also how vSphere sees the remote storage. Such a view will assist both groups in communicating productively. We refer to ESX within this chapter. Unless otherwise stated, this also refers to ESXi.

> **Best Practice**
>
> To maintain your capacity, it is best to use predictive monitoring tools that will trend how such capacity is being used, as discussed in Chapter 4, "Auditing and Monitoring."
>
> Review the storage compatibility guide at www.vmware.com/support/pubs/vi_pubs.html.

Overview of Storage Technology with ESX

To construct a storage infrastructure for your virtual environment that will operate easily, dependably, and optimally, it is extremely important to have a basic understanding of the storage technologies available for ESX and ESXi in today's market. With today's computing datacenter dealing with volumes of data in the gigabyte, terabyte, and possibly the petabyte range, organizations will be faced with dealing with larger, faster, more reliable storage products to get the job done. As mentioned in Chapter 1, the storage technologies include local attached storage (either SCSI, SAS, or SATA), SAN (either FC, SCSI, SAS, or SATA), iSCSI, and NAS-based NFS storage. Storage within ESX refers to where a VM disk file (VMDK) can live.

From an ESX perspective, VMs generally access the storage components through SCSI devices within the VMs. When a VM issues a read or write command to what the VM thinks is a local SCSI controller with locally connected drives, the guest OS accesses this storage just like it does on a physical server. When an OS receives a request from an application for a file read/write operation, this request is handled by the OS as a file-to-block translation, and the request is then passed to the driver serving the OS. Because the VM driver does not directly access the hardware, the driver subsequently passes the block read/write request on to the vmkernel, where another translation takes place, and then it is passed on to the physical hardware device driver and sent to the storage controller. This storage controller could be a local onboard SCSI controller serving SCSI devices local to a server, external SCSI RAID devices, a FC HBA accessing a SAN array via multiple paths, or network cards serving access to an iSCSI target or via NFS. If NFS is in use the block translation does not happen because it is a file system transport not a block transport. No matter what the physical storage devices are, the VM knows nothing about their attributes or access methods, and ESX does a great job of making the guest operating systems believe the storage is the same as a physical server. On the ESX host, all storage bus traffic from all the hosted VMs appears to be coming from a single source from the storage controller's perspective. The two ways of making storage presented to ESX or ESXi available to VMs is to use a VMDK or raw disk map, which is a LUN formatted with the one of the VM operating system's native file systems.

In production, most ESX installations use local storage for the service console or management appliance, and local backups for disaster recovery, incorporating an external datastore to access VM disk files, VM swap files, VM snapshot files, and so on. The choices of storage available with ESX or ESXi for formatting as a VMFS volume are FC-SANs, iSCSI, and local SCSI storage. NFS-based NAS is also supported but not for a VMFS volume but as a file store. These are essential components of a virtual environment as a result of the sheer volume of disk space required to meet the demands of virtual computing, as well as providing the flexibility to manage VMs with ease. By implementing shared storage into the computing environment, administrators now have the capability for multiple hosts to access a common storage repository and uncoupling storage from single physical servers. The need for megabytes, terabytes, or petabytes of data space to store and run your VMs in an enterprise environment is simply not satisfactory when using local system storage, especially when you would like to use clustered servers, Dynamic Resource Load Balancing (DRLB), Business Continuity (BC), and Disaster Recovery (DR) technology. Equally important is having a common storage platform for all ESX hosts for ease of movement between and access to VMs from any host. Designing enough capacity and an easily accessible storage implementation complements any DR and BC plan, which is always critical in today's computing environment.

Administrators have many choices to assist in implementing the virtual environment such as FC-SAN, iSCSI, NFS, and local storage. As storage options become available with new releases of ESX, the potential for unanticipated problems and roadblocks increases, which makes understanding and planning storage imperative. Keeping on top of the technology is also very important because there are new storage endeavors going on every day that will change your design and either reduce or add complexity. One such new storage change is the introduction of EMC VPLEX, which will change how enterprises perform Business Continuity and Disaster Recovery tasks. We will discuss VPLEX later within this chapter. As VPLEX changes and other tools like it are introduced, the storage designs for the virtual environment will also change.

FC Versus SCSI Versus SAS Versus ATA Versus SATA, and So On

The data transport technology chosen to be used will impact performance. However when you compare 10G Ethernet running FC over Ethernet (FCoE) or iSCSI to 8Gbps FC transport speeds become a wash. Picking one transport over the other is at this moment usually political and based on cost and perceived improvements in performance. Always run tests using each transport within your environment.

After you have chosen a transport technology the issue with performance becomes the speed of the disks and the number of spindles within an array. The number of spindles, speed of disk, and disk controllers in use per RAID volume will affect performance. If you have the highest performing drives in use and you want to eke out even more performance then you may want to look at the connector. Connector speeds are ranked as such from fastest to slowest:[1]

- FC (optical) (2000MB/s)

- SATA v3 (600MB/s)

- FC (copper) (400MB/s)

- USB 3.0 (400MB/s)

- FireWire 3200 (393MB/s)

- SCSI u320 (320MB/s)

- SAS 300 (300MB/s)

- SATA v2 (300MB/s)

- SAS 150 (150MB/s)

- SATA v1 (150MB/s)

- PATA (133.5 MB/s)

- FireWire 800 (98.25 MB/s)

- USB 2.0 (60MB/s)

As you can see from the previous list, FC optical connectors are still the fastest but these tend to be available only within high end storage arrays. It should be noted, however, that most disks are saturated at very low speeds, somewhere around 150MB/s. The key to higher speeds for traditional platters and spindle disks is the number of simultaneous writes/reads they can make across the number of platters within the disk. Reads and writes use different heads within these disks, and there are often at least six platters if not more. This is why the local disk cache becomes very important. The more local cache, the faster the data can be sent over the connector to the host or array.

Solid state drives (SSD) can achieve far more performance, and the connector used to access the SSD will make a difference. SSD drives can easily saturate

---

[1]Data from http://en.wikipedia.org/wiki/SATA

the lower speed connectors because they run roughly at 500 MB/s. So SATA 3 and FC are the best connectors for these types of devices. In addition, with SSD, there is no longer the concept of a spindle, just controllers, so to improve performance the controller, and hence the connector, chosen will make a huge difference. When you choose SSD storage when we say spindle, we will start to mean controller.

Best Practice

More spindles/controllers implies more performance, yet some arrays have limits on the number of spindles per RAID volume before performance starts to drop (generally older arrays).
Verify the limits associated with your arrays.
Use SSD over SATA v3 or FC where ever possible.

Choose drives with a high mean-time-between-failure that have a higher speed. 15K drives are much better than slower drives.

Storage tiering is becoming a must as the higher performing drives and connectors tend to also be very expensive, so in general it is best to mix disk types within an array and employ auto-tiering technologies such as fully automated storage tiering (FAST) from EMC to make the most use of your drives. With auto-tiering technologies your most-used virtual machines would end up on the highest performing drives, whereas less-used VMs would end up on slower performing drives and connectors.

FCoE and Converged Network Adapters (CNAs)

FCoE transports FC packets over Ethernet and is enabling the storage networking space to enter into a new paradigm on how connectivity will be handled in the data center. It is unique in that it does not require us to decide between block based (FC, iSCSI) or file based protocols (NFS) but instead allows for a unique mixing of those connections over a single wire through Converged Enhanced Ethernet (CNAs). FCoE, unlike traditional TCP, requires lossless, low jitter, high bandwidth physical layer connections. FCoE is typically delivered over optical links (similar to Fibre Channel) and Twinax (coax copper cables).

iSCSI (SCSI over IP)

iSCSI appliances are low cost, very simple to use, and utilize SCSI protocols over TCP/IP. iSCSI disk arrays or servers are accessible from IP network-attached processors that allow direct access to a networked LUN that hosts a VMFS from which to run VMs. In effect, iSCSI uses Ethernet rather than Fibre to form a storage fabric. iSCSI, as compared to SAN, is generally less expensive and integrates with existing networks. However, for best performance, iSCSI usually has its own network. Another key attribute of having your VMs on iSCSI is now VMs can run from an ESX host that is on a LAN (local area network) or WAN (wide area network) to enable data access across long distances, which is beneficial for utilizing remote resources and disaster recovery. iSCSI is comparable to Fibre Channel when using bonded network devices or a single or pair of 10G cards. iSCSI has gained a lot of attention, with HP, EMC, Cisco, NetApp, along with many other smaller companies, producing iSCSI components in hopes of competing with the SAN market at a lower cost. The low-cost benefit of iSCSI is a result of the capability to use existing hardware and topologies to now act as datastores, and in addition, current network administration organizations do not need to add new skills or hardware to manage iSCSI. iSCSI uses authentication and encryption available through IP and can also utilize VPN connections. Because iSCSI uses IP, any standard firewall can control access to the iSCSI servers or network.

iSCSI is a client/server technology where the initiator, or client (a host), initiates requests to a server, or storage device, which is the target. There are two types of initiators: software and hardware. The software initiator is a driver that manages all requests and matches them with the network interface drivers and SCSI drivers. The downside to the software initiator is that the OS implements the whole stack, which is processor intensive. A hardware initiator is an iSCSI HBA that is essentially an Ethernet card containing a SCSI ASIC (application-specific integrated circuit) board designed to manage the SCSI requests rather than the server's CPU assuming this job. VMware uses a software initiator, which is a port of the SourceForge-based Cisco initiator. The initiator management lives inside the management appliance with the drivers in the vmkernel. For ESXv3 it is important to have the service console network participate in the iSCSI network as this is the network used for iSCSI authentication whether CHAP is in use or not. There is an iSCSI HBA for ESX, the QLogic 4010. This device appears just like any other SCSI HBA and acts as a TCP Offload Engine (TOE) with its own network stack to offload iSCSI protocol from the system processor.

Additionally, it is a good idea within ESX and ESXi to enable Jumbo Frames when iSCSI is in use to enable larger data packets to be sent over the wire without splitting the data across many smaller packets. Jumbo Frames increases the performance of iSCSI.

NAS (Network-Attached Storage)

NAS devices can share many different protocols, with the most prevalent being NFS (Network File System), CIFS (Common Information File System), and iSCSI. ESX can make use of NFS and iSCSI, but not CIFS. iSCSI can be fully used by ESX, but it has some slight auditing and networking considerations, as covered in Chapter 4 and Chapter 8, "Configuring ESX from a Host Connection." NFS, on the other hand, has its own limitations, including the NFS protocol to use. ESX supports NFS over TCP only. NFS can store ISO images used to build VMs and VMDKs. In future discussions, iSCSI and SAN are synonymous as SCSI block technologies while NFS is a file sharing technology and as such treated much differently.

SANs (Storage Area Networks)

SANs can meet the extreme requirements of data storage for ESX. SANs make use of dedicated network connections to one or many variable-sized disk arrays, which provide ESX hosts and many other systems in a datacenter with a common, shared data access container. SANs provide an optimum storage area that ensures high availability, desired performance, and ease of Disaster Recovery for data accessed from the applications running on VMs. SANs provide an ideal complementary technology to run, manage, and store VMs with the capability to grow far into the future. SANs are similar in concept to Ethernet networking connecting hosts, but the difference is we are not connecting servers together. We are connecting servers to a data space that is larger than is achievable with locally attached storage with SANs, often providing data access that is as fast or faster than that of locally attached storage. In addition to directly presenting storage to a physical host, many SANs can present iSCSI to hosts via a dedicated Ethernet connection to connect hosts to the data space. SANs connecting directly to hosts use a Fibre Channel card utilizing 2Gb, 4Gb, 8Gb, or 12Gb connections. On average, iSCSI connects using 1Gb or 10Gb via network cards.

Although this might be a review for some readers, I believe that a review of what makes up a SAN would be useful. So, in short, here we go.

Gigabit Interface Converters (GBICs)

GBICs enable Fibre Channel devices such as HBAs, switches, and routers to interconnect with the Fibre Channel cable. The reason for the GBIC is to translate a Fibre Channel signal from the Fibre Channel cable into a format that is interpretable by the HBA or Fibre Channel switches. What GBICs provide is the capability to interconnect physical media such as optical and copper in the SAN. Because of the lack of standardization for SAN connectivity, the GBIC allows switch manufacturers to focus their products on solutions and not on a specific medium type. This can be handy when changing the Fibre Channel type; just upgrade the GBIC instead of upgrading a switch. This is a great advantage considering the price of Fibre Channel switches.

Fibre Channel Switch

Fibre Channel switches are the intelligent devices that create what is called the "SAN fabric" by interconnecting all the Fibre Channel devices making up the SAN: the servers, storage arrays, hubs, and routers to tape libraries. Fibre Channel switches provide the capability to create arbitrated-loop and switched-fabric SAN designs. Ports on some switches use GBICS, whereas others permit a direct Fibre Channel cable connection. The type of ports available on switches dictate what type of Fibre Channel network may be connected.

The types of Fibre Channel switch ports are as follows:

- FL_PORT—For Fibre Channel arbitrated loop (FC-AL) designs

- F_PORT—For switched-fabric designs

- U_PORT—For universal port (FC-AL or fabric) designs

- E_PORT—For connecting Fibre Channel switches together

Newer Fibre Channel switches now provide additional switch ports that allow connectivity for IP networks to support protocols such as iSCSI.

Bridge

The bridge, or what is referred to as a *router*, is used to connect a Fibre Channel SAN to SCSI devices such as a tape library, jukeboxes, or disk arrays. The purpose of this device is to bridge or route Fibre Channel protocol communication to a SCSI bus, which allows interconnection between the SAN and backup or secondary storage. This device is beneficial when you have existing investment in secondary storage and you want to integrate these devices for use in your SAN.

Topologies

Now that we have a brief description of SAN components, let's take a moment to review the manner in which these components interconnect in the SAN fabric.

Point-to-Point Topology

Point-to-point topology, as depicted in Figure 5.1, is the simplest method for connecting a SAN array to a server by connecting a Fibre Channel cable from the storage array's storage processor (SP) port directly to the server's FC HBA. This is the lowest-cost solution, but this topology has a high risk of failure simply because there is no redundancy available. You may connect an MSA1000 to a server in this topology, but many other SAN storage arrays do not support this connection (for example, the EVA and HP series). This topology, although supported by VMware, is highly discouraged, and suggested only for testing and proof of concept. Another problem with this topology is that to expand you must do a total shutdown.

Point-to-Point

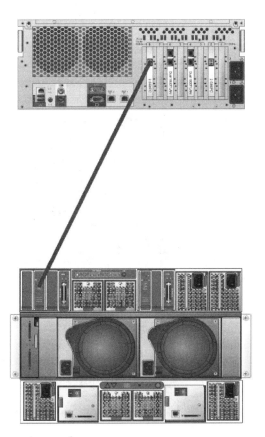

Figure 5.1 *Point-to-point topology*

Switched Fabric

The switched fabric or trivial fabric topology, as shown in Figure 5.2, shows an addition to the direct connect topology by adding a Fibre Channel switch, which allows several point-to-point connections for more storage and servers. The problem with this topology is that it still presents many points of failure, making this topology a non-fault-tolerant solution. Although not a best practice for an ESX environment, it is supported.

Switched Fabric

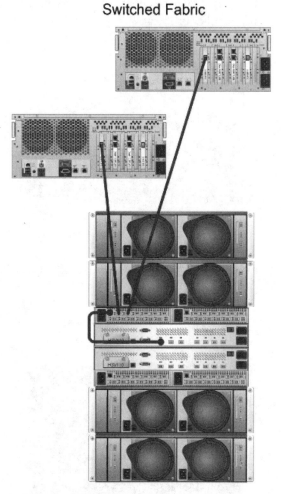

Figure 5.2 *Switched fabric topology*

Arbitrated Loop

The Fibre Channel arbitrated loop topology is similar to the networking topology known as Token Ring, as illustrated in Figure 5.3. Each component in the ring transmits data during an interval. This topology is popular because of the lower costs of Fiber Channel hubs compared to switches, even though the downside to this topology is the lack of scalability and efficiency. The arbitrated loop has no support within ESX and will have no support in the near future because of the performance limitations of this architecture.

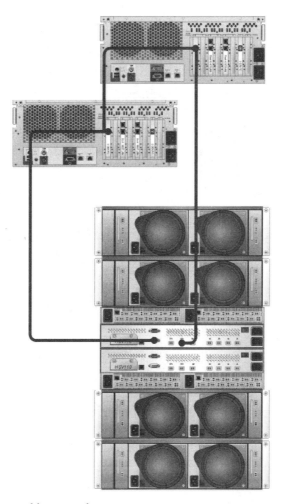

Figure 5.3 *Arbitrated loop topology*

Multipath Fabric

Multipath fabric, or multipath switched-fabric topology, introduces a highly fault-tolerant design with redundant storage processors on the storage array and FC HBAs on the servers, as shown in Figure 5.4. With multipath fabric topology, if an FC HBA or a storage processor fails, the ESX Server has a backup path to fail over to continue to access virtual disk files on the VMFS. ESX Server supports failover aspects of multipath but not automated load balancing and port aggregation.

Multipath Fabric

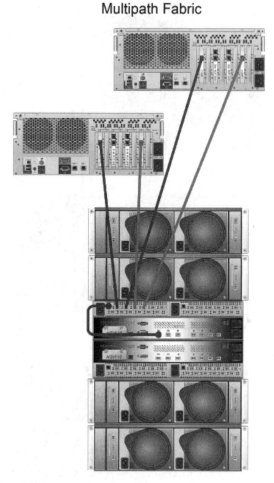

Figure 5.4 *Multipath fabric topology*

Redundant Fabric

The redundant fabric is the most popular topology and the preferred SAN topology for the ESX Server environment. It is illustrated in Figure 5.5. When a second Fibre Channel switch is included into the topology, the fabric becomes completely redundant. Fault-tolerant fabric eliminates all single points of failure. However, when using a single active/passive SAN, where only one storage processor (SP) is active at a time, ensure that all primary FC HBAs on every ESX

Server in the same farm point at the same SP, while the secondary FC HBAs point to another SP. This is extremely important to pay attention to, to prevent "LUN thrashing." This is a situation where the storage ports ping-pong connections back and forth, creating storage access degradation. However, this is not necessary when using an active/active SAN or multiple active/passive SANs. Active/passive and active/active describe the state of the storage processors. The SP is either active or passive. Active processors imply that it can handle storage requests, whereas passive processors cannot immediately do so. Passive SPs must first become active to handle requests. When a passive SP becomes active, it moves all the connections in use on the previous active SP to itself and then handles the request. So, be sure to present all LUNs for an ESX Server on an active/passive SAN through the same SP to alleviate LUN thrashing. Examples of active/active arrays are Hitachi 9900, EMC Symmetrix, HP XP (Hitachi), and IBM ESS. Examples of active/passive arrays are HP MSA1x00 (HP has active/active firmware available now for all MSA1x00 devices), HP EVA, IBM FAStT, and EMC Clarion.

Other SAN Options and Components
Other SAN options and components include replication, zoning, and multipath.

Auto Tiering
Auto tiering enables the array to move blocks of data around so that the most widely used data is on the fastest disks within the array. In most cases, the fastest disks will be SSD or flash drives.

Deduplication
Deduplication is a way to save space on storage by compressing all identical blocks on a storage array to just one block with a list of pointers to that block. The block is not deleted unless all the pointers are also deleted. So if your VMs are composed of the same exact operating system, this will save you space on your array.

Replication
If a company has an interest in Disaster Recovery, to ensure high data availability for its VMs, it might consider using replication for its SAN array data. It may be stored at one or more separate locations that are strategically selected to provide data availability when any one or more locations are compromised, rendering them inoperable. As discussed in Chapter 12, "Disaster Recovery, Business Continuity, and Backup," Disaster Recovery can be achieved with the use of clustering, snapshots, backups, and, when using SANs, replication to a remote site or sites using WAN technologies.

Redundant Fabric

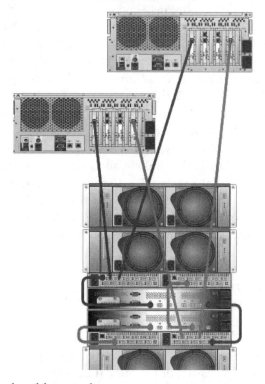

Figure 5.5 *Redundant fabric topology*

Fibre Channel over IP (FCIP) is the lowest-cost solution, which allows the use of the IP over the Internet to interconnect SAN arrays for replication. Some Fibre Channel switches provide the transfer link to allow Fibre Channel data to pass to FCIP across the Internet to a remote SAN to mirror the disk array data. In essence, SANs are connected to each other using an IP network protocol similar to the way servers are connected using Ethernet. Applications such as EMC's Symmetrix Remote Data Facility (SDRF), Peer-to-Peer Remote Copy (PPRC), and HP's Continuous Access provide the software to manage array-based SAN replication by synchronizing data at a remote site. ESX does have some replication limitations because there is no direct integration with third-party replication tools. In most cases, array vendors support synchronous replication up to 10 kilometers, whereas asynchronous replication can be over any distance. Failover to a backup site often requires manual intervention to change remote volumes to accessible mode.

New to this category is EMC VPLEX, which in the first release maintains a synchronous storage cache across a large distance (maximally 100 kilometers). In essence, they have stretched the storage network to be synchronous within two sites. This type of synchronous replication provides an active-active environment that spans two distinct arrays within two distinct data centers. VPLEX works with SAN as well as iSCSI storage.

Zoning

It is not desirable that any server on the SAN fabric arbitrarily access any data on a VMFS volume, whether intentional or accidental. This presents a data-integrity issue for the whole datastore, but it also presents a major security concern, and it promotes the spread of viruses and worms. A solution is zoning. Zoning controls the specific allocation of data path access to the LUNs or devices on the storage array. Zoning ensures that certain servers or users can only access the LUNs or devices they should be accessing on a SAN. Zoning also provides the service of device load balancing. Another attribute is that zoning reduces the number of LUNs or targets that the ESX Server sees, thereby reducing the amount of boot time for ESX or any servers scanning storage on the array. Think of a zone as essentially equivalent to a file system folder, or directory, or similar to network VLANs, or the concept of segmenting a network into many logical subnetworks that cannot cross data paths. When a SAN has many ESX Servers that all need to have data access to a common VMFS, it is essential to implement zoning correctly. To use vMotion in an ESX environment, all the ESX Servers have to have access to the same zone.

There are two types of SAN zoning: hard and soft zoning. With hard zoning, assign each device to a specific zone at the switch level. A method of hard zoning is to allow selected switch ports to communicate with other switch ports. Soft zoning allocates each device based on different server needs in the SAN topology. Soft zoning is at the storage processor level; for example, soft zoning uses World Wide Names (WWNs) to identify the storage processor on the fabric. A WWN is a unique 64-bit address represented in hexadecimal format that identifies an individual storage processor on the fabric. In some cases, storage arrays have multiple ports, each identified with an individual WWNN (World Wide Name Number). Similar to PCI networks cards that use MAC (Media Access Control) addresses to identify the ports on a LAN, WWNs are similar in concept to a SAN fabric. The advantage of zoning using a WWN is that all device or device ports have the flexibility of moving to another location on the fabric, while changing the device switch port but not changing the current zoning configuration. With ESX, it is essential that all servers in a farm be located in the same zone, so it is best to use soft-zoning policy if possible.

ESX Server provides a third zoning mechanism: LUN masking. LUN masking reduces the number of LUNs seen by the ESX Server, which may take a long time to boot if there are many LUNs to scan. All servers in a farm must see all LUNs for vMotion, and it is best to perform LUN masking at the storage processor level.

Multipath

Multipath failover allows a LUN on the SAN to be available, through multiple fabric paths, to an OS or application in the event of a failure somewhere in the fabric. If there is an event such as an FC HBA, switch, storage controller, or a Fibre Channel cable failure that causes the current path accessing a LUN to be severed, a failover happens automatically, with a configurable delay. With multipath failover, only one path to any particular LUN is active at any time. There are two other aspects of multipath: port aggregation and load balancing. Port aggregation enables, in the case of an active/active SAN, multiple HBAs, and hence multiple paths to the SPs, to be used, thereby gaining at least roughly a 2x performance improvement with storage queries and replies. Load balancing also makes use of multiple paths to the SPs and balances the traffic over all the paths to alleviate fabric bottlenecks.

ESX does support multipath failover and a basic form of load balancing, but it does not support port aggregation. Path management is an important topic when it comes to multipath functionality within ESX. ESX has made two policies available: MRU (most recently used), which is the default; and fixed (preferred path). Because the default policy is MRU, there could be problems with path management if using the default setting with an active/active array. When using the ESX MRU setting, which is used with active/passive arrays such as the MSA1x00, after a failover occurs to the backup path, that path will continue to remain in use until an administrator changes it back to the original preferred path. When you are using active/active arrays or multiple arrays, the "fixed" failover policy is best. In the event of a path failure with the selected preferred path, ESX attempts the alternative path to maintain access to the storage, but as soon as the preferred path regains connectivity, ESX reverts to the preferred path.

> ### Best Practice Path Management
>
> Use an MRU policy only for instances where there are single active/passive arrays or where multiple active/passive arrays are in use and zoned through to the same FC HBA.
>
> Use a fixed policy for instances where there are active/active arrays or when multiple active/passive arrays are in use and zoned through multiple FC HBAs.

When adding in multiple FC HBAs to an ESX Server, be sure to use the same type of adapter, because there is limited support for multiple types of adapters. As an example, it is not possible to set up multipath failover when using an Emulex and a QLogic FC HBA. The limitation is inherent in the drivers used. The FC HBAs must share the same driver to allow multipath failover functionality.

For ESX, there are several ways to investigate the state of multipath failover. The first is to log in to the management appliance and use the `esxcfg-mpath` command (output shown in the following listing). The other method is to use the vSphere Client (vSC) (see Figure 5.6).

```
# esxcfg-mpath –b
naa.600a0b80004972e3000006024be19053 : IBM Fibre Channel Disk
(naa.600a0b80004972e3000006024be19053)
    vmhba1:C0:T0:L2 LUN:2 state:active fc Adapter: WWNN:
50:01:43:80:02:9a:b6:75 WWPN:
50:01:43:80:02:9a:b6:74  Target: WWNN:
20:04:00:a0:b8:49:73:59 WWPN: 20:25:00:a0:b8:49:73:59
    vmhba2:C0:T0:L2 LUN:2 state:standby fc Adapter: WWNN:
50:01:43:80:02:9a:b6:77 WWPN: 50:01:43:80:02:9a:b6:76  Target:
WWNN: 20:04:00:a0:b8:49:73:59 WWPN: 20:24:00:a0:b8:49:73:59
```

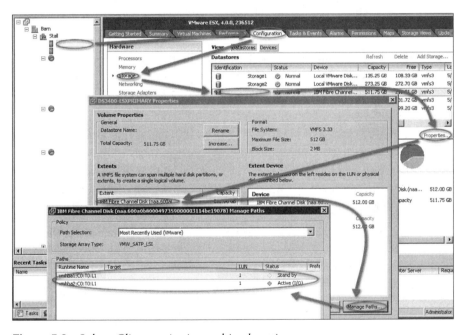

Figure 5.6 *vSphere Client, reviewing multipath settings*

Support for third-party multipath software products is *not* available for ESX v3, including HP's SecurePath and EMC's PowerPath. However, support for EMC's PowerPath is available for ESX v4 via the multi-path plug-in functionality that is available with the Enterprise Plus license level.

Storage Best Practices for ESX

Storage technology can be divided into SAN and iSCSI/NFS.

SAN/iSCSI Best Practices

SANs are extremely flexible and provide a common large datastore for use by the datacenter.

There are also some limitations and best practices:

- If implementing boot from SAN (BFS) on ESX, do not include on the boot LUN, presented by the SAN, any form of VMFS. VMFS SCSI Reservations lock the whole LUN and not just the assigned partition, which will contribute to contention for SAN resources. For ESX v4, the boot volume is very small but then loads the service console VM off a VMFS. For ESXi, the boot volume is very small, and it loads boot images off a VMFS.

- ESX does not contain true multipath capability, just failover and load balancing modes. Multipath can include some form aggregation among all FC HBAs. Therefore, more than two ports add more failover and load balancing paths and not necessarily more bandwidth.

- The "sort of" exception to the preceding practice is this: When there is an active/active SAN or multiple active/passive SANs, it is possible to zone LUNs presented through each available FC HBA. However, this is *not* multipath, but a zoning and presentation possibility, which then requires some form of failover.

- When placing FC HBAs in a server, be sure to place each card in its own PCI bus. Most servers have more than one PCI slot. Review Chapter 1 for more details on this.

- It is important to use the SAN array BIOS recommended by the vendor. If you use the wrong BIOS, ESX will fail to work properly with a SAN.

- When using multipath failover, always match FC HBA cards make and model.

- If using a multipath product via the Multi-path plug-in, always use the code specifically designed and available for ESX and ESXi.

- Most modern arrays support virtual LUNs. It is best to create smaller virtual LUNs striped across large physical LUNs. As disk sizes increase it is important to maintain the spindle/controller count with the RAID volumes in use.

- It is important to keep your FC HBA BIOS at the latest approved and supplied by the vendor for ESX, which is available from the vendor's website. Because there is no current method available to update firmware from the COS, reboot the server and use the maintenance mode kernel.

iSCSI/NFS Best Practices

iSCSI and NFS additions to ESX increase flexibility and provide more options for a common large datastore for use by the datacenter.

There are also some limitations and best practices:

- For ESX v3 ONLY: The iSCSI vmkernel device *must* be part of at least one service console vSwitch, which implies that the service console must be on the same network as the iSCSI servers. This is required whether using CHAP authentication, or not, to pass credentials to the iSCSI server.

- The NFS vmkernel device can be separate from the service console vSwitch.

- The vmkernel default route and netmask must include both the iSCSI and NFS servers. For ESX v3, this implies the service console default route and netmask should include at least the iSCSI server.

- Adding more NICs to the iSCSI vSwitch does not necessarily increase bandwidth. See Chapter 7, "Networking," for complete details on vSwitches. targets.

Virtual Machine File System

VMFS is a simple, efficient, distributed file system that is used by the vmkernel to enable high-performance access to large files such as virtual disks for VMs with very low overhead. VMFS is the native file system in ESX that enables the vmkernel to perform read/writes as efficiently as performing operations on a raw disk, with fast data structures used exclusively by the vmkernel, whether the VMFS is located on a local server or remote storage. ESX can host monolithic VMDKs on a VMFS and multiple file VMDKs on NFS.

Versions of ESX earlier than v3 used either VMFS-1 or VMFS-2 depending on the build level. VMFS-1 and VMFS-2 are flat block file systems that did not permit a directory structure hierarchy for the reason of maintaining fast access to virtual disk files from the vmkernel. ESX v3 introduced VMFS-3, which adds a directory structure allowing for the storage of VM configuration, disk, and swap files in one place. A single LUN may only house exactly one VMFS, which in turn will provide a container for many VM disk files from many ESX Servers if the VMFS is located on shared or local storage. The vmkernel organizes access to the VMFS by using SCSI-2 Reservation on the entire volume or LUN. SCSI-2 Reservations are covered later is this chapter. ESX v4 introduced new features to the VMFS such as grow-able volumes. Whether or not you can grow the volume using VMware vCenter depends on the level of the VMFS in use. You can always grow the volume regardless of VMFS-3 version directly connected to the host.

A VMFS volume contains a metadata area to manage all the files that live in the VMFS, as well as the attributes of the VMFS volume. The metadata file includes the VMFS label, number of files in the VMFS, attributes about the files, and file locks. Creating, deleting, and modifying the size of a file or its attributes updates the metadata. Because the VMFS is a cluster (distributed) file system, any update to the metadata requires locking the LUN on which the VMFS resides using a SCSI-2 Reservation. ESX uses the lock to synchronize data across all the ESX nodes accessing the VMFS.

The primary reason for a VMFS is the storage of VMDK files and VM swap files. These files are often out on shared storage, and therefore require not only the intrinsic features of the VMFS, but the clustering features, too. Other files also exist on a VMFS. Table 5.1 lists important file extensions, their use, and the version of ESX that uses them. A full list is available in Chapter 9, "Configuring ESX from a Virtual Center or Host."

Table 5.1 *VMFS Files by Extension*

Extension	Usage	Notes
.dsk	VM disk file	Early versions of ESX
.vmdk	VM disk file	
.hlog	Log file formed by VMotion	Often left hanging around, safe to remove
.vswp	Virtual swap file	Per VM, per host before ESX v3
.vmss	VM suspend file	
.vmsn	VM snapshot file	
.vmtd	VM template disk files	Exported form of a VMDK (prior to version 3)
.vmtx	VM template configuration files	Prior to version 3 only
.REDO	Files produced when VM is in REDO mode	Should disappear on a commit. Prior to version 3 only.

Extension	Usage	Notes
.vmx	VM configuration files	
.log	VM log files	
.nvram	Nonvolatile RAM file	

VMDK and VMFS Manipulation

VMFS volumes are managed by the vmkernel, but are also available from the service console. They are available from the /vmfs mount point, which is automatically created when VMFS volumes are added or created by ESX. The mount point is handy when working in the service console. However, normal Linux commands do not report anything about the mounted VMFS LUNs, so be sure to use the vdf command to see disk usage information, and the vmkfstools command to manage the VMFS volume(s). In addition, manipulating VMDKs using normal Linux could result in corrupt virtual disks. The safest way to move VMDKs from machine to machine other than using SVMotion and Cold Migration is to either use secure copy (scp) for transferring disk images from VMFS to VMFS or first export the VMDK or convert it to the 2Gb sparse disk type or export it as an OVF using the vSC. The 2Gb sparse VMDK type is safe to move using any Linux-based tool. 2Gb sparse VMDK files can be executed within the vmkernel from an NFS volume on ESX v3 while NFS support for standard VMDKs is available as of ESX v3.5. The following is the way to convert to 2Gb sparse files:

```
ESX 3: vmkfstools -i /vmfs/volumes/VOLUMENAME/file.vmdk -d
2gbsparse/tmp/file.vmdk
```

In addition, it's simple to create a VMFS from the command line. First, it is important to remember that there is a basic rule of one VMFS per LUN because of the way ESX invokes SCSI-2 Reservations. See Chapter 8 for information about creating VMFS volumes from the command line, but for performance reasons it is best to use the vSC to create a VMFS because it provides 64K track-boundary alignment.

> ### Best Practice for VMDK Movement
>
> Use scp to move VMDKs from VMFS on one host to VMFS on another host only if you cannot use Cold Migration or SVMotion from within vSC. To move VMDKs to a non-VMFS location, convert the VMDK to a 2Gb sparse file first or export the VM as OVF from within the vSC. Then use any tool to move the resultant VMDK files.

VMFS Types

The VM file system has gone through three forms (see Table 5.2) and has been designed to optimize VM runtime. The VMFS is a clustered file system shared among ESX Servers.

Table 5.2 *Virtual Machine File System Differences*

VMFS Type	Notes
VMFS-1	No directory structure, limited files per VMFS, public access mode
VMFS-2	No directory structure, configuration files stored on boot storage device, BFS supported, public and shared access modes, raw disk map support, enhanced to support multiple ESX Servers
VMFS-3	Directory structure, configuration, and vSwap files stored with VM disk file, public access mode only enhanced to support multiple ESX Servers

Structure of VMFS

VMFS contains a header of the VMware file system metadata that includes all the attributes for the VMFS volume and holds the files within the volume. When a metadata update is required, the vmkernel of the ESX Server places a non-persistent SCSI-2 Reservation on the complete VMFS volume, which creates a lock until the operation is completed. This is essential to keep other ESX Servers accessing the same VMFS volume from updating the metadata while another update is happening, which prevents metadata corruption, which is necessary for any clustered file system. The VMFS metadata attributes include the size, type, and extents of the VMFS, and information about each file. The file attributes within the metadata are a file's types, permissions, ownerships, access and modification times, sizes, names, locations within the VMFS, or if a raw disk map (RDM), a direct pointer to the LUN location. After the metadata are the actual files and directories within the VMFS. The overall VMFS layout is shown in Figure 5.7.

Storage IO Control

Storage IO Control (SIOC) was introduced in vSphere 4.1 as a way to traffic shape storage requests clusterwide. SIOC works by having each host within the cluster write latency data into the metadata of the attached LUNs, This data is then used to determine if the latency is too high (20ms at this time). If the latency is too high SIOC comes into play and puts into place a rudimentary traffic shaping that allows the most important virtual disks to write data more often than others. The most important virtual disks are set by increasing the disk shares number above all other virtual disks. The higher the number of disk shares, the more important the virtual disk. See Chapter 10, "Virtual Machines," for how to set these shares.

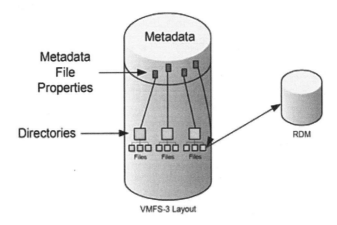

Figure 5.7 *VMFS layout*

SIOC is limited at this time to Fibre Channel and iSCSI–based LUNs, and is designed to alleviate contention within the Fibre Channel and iSCSI storage subsystem cluster wide not specific to any given host. In addition, SIOC does not affect physical raw disk maps but could be used on virtual raw disk maps because they show up as a virtual disk.

VMFS Accessibility Modes

For ESX versions earlier than version 3, there are two types of VMFS access modes, which define how the ESX Servers may access the VMFS and files in the volume. The two types of access modes in are public and shared, and it is important to understand the difference between these modes. VMFS-1 used public mode exclusively because only a single ESX Server would be accessing the VMFS volume, and so the file read/writes locked the whole volume. With VMFS-2, public mode has enhanced the locking algorithm that allows multiple ESX Servers to access the VMFS volume in an atomic mode by only locking at the file level during reads/writes. In shared access mode, the VMFS is in read-only mode, where the vmkernel controls file accesses. Public mode locks the entire VMFS only during a metadata update. As of ESX v3, shared access mode goes away, leaving only public access mode. Because the shared access mode was exclusively available for VMDKs used as shared disks of clustered VMs, a new shared-disk mechanism is available with ESX v3. That is the use of RDMs. The same holds true for ESX v4 as it does for ESX v3.

Raw Disk Maps

RDMs provide VMs direct access to the underlying LUN presented by remote storage, either iSCSI or SAN. RDMs either use a physical mode, where the VM controls all access and ESX places the virtual SCSI adapters in pass-through mode, or the ESX host can manage the RDM, providing all the normal disk-level functionality, including snapshots and other virtual disk modes. The latter occurs only if the RDM is a virtual RDM.

Growable VMFS

VMware has implemented the capability to grow a VMFS in size after the underlying LUN has been grown by the storage administrator. There is no longer a need to string together many small LUNs using extents; just extend the LUN and then extend the VMFS.

SCSI Pass Thru

Similar to RDMs in physical mode, SCSI pass thru mode allows a VM direct access to any SCSI device attached to the ESX host. The main use is to gain access to a tape device and other non-disk SCSI devices. Tape devices are only supported using Adaptec SCSI host adapters. Fibre Channel tape devices are accessible through Fibre Channel switches and are presented like any LUN.

VMFS Error Conditions

ESX VMFSs can have several error conditions that are important to understand. Understanding the causes of these errors will help to govern how to implement ESX with remote storage. Some of the error conditions do not actually point to a problem on the ESX host, but they will nonetheless cause problems on ESX and need to be addressed at the SAN and ESX host levels. All these errors will show up in the `/var/log/vmkwarning` file, or via the MUI under the Options tab and its System Logs link (for ESX versions earlier than version 3). What follows in the rest of this section is a breakdown of the common errors, their implications, and steps to alleviate them. As of ESX v3, the VMFS non-VM I/O is throttled in an attempt to alleviate any of these conditions.

VMware has done quite a bit of work with VMware ESX v3.x and v4 to make the errors within the error logs more readable. One error in particular stands out in bold when it happens and that is SCSI RESERVATION CONFLICT. You absolutely never want to see this error; when you do, you have disk/array/IO contention within your virtual environment and it should be addressed quickly. Continued SCSI RESERVATION CONFLICTS can lead to VMs blue screening or crashing. The most interesting way VMware approached alleviating SCSI reservation conflicts is to increase the `scsiconflictretries` advanced option to 80 where it used to be a value of 8. The maximum allowable value is now 200.

A SCSI Reservation occurs whenever there is a request to update the metadata of a VMFS with new information or modification of old information. These reservations will lock the entire LUN, and although the standard states that a SCSI-2 Reservation can lock an extent or partition, it is important to realize that in ESX it requests a lock of the entire LUN. Because multiple machines can update the metadata per LUN at any time, these reservation requests can occur quite often and at the same time (and thus the possibility of SCSI Reservation conflicts occurs). Each reservation request that occurs will, after it is accepted, take anywhere from 1 millisecond to 12 milliseconds to complete, with an average of 7 milliseconds. Some operations take only 1 to 2 milliseconds from SCSI Reservation request, acceptance, and release. These fast operations are generally ones that change permissions, access and modification times, owner, and group names. All other operations generally lock the LUN for 7 milliseconds.

Operation changes are often the only ways to alleviate a SCSI Reservation conflict. To do so, it is best to understand what can cause them. Because SCSI Reservations are issued only for those items that modify the metadata of the VMFS, there is a definitive list of operations that can cause these. That list is as follows:

- When a file is first created.

- When a file is deleted.

- When a snapshot is created.

- When a 2Gb sparse or thin-formatted VMDK changes size on a VMFS, the size increase happens in 15MB chunks. If a 2Gb sparse or thin-formatted VMDK resides on an NFS partition, no SCSI-2 Reservation is made, only an NFS lock.

- When the VMDK is migrated, two reservations are actually required: one on the source system, and one on the target to make sure the files do not change in the middle of an operation, whether via a hot migration (VMotion) or a cold migration. Conflicts can cause the VMotion to fail outright.

- When the VMDK is suspended because there is a suspend file written.

- When the VMDK is created via a template. If the template also resides on a VMFS, there is a SCSI Reservation for the source and also one for the target so that the template does not get destroyed in the middle of a deployment.

- When a template is created from a VMDK. If the template target is also on a VMFS, there is a SCSI Reservation every 16MB for the target and a single lock for the source. The source SCSI Reservation is to ensure that the VMDK is not modified as it is made into a template.

- When the VMDK is exported.

- When the file system is modified via `fdisk` or similar disk-manipulation tools run from the service console.

- When `vm-support` is run from the service console.

- When running `vdf` from the service console after a modification to the file system is made. This is a nonexclusive reservation.

- When a file on the VMFS has its ownership, permissions, access times, or modification times changed.

- When a file on the VMFS changes its size, a reservation is requested every 15MB.

- When a LUN is first attached to ESX.

The problem is not only an issue of a SCSI Reservation conflict, but the time it takes to return a status that the reservation request is good. SCSI Reservation requests are immediately handled by all arrays, but it could take up to 200ms for the status to be reported back to ESX. Running a Fibre analyzer against an array leads to the results shown in the rest of this section. Here the reservation request was issued, and 70ms later there was a response to the ESX host. The time for this type of situation ranges from 1ms to 120ms. There is no way currently available to predict the exact time that a lock request will report back to ESX.

```
00:30.243_596_192,SCSI Cmd = Reserve(6); LUN = 0000; FCP_DL =
00000000; ,00,4AD8
00:30.313_070_422,SCSI Status = Good; ,,4AD8
70ms response on lock.
```

Here the reservation release request was issued, and .340ms later the array responded to the ESX host:

```
00:30.313_652_818,SCSI Cmd = Release(6); LUN = 0000; FCP_DL =
00000000; ,00,4B20
00:30.313_922_280,SCSI Status = Good; ,,4B20
.340 ms response on lock release.
```

Here is a case in which two locks were requested at the same time from different machines. There is a 107ms lock response delay, which results in a SCSI Reservation conflict. This will exhaust the `scsiconflictretries` setting of 20 in ESX v3 and result in a SCSI Reservation conflict within ESX, and the operation on the LUN metadata will fail outright. However, with the new value of

80 within ESX v4, there is no conflict because the retry is performed a sufficient number of times.

```
00:31.955_514_678,FC_i7 1,SCSI Cmd = Reserve(6); LUN = 0000;
FCP_DL = 00000000; ,00,2630
00:32.015_103_122,FC_i6 3,SCSI Cmd = Reserve(6); LUN = 0000;
FCP_DL = 00000000; ,00,30F8
00:32.015_391_568,FC_i6 4,SCSI Status = Resv Cnft; ,,30F8
00:32.062_289_994,FC_i7 2,SCSI Status = Good; ,,2630
107ms for Lock response.
```

Storage Checklist

Now that you understand storage hardware and concerns, it is possible to formulate a checklist for the use of storage with ESX. SANs, iSCSI, and NAS are truly complementary technologies to virtualization, providing increased flexibility in addition to what VMs already offer. After presentation of storage to the server by the storage administrator (SAN, iSCSI, or NFS), ESX does not need any other changes to manage the LUNs. A benefit of remote storage is that it provides the capability to create any amount of storage for all ESX hosts to share and disperse workloads evenly and effectively. The benefits include provisioning VMs from template, convenient backup and disaster recovery, boot from SAN or iSCSI for various environments, providing storage for diskless environments, and providing a common storage interface needed for clustering using SCSI reservations.

Having NAS, iSCSI, or SANs being able to traverse long distances means that ESX hosts from many locations can access the same datastore. There is also an advantage to spreading storage and backup server to many different facilities because doing so can also reduce the risk of disasters. When VM disks and configuration files are stored on a remote datastore, any VM can run on any host and have the capability to migrate to another host at will. Discussion of these possibilities occurs in later chapters. However, one of the main drawbacks of remote storage is the lack of standardization with SAN and NAS technologies. Granted, SCSI and iSCSI are standards, but the implementation by vendors is by no means standard. Just look at SCSI-2 Reservation request response times. No standard governs how fast these need to be. Each array has different mechanisms to control the storage, so VMware is continuously working to validate as much storage vendor equipment as possible. Table 5.3 presents a checklist to follow when using remote storage with ESX.

Table 5.3 *Storage Checklist*

Element	Comments
Storage arrays	Determine supportability of the array by finding the make and model on the SAN compatibility guide. This includes iSCSI devices. If the SAN is not in the ESX storage compatibility matrix, do not use it.
Firmware	Verify the minimum firmware levels recommended by the storage vendor. This includes any switch and FC HBA or iSCSI TOE HBA firmware.
Multipath-ing (SAN)	There is no specialized multipath software for ESX. When there is more than one active SP for ESX, there is the capability to zone through multiple HBAs by the array. ESX cannot perform this zoning. Be sure not to zone through multiple HBAs on the same ESX Server because there is only an active/passive array. Be aware of the limited number of targets ESX can "see," and know that multipathing counts against the target limit.
Multipath-ing (MPP)	Does your array have a multipath plug-in driver to perform full multi-pathing for use with ESX and ESXi with an Enterprise Plus license?
LUN masking	Mask all LUNs at the storage level. Never mask off LUN 0 or the controlling LUN for the array.
Switches	Outside of ensuring the proper level of firmware for a switch concerning an array, there is nothing to consider from an ESX perspective.
Cabling	Ensure cabling is performed to avoid LUN thrashing, which occurs when an active HBA is connected to a passive storage processor when there are only two paths to an array (multipath fabric). In four-path configurations, this is not a big issue (redundant fabric).
HBA (FC/iSCSI)	Verify the supportability of the HBA by reviewing the I/O compatibility guide. If an HBA is not in the compatibility matrix, do *not* use it.
Clustering	ESX version 3 requires remote storage for an RDM for *all* shared disk clusters. Ensure there is enough LUN to support this. Also confirm that the array supports clustering by looking at the HCL. In addition, shared disk clusters require the boot volume of the VM to be on local storage.
Storage processors	Understand which storage processors are active and passive and how they are zoned and presented to ESX.
RAID level	Ensure a LUN is at the proper RAID level. RAID 5 or ADG are generally best.
Virtual LUNs	Use Virtual LUNs striped across larger multi-spindle/controller physical LUNs.
Connection type	When presenting to ESX, a SAN will need the proper connection type, which is a value used during LUN presentation. This information is available from the SAN vendor.
Limitations	Review and understand all limitations from the storage compatibility matrix and from the storage vendor.

Element	Comments
Access	Record the WWPN or network IP and netmask for the ESX Server for use by the storage device.
ESX/ESXi	Verify the patch level and configuration of ESX against the storage compatibility matrix for the remote storage device in use.
Storage topology	When formulating a storage topology design, consider all forms of available storage and LUN sizes for ESX: SAN, iSCSI, local storage, direct attach storage, NAS, SATA usage, and so on.
VMotion/ SVMotion	Which LUNs are visible to which servers.
LUN 0	Is there a LUN 0 or controlling LUN associated with the storage device? This can affect BFS. In addition, this LUN is always presented to every host.
Control	Who controls the storage device? Ensure there are clear lines of communication.
Documentation	Is there supporting documentation for re-creating the ESX/ESXi environment as needed? Include diagrams highlighting any possible single points of failure.
Space	Are there enough LUNs and LUN space for Business Continuity and Disaster Recovery? See Chapter 12 for full details.

Assessing Storage and Space Requirements

When considering what ESX storage needs may be, many people look past the assessment of their VM requirements and concentrate only on the storage product suite. The question is, "From where are the VMs going to run and therefore be stored?" When designing an ESX storage infrastructure from the ground up, or utilizing an existing storage implementation, it is vital to categorize and validate the storage on which to run VMs. Even though the perception of how important an organization's VMs are depends upon criticality, performance, availability, or DR requirements, this same information will assist in determining what storage design will be appropriate.

It is best to perform an unbiased poll for each VM's requirements as to the criticality of the applications that are running. How fast does this VM need to perform? Will this VM need point-in-time recovery? How does this VM need to be backed up? Would this VM ever need to be replicated? By collecting this data about the VM that will be running today, tomorrow, and down the road, the data will aid in answering these important questions:

- Is the current storage configuration acceptable, and if so, what limitations may be expected or is all-new storage required to accomplish your goal?

- What level of storage will meet all virtualization goals, and which storage solution is most cost-effective?

One problem is, over time, the level of storage may change due to technology advances; in addition, your VM requirements may change as applications become less or more important, and therefore storage will also change. In addition, peak storage needs could be different depending on what is running, specifically backups. This can be a difficult task because many VMs accessing a VMFS have varied peak characterization attributes to optimize your storage access. The more VMs accessing a VMFS, the greater the possibility of high I/O contention leading to performance degradation. A suggestion to manage possible I/O contention is to create LUNs or volumes that separate test, development, template storage, and production.

Be sure to test your entire workload and not just a part, and as close to production values as possible. When it comes to storage there are many aspects of the virtual environment that will impact I/O. The transport you choose will dictate how much bandwidth is available, and if you find one VM uses the entire bandwidth amount, you may need to switch to another transport or redesign the application in order to virtualize it.

SIOC will help in this area as you can then mark VMs for higher quality of service in terms of storage contention (at the moment this works for just block devices). You want to base your storage choices on I/O workload. Any tests we discuss later depend on having enough I/O to complete all necessary tasks. LUN size has something to do with the amount of available I/O (or at least per server queues for data transfer), but so does the amount of disk I/O you need to have available for your applications.

LUN Sizes

A topic that is certain to appear when configuring storage for ESX hosts is the size of the LUN. Should the VMs use many small LUNs or a few large LUNs?

The claims made in support of many smaller LUNs or volumes center around the idea that with more LUNs per ESX host, there is an increase in the number of simultaneous actions (thus possibly reducing the number of SCSI Reservations). Small LUNs could equate to less wasted space when managing the SAN. Different types of application may require different levels of RAID, so you may need specific LUNs for these scenarios. If you need to use clusters across ESX hosts, these will need their own LUNs for quorum and data access.

The claims made for support of fewer, larger LUNs for VMFS are based on the idea that a SAN administrator can create large LUNs to provision disk space ahead of time, which allows the ESX host administrator to use the space as desired. An advantage of fewer LUNs is the reduction of the amount of heap used by the server to manage many LUNs. If there are fewer LUNs to view, you have less to worry about concerning the visibility of LUNs because of zoning or LUN masking policies. Also, with large VMFSs, there is the freedom to resize virtual disks to larger sizes and use snapshot files.

It is common to have a difficult time choosing whether to use big or small LUNs. It is important to characterize the VMs to choose to go with many small LUNs or just a few large LUNs. Consider testing the VMs in both scenarios, and collect some data that will assist in deciding which size LUN to use for production. First, choose a sample set of applications from the production environment.

For one testing datastore, create a large LUN with RAID 5 or RAID 1+0 and make sure it is write-cache enabled. Format VMFS -3, on this LUN, and deploy three virtual disks, and monitor the disk performance on the datastore. If all is running well, increase the number of virtual disk files by three more, and continue to monitor disk performance while running the appropriate applications within the VM. Continue to add virtual disk files until there is an unacceptable level of application performance. This adding of virtual disk files is actually adding VMs with only a single VMDK. This will flesh out a threshold as to how many virtual disks with the chosen applications running in them. It could be possible to have up to 32 lightweight VMs, meaning very low resource-consuming VMs, or 10 heavyweight VMs with high-resource usage.

On the other test datastore with many small LUNs or volumes, create many small LUNs with various storage characteristics and format a VMFS -3 in each LUN, and be sure to label each LUN with its respective characteristic. Place each virtual disk file in the VMFS appropriately configured for the application the VM is running, and again monitor disk usage. Add VM disk files once more to find the threshold.

A third test is whether VMFS extents can be used to gather a bunch of smaller LUNs into one large LUN. Although extents allow multiple LUNs to be part of a single VMFS, there are issues when trying to remove an extent. However, this is also a valid test for comparison with the other two mechanisms. Yet, the extent size should be at least the common size of a VMDK. Extents perform just as well as standard VMFS volumes; however, they become harder to manage from the storage administrator's point of view unless the LUNs are well labeled within the storage as belonging to a VMFS and which one.

How big a LUN is, is a fundamental question of storage, and unfortunately not easily answered because the answer is a moving target based on VM resource utilization. The method outline previously is one method to try. The next big question is how many VMs to place on each LUN, and this can also define LUN size. If each VM is 200GB, for example, the size of the LUN could be rather large and still accommodate only a few VMs. Five VMs implies at least 1TB of storage for a given LUN. This number is a minimum, because the following should also be part of any consideration: the size of snapshots, vMotion logs, vSwap, VM log files, suspend files, and so on. Table 5.4 shows all the possible files. Consider the sizes of all these files when sizing a LUN. Although five 200GB VMs may be possible on a 1TB LUN, it might be better to only place 3VMs on this LUN to accommodate all the other files. Deduplication within the hardware and your LUN utilization will actually decrease. That 1TB of space used could end up being 750MBs of space or less in use. If this space does not represent "data" but instead just OS, and all OSes are identical, that disk utilization may not change. After data is involved, disk utilization will change and often increase. Use the checklist presented in Table 5.4 to size LUNs.

Table 5.4   *LUN Size Checklist*

Element	Common Size/Value	Notes
Performance threshold	None	This is the results of the tests defined previously.
Default size of individual VMDKs	None	Calculate based on the real values. Many implementations standardize on a single VMDK size and always use increments of that size.
RDM size	None	An RDM will use a slot in the VMFS table of contents but take up no other VMFS space. Many implementations choose a default lower limit with which to decide whether a VMDK should actually be an RDM. Anything over 200GB is common.
Snapshot file size	15MB	A snapshot creates a point-in-time copy of the changed blocks from the master VMDK. A snapshot can grow up to the size of the original VMDK.
VM configuration file	2K	There are two per VM as the VM configuration file is stored with the VMDK.

Element	Common Size/Value	Notes
VMDK configuration file	.5K	There is one VMDK configuration file per VMDK.
vSwap file	Size of VM memory	There is always one per VM, the size of the VM memory.
NVRAM file	8K	There is one NVRAM file per VM.
VM log file	20K min	The VM log file can be any size from 20K to the largest file allowed on the file system. This file can remain less than 100K, and there are up to seven of them. If there is a problem, this log file can grow to gigabytes very quickly.
Snapshot configuration file	.5K	There is usually one file per VM.
vMotion log file	.5K	There is one file per vMotion.

It is important to realize that most of the values used are based entirely on the environment being modeled. There is only one hard-and-fast rule: The more VMFS there are, the more actions that can happen simultaneously, as described in Chapter 6, "Effects on Operations."

Example of LUN Sizing

As an example, let's review the following possible configuration. In the nonvirtualized world, each of 12 servers has 2GB of memory and 200GB of hard disk space allocated per machine. However, when the usage statistics for the hosts were uncovered, it was discovered that only 512MB of memory and 20GB of disk space were actually used. From Table 5.4, the static size of a VM's disk usage is around 31.5K of disk space. Because the limit on the memory was only 512MB, we may want to only allocate that much memory for the VM so that a vSwap file would be created of that size. Then, because the disk usage is 20GB, it might be wise to start off with 25GB VMs. The math leads to 25GB + 512MB + 31.5K of necessary disk space, or roughly 25.6GB. However, it has been decided that snapshots will be used and that two snapshots will be necessary for recovery purposes. This implies that now at most 25.6GB * 3 or 76.8GB of space will now be required per VM. If a snapshot memory image will be required, an addition 1GB of space is required. With 12 VMs, the total required disk space is now 933.6GB.

The next decision point is whether to keep all 12 VMs on the same LUN. The suggested answer is *no,* which implies using less disk space per LUN. Assuming it was decided to split the 12 VMs between 2 LUNs, each LUN could be .5TB or some value greater than or equal to 466.8GB. Increasing this value to 600GB gives some leeway for increasing memory and increasing a VMDK file or adding another VMDK as necessary to a VM.

In this example, it is important to realize what the minimums are and increase that value to allow for future growth of the VM. ESX has a VMFS size limit of 2TBs – 512 bytes. The "– 512 bytes" was added as of ESX v4. There is also a file and directory count limit of just over 31,000 files and directories also to add into your model the use of deduplication if present. In our example, the total disk size could be reduced to 400GB with the use of hardware deduplication. It is also important to realize that you should never fill a VMFS past 90%. The best suggestion for an upper limit is 80%. After you do this, there could be issues with virtual machines.

> ### Best Practices
>
> There is a limit to a single VMFS of 2TB–512 bytes within ESX v4, and 2TB within ESX v3. Migrations between ESX v3 and ESX v4 MUST account for this change.
>
> Do not forget about deduplication benefits within arrays.
>
> Each extent is a different VMFS and you can have 32 extents for a single ~63TB VMFS.
>
> Never fill a VMFS past 90%.
>
> Use 80% full as a warning that you need more LUN space.

Storage-Specific Issues

Some of the most common storage issues encountered while using ESX are discussed in this section, as are several solutions. There are usually three ways to address each storage problem; however, the most useful happens to be the use of the service console or command line. Although not a definitive list of issues, they are common. Most storage solutions will use the `vmkfstools` command-line tool. `vmkfstools` is the VMDK and VMFS management tool for the command line to create, modify, or delete VMDKs, RDMs, VMFS, and vSwap files (for those ESX versions that need them created).

Increasing the Size of a VMDK

There are mixed feelings about the need to increase VMDK sizes when it is easily possible to add a new virtual disk to a VM, and with ESX version 3 it is possible to add a VMDK on-the-fly while the VM is running from the Virtual Infrastructure Client. Earlier versions of ESX required the VM to be shut down prior to VMDK addition. To change the size of a VMDK, you must shut down the VM. Note that changing the size of the VMDK does *not* change the size of the file system or systems held within the VMDK. Resizing a VMDK is extremely dangerous, and in most cases should never happen. Add a new VMDK instead, or create a new VMDK and copy the contents from the old to the larger using the standard VM OS tools.

As an example, let's look at a VMDK holding an NTFS for the Windows 2003 OS used by the VM. Because this VM has one file system and it is the C: partition, the OS does not necessarily allow the resizing of this partition directly. A third-party tool will be required to do so, such as DiskPart, which must be used from other boot media. That aside, the command to use to resize the VMDK follows. Note that it is also possible to shrink a VMDK, which *will* destroy data. Any use of the following commands is risky and should only be performed if you can safely answer this question:

Are you satisfied with your backup?

If you can answer yes to the preceding question, proceed. Otherwise, do not, because these commands are destructive.

```
vmkfstools -X xxG /vmfs/vmhbaC:T:L:P/yyyyy.vmdk
```

Note that xx is the number of gigabytes to which to set the size of the VMDK, and yyyyy is the name of the VMDK to manipulate. If xx is less than the original size of the VMDK, it is possible to shrink the VMDK, and that would result in data loss. ESX version 3 prevents the shrinking of files. The next step is to boot from a virtual floppy or CD-ROM that contains DiskPart or equivalent utility and manipulate the VMDK partitions by either increasing the size of the original partition or by creating secondary partitions. However, if creation of secondary partitions is to be performed, it is much safer and recommended that a new VMDK be created instead. If the OS within the VM supports some form of logical volume or dynamic disk technology, however, it is possible to add the new partition to the existing file system. Linux has this capability for its partitions, whereas Windows has this functionality only for nonboot partitions or C: drives.

As of ESX v3.5, this task can now be performed within the vSC but requires the VM to be powered off to perform. However, you will still need a third-party tool to resize the filesystem for you using the vSC. An alternative graphical mechanism is to use VMware Converter to export the VM and then re-import the VM, at the same time changing the size of the VMDK. VMware Converter will not only change the size of the VMDK, but change the filesystem sitting within the VMDK as well.

Lastly, you should realize that adding another VMDK may be the better solution and this can happen while the VM is actually running via the vSC.

Increasing the Size of a VMFS

Similar to increasing the size of a VMDK, increasing the size of a VMFS should be approached with care. In general, the recommendation for ESX v3 is *not* to resize a VMFS, but instead to create a new VMFS and copy over all the files from one to another, or even better, use multiple VMFSs to increase the number of simultaneous operations. To increase a VMFS, first the LUN size must be increased, but this does not automatically increase the size of the VMFS; however, it does allow multiple partitions on the LUN to be created. But, because there is a rule of one VMFS per LUN, doing this will cause contention and, therefore, performance issues. ESX has three means to increase the size of the VMFS by either extending a VMFS across multiple LUNs, referred to as extents, by growing the VMFS onto another partition of the SAME LUN that was increased by the storage administrator, or if using ESX v4, grow the VMFS which requires space within the LUN on which the VMFS resides.

Adding Extents

To add an extent use the vSC, review the VMFS properties in question, and then use the Add Extent Wizard.

Deleting Extents

Do not delete an extent unless you can first answer the following question:

Are you satisfied with your backup?

If you can answer yes to the preceding question, proceed. Deleting an extent is destructive as there is only one way to delete an extent that is by deleting the entire VMFS.

Searching for New LUNs

To search for new LUNs presented to the ESX host, just use the Rescan buttons the vSC.

The c in the following command implies the controller to rescan listed when running the command `esxcfg-vmhbadevs`. If the controller was not used prior to the rescan, finding the controller is based on extrapolating the results of the `esxcfg-vmhbadevs` command results:

```
esxcfg-rescan vmhbaC
```

VMFS Created on One ESX Host Not Appearing on Another

In some cases, a VMFS does not appear on all ESX hosts when a rescan is issued. This common storage problem is not really an ESX issue but could be related to the advanced options DiskMaskLUN (for ESX v3 only) or DiskMaxLUN settings. If the LUN to be presented is greater than eight in ESX v3 or 128 in ESX v4, it is related to DiskMaxLUN. If DiskMaxLUN and DiskMaskLUN are set properly, it is related to how the LUN is zoned or presented, and that points directly to the storage array and the WWID (World Wide ID) and WWPN (World Wide Port Number) used in zoning and presentation. It is possible to find the WWPN of all the ESX hosts by visiting the Storage Controllers buttons and tabs in the vSC (see Chapter 9, "Configuring ESX from a Virtual Center or Host," section) to relay this information to the storage array administrators.

When using iSCSI or NFS mounts within ESX, this problem is often related to mismatched IP networks in use between the servers and the storage device. Remember, iSCSI and NFS do not use the management appliance or service console for data traffic; they use the network assigned to one of the vmkernel NICs based entirely on IP address and netmask. So if this problem exists, you may need to check your network cabling and the IP subnet of the vmkernel device and make use of the vmkping command to ensure you can reach the storage device from the ESX host.

How to Unlock a LUN

In some cases, when attempting to manipulate a VMDK the result is that there is a lock imposed by another host and the action cannot occur. Remember from our initial discussion on SCSI Reservation conflicts that a lock is imposed on the entire LUN, not just on a single file. To reset the LUN and release the lock, run the following command:

```
vmkfstools -L release /vmfs/devices/disks/vml-ID
```

You must use the vml-ID which is seen when using `esxcfg-scsidevs` command. Note that the first command uses 0 for the partition number to address the whole LUN, and the second command will have a partition to address the extent or VMFS only. Because ESX locks the whole LUN when it performs SCSI Reservations, it is never suggested to have more than one partition per LUN for a VMFS, so the P should always be 1 in this case. The only exception to this is a VMFS on a local SCSI controller that does not have the same locking issues, because they can never be shared.

If the `release` option does not work there are several other more destructive options available such as `lunreset`, `busreset`, and `targetreset`. Whereas `release` works on just the SCSI lock, `lunreset` resets the entire line, while `busreset` resets the entire bus, and `targetreset` resets the target. These are increasingly less granular and as such can be destructive in nature. The ultimate option is to use the `-B` option for `vmkfstools` which will destructively force a break of the lock held. This should be done ONLY when you target the only host with a lock.

There is no method to release a lock from anywhere but the command line of the host that currently holds the lock, short of rebooting every ESX host attached to the LUN. In extremely rare cases, a reboot is necessary. See the discussion in Chapter 6 to alleviate the need to play around with LUN resets.

Boot from SAN or iSCSI

Boot from SAN and boot from iSCSI share similar issues. As previously mentioned, ESX locks the entire LUN when operating upon the metadata of a VMFS, and because at least one VMFS will be available when BFS is enabled, it is vitally important that the disk layout for the boot device *not* include a VMFS. If this happens, an operation on the VMFS will also lock the file systems for the console operating system and ESX generally becomes unstable. To alleviate this problem, always make sure there are at least two LUNs available for BFS. The first is private to the host in question and is the boot LUN; the second is the LUN to use for VMFS.

In odd cases with those arrays that have a controlling LUN, usually 0 or 31, that must be presented to every host attached to the SAN, it might be necessary to have three LUNs mapped to the host (LUN 0 and two others) to even install ESX .

Conclusion

With careful planning and diligence, it is possible to have a very strong SAN-, iSCSI-, or NFS-based storage network for ESX host. The key to all this is understanding how storage works within ESX to help plan around any issues that could occur. This chapter complements the storage whitepapers provided by VMware on their documentation website. The next chapter reviews some operational concerns to assist in better planning of the virtualized storage network.

Chapter 6

Effects on Operations

The introduction of virtualization using VMware ESX and ESXi creates a myriad of operational problems for administrators, specifically problems having to do with the scheduling of various operations around the use of normal tools and other everyday activities, such as deployments, antivirus and other agent and agentless operational tasks (performance gathering, and so forth), virtual machine agility (vMotion and Storage vMotion), and backups. In the past, prior to quad-core CPUs, many of these limitations were based on CPU utilization, but now the limitations are in the areas of disk and network throughput.

The performance-gathering issues dictate which tools to use to gather performance data and how to use the tools that gather this data. A certain level of understanding is required to interpret the results, and this knowledge will assist in balancing the VMs across multiple ESX or ESXi hosts.

The disk throughput issues are based on the limited pipe between the virtualization host and the remote storage, as well as reservation or locking issues. Locking issues dictate quite a bit how ESX should be managed. As discussed in Chapter 5, "Storage with ESX," SCSI reservations occur whenever the metadata of the VMFS is changed and the reservation happens for the whole LUN and not just an extent of the VMFS. This also dictates the layout of VMFS on each LUN; specifically, a VMFS should take up a whole LUN and not a part of the LUN. Disk throughput is becoming much more of an issue and will continue to be. Which is why with vSphere 4.1, Storage IO Control (SIOC) was introduced to traffic shape egress from the ESX host to Fibre Channel arrays. SIOC comes into play if the LUN latency is greater than 20ms. SIOC should improve overall throughput for those VMs marked as needing more of the limited pipe between the host and remote storage.

The network throughput issues are based on the limited pipes between the virtual machines and the outside physical network. Because these pipes are shared among many VMs, and most likely networks, via the use of VLANs, network I/O issues come to the forefront. This is especially true when discussing operational issues such as when to run network intensive tasks: VM backups, antivirus scans, and queries against other agents within VMs.

Virtual machine agility has its own operational and security concerns. Basically, the question is, "Can you ever be sure where your data is at any time?" Outside of the traditional operational concerns, virtual machine agility adds complexity to your environment.

Note that some of the solutions discussed within this chapter are utopian and not easy to implement within large-scale ESX environments. These are documented for completeness and to provide information that will aid in debugging these common problems. In addition, in this chapter unless otherwise mentioned we use the term ESX to also imply ESXi.

SCSI-2 Reservation Issues

With the possibility of drastic failures during crucial operations, we need to understand how we can alleviate the possibility of SCSI Reservation conflicts. We can eliminate SCSI Reservations by changing our operational behaviors to cover the possibility of failure. But what is a SCSI Reservation?

SCSI Reservations occur when an ESX host attempts to write to a LUN on a remote storage array. Because the VMFS is a clustered file system, there needs to be a way to ensure that when a write is made, that all previous writes have finished. In the simplest sense, SCSI Reservation is a lock that allows one write to finish before the next. We discuss this in detail in Chapter 5.

Although the changes to operational practices are generally simple, they are nonetheless fairly difficult to implement unless all the operators and administrators know how to tell whether an operation is occurring and whether the new operation would cause a SCSI Reservation conflict if it were implemented. This is where monitoring tools make the biggest impact.

VMware has made two major changes within the VMFS v3.31 to alleviate SCSI-2 Reservation issues. The first change was to raise the number of SCSI-2 Reservation retries that occur before a failure is reported. The second change was to allocate to each ESX host within a cluster a section of a VMFS so that simple updates do not always require a SCSI-2 Reservation. Even with these changes, SCSI-2 Reservations still occur, and we need to consider how to alleviate them.

The easiest way to alleviate SCSI-2 Reservations is to manage your ESX hosts using a common interface such as VMware vCenter Server, because vCenter has the capability to limit some actions that impact the number of simultaneous LUN actions. However, with the proliferation of PowerShell scripts, other vCenter management entities, and direct to host actions, this becomes much more difficult. Therefore, as we discussed in Chapter 4, "Auditing and Monitoring," it behooves you to perform adequate logging so that you can determine what caused the SCSI-2 Reservation, and then work to alleviate this from an operational perspective.

> **Best Practice**
>
> Verify that any other operation has first completed on a given file, LUN, or set of LUNs before proceeding with the next operation.

The primary way to avoid SCSI-2 Reservations is to verify in your management tool that all operations upon a given LUN or set of LUNs have been completed before proceeding with the next operation. In other words, serialize your actions per LUN or set of LUNs. In addition to checking your management tools, check the state of your backups and whether any current open service console operations have also completed. If a VMDK backup is running, let that take precedence and proceed with the next operation after the backup has completed. The easiest way to determine if a backup is running is to look on your backup tool's management console. However, you can also check for a snapshot that is created by your backup software using the snapshot manager that is part of the vSphere client or one of the snapshot hunter tools available. Most snapshots created by backup tools will have a very specific snapshot name. For example, if you use VCB, the snapshot will be named "_VCB-BACKUP_."

Multiple concurrent vMotions or Storage vMotions are a common cause for SCSI-2 Reservations, and this is why VMware has limited the number of simultaneous vMotions and Storage vMotions that can take place to six (increased to 8 in vSphere 4.1). Note that although vSphere will allow this number of migrations take place concurrently, it is not recommended for all arrays. For high-end arrays, the maximum can be performed simultaneously.

To check to see whether service console operations that could affect a LUN or set of LUNs have completed, judicious use of `sudo` is recommended. `sudo` can log all your operations to a file called `/var/log/secure` that you can peruse for file manipulation commands (`cp`, `rm`, `tar`, `mv`, and so on). Hopefully, this is being redirected to your log server, which has a script written to tell you if any LUN operations are taking place. Additionally, as the administrator, you can check the process lists for all servers for similar operations. No VMware user interface combines backups, vMotion, and service console actions. However, the HyTrust appliance is one such device that does provide a central place to audit for LUN requests (but not the completion of such requests).

When you work with ESXi, filesystem actions can still take place via Tech Support Mode, VMware Management Appliance (vMA) and the use of the vifs command. Even for ESXi, logging will be required.

For example, let's look at a system of three ESX hosts with five identical LUNs presented to the servers via Hitachi storage. Because each of the servers shares LUNs we need, we should limit our LUN activity to one operation per LUN at any given time. In this case, we could perform five operations simultaneously as long as those operations were LUN specific. After LUN boundaries are crossed, the number of simultaneous operations drops. To illustrate the second case, consider a VM with two disk files, one for the C: drive and one for the D: drive. Normally in ESX, we would place the C: and D: drives on separate LUNs to improve performance, among other things. In this case, because the C: and D: drives live on separate LUNs, manipulation of this VM, say with vMotion, counts as four simultaneous VM operations. This count is due to one operation affecting two LUNs, and the locks need to be set up on both the source and target of the vMotion. Therefore, five LUN operations could equate to fewer VM operations.

This leads to a set of operational behaviors with respect to SCSI Reservations.

Using the preceding examples as a basis, the suggested operational behaviors are as follows:

- Simplify deployments so that a VM does not span more than one LUN. In this way, operations on a VM are operations on a single LUN. This may not be possible because of performance requirements of the LUNs.

- Determine whether any operation is happening on the LUN you want to operate on. If your VM spans multiple LUNs, check the full set of LUNs by visiting the management tools in use and making sure that no other operation is happening on the LUN in question.

- Choose one ESX host as your deployment server. In this way, it is easy to limit deployment operations, imports, or template creations to only one host and LUN at a time.

- Use a naming convention for VMs that also tells what LUN or LUNs are in use for the VM. This way it is easy to tell what LUN could be affected by VM operation. This is an idealistic solution to the problem, given the possible use of Storage vMotion, but at least label VMs as spanning LUNs.

- Inside vCenter or any other management tool, limit access to the administrative operations so that only those who know the process can enact an operation. In the case of vCenter, only the administrative users should have any form of administrative privileges. All others should have only VM user or read-only privileges.

- Only administrators should be allowed to power on or off a VM. A power-off and power-on are considered separate operations unrelated to a reboot or reset from within the Guest OS. Power on and off operations open and close files on the LUN. However, more than just SCSI Reservation concerns exist with this case—there are performance concerns. For example, if you have 80 VMs across 4 hosts, rebooting all 80 at the same time would create a performance issue called a boot storm, and some of the VMs could fail to boot. The standard boot process for an ESX host is to boot the next VM only after VMware Tools is started, guaranteeing that there is no initial performance issue. However, this does not happen if VMware Tools is not installed or does not start. The necessary time of the lock for a power-on or -off operation is less than 7 microseconds, so many can be done in the span of a minute. However, this is not recommended, because the increase in load on ESX could adversely affect your other VMs. Limiting this is a wise move from a performance viewpoint.

- Use care when scheduling VMDK-level backups. It is best to have one host schedule all backups and to have one script to start backups on all other hosts. In this way, backups can be serialized per LUN. The serialization problem is solved by using the VMware Consolidated Backup, VMware Data Recovery, and many third-party tools such as Veeam Backup, Vizioncore vRangerPro, and Symantec BackupExpress. It is better for performance reasons to have each ESX host doing backups on a different LUN at any given time. For example, our three machines can each do a backup using a separate LUN. Even so, the activity is still controlled by only *one* host or tool so that there is no mix up or issue with timing so that each per LUN operation is serialized for a given LUN. Let the backup process limit and tell you what it is doing. Find tools that will

- Never start a backup on a LUN while another is still running.

- Signal the administrators that backups have finished either via email, message board, or pager(s). This way there is less to check per operation.

- Limit vMotion (hot migrations), fast migrates, cold migrations, and Storage vMotions to one per LUN. If you must do a huge number of vMotion migrations at the same time, limit this to one per LUN. With our example, there are five LUNs, so there is the possibility of five simultaneous vMotions, each on its own LUN, at any time. This assumes the VMs do not cross LUN boundaries.

- vMotion needs to be fast, and the more you attempt to do vMotions at the same time, the slower all will become. The slower the vMotion process, the higher the chance of the Guest OS having issues such as a blue screen of death for Windows. Using vMotion on 10 VMs at the same time could be a serious issue for the performance and health of the VM regardless of

SCSI Reservations. Make sure the VM has no active backup snapshots before invoking vMotion.

- Use only the default VM disk modes. The nondefault persistent disk modes lead to not being able to perform snapshots and use the consolidated backup tools. Nonpersistent modes such as read-only create snapshot files on LUNs during runtime and remove them on VM power-off so as to not affect the master disk file.

- Do not suspend VMs, because this also creates a file and therefore requires a SCSI Reservation.

- Do not run vm-support requests unless all other operations have completed.

- Do not use the vdf service console tool when any other modification operation is being performed. Although vdf does not normally force a reservation, it could experience one if another host, because of a metadata modification, locked the LUN.

- Do not rescan storage subsystems unless all other operations have completed.

- Limit use of vmkmultipath, vmkfstools, and other VMware-specific service console and remote CLI commands until all other operations have completed.

- Create, modify, or delete a VMFS only when all other operations have completed.

- Be sure no third-party agents are accessing your storage subsystem via vdf, or direct access to the /vmfs directory.

- Do not run scripts that modify VMFS ownership, permissions, access times, or modification times from more than one host. Localize such scripts to a single host. It is suggested that you use the deployment server as the host for such scripts.

- Run all scripts that affect LUNs from a management node that can control when actions can occur.

- Stagger the running of disk-intensive tools within a VM, such as virus scan. The extra load on your SAN could cause results similar to those that occur with SCSI Reservations but which are instead queue-full or unavailable-target errors.

- Use only one file system per LUN.

- Do not mix file systems on the same LUN.

What this all boils down to is ensuring that any possible operation that could somehow affect a LUN is limited to only one operation per LUN at any given time. The biggest hitters of this are automated power operations, backups, vMotion, Storage vMotion, and deployments. A little careful monitoring and changes to operational procedures can limit the possibility of SCSI Reservation conflicts and failures to various operations.

A case in point follows: One company under review because constant, debilitating SCSI Reservation conflicts reviewed the list of 23 items and fixed one or two possible items but missed the most critical item. This customer had an automated tool that ran simultaneously on all hosts at the same time to modify the owner and group of every file on every VMFS attached to the host. The resultant metadata updates caused hundreds of SCSI-2 Reservations to occur. The solution was to run this script from a single ESX host for all LUNs. By limiting the run of the script to a single host, all the reservations disappeared, because no two hosts were attempting to manipulate the file systems at the same time, and the single host, in effect, serialized the actions.

Hot and cold migrations of VMs can change the behavior of automatic boot methodologies, which can affect LUN locking. Setting a dependency on one VM or a time for a boot to occur deals with a single ESX host where you can start VMs at boot of ESX, after VMware Tools starts in the previous VM, after a certain amount of time, or not at all. This gets much more difficult with more than one ESX host, so a new method has to be used. Although starting a VM after a certain amount of time is extremely useful, what happens when three VMs start almost simultaneously on the same LUN? Remember, we want to limit operations to just one per LUN at any time. We have a few options:

- Stagger the boot or reboot of your ESX host and ensure that your VMs start only after the previous VMs' VMware Tools start, to ensure that all the disk activity associated with the boot sequence finishes before the next VM boots, thereby helping with boot performance and eliminating conflicts. VM boots are naturally staggered by ESX when it reboots anyway if the VM is auto-started.

- Similar to doing backups, have one ESX host that controls the boot of all VMs, guaranteeing that you can boot multiple VMs but only one VM per LUN at any time. If you have multiple ESX hosts, more than one VM can start at any time on each LUN, one per LUN. In essence, we use the VMware vSphere SDK to gather information about each VM from each ESX host and correlate the VMs to a LUN and create a list of VMs that can start simultaneously; that is, each VM is to start on a separate LUN. Then we wait a set length of time before starting the next batch of VMs. This method is not needed when VMware Fault Tolerance fires because the shadow VM is already running. Also, VMware HA uses its own rules for starting VMs in specific orders.

All the listed operational changes will limit the number of SCSI subsystem errors that will be experienced. Although it is possible to implement more than one operation per LUN at any given time, we cannot guarantee success with more than one operation. This depends on the type of operation, the SAN, settings, and most of all, timings for operations.

Yet you may ask yourself, "Wouldn't using ESXi solve many of these issues because there is no service console?" The answer is, "Partially." Many of the "scripting" issues that occur within a service console are no longer a concern. Scripting issues can come up using the new VMware Virtual Management Appliance (vMA) or by using the remote CLI directly if there is not a single control mechanism for when these scripts run against all LUNs in question. So the problems can still occur even with ESXi. On top of this, it is still possible to run scripts directly within the ESXi Posix environment that comprises the ESXi management console. Granted, it is much harder, but not impossible.

There are several other considerations, too. Most people want to perform multiple operations simultaneously, and this is possible as long as the operations are on separate LUNs or the storage array supports the number of simultaneous operations. Because many simultaneous operations are storage array specific, it behooves you to run a simple test with the array in question to determine how many simultaneous operations can happen per LUN. As ESX improves, arrays improve, vStorage API for Array Integration is used within arrays, and transports improve in performance the number of simultaneous operations per LUN will increase.

With vSphere, the number of SCSI Reservations have dropped drastically but they still occur; when they do, this section will help you to track down the reasons and provide you the necessary information to test your arrays. You should also test to determine how many hosts can be added to a given cluster before SCSI Reservations start occurring. On low-end switches, this value may just be 2, whereas on others it could be 4.

Best Practice

Verify the number of simultaneous LUN activities that can occur on the remote storage arrays chosen for use.

Performance-Gathering and Hardware Agents Within a VM

Performance and other types of monitoring are important from an operational point of view. Many customers monitor the health of their hardware and servers by monitoring hardware and performance agents. Although hardware agents monitor the health of the ESX host, they should not monitor the health of a VM, because the virtual hardware is truly dependent on the physical hardware. In addition, most agents are talking to specific chips, and these do not exist inside a VM. So using hardware agents will often slow down your VM.

> ### Best Practice for Hardware Agents
>
> Do *not* install hardware agents into a VM; they will cause noticeable performance issues.

Measuring performance now is a very important tool for the Virtual Environment; it will tell you when to invest in a new ESX host and how to balance the load among the ESX hosts. Although there are automated ways to balance the load among ESX hosts (they are covered in Chapter 11, "Dynamic Resource Load Balancing"), most if not all balancing of VM load across hosts is performed by hand, because there are more than just a few markers to review when moving VMs from host to host.

There is an argument that Dynamic Resource Scheduling (DRS) will balance VMs across all hosts, but DRS does balancing only when CPU contention exists. If you never have contention, you may still want to balance your loads by hand, regardless of DRS settings.

The first item to understand is that the addition of a VM to a host will impact the performance of the ESX host—sometimes in small ways, and sometimes in other ways that are more noticeable. The second item to understand is how performance tools that run within a VM, for example Windows, calculates utilization. It does this by incrementing a tic counter in its idle loop and then subtracts that amount of time from the system clock time interval. Because the VM gets put to sleep when idle, the idle time counter is skewed, which results in a higher utilization representation than typical. Because there are often more VMs than CPUs or cores, a VM will share a CPU with others, and as more VMs are added the slice of time the VM gets to run on a CPU is reduced even further. Therefore, a greater time lag exists between each usage of the CPU and thus a longer CPU cycle. Because performance tools use the CPU cycle to measure performance and to keep time, the data received is relatively inaccurate. When the system is loaded to the desired level, a set of baseline data should be discovered using VMware vCenter or other Performance Management tools.

After a set of baseline data is available, internal to the VM performance tools can determine whether a change in performance has occurred, but it cannot give you raw numbers, just a ratio of change from the baseline. For example, if the baseline for CPU utilization is roughly 20% measured from within the VM and suddenly shows 40%, we know that there was a 2x change from the original value. The original value is not really 20%, but some other number. However, even though this shows 2x more CPU utilization for the VM, it does not imply a 2x change to the actual server utilization. Therefore, to gain performance data for a VM, other tools need to be used that do not run from within the VM. VMware vCenter, a third-party tool such as Vizioncore vFoglight, or the use of esxtop from the command line or resxtop from the remote CLI are the tools to use because these all measure the VM and ESX host performance from outside the VM. In addition, they all give a clearer picture of the entire ESX host. The key item to realize is that when there is a sustained over 80% utilization of CPU for an ESX host as measured by vCenter or one of the tools, a new ESX host is warranted and the load on the ESX host needs to be rebalanced. This same mechanism can be used to determine whether more network and storage bandwidth is warranted.

Balancing ESX hosts can happen daily or even periodically during the day by using the vMotion technology to migrate running VMs from host to host with zero downtime. Although this can be dynamic (see Chapter 11), using vMotion and Storage vMotion by hand can give a better view of the system and the capability to rebalance as necessary. For example, if an ESX host's CPU utilization goes to 95%, the VM that is the culprit needs to be found using one of the tools; once found, the VM can be moved to an unused or lightly used ESX host using vMotion. If this movement becomes a normal behavior, it might be best to place the VM on a lesser-used machine permanently. This is often the major reason an N+1 host configuration is recommended.

Deployment of VMs can increase CPU utilization. Deployment is discussed in detail in a later chapter, but the recommendation is to create a deployment server that can see all LUNs. This server would be responsible for deploying any new VM, which allows the VM to be tested on the deployment server until it is ready to be migrated to a true production server using vMotion.

For example, a customer wanted to measure the performance of all VMs to determine how loaded the ESX host could become with the current networking configuration. To do so, we explained the CPU cycle issues and developed a plan of action. We employed two tools in this example, VMware vCenter, and `esxtop` running from the service console or from the vMA in batch mode (`esxtop -b`). For performance-problem resolution, `esxtop` is the best tool to use, but it spits out reams of data for later graphing. vCenter averages things over 5-minute or larger increments for historical data, but its real-time stats are collected every 20 seconds. `esxtop` uses real and not averaged data gathered as low as every 2 seconds with a default of 5 seconds. The plan was to measure performance using each tool as each VM was running its application. Performance of ESX truly depends on the application within each VM. It is extremely important to realize this, and when discussing performance issues to not localize to just a single VM, but to look at the host as a whole. This is why VMware generally does not allow performance numbers to be published, as the numbers are workload dependent. It is best to do your own analysis using your applications, because one company's virtualized application suite has nothing to do with another company's; therefore, there can be dramatic variations in workload even with the same application set.

If you do want to measure performance of your ESX hosts for purposes of comparison to others, VMware has developed VMmark, which provides a common workload for comparison across multiple servers and hypervisors. Unfortunately, VMmark is not a standard yet. There also exists SPECvirt_sc2010 from the Standards Performance Evaluation Corporation located at www.spec.org/virt_sc2010/.

Network Utilization

Network utilization or I/O is a constant operational concern within the physical data center, and this does not change within the virtual environment. What does change is that network concerns are now affected by ALL virtual machines using the link in question and that the virtual switches are tied to CPU utilization of the ESX host in question. Many people claim that no one VM would ever saturate a single gigabit connection, and now with 10 gigabit connections this is impossible. Neither of these are impossible; there is more than enough capability in modern hypervisors to saturate any link. However, as with the discussion of disk I/O and CPU performance, we must remember that many VMs are sharing those same network links and that the bandwidth used by one VM will affect all other VMs using the same link.

Even when you use VLANs, the traffic for all those VLANs is running over a single wire, perhaps a few wires if you are using the built in ESX load-balancing methods. Even so, it is possible for all VMs to adversely affect overall network utilization. Now when we throw into the mix VMsafe-Net and other network and security virtual appliances, we can throttle down bandwidth even more. At the very least we are adding to the overall CPU requirements for networking.

In a recent class, I was asked, "Why is this the case when virtual switches are 100% in memory?" The problem is that while the data and virtual switch code is in memory, that code must still run within the CPU as the vmkernel. So as you add more VMs, virtual switches, and snapshots, there is an increase in overall

CPU utilization because now the vmkernel has to do more to handle virtual networking (an increase in snapshots implies that the CPU has to do more work to handle disk blocks, which includes change block tracking modes in vSphere because there is now more to do within the CPU for snapshots).

Anything happening within the vmkernel will impact CPU requirements just as VMsafe will impact virtual switch performance and therefore directly impact a host's virtual networking. What happens within a given VM can impact a host's virtual networking. Solutions like Intel-VT and AMD RVI reduce overall CPU overhead as they offload what the vmkernel needs to do. vStorage API for Array Integration (VAAI) will also decrease overall vmkernel needs because repetitive actions for storage will be placed into the arrays.

Virtual Machine Mobility

Virtual machine mobility is becoming an increasing concern for operations and compliance tracking because we often need to answer the question: "Where is our data?"

Given VMware vMotion, DRS, DPM, FT, HA, and Storage vMotion, we could surmise that our virtual machines are always in motion and therefore the data within the VM is never actually at rest. Given this, it is becoming more of an issue to know exactly where that VM is at all times. Did the VM end up on a host where it should not be running because of compliance, networking, or other concerns?

The current guidance with respect to compliance and virtualization security is to silo VMs within security zones contained within specific clusters. One way to enforce this is to tag the VMs, hosts, virtual switches, and other virtualization host objects with security zone tags (such as how the HyTrust Appliance and Reflex Systems approaches compliance) so that a VM cannot be placed on a host, virtual switch, and so forth that does not share the same tag.

Without these types of tags, a VM could end up on a host that does not have the proper virtual trust zones configured. Host Profiles can help to solve many of these configuration issues for the same cluster, but does not solve the problem for a different cluster, enclave, datacenter, and so on. However, tags apply to manual operations. The automatic operations from HA, DRS, and DPM are limited to only those hosts within the cluster. Hence, we see the oft-required security zone silo per cluster.

If tags are not in use, and they are not in use for the vast majority of virtualization systems today, there is an increasing risk that VMs end up on misconfigured hosts, and therefore application availability is impacted. In addition, a VM could end up somewhere else within your virtual environment. Perhaps it ends up on a single development host that is part of the virtual environment but shares the same LUNs as your production hosts.

Operationally, it is important to know where a virtual machine is at all times. To aid in this there are tools such as the HyTrust Appliance, VMware vCenter, and Hyper9, as well as any other virtualization search tools. For large environments, you may need to search for the location of your critical virtual machines or have canned reports that report on anomalies caused by vMotion and Storage vMotion. Anomalies to look for could be VMs for one trust zone ending up on hosts not vetted for that trust zone (DMZ VMs are a good point). These anomalies can happen to hosts outside a given cluster but within the same datacenter, as defined by VMware vCenter.

Data Store Performance or Bandwidth Issues

Because bandwidth is an issue, it is important to make sure that all your data stores have as much bandwidth as possible and to use this bandwidth sparingly for each data store.

"As much bandwidth as possible" and "use sparingly" may sound counter intuitive, but they are not from an operational perspective. Normal operational behavior of a VM often includes such things as full disk virus scans, backups, spyware scans, and other items that are extremely disk-intensive activities. Although none of these activities will require any form of locking of the data store on which the VMDK resides, they all take a serious amount of bandwidth to accomplish. The bandwidth requirements for a single VM are not very large compared to an ESX host with more VMs. All activities are fairly additive in nature. What you do within one VM, from a disk perspective, affects all other VMs on the same datastore and, depending on the storage solution, all VMs on other data stores. How is this possible? Think about the networks involved, with traditional iSCSI over the network and NFS; your ultimate bandwidth is limited to the speed of the links used, so a single gigabit ethernet link is much more limited than links that use Fibre Channel host bus adapters (FC or iSCSI). This is why it is important to have as much bandwidth as possible, including using load balancing of your storage links for each data store in use. If you have access to a multipath plug-in driver, you may also be able to aggregate your storage links to form one larger trunk of pipes to your storage device and at the same time increase your overall storage bandwidth. Even with MPP and bandwidth aggregation, load balancing, either by hand or automatically, is a step in the proper direction.

Staggering storage-intensive activities in time will greatly reduce the strain on the storage environment, but remember that staggering across ESX hosts is a good idea as long as different data stores are in use on each ESX host. For example, it would cause locking issues for VMs that reside on the same LUN but different ESX hosts to be backed up at the same time, unless you are using in-VM agents; in that case, no locking issues would exist. Locking should be avoided. However, virus scans will not cause many issues when done from multiple VMs on the same LUN from multiple ESX hosts, because operations on the VMDK do not cause locks at the LUN level. By running backup and vStorage based antivirus tasks on different ESX hosts, you are using different links to the SAN and therefore are spreading your overall bandwidth usage across multiple links and hopefully using less of each link than running everything on a single ESX host.

It is possible that running of disk-intensive tools within a VM could cause results similar to those that occur with SCSI reservations, such as overloaded links that return errors instead of completing the operational task. These types of failures are not SCSI reservations. Instead, they are load issues that cause the SAN or NAS to be overworked and therefore present failures similar to SCSI-2 reservations.

> ### Best Practice for Internal VM Disk Operations
> Stagger all disk-intensive operations internal to the VM over time and ESX hosts to reduce strain on the storage network.
> Spread the load across multiple ESX hosts and storage links.

Other Operational Issues

ESX makes extensive use of memory. There are operational concerns regarding the use of memory, too. The main issue with memory is to prevent the swapping of memory during runtime of VMs. The runtime covers the memory actually used, and not always what is allocated. A VM may have 256GB of memory allocated to it. If we allocate 64Gbs to a VM, and this much memory is allocated to all the VMs, on a 64GB ESX host, only one VM could be created and the memory will be overcommitted as the ESX takes some memory. If the goal is to run 20 VMs, there is a memory requirement of 1280GB, which is quite a bit over the 1TB server memory limit inherent in ESX. Which means that if all the 64GB of memory is actually used by a VM, the ESX host will need to start swapping (or paging) memory out in large chunks to accommodate the running of another VM.

If in reality only 1GB of each VM is used, only 20GB of the available 64GB of memory is in use at any time, allowing more VMs to be created and used without swapping memory, even though there is potential for up to 1280GB of memory to be used. In this case, it is best to assign memory sparingly and to give a VM only what it needs to run. This way, memory management will allow a denser population of VMs to run.

Consider the following thought: With ESX, we are now back in time to the realm of limited resources. There are no longer gobs of memory and disk available for any particular machine, but a realm where memory and disk can be vast; but as more VMs are added, more resources are used. The goal is now to preserve memory. For example, consider programming the old Commodore 64, where no more than 360K would fit on a single floppy; to go past this, more than one floppy had to be used. Everyone programmed to the 360K limit of the floppy so that code would fit on a single disk. After another floppy was in use, the applications usage went downhill, performance suffered, and wait time increased. With ESX, we are back in this realm where we need to be cognizant of the limitations of the host, which is trying to do much, much more with less than ever before.

> ### Best Practice for ESX
> The mindset for ESX is to give out only the necessary resources to each VM, rather than give out all the resources.

All VMs affect the resource limits of the host. Therefore, resource management becomes a huge issue (as covered in another chapter). Note, however, that changes to the way resources are used, assigned, and managed can inadvertently affect all VMs on a host or in a farm.

Limiting memory assignment to VMs can allow more VMs to run in a single ESX host without impacting memory or performance limits.

Life-Cycle Management

Because it is easy to overuse resources besides memory, it is very important to have some sort of life-cycle management tool in place, so that VMs can be ordered and approved by the responsible parties. With VMware vSphere vCenter Server, now the VMware vCenter Orchestrator product can provide a limited form of life-cycle management. The VMware Life-Cycle Manager product requires its own license, and it provides a necessary life-cycle management process.

A life-cycle management tool is, however, only as good as the process backing it up. A tool is not useful without a written life-cycle process. At the very least, such a process should include the following:

- Virtual machine request with the resources required in terms of memory, CPU, disk, and network.

- Virtual machine request with justification, lifetime of VM, VM owner, application owner, and manager involved. This should also include what to do with the VM after the lifetime is over, such as archive, delete, and so on.

- Management approval of the justification.

- Architectural review of the virtual machine resource requirements with the results being whether a new ESX host is required, as well as the actual resources to allocate, which most likely will be lower than the requested amounts. This should include exactly which networks and storage devices should be used, as well as the ESX host to initially place the VM. Architectural review should consider FT, DPM, DRS, SRM, EVC, SIOC, NetIOC, and HA, as well the VM's impact on any other VM. Has this VM superseded another VM?

- Application design review for the application and operating system to be placed within the VM. This should include a review of all agents required within the virtual environment.

- Placement of the VM within a development cluster for testing.

- Staging the VM through QA to determine that all is working as expected.

- Staging the VM into production with a final review before going live.

- Final sign off on live VM by VM owner.

- VM decommission and disposition.

Throughout a VM's life cycle, the ownership of the VM may change. It is very important to track such changes. If a VM has issues, a virtualization administrator will need to go to this VM owner to assist in solving the problem. It could also be that the VM has now become obsolete and as such is at the end of its life cycle. Life-cycle management will help control your ever-growing number of VMs and limit dependency issues.

Such controls often exist for physical machines, and they should be translated into the virtual environment. Although it is very easy to create a VM, it should never happen at the request of anyone directly but should follow a life-cycle process.

The virtual machine life-cycle process is the one process that will aid in debugging operational issues caused by the politics behind virtual machine creation.

Conclusion

By paying careful attention to operational issues, it is possible to successfully manage ESX and remove some of the most common issues related to poor operational use of ESX. ESX is designed to be centrally managed and care should be taken to do so. It is also important to realize that each implementation of ESX has different operational concerns.

Chapter 7

Networking

As mentioned in Chapter 1, "System Considerations," there are certain best practices in relation to networking, particularly the physical network interface card (pNIC) count associated with ESX and ESXi with respect to use of 1Gb, 10Gb, and Converged Network Adapters (CNAs) such as those used with Fibre Channel over Ethernet (FCoE). We look at networking in more detail to explain the capabilities of ESX and ESXi in this arena. In this chapter, we begin with some of the basic building blocks that make up a virtual and physical network. Then we turn to network definitions and generally how everything is recommended to be connected. In this section, we will also discuss the differences between ESX and ESXi and how VMware vShield, VMsafe, vNetwork Distributed Switch, and VMDirectPath all fit into the picture. Discussion of a network requirements checklist follows. Next, some brief examples of networks are presented. Finally, we spend some time on the subject of configuration.

Basic Building Blocks

In the physical world, there are basic building blocks to a network, and this does not change in the virtual world. The most basic of building blocks exist within the virtual world: NICs and switches. Table 7.1 shows a mapping of the physical to virtual building blocks of a network.

Table 7.1 *Basic Network Building Blocks*

Physical	Virtual (ESX 4)	Virtual (ESX 3.x)	Comments
Network Interface Card (pNIC)	Network Interface Card (vNIC)	Network Interface Card (vNIC)	VMs are limited to pcnet32, e1000, vmxnet, and vmxnet3 devices.

continues

Table 7.1   *(Continued)*

Physical	Virtual (ESX 4)	Virtual (ESX 3.x)	Comments
	VMDirectPath	N/A	VMs can talk directly to very specific SRIOV network adapters.
Network Switch (pSwitch)	Virtual Switch (vSwitch)	Virtual Switch (vSwitch)	vSwitch has less functionality than pSwitch.
	Cisco Nexus 1000v (N1KV)	N/A	Similar to Cisco Nexus pSwitches.
	Virtual Distributed Switch (vDS)	N/A	Global Virtual Switches spanning multiple ESX and ESXi hosts.
Network Router	N/A	N/A	Performed VIA software in a VM.
Firewall	VMware vShield	N/A	Performed VIA software in a VM.
	VMware VMsafe-Net	N/A	VMsafe-Net sits before each vNIC of a VM and is part of the vmkernel.
Gateway	N/A	N/A	Performed VIA software in a VM.

As you can see in Table 7.1, the virtual environment appears to have in some cases less functionality than the physical equivalent, and vSphere ESX and ESXi 4 have more options available. Some of the lack of functionality has been addressed by implementations of the N1KV and the new Firewall options. VMware vSphere has specifically addressed the following issues:

- Lack of physical switch equivalence solved by creating the vNetwork API used by the Cisco Nexus 1000V, which can be purchased from Cisco

- Lack of firewalls for the virtual network, which has been addressed in two ways: use of VMware vShield, as well as by the VMsafe-Net API, which allows third parties to add to the vmkernel firewall capability

- Lack of high performance capability within the virtual network, which has been addressed by the inclusion of the default Intel e1000 NIC, the much improved vmxnet3 NIC, and by the inclusion of Single Root IO Virtualization (SRIOV) support via VMDirectPath, which in essence bypasses the virtual network completely

- Misconfiguration issues caused by requiring network labels to be the same across all virtualization hosts by implementing the distributed virtual switch as well as host profiles

- Lack of Private VLAN support by adding the support for distributed virtual switch filters (dvFilter) support within the Distributed Virtual Switch

These changes to the virtual network (vNetwork) building blocks greatly increase the availability and capability of your virtual networks. There still are very few limits and caveats associated with the virtual hardware. The most interesting and handicapping limitation is that the vSwitches cannot be layered; however, this is only a minor hiccup. Similar to blocks played with by children, the vNetwork components can be placed together to create complex networks.

Consider the following example presented by a customer: The customer usually took infected physical boxes to a lab bench on a stand-alone network for testing, cleaning, rebuilding, and staging before placing them back into the wild. The customer wants to be able to do similar things in a virtual environment, but the machines on the lab bench must have access to the administrative VMs and other installation server VMs that the whole enterprise uses. However, everything must be secure, and viruses cannot infect other parts of the network.

Figure 7.1 lays out a possible network to meet our customer requirements. As shown in Figure 7.1, we used our basic building blocks to interconnect our networking bits. We have used pNICs, vNICs, pSwitches, and vSwitches, and a VM that acts as a Network Address Translation (NAT)–based firewall (vFW-NAT) between the lab bench and the real world. Several operating systems provide this type of firewall capability, including Linux and Windows, but not VMsafe-Net or VMware vShield Zones but is available when using VMware vShield Edge. The customer used Linux as the packet-filtering firewall, allowing access only to what was absolutely necessary. In addition, the firewall was designed to block all outgoing traffic to prevent further spread of infections. In this way, if a VM became infected for some reason, it could quickly be moved to a quarantined network. Figure 7.1 does depend on an external firewall for those VMs not in the internal quarantined network. The use of two independent pNICs each connected to their own vSwitch allows the lab bench to connect independently of the enterprise. The vFW-NAT between the two vSwitches allows traffic from the installation servers to reach the lab bench but does not allow infections to reach the enterprise.

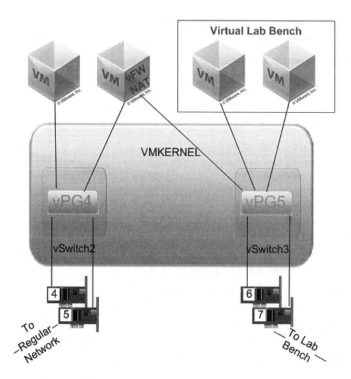

Figure 7.1 *Customer example using basic network building blocks*

But how could the same be done using the new vSphere building blocks? The current issue with VMware vShield Zones, PVLAN, and VMsafe-Net is that they do not provide NAT or router functionality but do provide firewall capability between different zones within your virtual network, perhaps using the same address space, or if you want, between multiple address spaces, by using virtual router functionality. After we discuss how these new functionalities work, you'll see an example of each.

Details of the Building Blocks

Given the example just discussed and Figure 7.1, we should define our basic building blocks more and list out any limitations or characteristics. Let's look at Figure 7.2 when defining the basic building blocks. Figure 7.2 is a simplified network that displays a segment of a full virtual network so that we can fully discuss each of the basic building blocks.

Physical Switch (pSwitch)

The pSwitch can be any network switch from any vendor. The best practice is to have at least two pSwitches attached for VMs so that if one goes down the other can handle the load and provide a level of load balancing and redundancy. The best practice for all pSwitches is to have gigabit ports unless you are now using 10G network cards; in that case the pSwitches need to have 10G ports. Use of FCoE will also change the types of pSwitches that can be used.

> ### Best Practices for pSwitches
>
> Use redundant switches for each network interface that is a part of a vSwitch.
>
> Match pSwitch port speeds to physical NIC port speeds and types.

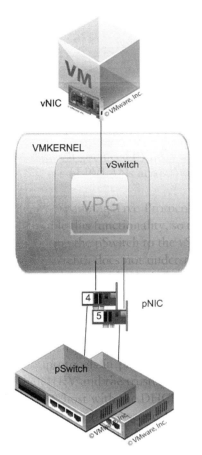

Figure 7.2 *ESX physical and virtual network layout*

Physical NIC (pNIC)

The pNIC is the most basic of building blocks and comes in a myriad of forms from twisted-pair to Fibre with speeds from 10Mbps to 100Gbps. Thousands of different types of these are available from almost the same number of vendors. As listed in Chapter 1, support exists only for a few vendors and flavors with ESX and ESXi. ESX and ESXi use the pNIC to communicate to the physical network. Most pNICs will be attached to one or more vSwitches.

When looking at Figure 7.2, note that each vSwitch could have associated with it any number of pNICs to provide redundancy and load-balancing capabilities for virtual machines and other virtual networks.

In addition to the capability of pNICs to attach to vSwitches, they can also be directly connected to a virtual machine using the VMware VMDirectPath functionality of vSphere. VMDirectPath, in essence, bypasses the completed vNetwork stack.

> ### Best Practice for pNICs
>
> Assign pNICs in pairs to vSwitches to increase redundancy and possibly load balancing within the limitations of the chosen hardware. pNICs should be at least gigabit to the pSwitch.

Virtual Switch (vSwitch)

Three flavors of virtual switches are available to vSphere in each pNIC that provide uplinks from pSwitches to the vSwitch: the VMware vSwitch, the Cisco Nexus 1000V (N1KV), and the vNetwork distributed switch, which keeps the vNetwork in sync across multiple virtualization hosts and provides extra functionality. The Cisco N1KV is an add-on switch from a third-party, Cisco, and requires licenses purchased from Cisco.

In this section, each virtual switch type is broken out with its functionality listed within a corresponding table. After we delve into each vSwitch, there is a comparison table (see Table 7.5) so that you can determine which functionality is within each virtual switch.

VMware vSwitch

The standard VMware vSwitch provides the capability to link multiple VMs to one or more pNICs via portgroups. Portgroups are constructs that can be viewed as virtual switch segmentation where each segment can have its own VLAN ID or not. Unlike pSwitches there is no need to provide VLANs when segmenting the VMware vSwitch to group like virtual machines together. It is a logical grouping so that it is easier to determine which VMs are connected to which portgroups. However, portgroups also have their own functionality.

Portgroups can have a VLAN assigned to them, which will limit the data any vNIC on the portgroup can see based on the VLAN ID seen by the portgroup. In addition, a VLAN ID of 4095 allows a portgroup to act similar to a SPAN port and see all traffic on the vSwitch. In actuality, it allows promiscuous mode vNICs to see all traffic on the vSwitch. There can also be multiple vSwitches per ESX or ESXi host, and each vSwitch may or may not be connected to physical NICs.

Table 7.2 lists the basic functionality available to every VMware vSwitch.

Table 7.2 *VMware vSwitch Functionality*

Function	Definition in vSwitch Terms
802.3ad	802.3ad bonds two or more pNICs together with a single IP address. Each end of the connection (pSwitch and vSwitch) must agree that this bond exists. This is static 802.3ad because no support exists for LACP or other negotiation protocols.
VMware NIC teaming	This functionality is very similar to Linux bonding drivers and differs from 802.3ad in that both ends do not need to agree that the bond exists. The only side that needs to know that a bond exists is the vSwitch side of the network. VMware NIC teams can be attached to the same or multiple pSwitches.
pNIC failover	Each vSwitch can failover a network connection if there is more than one pNIC connected to it. This is a feature of VMware NIC teaming. This failover occurs at the pNIC level after a network path disappears from a failed pNIC, pNIC port, pSwitch, or cable issue.
Traffic shaping	Capability to limit transmit-rate from the virtual machine.
Multicast Support	Via the equivalent of IGMP v2 and v3; it is not actually IGMP, but via a proprietary mechanism.
Security Features	
Port Security	Capability to disable a port from being placed into promiscuous mode, modify the MAC address assigned, or forge transmits from within the VM.

continues

Table 7.2   *(Continued)*

Function	Definition in vSwitch Terms
Load Balancing	
Out-mac	Distribute load based on source MAC addresses (default for ESX versions earlier than 3).
IP address	Distribute load based on source and destination IP address; all other protocols are load balanced sequentially.
Port ID	Distribute load based on the source virtual port ID (the default).
IP Hash	When using IP Hash, if the protocol is other than IP (that is, IPX), the data at the equivalent offset within the frame is used to identify conversations and perform load balancing of the conversations.
802.1Q	
EST	With external switch tagging, the trunk leads to the pSwitches and from there to a pNIC pair that exists for each VLAN; in essence, there is one vSwitch per VLAN. Each VM connects to the vSwitch, and no portgroups are needed on the vSwitch. This requires more pNIC availability across all hosts, 2 per VLAN on the pSwitch.
VST	The most common use of 802.1q is the virtual switch tagging, which passes the trunk from the pSwitch through the pNICs and to the vSwitch. On the vSwitch, the VMs connect to virtual portgroups. This method reduces the hardware requirements to only the pair of pNICs needed for redundancy and moves possible complex network management to the hands of the ESX administrators.

Function	Definition in vSwitch Terms
VGT	In virtual guest tagging, the trunk goes from the pSwitch to the pNIC to the vSwitch and then to the vNIC for the VM in question, and special drivers on the VM will decide how to handle the trunk. Windows by default does not support this, and there are very few drivers for any operating system to handle the trunk directly.
Management Functions	
Network Policy Groups	VMware Portgroups with portgroup security policy settings.
Port Mirroring	N/A
SPAN	Use of a VMware Portgroup with a VLAN ID of 4095 and vNICs on this portgroup allowed to be promiscuous.
Netflow	Experimental support is provided for Netflow v5 in vSphere.
CDP	Cisco Discovery Protocol support.
Remote Syslog	Via standard vmkernel log files where each virtual switch, pNIC, and vNIC event is tracked.
Packet Capture and Analysis	Using a virtual machine using a port mirroring setup.

vNetwork Distributed Switch

vNetwork Distributed Switches (vDS) can be seen as a superset of the standard Virtual Switch with advanced functionality. Even so, it has one very nice feature: the capability to ensure that all underlying virtual switches on a host that comprise the vDS have the same network labels so that vMotion, FT Logging, and other features work seamlessly as your VMs move from host to host.

It is easiest to picture vDS as a control structure above the virtual switch. Even though you create a single vDS within the vSphere Client, underlying virtual switches represent that vDS on the local host. The control structure enables a greater degree of functionality, such as Network vMotion where the network policy associated with the VM is migrated during a vMotion from host to host. It also enables the capability to implement private VLANs.

PVLANs are implemented by applying distributed virtual switch filters (dvFilters) within the virtual switch on the host to which the traffic is destined.

Note that vDS-based PVLANs cannot extend into the physical network as they can with the N1KV. dvFilters are similar in nature to ACLs but are limited to PVLANs unless you also use VMware vShield Zones.

Table 7.3 lists the basic functionality available to every vDS.

Table 7.3 *vNetwork Distributed vSwitch Functionality*

Function	Definition in vSwitch Terms
802.3ad	802.3ad bonds two or more pNICs together with a single IP address. Each end of the connection (pSwitch and vSwitch) must agree that this bond exists.
Traffic shaping	Capability to limit the transmit rate from a virtual machine and receive rate to a virtual machine.
Multicast Support	Via the equivalent of IGMP v2 and v3; it is not actually IGMP, but via a proprietary mechanism.
Network vMotion	Network policy and state of the virtual port is saved during a vMotion when used in conjunction with vDS.
Security Features	
Port Security	Capability to disable a port from being placed into promiscuous mode, modify the MAC address assigned, or forge transmits from within the VM.
PVLAN	Private VLAN support using dvFilters on the destination host.
Load Balancing	
Out-mac	Distribute load based on source MAC addresses (default for ESX versions earlier than 3).
IP address	Distribute load based on source and destination IP address; all other protocols are load balanced sequentially.
Port ID	Distribute load based on the source virtual port ID (the default).
IP Hash	When using IP Hash, if the protocol is other than IP (that is, IPX), the data at the equivalent offset within the frame is used to identify conversations and is used to perform load balancing of the conversations.

Function	Definition in vSwitch Terms
Load Based Teaming	vSphere 4.1 only: If network contention exists within the vDS, the vNIC to pNIC mapping setup for the other load balanced mechanisms will be adjusted to the least used pNIC.
802.1Q	
EST	With external switch tagging, the trunk leads to the pSwitches and from there to a pNIC pair that exists for each VLAN; in essence, there is one vSwitch per VLAN. Each VM connects to the vSwitch, and no portgroups are needed on the vSwitch. This requires more pNIC availability across all hosts, 2 per VLAN on the pSwitch.
VST	The most common use of 802.1q is the virtual switch tagging, which passes the trunk from the pSwitch through the pNICs and to the vSwitch. On the vSwitch, the VMs connect to virtual portgroups. This method reduces the hardware requirements to only the pair of pNICs needed for redundancy and moves possible complex network management to the hands of the ESX administrators.
VGT	In virtual guest tagging, the trunk goes from the pSwitch to the pNIC to the vSwitch and then to the vNIC for the VM in question, and special drivers on the VM decide how to handle the trunk. Windows by default does not support this, and there are very few drivers for any operating system to handle the trunk directly.
Management Functions	
Network Policy Groups	VMware Portgroups with portgroup security policy settings.
Port Mirroring	
SPAN	Use of a VMware Portgroup with a VLAN ID of 4095 and vNICs on this portgroup allowed to be promiscuous.
Netflow	Experimental support is provided for Netflow v5 in vSphere.

continues

Table 7.3   *(Continued)*

Function	Definition in vSwitch Terms
CDP	Cisco Discovery Protocol support.
Network IO Control	vSphere 4.1 only, NetIOC provides egress traffic shaping across the pNICs associated with the vDS.
Remote Syslog	Via standard vmkernel log files where each virtual switch, pNIC, and vNIC event is tracked.
Packet Capture and Analysis	Using a virtual machine using a port mirroring setup.

Cisco Nexus 1000V

The Cisco Nexus 1000V brings network administrators familiar with Cisco Nexus hardware directly into the vNetwork so that they can control the vNetwork just like they control the physical network.

Unlike the VMware vSwitch, there is only one Cisco N1KV per ESX or ESXi host. All network segmentation works just like a physical switch by using VLANs.

Table 7.4 lists the basic functionality available to every Cisco Nexus 1000V.

Table 7.4   *Cisco Nexus 1000V vSwitch Functionality*

Function	Definition in vSwitch Terms
802.3ad	802.3ad or EtherChannel bonds two or more pNICs together with a single IP address. Each end of the connection (pSwitch and vSwitch) must agree that this bond exists.
802.1AX	Link aggregation or Virtual PortChannel bonds
LACP	Link Aggregation Control Protocol
Traffic shaping	Capability to limit the transmit rate from a virtual machine as well as the receive rate to a virtual machine.
QoS	Quality of Service marking based on differentiated services code point (DSCP), type and class of service.
802.1Q	Standard 802.1q VLAN tagging is supported.

Function	Definition in vSwitch Terms
Multicast Support	Via IGMP v2 and v3
IGMPv3 Snooping	To protect against multicast attacks.
Network vMotion	Network policy and state of the virtual port is saved during a vMotion when used in conjunction with vDS.
Security Features	
Port Security	Capability to disable a port from being placed into promiscuous mode, modify the MAC address assigned, or forge transmits from within the VM.
PVLAN	Private VLAN support and Local PV-LAN enforcement.
ACLs	Access control lists for each port on the Cisco Nexus 1000V.
DHCP Snooping	Dynamic Host Configuration Protocol Snooping to protect against DHCP server attacks.
IP Source Guard	
DAI	Dynamic Address Resolution Protocol (ARP) Inspection to protect against ARP cache poisoning attempts.
Load Balancing	
Out-mac	Distribute load based on source MAC addresses (default for ESX versions earlier than 3).
IP address	Distribute load based on source and destination IP protocol; all other protocols are load balanced sequentially.
Port ID	Distribute load based on the source virtual port ID.
Nexus 1000V Only	Distribute load based on source and destination MAC addresses instead of just on the source MAC address.
	Distribute load based on source and destination port IP instead of just the source IP address.
Management Functions	
Network Policy Groups	Via Nexus Policy Controls, including multitier policy group controls.
Port Mirroring	SPAN and ERSPAN support.

continues

Table 7.4   *(Continued)*

Function	Definition in vSwitch Terms
Netflow	v5 and v9 support.
SNMP	SNMP v3 read and write support.
CDP	Cisco Discovery Protocol support.
Remote Syslog	Only Cisco Nexus 1000V events.
Packet Capture and Analysis	Built into Nexus 1000V.
RADIUS/TACACS+	Built in authentication and logging modules.

Table 7.5   *Feature Comparison Between Virtual Switches*

Function	VMware vSwitch v4	VMware vDS	Cisco N1KV	VMware vSwitch v3
802.3ad (Static)	Yes	Yes	Yes	Yes
802.3ad (Dynamic)	No	No	Yes	No
802.1AX	No	No	Yes	No
LACP	No	No	Yes	No
Transmit Rate Limiting	Yes	Yes	Yes	Yes
Receive Rate Limiting	No	Yes	Yes	No
QoS	No	No	Yes	No
802.1Q	Yes	Yes	Yes	Yes
Multicast Support	Yes	Yes	Yes	Yes
IGMPv3 Snooping	No	No	Yes	No
Network vMotion	No	Yes	Yes	No
Security Features				
Port Security	Yes	Yes	Yes	Yes
PVLAN	No	Yes	Yes	No
ACLs	No	No	Yes	No
DHCP Snooping	No	No	Yes	No

Function	VMware vSwitch v4	VMware vDS	Cisco N1KV	VMware vSwitch v3
IP Source Guard	No	No	Yes	No
DAI	No	No	Yes	No
Load Balancing				
Out-mac	Yes	Yes	Yes	Yes
IP address	Yes	Yes	Yes	Yes
Port ID	Yes	Yes	Yes	Yes
Source and Destination MAC	No	No	Yes	No
Source and Destination Port IP	No	No	Yes	No
Additional Hash Algorithms	No	No	Yes	No
Load Based Teaming	No	Yes (vSphere 4.1)	No	No
Management Functions				
Network Policy Groups	Yes	Yes	Yes	Yes
Network IO Control	No	Yes (vSphere 4.1)	No	No
Multi tier Network Policy Groups	No	No	Yes	No
Port Mirroring	Yes	Yes	Yes	Yes
Netflow	V5 (Experimental)	V5 (Experimental)	V5/v9	No
SNMP	No	No	Yes	No
CDP	Yes	Yes	Yes	Yes
Remote Syslog	Via vmkernel	Via vmkernel	Yes	Via vmkernel
Packet Capture	Via VM	Via VM	Yes	Via VM
RADIUS/ TACACS+	No	No	Yes	No

Virtual NIC (vNIC)

The vNIC is the last bit of the puzzle because it is used to connect the VMs to the vSwitch and thereby possibly to a pNIC. The vNIC comes in four flavors (internal to the VM): AMD PC-NET32, Intel e1000, vmxnet, and vmxnet 3. The PC-NET32 vNIC is a simple 10/100Mbps network adapter that is easy to virtualize because it does not have much complexity to it. It is not a smart NIC, but nearly every operating system has a driver for this NIC; therefore, it was a perfect candidate for virtualization. The PC-NET32 reports as 10Mbps, but is not limited to that speed. It will pass traffic as quickly as it can, but has significant amounts of overhead because of a literal implementation of the LANCE chipset.

Modern operating systems also have support for the very common Intel e1000 device, which is a gigabit network adapter. The e1000 device reports as 1Gb but is not bound by this "limit." The other vNICs are the vmxnet and vmxnet3 developed by VMware. The vmxnet vNIC has more smarts than PC-NET32 because it will take some shortcuts in the virtualization as it truly understands the virtualization layer and can hook directly into it to get better performance. The vmxnet3, on the other hand, has more smarts than the Intel e1000 and adds many more performance improvements into the vmxnet as well as much of the new VMware vSphere vNetwork functionality. The choice of which to use depends on the VM configuration and is discussed in Chapter 10, "Virtual Machines."

Virtual Firewall (vFW)

ESX does not contain a vFW built in to the vSwitch. Even so, two possible virtual firewalls are available. The first one is the standard mechanism of using a virtual machine as a firewall that sits between multiple virtual switches. This is the way VMware vShield Zones v1.0 and vShield Edge is implemented. The second one can be implemented by using VMsafe-Net functionality or the way VMware vShield Zones v2.0 and vShield App is implemented. VMsafe-Net is an introspection API that enables packets to be inspected and either blocked or allowed through prior to being delivered to the vNIC. VMsafe-Net lives within the vmkernel, but in the network stack it sits just before each active vNIC within the host. To make use of VMsafe-Net requires the use of a third-party VMsafe-Net driver such as ones from Altor Networks (VF3), Reflex Systems (vTrust), IBM (VSP), or TrendMicro (Deep Security). There are other VMsafe-Net vendors available as well. As such, VMsafe-Net is available for use, but the firewall functionality is not part of vSphere.

Virtual Router (vRouter)

The vRouter, like the vFW, is not built in to ESX or ESXi, but would be a VM with an OS that would support routing. Again, Linux systems often fill this software role, and VM appliances exist, based on a form of Linux (www. vmware.com/appliances/).

Virtual Gateway (vGateway)

The vGateway is like the vRouter, and again would be a form of a VM. Linux systems often fill this software role, and VM appliances based on a form of Linux do exist.

vNetwork Functionality

Other than the basic functionality of each vSwitch listed, certain intrinsic behaviors also apply to all virtual switches. You need to understand these before you plan any vNetwork. Specifically, you should understand how data flows around the virtual network and how PVLANs and security measures are implemented within each of the virtual switches. Assumptions about traffic flow and implementation of virtual switch building blocks have lead to many misconfigurations and inconsistencies within vNetworks.

802.1Q VLANs

802.1Q is the same as VLAN tagging and is an important consideration for the design of an ESX Server network because it could change the physical and virtual networking within or outside of ESX. 802.1Q transfers multiple networks or subnetworks over the same set of cables, thereby limiting the number of cables used, VLANs, pSwitches, and hopefully the number of pNICs in use on the network. For low-port-density devices such as blades, 802.1q can be very important. ESX supports three mechanisms for 802.1q, and each contains different constraints and requirements. EST has a higher hardware investment, VST has a higher configuration investment, and VGT has a high driver investment.

External Switch Tagging (EST)

EST (external switch tagging) is configured so that the trunk comes to the pSwitches, and then each network in the trunk needed by ESX is sent over network card(s) that act as uplinks to the virtual switches in use. Figure 7.3 displays a trunked network with five VLANs going to ESX via a pair of network cards used by all VLANs. Even with quad-port pNICs, ESX can only handle up to a reduced number of networks or subnetworks based on the type of NICs in use, and this could lead to requiring more server hardware to satisfy all network requirements. In general, you can have up to 32 pNICs for host, which implies up to 32 networks or subnetworks when using EST.

When using EST, the packets coming into the switch are tagged with the appropriate VLAN but untagged when sent from the pSwitch to the pNICs within the ESX host.

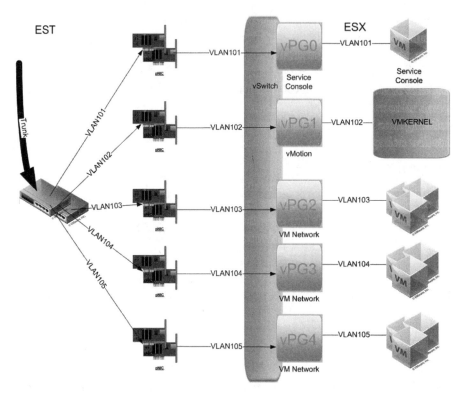

Figure 7.3 *External switch tagging with five VLANs*

Virtual Guest Tagging (VGT)
Virtual guest tagging (VGT) requires the VM to host specialized software drivers to interpret the 802.1q packets (see Figure 7.4). In this case, the trunk goes from the pSwitch directly to the VM without interpretation by any other device. Although this is possible with some operating systems, it is not a commonly available driver for Windows. VGT is useful for vFW and other security devices.

Virtual Switch Tagging (VST)
Virtual switch tagging (VST) is the commonly recommended method of implementing 802.1q because there is no need to purchase more hardware, yet it moves some network configuration out of the hands of networking teams and into the hands of the ESX Server administrators unless you are using the Cisco N1KV. In Figure 7.5, all networks are trunked until they reach the vSwitch, which has four portgroups representing the five VLANs/networks trunked together. In many cases, VST is recommended by networking teams who are only concerned about the hardware connectivity and not the virtual environment. VST reduces the number of physical cable pulls, pNICs, and pSwitches required

and moves these items into the virtual environment, because now the wiring is virtual. With just the click of a button it is now possible to connect a VM via its vNIC to a portgroup and vSwitch.

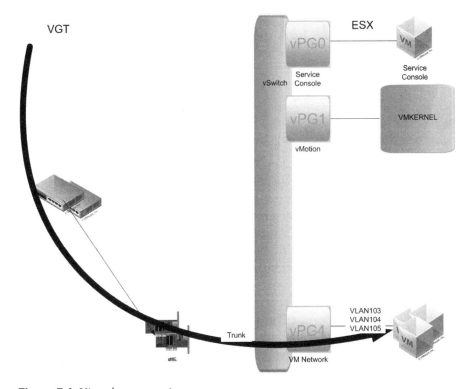

Figure 7.4 *Virtual guest tagging*

Although adding complexity to an ESX Server administrator's job, the network administrator's job gets quite a bit simpler when VST is in use, unless the Cisco N1KV is in use. The ESX Server administrator only needs to define portgroups on the vSwitch and assign VMs to the required portgroups for VST to be configured.

Virtual Switch Layering

It is not possible to layer vSwitches and to trunk between them. This greatly simplifies the vNetwork because it makes it impossible to form a spanning tree loop, which means that there is no need for spanning tree code necessary within the VMware vSwitches, and makes it impossible (without adding a VM) to create a spanning tree loop.

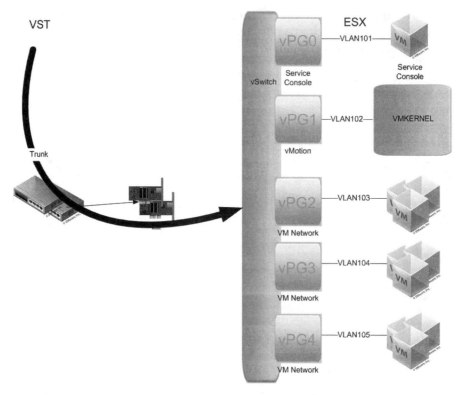

Figure 7.5 *Virtual switch tagging*

Unlike pSwitches, the vSwitch is not a true switch and does not have the same capabilities. At best, they are just connection points on a network and cannot be layered without first going through a VM. It is important to consider your virtual networking (vNetwork) layout before you begin creating VMs. The network needs to be thought out before VMs are created, because the vNIC selections within the VM must exist before the VM can have any network connections. If networking is not required for the VMs, nothing needs to be done. However, we have yet to see this as an implementation used by customers, even though most, if not all, of the vNetwork can be changed throughout the life of an ESX host.

Load-Balancing pNICs

vSwitches can load balance the network packets between multiple pNICs and pSwitches as a feature of VMware NIC teaming. The type of load balancing employed can be chosen by the creator of the vNetwork. All VMware vSwitches default to load balancing based on the source port ID. The following load balancing mechanisms are available.

- Out-mac—Distribute load based on source MAC addresses (default for ESX versions earlier than 3).

- IP address (out-ip)—Distribute load based on source and destination IP address; all other protocols are load balanced sequentially.

- Port ID—Distribute load based on the source virtual port ID (the default).

- IP Hash—When using IP Hash, if the protocol is other than IP (that is, IPX), the data at the equivalent offset within the frame is used to identify conversations and is used to perform load balancing of the conversations.

When you choose a load-balancing mode, the vNIC associated with the VM is associated with a pNIC, and all traffic goes out that pNIC until the VM is rebooted. VMware vSphere 4.1 introduces Load Based Teaming to the vDS to allow this vNIC/pNIC binding to be modified if one pNIC link is congested. The modification can occur only every 30 seconds.

VMware NIC Teaming Redundancy

To use load balancing, the vSwitch must have multiple pNICs associated with it. With more than one pNIC, it is possible to determine which pNICs should be used for load balancing and which for redundancy. If, for example, four pNICs were attached to a given vSwitch, you could enable two for load balancing and two for redundancy or any combination that leaves at least one pNIC active at all times.

What is really interesting and useful is that it is possible to make these selections for each individual portgroup of a vSwitch, thereby giving you greater control of which pNICs are used for a given portgroup and their redundancy settings. In essence, you could have four portgroups and four pNICs and ensure that each portgroup uses its own pNIC unless there is a failure case (the pNIC, cable, or pSwitch port fails). Failures are detected when the link state of the network path appears to be dead. When a link state failure is detected, the best debugging technique is to look physically at the box to determine whether the link state light is lit, something that should be a feature on any modern pNIC and pSwitch port.

When a failure mode is detected, a vSwitch, and hence portgroup, can also be set to failback to the original configuration after the problem that caused the failure is fixed. In this way, your optimal configurations can be maintained.

Beacon Monitoring

ESX can use beacon monitoring as a secondary method to determine whether network paths are dead in addition to the link state it automatically detects. Beacon monitoring needs to be specifically configured. Using beacon monitoring could determine whether the pSwitch is down for some reason, a pNIC or cable is bad. A beacon is sent out on all network paths attached to the vSwitch. ESX then waits for the beacons to return. If there is a failure to return, it determines that the network path in question is dead. If a pSwitch traps beacon packets and does not forward them, beacon monitoring within ESX can detect this as a dead network path and resend data down one of the other network paths, which could mean duplicate data is received by the target. This could cause the target to get fairly confused quickly. This will cause false positives, and it might be necessary to change the type of beacon to send another value. In most cases, beacon monitoring should not be used for everyday use. If the link state appears to be good and you're still not able to communicate on the network, beacon monitoring can be a valuable debugging tool.

It is possible to have redundant switches and still have a network failure because one of the switches would hang and still indicate link up. A solution is to use beacon monitoring with two links to each switch for true redundancy.

Traffic Shaping

Each vSwitch has basic traffic-shaping capabilities or the capability to control or shape what runs over the network on a per-vSwitch and portgroup level. There are three basic rules to traffic shaping within ESX. These rules in effect implement a subset of traffic shaping that implements bandwidth limiting and not any form of service differentiation. Traffic shaping on a vSwitch is based on data coming into the vSwitch or portgroup and is referred to Ingress Traffic Shaping on a vDS. A vDS further has Network IO Control (NetIOC), which is used to configure Egress Traffic Shaping or traffic shaping for data going out the pNICs to the pSwitches. Each mechanism has its own settings that follow.

Average Bandwidth

The average bandwidth is specified in kilobits per second (Kbps). A GbE network has 102,400Kbps or 1Gbps, and a 10GbE network has 102,400,000Kbps or 10Gbps. Because currently available ESX network speeds are no more than 10Gbps, the upper limit for the average bandwidth can have a setting of 102,400,000Kbps. The lower limit is a value of 0Kbps, which will not allow any traffic through the portgroup or an entire vSwitch. Note that this value is an average, so the bandwidth utilization can go above this value and even below this value, and the average is over one second. For example, if you want to have a vSwitch that is in effect a .5Gbps network, the value for this is 51,200Kbps.

Peak Bandwidth

The peak bandwidth is the maximum amount of bandwidth available at any time. The amount of bandwidth can never go above this value. The maximum and minimum limits are the same as for average bandwidth. If we follow the example for average bandwidth, we may want the vSwitch to peak at only half of a gigabit per second, so the value would be set to 51,200Kbps.

Burst Size

The burst size is set in kilobytes and represents the maximum amount of the data to be transmitted at any given time, or the size of a burst of data over the network targeted for the vSwitch. It is possible to set any limit on this value. However, remember this is not just the payload of the data packet sent over the network but includes the envelope. In essence, burst size limits the maximum size of the packets that can be sent through the vSwitch or portgroup.

Private VLAN

Private VLANs further segment the logical broadcast domain of a VLAN into private groups. Each private group can communicate with other VMs within the same private group and generally not between private groups. Given that PVLANs are subsets of VLANs, the VLAN is referred to as the primary PVLAN, and the PVLANs within that VLAN are referred to as the secondary PVLANs.

vDS and Cisco N1KV PVLANs can span multiple hosts, and therefore the physical switching network must be PVLAN aware and most likely modified to accommodate such behavior.

Traffic within a PVLAN is not encapsulated within the primary PVLAN because no VMware vSwitch handles double-encapsulated packets. Each secondary PVLAN can be of three types, and each has its own VLAN tagging rules.

Promiscuous

A promiscuous PVLAN may send and receive packets to any node in any other secondary VLAN associated to the same primary, and each vNIC would receive all packets on the PVLAN if the vNIC was in promiscuous mode. In general, router, firewall, and other security appliances are the only devices that require promiscuous mode vNICs. An exception is if you are using VGT; then a promiscuous mode PVLAN may be required as well. The VLAN ID for a promiscuous secondary PVLAN is the same as the primary PVLAN and as such is tagged with the primary PVLAN VLAN ID.

Isolated

An isolated PVLAN implies that nodes on an isolated PVLAN cannot talk to each other without going through a router (thus the promiscuous PVLAN). This is often used for backup networks. That way, all the hosts can talk to the backup server, but the network enforces isolation from each other.

Community

Those vNICs within a Community PVLAN will receive packets from other vNICs within the same PVLAN as well as any Promiscuous mode PVLAN within the same primary PVLAN. An isolated PVLAN's VLAN ID is different from the primary PVLAN's ID and as such traffic is tagged with the secondary PVLAN VLAN ID.

Traffic Flow

How data travels through the vNetwork is very important to understand because you should be able to determine when traffic will hit the physical network, stay within the virtual switch, portgroups, or have to go to the outside. Remember that the virtual switches available are nothing more than Layer-2 devices and as such do not act as routers or gateways. Yet, with VMsafe, PVLANs and access control lists can act as basic firewalls. We will discuss each of these further in this chapter. For now we will concentrate on the basic traffic flow of data through the vSwitch. There are many issues to consider with respect to vNetwork traffic flow.

For all these discussions on traffic flow, we need to think of the vDS as a control construct and not a vSwitch construct. For each defined vDS across all nodes in a ESX or ESXi cluster, there are corresponding virtual switches for each host. We are looking at the per host traffic flow between multiple VMs and the network outside the host. When we bring vDS into the equation, we must remember that the vSwitch on one host cannot directly communicate to a vSwitch on another host without first going out the pNIC to a pSwitch and then through the physical network to reach the other host.

VM to VM Traffic on Same Portgroup/Same vSwitch/Same Host

The most basic of VM to VM traffic flows is depicted in Figure 7.6. Figure 7.6 depicts the traffic flow when data moves from VM to VM, where each VM is a connected to the same portgroup on the same VMware vSwitch. In this case, all traffic stays within the portgroup and vSwitch in use by the VMs.

Technically, however, the traffic hits the portgroup, then the vSwitch, then goes back out the same portgroup. When vDS is in use, this is for VMs within the same host, not spanning hosts.

VM to VM Traffic on Same vSwitch/Different Portgroups w/NO VLANs/ Same Host

Now we move to a slightly more complex configuration of a vNetwork on the same host. This is depicted in Figure 7.7, where there is more than one portgroup defined within a given vSwitch, and each portgroup hosts at least one VM. At the same time there are no VLANs defined for each of the portgroups.

Although it is a slightly more complex configuration, the traffic flow for VM to VM traffic on the same vSwitch is the same as in the previous discussion.

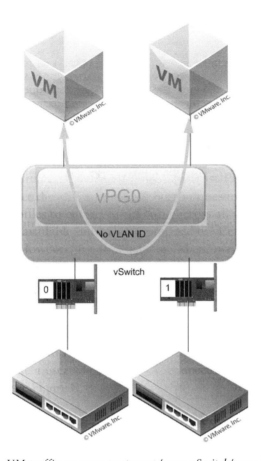

Figure 7.6 *VM to VM traffic on same portgroup/same vSwitch/same host*

The traffic flows from the source VM to the portgroup, then to the vSwitch, then to the portgroup for the target VM, and then into the vNIC for that VM. In essence, when the VMs are on the same host and there are no VLANs, the traffic flows through the vSwitch from VM to VM.

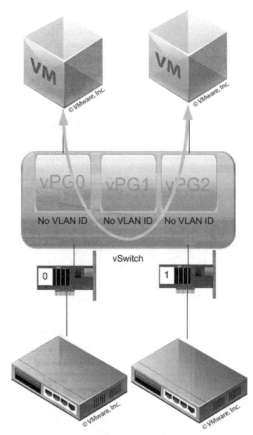

Figure 7.7 *VM to VM traffic on different portgroups/no VLANs/same vSwitch/same host*

VM to VM Traffic on Same vSwitch/Different Portgroups w/ VLANs/Same Host

Building on the previous discussion, we now add VLANs into the picture, as depicted in Figure 7.8. VLANs add quite a bit of complexity to the traffic flow because a vSwitch is nothing more than a Layer-2 device and not a router or gateway. Therefore, the traffic flow of one VLAN to another, although they share the same physical wire, is not the same as the traffic flow of portgroups with no VLANs defined.

The traffic for portgroups with VLANs defined goes from the VM to the portgroup, to the vSwitch, to the pNIC, and then to some form of router or gateway device that bridges between the two VLANs; then back into the host via pNIC to the vSwitch and to the target portgroup as defined by portgroup, and then finally into the target VM. There is a special case we will discuss shortly where the bridge is within the vSwitch. Just remember that if no bridge exists between the VLANs, the traffic looks like that of Figure 7.8.

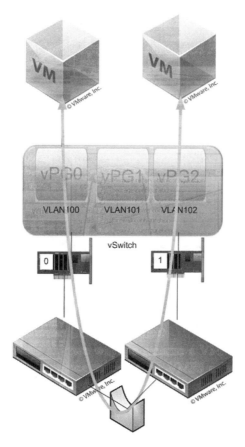

Figure 7.8 *VM to VM traffic on different portgroups/VLANs/same vSwitch/same host*

VM to VM Traffic on Different Hosts

Note that the previous traffic flow is the best description of how traffic flows between multiple hosts using VLANs as depicted in Figure 7.9. The only difference between use of VLANs and no use of VLANs is that the traffic may not actually go through a bridge, router, gateway, or firewall. When using the same VLAN, or when no VLANs are in use, the Layer-2 physical switch network will transfer the packet within the pSwitch instead of requiring some sort of gateway device because the VLAN used is known by the switch and can deliver the traffic between two ESX hosts connected to the same pSwitch fabric. In the case of no VLAN in use, this uses the pSwitch's default VLAN.

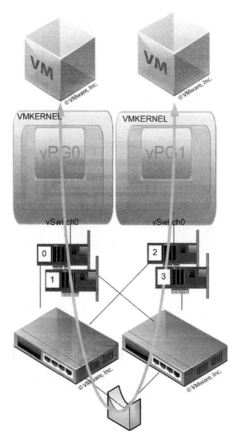

Figure 7.9 *VM to VM traffic on different hosts*

Traffic flows from the source VM to the portgroup through the vSwitch to the pNIC, through the pSwitch. If VLANs are involved, the traffic flows through some sort of bridge device; otherwise, it gets passed through the physical switching network to the pSwitch connected to the pNIC on the device hosting the target VM, where the traffic flows from the pSwitch, to the pNIC, to the vSwitch and the subsequent portgroup, and finally to the VM.

When going from host to host, the physical switch network is always involved, and traffic flows out of one host and into another.

VM to VM Traffic on Different Portgroups/Same VLAN ID/Same vSwitch/ Same Host

There is an interesting case where multiple portgroups are in use and more than one portgroup shares the same VLAN ID as another portgroup on the same vSwitch. This is depicted in Figure 7.10.

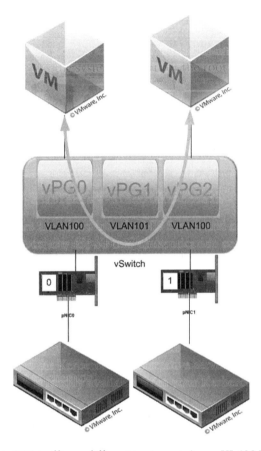

Figure 7.10 *VM to VM traffic on different portgroups/same VLAN ID/same vSwitch/ same host*

The traffic flow leaves the source VM through the source portgroup and moves into the vSwitch. It then goes into the target portgroup that has the same VLAN ID and finally into the VM via the vNIC. In reality, the traffic never leaves the vSwitch.

VM to VM Traffic on Different Portgroups/Different VLAN/Virtual Bridge/ Same Host

Figure 7.11 depicts another interesting case of traffic flow, where the bridge, gateway, router, or firewall device for bridging between different VLANs is a VM with multiple vNICs that live in each VLAN. An example of this type of device is VMware vShield Zones 1.0.

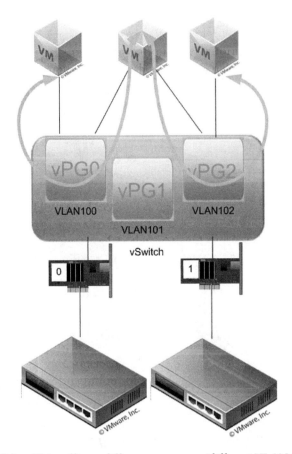

Figure 7.11 *VM to VM traffic on different portgroups/different VLAN ID/same vSwitch/same host/virtual bridge device*

In this case, the traffic flows out of the VM to the portgroup, then to the bridge VM, then from the bridge VM into the target portgroup, and finally into the target VM. The traffic never leaves the vSwitch and therefore never leaves the host. This use case, instead of bridging between different portgroups, can also bridge between different virtual switches, as depicted in Figure 7.12.

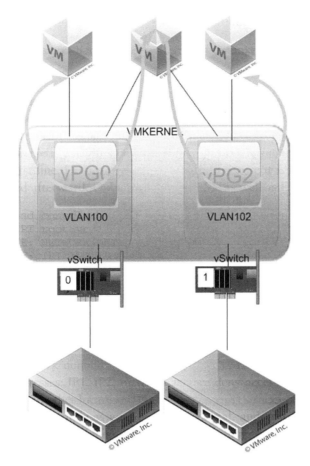

Figure 7.12 *VM to VM traffic on different portgroups/different VLAN ID/different vSwitch/same host/virtual bridge device*

PVLAN Traffic Flow

Traffic flowing over a Cisco Nexus 1000V or vNetwork Distributed Switch flows in the same ways as previously discussed. The location of the source and targets of the packet become important. Traffic within PVLANs is no different from traffic within a VLAN, except that there is the need for a new vSwitch type (vDS) to support this type of tagging.

Traffic Flow Conclusion

Knowing when traffic flows outside of each portgroup, vSwitch, and host is very important to understand but follows some basic rules, as outlined in Table 7.6. It is also important to realize that when a vDS is involved, the traffic flows do not change. Table 7.6 tells you when the traffic will leave the vSwitch. If there is an asterisk by the Yes or No, the traffic would also leave the host.

Table 7.6 *Table of Traffic Flows*

	No VLAN Same vSwitch	Same VLAN ID Same vSwitch	Different VLAN ID Same vSwitch	No VLAN Different vSwitch	Same VLAN ID Different vSwitch	Different VLAN ID Different vSwitch
Same Port-group	No	No	N/A	Yes	Yes	N/A
Different Port-group	No	No	Yes *	Yes *	Yes *	Yes *
Same vSwitch	No	No	Yes *	Yes	Yes	Yes
Different vSwitch	Yes *	Yes *	Yes *	Yes *	Yes *	Yes *
Different Host	Yes *	Yes *	Yes *	Yes *	Yes *	Yes *
With VM Bridge	Yes	Yes	Yes	Yes	Yes	Yes
Bridge in Physical Network	N/A	N/A	Yes *	Yes *	Yes *	Yes *

What is interesting about Table 7.6 is that when you use different VMware vSwitches, you almost always need to exit the host unless a VM bridge is in use. Note that these cases do not apply to the Cisco N1KV because there is only one N1KV per host.

vNetwork Security

Each vSwitch (VMware, vDS, Cisco N1KV) has various security mechanisms as well as some that appear to be part of the vSwitch but in actuality are not (such as VMsafe and vShield Zones). In this section we use vSwitch to refer to all three available vSwitches and not just one unless otherwise specified. It is best to understand all these aspects of vNetwork Security when designing any vNetwork, because some security appliances require that you break best practices.

It should be noted that vNetwork security is not all that different between how standard kernels work and the hypervisor itself. The differences are that the vSwitch adds more to the network stack than would normally be there, and the vSwitches have some intrinsic security built in to them to protect the data flowing over them from attack by other vSwitches on the same host.

Figure 7.13 depicts the hypervisor network stack when only VMware vSwitches are in use and with two distinctly different network devices (Broadcom and Intel) in use. The physical devices each have device specific drivers that tie into the kernel network stack, which contains common networking driver code. This is, in effect, all the bits necessary to bridge from Layer 1 (physical NICs) to Layer 2 (data link layer). When you use the VMware vSwitch, there is one Layer 2 control plane because the VMware vSwitch is a Layer 2 device. Within this control plane, live forwarding structures for each of the created vSwitches. Built-in security within the control plane of each vSwitch denies the capability for traffic from one vSwitch forwarding structure to appear on another vSwitch.

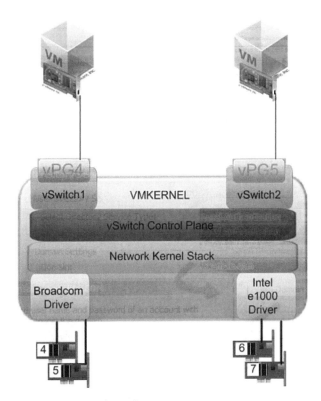

Figure 7.13 *Hypervisor network stack*

Further, a secondary level of forwarding structures enables each defined vSwitch to be subdivided into portgroups. Portgroups represent even more forwarding structures on top of the single vSwitch control plane. If it were not for the built-in security, defining multiple vSwitches and portgroups, the single control plane would act and behave just like any other physical switch. These forwarding structures would represent nothing more than VLANs. In many ways, they do represent VLANs with some level of security.

Figure 7.14 represents how the network stack would look if you were to combine the VMware vSwitch with the Cisco Nexus 1000V. Note that now two distinct vSwitch control planes are in use, yet the network kernel stack and driver layers remain the same. Just like the VMware vSwitch built-in security of denying one vSwitch construct from talking directly to another vSwitch construct, it is not possible for these two control planes to talk to one another, thereby gaining some level of separation, but because they share the same kernel network stacks, we are now back to segregation via VLAN-like constructs.

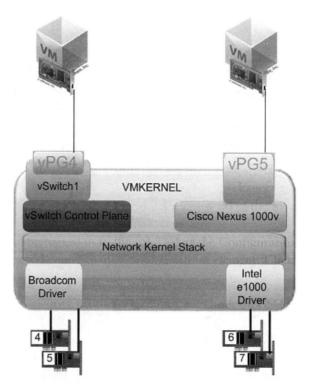

Figure 7.14 *Hypervisor network stack with Cisco Nexus 1000V*

From a security perspective, you are trusting that the VMware vSwitch constructs will *never* talk to each other unless purposely bridged using external devices or virtual machines. Furthermore, you trust that the segregation within the kernel network stack and drivers in use always provides proper separation or segregation.

Port Security
There are three port security settings available for the VMware vSwitch; however, they apply only to the VM ports on the vSwitch and are used to protect your network from hostile virtual machines. In addition to these basic capabilities, the Cisco N1KV has other protections that when applied increase the overall security of your virtual network.

Deny MAC Spoofing by VMs (VMware vSwitch)
Each portgroup and vSwitch has a mechanism to limit the capability of a VM to change the MAC address of its vNICs. This is not enabled, by default, to legacy licensing models that depend upon a specific MAC address. The current security recommendation is to change this behavior and deny the capability of VMs from changing their vNIC MAC address.
    The Cisco N1KV has its own mechanism to Deny MAC spoofing by VMs.

Deny Forged Transmits by VMs (VMware vSwitch)
Each portgroup and vSwitch has a mechanism to limit the capability of VMs to send traffic where the source MAC is different from the one currently registered within the vSwitch. This is enabled by default; however, the current security recommendation is to change this behavior and deny the capability of the VM to forge transmits.
    The Cisco N1KV has its own mechanism to Deny forged transmits by VMs.

Deny Capability of vNICs to Enter Promiscuous Mode (VMware vSwitch)
Each portgroup and vSwitch has the capability to limit whether virtual machine vNICs can receive all data traversing the portgroup after entering promiscuous mode. Promiscuous mode vNICs are often required by security appliances but in general not by any other type of device. A promiscuous mode vNIC can be used as a way for a VM to see more network traffic than should be seen by the VM, because a promiscuous mode vNIC gets sent all traffic that passes over the portgroup. The default is to disable this capability, and the security recommendation is to change this behavior very carefully.
    The Cisco N1KV has its own mechanism to Deny promiscuous mode traffic across the port.

DHCP Snooping (Cisco N1KV)
DHCP Snooping provides a way to filter untrusted DHCP server responses from reaching your virtual machines, either from outside your network or from VMs suddenly acting as DHCP servers. This is done by configuring a specific interface on the N1KV as a trusted port that is allowed to pass DHCP requests. By default, DHCP Snooping is disabled. DHCP Snooping can be applied only to the ports on the N1KV, which could be the uplink from a physical switch. This

would prevent VMs from acting as a DHCP server but not prevent any physical host from acting as one. The key is to ensure that DHCP Snooping is available on both the physical and virtual network.

IP Source Guard (Cisco N1KV)
IP Source Guard prevents a VM from spoofing the IP Address of another virtual machine or host on the physical or virtual networks. IP Source Guard works with DHCP Snooping or static settings to prevent the VMs from spoofing other IP addresses.

Dynamic ARP Inspection (DAI within Cisco N1KV)
DAI validates ARP packets within the network based on trusted tables created by DHCP Snooping or static entries. DAI is used to limit the effectiveness of ARP Cache poisoning and other ARP cache attacks.

VMsafe Net/dvFilters
VMsafe-Net or dvFilters is a vmkernel module that sits just before each active vNIC on a given host and is therefore host specific. What is also interesting about VMsafe-Net modules is that with the exception of VMware vShield Zones 2.0, App, and Endpoint, most are available directly from third parties. You can find VMsafe-Net modules from third parties such as Altor Networks, Reflex Systems, TrendMicro, IBM, and others.

Figure 7.15 shows where VMsafe-Net fits within the networking stack as a firewall icon. In essence, it sits just before the vNIC if traffic is flowing from a vSwitch, or just after the vNIC if the traffic is flowing from the vNIC. As an introspection API, VMsafe-Net modules can inspect the traffic to determine if it should enter or leave the vNIC and therefore makes a perfect per vNIC firewall.

Unfortunately, some standard firewall controls you expect, such as NAT and port redirection, do not currently exist within the VMsafe-Net modules, and given the location of the VMsafe-Net within the network stack, they may be difficult to implement easily.

The other common issue when using VMsafe-Net modules is that there is always a virtual appliance that runs on the host it is protecting. This virtual appliance is used to control the VMsafe-Net module and to set per host security policies. Whether all these modules within the virtual environment talk to each other depends on the VMsafe-Net product chosen.

Access Control Lists
Access control lists (ACLs) exist solely within the Cisco N1KV and not within the concept of the VMware vSwitch or vDS. ACLs for the N1KV follow the rules defined for the Cisco Nexus family of switches. ACLs provide a mechanism to limit access to ports based on source or destination IP, MAC, Protocol, and so on.

ACLs are applied either when traffic arrives at a N1KV or leaves a N1KV, based on how the rules are written. ACLs can filter out traffic before it leaves the Cisco N1KV, which is unlike VMsafe-Net. With VMsafe-Net, the traffic is filtered out after it has traversed the virtual switch in use. When you use a combination of the N1KV and VMsafe-Net, you can filter traffic as it enters the N1KV, as well as when it leaves the N1KV and before it enters the virtual NIC via VMsafe-Net. This implies that you have three sets of ACLs in use: ingress and egress from the Cisco N1KV and the rules defined for VMsafe-Net.

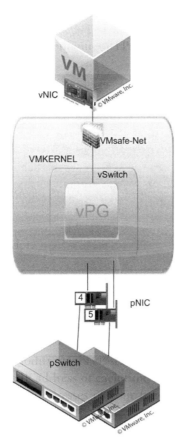

Figure 7.15 *VMsafe-Net*

VMware vShield

VMware vShield Zones 1.0 is a virtual firewall that is implemented as a Linux-based virtual machine that provides firewall capability between two or more portgroups, VLANs, or virtual switches. In other words, unlike VMsafe-Net, VMware vShield Zones 1.0 is a single virtual appliance with no driver component. It was depicted earlier (refer to Figure 7.11). Yet, like VMsafe-Net, there are no NAT or port-redirection capabilities within VMware vShield Zones 1.0. In addition, you need a VMware vShield Zones virtual appliance per ESX or ESXi host as well as one per every nine portgroups. If vShield Zones is used in conjunction with vDS, you gain the capability to have one set of security policies for all hosts participating within the vDS.

Although vShield Zones is not vSwitch functionality per se, it should be grouped with all the other vSwitch security mechanisms. vShield Zones could be considered one of our basic building blocks: vFW.

As of the writing of this book, VMware announced a beta for vShield 2.0 that includes edge firewall capabilities as well as a VMsafe-Net implementation. vShield Edge is a virtual appliance like vShield Zones 1.0. vShield App is a VMsafe-Net firewall module.

Network vMotion

When you use vDS, there is now the concept of Network vMotion. Network vMotion transfers the security policy associated with a given VM and network between ESX or ESXi hosts as the VM is migrated to the target host. This is also supported natively within the Cisco N1KV, whether using vDS or not.

This aspect of vSphere improves the overall security of your network by ensuring that network security policies are transferred with each VM. Although vDS maintains like network labels across all participating ESX or ESXi hosts, the security policy as set by dvFilters and vShield Zones needs to also be transferred.

Network vMotion unfortunately does not apply directly to third-party VMsafe-Net modules because the network policy is maintained outside of vCenter by the third-party products.

SPAN Ports

Cisco N1KV supports Switch Port Analyzer (SPAN) and Encapsulated Remote SPAN (ERSPAN) ports using the standard Cisco Nexus configuration for such ports. SPAN provides a mechanism for all traffic destined for one port to be also sent to a SPAN port for packet inspection. SPAN is used mainly for security tools such as IDS and IPS. Within the VMware vSwitches and vDS, SPAN ports do not exist per se. However, it is possible to create a vSwitch portgroup that can achieve similar functionality as shown within Figure 7.16, which shows data destined for one portgroup also being sent in tandem to the portgroup with a VLAN ID of 4095.

As you can see, creating a portgroup with SPAN functionality requires using a portgroup with a VLAN ID of 4095, which is vPG2 within Figure 7.16. In addition, that portgroup must allow promiscuous mode vNICs. After both conditions are met, all traffic traversing the vSwitch can be seen by any virtual machine that is attached to the portgroup with a VLAN ID of 4095.

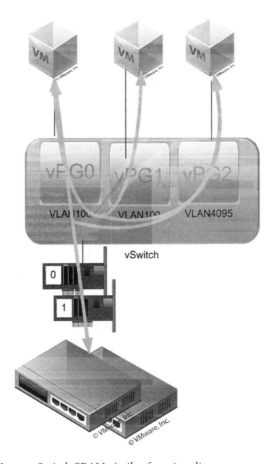

Figure 7.16 *VMware vSwitch SPAN-similar functionality*

Another use for the portgroup with a VLAN ID of 4095 is to implement virtual guest tagging (VGT) implementation of 802.1Q supported by VMware virtual switches. All those VMs that participate in VGT must be attached to a portgroup with a VLAN ID of 4095; otherwise, the traffic will not be delivered to the listening VMs. Most non-VMsafe-Net security appliances implement VGT in order to gain access to all the VLAN data traversing the vSwitch.

Network Definitions

Each ESX or ESXi host contains many networks. Each of these predefined networks has its own inherent risks and, to many security specialists, represents a different security zone. All these networks may exist whether you are using ESX or ESXi (refer ahead to Figure 7.18). The major difference between ESX and

ESXi from a networking perspective is how each of the management consoles is seen from a networking perspective.

Within ESX, the service console represents the management console; it is contained fully within a VM and obeys all the rules for traffic flow and other basic functionality we have discussed for virtual machines. However, for ESXi, the management console sits on a new type of device named a vmkernel NIC (vmknic). A vmknic is a direct link from a pNIC to an object within the hypervisor, as depicted by Figure 7.17.

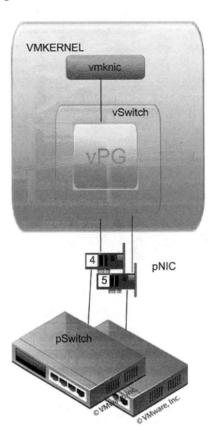

Figure 7.17 *vmknic connectivity*

A vmknic, like a vNIC connects to a portgroup within a vSwitch, but the vmknic lives entirely within the vmkernel and is used to connect vmkernel networks to the outside world (vMotion, FT Logging, iSCSI, and NFS). After a portgroup is attached to a vmknic, the portgroup can no longer be used for virtual machines or the service console. In addition, each vmknic must live on its own IP subnet even if VLANs are in use. This aids in routing between vmknic's and external devices.

Figure 7.18 shows the basic connections of all the different networks within an ESX and ESXi host. The only difference between ESX 3 and ESX 4 is the inclusion of the FT Logging Network, which is highlighted. Each network is represented by its own portgroup and shows to what these portgroups connect. Some could argue that each vNetwork mentioned does not require its own portgroup. However, except for NFS and iSCSI traffic (which can refer to storage network) this is actually true. When you create one of these networks within your environment, you are required to connect to different portgroups when using any of the VMware virtual switch constructs. Storage networking is the only exception. Whether or not these portgroups are connected to the same vSwitch construct is a matter of trust zone definitions and networking policies within your environment.

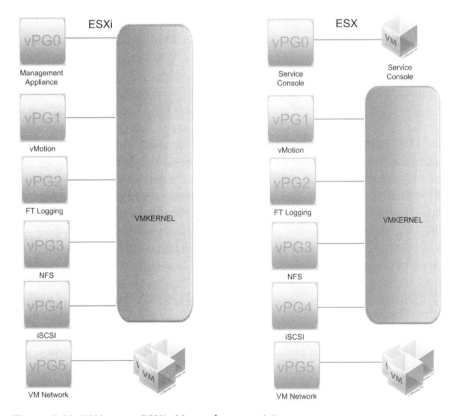

Figure 7.18 *ESX versus ESXi vNetwork connectivity*

The last part of the vNetwork is often the most complex, and that is the VM Network. Each VM Network can contain, in addition to the standard ESX or ESXi networks, DMZs, Production, QA, Test, Development, and other networks. Whether multiple network security zones exist within the VM Network is determined by your entity's security policies. What follows is a list of various networks and their definitions with respect to the virtual environment.

Virtual Environment Management Network

The virtual environment management network should be a secure, firewalled network that in general only virtualization administrators should access directly. The VMware vCenter Server, ESX service consoles, and ESXi management appliances should be on this network. There is some discussion as to whether remote access devices like Dell RAC or HP ILOs should also be on this network or a different network. In theory, those who need to use the remote access devices are generally virtualization administrators as well.

The utility of the virtual environment management network is to create, deploy, and manage VMs and hosts within the virtual environment. Access to this network should be segregated to only those who have the need for this access. This access could also be encrypted over a VPN for enhanced security. In either case the virtual environment network should be firewalled from all other networks. All cold migrations, which are unencrypted, the initial instructions for a vMotion, and every other action carried out by an ESX host including all forms of monitoring travel over this network.

The ESX service console uses an internal device called a vSwif to represent the vNIC used. There can be as many vSwif devices as needed to attain the necessary redundancy. However, NIC teaming is recommended over multiple vSwif devices unless you create a second service console attached to the secondary vSwif.

The alternative option for creating a redundant admin network is to have two pNICs for the service console, but to have only one operational at any time and to write a script to do IP-based failover from within the service console. Both pNICs would be configured with the same IP address and with only one active at the same time. Failover would consist of bringing down the primary network and then after it is down, bringing up the secondary network. This option provides IP-based failover only and does not support 802.1Q VLAN tagging, the various forms of load balancing, or 802.3ad, because there are no drivers for any of this functionality within the service console. The following script can be run from an ESX service console but not from an ESXi management console to achieve IP-based network failover:

```
#!/bin/sh
running=vswif0
second=vswif1
GatewayIP=10.0.0.141
while [ 1 ]
do
```

```
            data=`ping -c 1 $GatewayIP | grep -i unreachable`
            if [ X$date != "" ]
            then
                    # reset
                    ifdown $running
                    ifup $second
                    # reset running device
                    foo=$running
                    running=$second
                    second=$foo
            fi
            sleep 300
    end
```

The preceding code assumes that devices vswif0 and vswif1 of the service console are defined with exactly the same information, but vswif1 is not configured to start on boot. The script will attempt to ping the gateway, and if it cannot be reached it will bring down the network device and start the secondary device. It should be noted that VMware NIC Teaming performs this failover within the virtual switch and is the preferred mechanism for failover.

It is also possible, as stated earlier, to add many more than one network device to your ESX or ESXi management console using the standard interface. However, you cannot attain IP address redundancy using this method. You can gain access to the service console using multiple networks; however, management will generally come in only through a single network. The benefit of multiple IP addresses, however, is to give VMware High Availability (HA) different networks to check to see whether a host is alive or dead.

VMware HA requires that it can accurately determine whether a host is alive or dead because after it determines that a host is unavailable, HA could fire the rules you have set. If the host was actually still alive but a pSwitch went bad, it is possible that HA could attempt to fire. With vSphere this would fail because of file locking on the datastores where the VMs reside; yet for older versions of HA, you could end up with multiple instances of VMs. This would cause definite failures as VMs go to write data to disk. We will cover this in Chapter 11, "Dynamic Resource Load Balancing."

> *Best Practice for Virtualization Management Network*
>
> Use NIC teams to attain redundancy.
>
> Secure this network with some form of firewall.

ESX and ESXi 3 also required that the management consoles participate within the iSCSI network, because half the iSCSI code lives in the management console. This generally implies sharing the same vSwitch between the iSCSI device and the service console or management appliance. The use of iSCSI throws a huge monkey wrench into the security of the service console and the need to have the administrative network handle nonadministrative traffic. At this time, only one way exists to alleviate the possible conflicts between administration and iSCSI: Use port ID-based load balancing so that each port has its own pNIC. Even so, there is no guarantee that the iSCSI server will end up coming in over a different pNIC than the standard management console traffic. Another option, perhaps, is to use two service console vSwitches on two distinct networks, thereby having one vSwitch for the admin network and a second for the iSCSI network.

The iSCSI limitation has gone away with the use of vSphere but should still be considered if you are migrating from ESX or ESXi v3 to ESX or ESX v4.

Out-of-Band Management Network

The Server Console Network is the network used by HP ILO and Dell DRAC devices for presenting the system console to administrators over the network. These devices are also used by VMware Dynamic Power Management (DPM). Given that DPM activity is over the Virtualization Management Network, the Server Console Network most likely is the same network. There may be a need to keep them separate from a security policy perspective, but when VMware DPM is in use, the two networks must interoperate.

vMotion Network

The vMotion network is used to transfer the memory image and VM configuration of a running VM from host to host, and therefore, for security reasons, requires its own private network. Placing this network unprotected within your public network would allow someone to grab the memory footprint of the VM, which in security circles would be considered catastrophic. It is recommended that this network be on a private pSwitch or pSwitch VLAN because this memory footprint is sent over the wire unencrypted. The vMotion network requires a pNIC connected to a vSwitch. This vSwitch should not be connected to any VMs for security reasons, but instead is connected to the ESX vmkernel for vMotion only. The vMotion network should be a redundant network where two pNICs are connected to the vMotion vSwitch. However, in this mode, there is only failover support and not load balancing.

Best Practice for vMotion Network

Connect pNICs of the vMotion network to their own private pSwitch or VLAN for performance and security reasons.

Fault Tolerance Logging Network

Like the vMotion Network, the Fault Tolerance (FT) Logging Network transfers critical data over a high speed network. FT Logging transfers the data necessary to keep the two VMs that compose a FT-enabled virtual machine in CPU lockstep with each other. FT creates a shadow VM on a secondary vSphere host and, as such, needs to send to the shadow VM all the nondeterministic events and some state information of the vCPU of the primary VM. This data could include enough information to discover exactly how an application runs, discover credentials in use, and perform any encryption or any other security and data manipulations. Access to this network could allow an attacker to reverse engineer an application or encryption mechanism in use. Combine this with access to the vMotion network and, in essence, you can capture the entire application, as well as the memory in use. Therefore, the FT Logging Network is very important to protect. The vSwitch used for FT Logging would not be connected to any VMs, but instead is connected to the ESX vmkernel for FT Logging only. The FT Logging Network should be a redundant network where two pNICs are connected to the FT Logging vSwitch. However, in this mode, there is only failover support and not load balancing.

> ### Best Practice for FT Logging Network
>
> Connect pNICs of the FT Logging Network to their own private pSwitch or VLAN for performance and security reasons.

NFS Network

The NFS vmkernel Network allows the vmkernel to talk to NFS Servers over NFS v3 Protocol using TCP instead of UDP. NFS is a file-based protocol and not a block-based protocol like SCSI, which is used for SAN and iSCSI, and as such NFS does not suffer from SCSI-2 Reservation issues. But it does have its own locking protocols for each file. Because the NFS Network is used to present a datastore to the ESX or ESXi host, it is important to configure this network with at least two pNICs and to connect those pNICS to multiple pSwitches. In addition, for security reasons, this network should be private to the ESX or ESXi hosts and not used by VMs.

> ### Best Practice for the NFS Network
>
> Use multiple pNICs and pSwitches for redundancy and bandwidth.
>
> The NFS Network should not be used by VMs.

If your NFS server supports network multipath, it would be possible to connect as many pNICs as necessary to gain the bandwidth you need for the VMs on the NFS datastore. However, be aware that you need to maintain redundancy for this network and that multipath functionality is not provided by ESX but by the NAS involved. ESX provides redundancy but not load balancing nor aggregation of the NFS network.

iSCSI Network

The iSCSI network is used to communicate with iSCSI servers (either SAN or hybrid NAS device) as long as it is over an ethernet cable, whether copper or optical. Note that SAN fabric is accessed through other means, not via this network. Because this is a datastore network, it is important to configure this network with at least two pNICs and to connect the pNICs to multiple pSwitches. In addition, for security reasons the networks should be private to the ESX or ESXi hosts. The iSCSI network should not have any VMs on it. For ESX 3, there is one caveat about the use of iSCSI: A port on the service console must participate in the iSCSI network.

> ### Best Practice for the iSCSI Network
> Use multiple pNICs and pSwitches for redundancy and bandwidth.
>
> The iSCSI network should not be used by VMs.

VM Network

The VM network by should consist of at least two pNICs connected to a single vSwitch. For redundancy reasons, each of these pNICs should be connected to different pSwitches, but it is not required. The VM network should always consist of a pair of pNICs, because the vSwitch will provide load balancing and failover functionality to increase throughput and redundancy for each VM. Each vSwitch for the VMs can handle all the various flavors of load balancing, VLAN tagging, and redundancy. In general, there is no need for more than two pNICs for the VM network even with a host full of machines because with load balancing there is at least a 2Gb pipe going out to the world. When talking to network people, most, if not all, of our customers firmly believe that no ESX host needs more than 2Gb of bandwidth. However, if a need exists for more bandwidth, it is strongly suggested that another pair of pNICs be added and another vSwitch added, and that the NIC team limit this to two pNICs per vSwitch. The round-robin approach used for assigning network paths, when there is a path failure, could cause what amounts to a fair amount of thrashing on the pSwitches until the system again balances out, with an elapsed time in minutes and not seconds. Granted, this thrashing is limited to poorly configured switching networks. Limiting the network paths to two alleviates this issue.

> ### Best Practice for VM Network
>
> Always connect two pNICs to each VM vSwitch that needs outside access for redundancy and load balancing. In addition, use multiple pSwitches.
>
> Do not use more than two pNICs per vSwitch.

Some special networks within the overall VM Network designation are discussed next.

Demilitarized Zone (DMZ) Network

The DMZ network consists of those externally facing servers that are used to access your organization from external sources. The DMZ often bridges from the externally facing servers to internal servers. Access to the DMZ is strictly controlled in many organizations. Yet, it can be virtualized but with quite a bit of care. It is very important to be aware of any possible security issues with this network. In fact, an often-recommended approach is to use a 100% segregated switching network for any DMZ traffic. This is one of the most hostile networks within any organization because it is the one exposed to the outside. Although an edge firewall is in use, there are still many attack points within any DMZ.

The best practices for securing your DMZ network within the virtual environment are many and varied and depend solely upon your external DMZ networking and associated security policies. A good reference to fully understand the security requirements for the virtual environment and their impact on virtualizing DMZ networks is the book *vSphere and Virtual Infrastructure Security*.

Build/Repair Lab Networks

Build or Repair Lab Networks is also an interesting network, as we showed in Figure 7.1. This network could contain extremely hostile or at-risk virtual machines. Therefore it is recommended that this type of network be 100% segregated from all other networks. In a build lab, the risk is zero day attacks based on missing patches that are staged to install within the build lab.

Storage Network

The virtual machine storage network should be segregated from the VMware ESX or ESXi host storage network. A VM, unless it's a management device (see "Management Network (Virtualization or Otherwise)"), should never share the same network as the host because it would be possible for a VM to adversely impact the performance and security of this network.

Backup Network

The backup network is a bandwidth-intensive network and should be segregated for performance reasons from the rest of the networks, perhaps even using a separate set of switches. With large datacenters, it is possible that a backup network could have a sustained high utilization because terabytes of data could be backed up every day. The backup network also includes such things as continuous data protection within the VMs but not with the host.

Management Network (Virtualization or Otherwise)

Another VM network of interest is the management network for either virtualization or other aspects of the datacenter. These virtual machines should be firewalled from other types of VMs because these types of VMs are high-value attack points. If you can break into a management node or network, it may be possible for an attacker to gain access to all aspects of your virtual environment. Such systems may include VMware vCenter and the vCenter management tools as well as vSphere Clients, VMware SDK Tools, storage control appliances, and any security appliances. We cover this in depth within the "Virtual Environment Management Network" discussion previously in this section.

Checklist

Now that we understand the components that make up networks within and outside of an ESX host, we can expand on this and break down our network requirements to a checklist. This checklist will display what is required for networking the ESX host and the VM guests. Without this information the implementation of ESX could be seriously delayed. For example, we went to a customer site that did not have all this information. The initial deployment of the server was delayed by two days, and then the final deployment by at least two weeks as new cables needed to be pulled, pNICs added, and IP addresses allocated. It is best to take care of this before you need them to speed up the deployment of an ESX host.

As shown in Table 7.7, quite a bit of information is needed before ESX installation, and although any change to the networking setup can occur after installation with judicious use of the appropriate commands and configuration files, it is always better to have this information prior to installation. In addition, the VM side of the network must be known prior to implementation so that the appropriate vSwitches can be created. As you can see, some decisions need to be made in order to properly configure the network for the VMs and for the host. Outside of the standard IP addresses for VMs and the host, there are some important items to consider and review. In Table 7.7, the Management Console (MC) mentioned refers to either the ESX service console of the ESXi management console.

Table 7.7 *ESX Networking Checklist*

Element	Host or Guest	Comments
pSwitch	Host	The recommendation is for two or more pSwitches for redundancy. The actual number depends on the security and performance requirements for your networking.
pNIC	Host	This depends on the number of networks involved, whether VLANs will be used, or separate pSwitches. You could use as few as four pNICs and as many as NICs as fits in your host. This depends on your security, performance, and redundancy requirements. In general, two pNICs per physical network is a good number. Physical networks could be ones that contain many VLANs.
MC IP address	Host	The IP address of the management console.
MC netmask	Host	The netmask of the management console.
MC gateway	Host	The IP address of the Default Gateway of the management console. Include any secondary gateways used by VMware HA.
MC DNS	Host	DNS servers for the management console.

continues

Table 7.7 *(Continued)*

Element	Host or Guest	Comments
MC redundancy Method	Host	VMware NIC Teaming or IP Based Failover. The recommendation is for VMware NIC Teaming with the default load-balancing method.
ILO/DRAC IP Address	Host	Record the IP address of your remote access device HP ILO, Dell DRAC, or similar devices for use with DPM.
vMotion IP address	Host	IP address for the vMotion network. This could be routable for long distance vMotion. vMotion requires its own subnet that should be separate from any other vmkernel network. It is recommended that this also be separate from the management console IP address.
vMotion Gateway	Host	Gateway of the vMotion Network.
FT IP Address	Host	Fault Tolerance IP Address, which must be a different subnet than any other vmkernel network.
NFS IP Address	Host	NFS Client IP Address, must be a different subnet than any other vmkernel network. Include the NFS Server IP address or hostname for use with accessing datastores.
iSCSI IP Address	Host	iSCSI Client IP Address must be a different subnet than any other vmkernel network. Include the iSCSI Server IP address or hostname for use with accessing datastores.
Beacon Monitoring	Host	If enabled, there may be a need for additional links to and between pSwitches.

Element	Host or Guest	Comments
802.1Q state	Host	Are the networks heading to the ESX host trunked to the pSwitch or through to the vSwitch? If 802.1Q is not in use, this is important to note.
vSwitch load-balancing method	Host	Are the vSwitches going to use port ID-, MAC address-, or IP address-based load balancing?
IP address for all the VMs	Guest	A list of IP addresses for the VMs.
Netmask for all the VMs	Guest	The netmask for the VM networks in use.
Gateway for all the VMs	Guest	The gateway to use for the VM networks in use.
DNS servers for all the VMs	Guest	The DNS server for use within the VM network.
vSwitch names	VMs	Naming your vSwitches appropriately will aid in finding which vSwitch to connect a vNIC to.
vSwitch portgroup names	VMs	If VST is in use, the portgroup names will be helpful before beginning.
pSwitch configuration	pSwitch	Is spanning tree disabled, PortFast enabled; are 802.1Q trunks defined, and are there enough ports?

Starting with the IP addresses required: We need an IP address for the management console; *not* for each vSwitch, but instead for the VMs attached to the vSwitch.

"But," you ask, "we have pNICs, so IP addresses are required for the pNICs?" The pNICs assigned to vSwitches are placed into a bridge mode that bridges the pSwitches to the vSwitches and thus do not require their own IP address. In this mode, the VMs require IP addresses as does the management console, but not the pNICs themselves. Nor do the vSwitches require IP addresses, because they are not IP-based managed switches.

pSwitch Settings Checklist

In Table 7.7, we list just the pSwitch configuration within the checklist. However, this expands to Table 7.8 and depends entirely on the pSwitches in use as well as the functionality you require within the virtual network.

Table 7.8 *ESX pSwitch Checklist*

Element	N1KV/vSwitch	Comments
Spanning Tree Protocol	vSwitch	Either disable STP when using VMware vSwitches or enable Portfast on the pSwitch, because the VMware vSwitch does not understand STP. This is not required when using the Cisco N1KV.
Portfast	vSwitch	If STP is in use, ensure that the pSwitch ports used by the VMware vSwitches have portfast enabled. This is not required for the Cisco N1KV.
PVLAN	N1KV	N1KV supports PVLANs, but if PVLANs within the N1KV span multiple ESX or ESXi hosts, then there needs to be network connections between the hosts through pSwitches that understand PVLANs.
PVLAN	vSwitch	dVS supports PVLANs, but if PVLANs within the dVS span multiple ESX or ESXi hosts, then there needs to be network connections between the hosts through pSwitches that understand PVLANs.
802.1Q Configuration	Both	Determine your 802.1Q connection to the ESX hosts and clusters: EST, VST, VGT.

Element	N1KV/vSwitch	Comments
Mapping pSwitch ports	Both	Ensure that you understand which pNIC ports connect to which vSwitch to host pNICs and pSwitch ports. In other words, map pSwitch ports to pNICs to vmknics.
Jumbo Frames	Both	Does the vSwitch support Jumbo Frames for IP Storage?
DHCP Snooping	N1KV	It is possible that DHCP Snooping implemented on the N1KV would require the same functionality within the pSwitches in use to prevent physical hosts from acting as untrusted DHCP servers.

There are not many items in Table 7.8, yet they are extremely important to verify and consider; otherwise, the virtual/physical network interface may not function as desired. For example, if you need PVLAN support and your pSwitch has no support for PVLANs, use of PVLANs across multiple hosts via the vDS would most likely fail.

The most important item is Spanning Tree Protocol. I do not know of any networking team that will disable this functionality, so the per interface portfast option is required when uplinking the pSwitch to the vSwitch over a pNIC. The reason is that the VMware vSwitches does not understand STP so it passes the STP packets throughout the virtual network untouched. The VMware vSwitches do not implement the Spanning Tree Protocol. It is impossible to create a STP loop with VMware vSwitches unless you configure a VM as a bridge between two vSwitches.

When using the Cisco N1KV, it may be necessary to ensure that the pSwitches also understand the security protocols in place. For example, if you are using DHCP Snooping within the N1KV and the trusted DHCP server is a VM, then all DHCP Snooping on the ESX host with the DHCP Server Guest would show that the trusted server is a VM. Yet on a second ESX host, the trusted server would end up coming over the uplink port. Because of this, the second server would need a physical switching network that also understands DHCP Snooping to ensure that no physical machine also acts as a DHCP server. Why is this necessary? Because the trusted interface for the DHCP Snooping would end up being the uplink interface and not an interface representing a VM on the second

ESX or ESXi host. Given this, it is quite possible that another VM or physical host could act as a DHCP server on a trusted port.

Little complexities like this exist when adding advanced security functionality from within virtual switches, so extra care should be used to ensure that these complexities do not break your current security policies.

vNetworking

Now that we know the basic building blocks, traffic flow, and functionality of virtual switches involved, it is time to put it all together. We will break out the functionality by traditional networking means, such as gigabit networking links and the new converged network adapters. These are the best practices for configuring your virtual to physical network interfaces. These best practices are based on achieving the highest level of performance, redundancy, and security based on the various networks previously described. We will work from the simplest networking case to the most complex.

vNetworks: The Great VLAN Debate

There is a great VLAN debate going on in the virtualization security community, as well as in the virtual networking community. VLANs tag data so that it can be delivered to the appropriate target if the switches, pNICs, and vNICs are all configured properly. This means that the data on the virtual or physical wire is, in effect, interleaved data with tags set. The weakness in using VLANs is that it is always possible to use a Man-in-the-Middle (MiTM) attack to see or perhaps even change the data traveling over these wires by introducing an unsanctioned device on the wire in question. Because the traffic is interleaved on the same wire, it is possible to configure a device to see all traffic, which is no different than if the traffic was untagged. Many Layer-2 attacks exist to also break pSwitches to broadcast the traffic for every VLAN to all hosts. Figure 7.19 shows this traffic on the wire (virtual and physical).

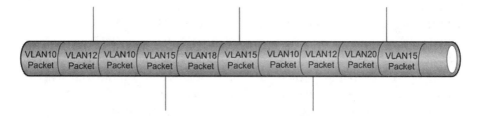

Figure 7.19 *VLAN traffic on a wire*

Physical and virtual switches themselves provide some level of security, referred to as port security, to limit the adverse impact of virtual and physical machines from acting as these MiTM attack platforms. Port security can be configured to detect NICs in promiscuous mode, which allows all traffic within a give VLAN to be seen by the NICs in this mode. If this is combined with a Layer-2 attack against the pSwitch, it could be possible for the NICs in question to see all traffic for all VLANs. Most switches are fail-open devices, which implies that they allow network traffic to flow if a failure occurs. One such failure discussed within the community is where the switch had a hardware failure that caused traffic for one VLAN to be seen and delivered to all ports regardless of VLAN in use. The solution was to replace the switch.

Many people look at the VMware vSwitches as nothing more than a logical segregation of packets much like VLANs on a physical switch, and this is quite true. There is, in essence, one code base with a separate network forwarding data structure per vSwitch and within each portgroup of a vSwitch. This sounds surprisingly like how VLANs are implemented on pSwitches, with one major difference. The VMware vSwitch is authoritative about what is connected to each of its ports, whereas a pSwitch must learn this data.

What this boils down to is that the security concerns of using VLANs depend entirely on the protections within the physical and virtual switches in use. VMware virtual switches are authoritative, so they do not need to learn MAC addresses, which is one of the major reasons VMware vSwitches are not susceptible to the well-known Layer-2 attacks to which other switches could be susceptible. The Cisco Nexus 1000V implements all Cisco's port and switch security to limit the impact of the well-known Layer-2 attacks from virtual machines as well as the outside. Like all other vSwitches the N1KV does not require a CAM table, so is not susceptible to all current Layer-2 attacks.

However, use of VLANs will always boil down to trust. Do you trust your network switches or not?

Even so, with the advent of 10G Ethernet, FCoE and Converged Network Adapters (CNAs) we should realize that VLANs are basically here to stay, and not accepting their use may imply either wasted bandwidth or the use of a plethora of physical NIC adapters.

The one thing we do know about VLAN usage is that the security policy applied to the physical network needs to also be applied to the virtual network with no exceptions. Consistency is your friend when it comes to auditing.

vNetworks: Network Splits

When we look at the plethora of virtual networks involved within the virtual environment, we see that if we were to apply a traditional non-VLAN approach to this to ensure redundancy and performance with a modicum of security, we could easily end up with at least 14 pNICS involved, or 2 per virtual network. Because we expect most of these networks to be physically separated, that equates to at least 14 pSwitches as well. That is just too many pNICs, vSwitches, and pSwitches. Stepping up to solve this problem are all the virtual IO and virtual network constructs that existed prior to and since the inception of the modern hypervisor. As we discussed in the previous section, "vNetworks: The Great VLAN Debate," VLANs are here to stay and help us to solve this problem.

But the question remains, how many pNICs and pSwitches should be used with your virtual network? That question can be answered based on the answer to several other questions:

1. How many security zones are there within your virtual and physical networks?

2. Do you have a security policy against the use of 802.1Q VLANs to segregate security zones?

3. Do you trust the VMware vSwitch and Network Kernel Stack to properly segregate and protect these security zones?

Within the virtual environment, and specifically within the VMware vSphere hypervisor, are six distinct networks (Management, FT Logging, vMotion, iSCSI, NFS, and Virtual Machine). Whether you use each of these networks will also dictate the necessary pNIC and pSwitch requirements. In addition, the split of networks within your Virtual Machine network will also dictate these numbers. How to segregate or separate your vNetworks will also be impacted by the various security zones involved. Figure 7.20 depicts these basic security zones.

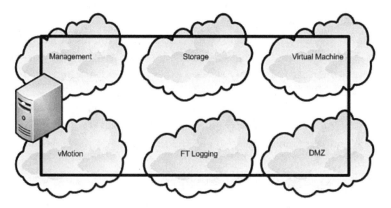

Figure 7.20 *Basic security zones*

But the big question on everyone's mind is usually how these zones can be combined to provide sufficient security while maintaining bandwidth and redundancy for necessary functionality. Figure 7.21 shows some combinations that can work to reduce the necessary pNIC requirements. It is possible to combine Management, FT Logging, and vMotion into the same security zone, but still ensure that the necessary performance and redundancy is available. The ultimate in combinations is shown in Figure 7.22, which adds to the previously combined zone the storage security zone.

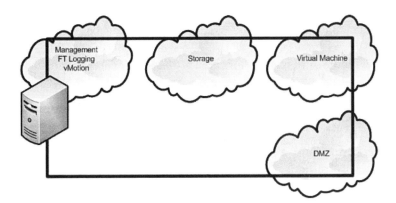

Figure 7.21 *Combining basic security zones*

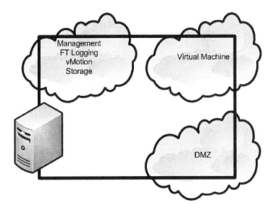

Figure 7.22 *Ultimate combination of basic security zones*

Others may also add virtual machines to this network, but I would do this only if they are actually virtualization management virtual machines. In essence, Figure 7.21 and 7.22 break down vNetworks into two or three classifications of networks. The first one is what we will refer to as Virtualization Networks

(Management, FT, and vMotion). The second is Storage, which we can combine with the Virtualization Networks, depending on performance requirements. The last is the Virtual Machine Networks, which can include other security zones such as DMZs. So now we have broken down the true number of security zones to maybe two or three.

How you achieve this segregation of traffic depends on how you answer the questions presented earlier. If you answer question 2 that you do not trust VLANs to separate security zone traffic, you will need more pNICs than you otherwise would if you trust VLANs to segregate security zone traffic.

If you do not trust the VMware vSwitch and Network Kernel Stack to properly segregate and protect traffic, you need to look further for compensating controls, such as encryption of all communication between all VMs and servers involved with the virtual environment. The issue with encryption is that it adds overhead to each VM's use of the network, which will increase overall CPU load. The other issue with encryption is key management. Apani has one solution to this problem within the virtual network. If you use encryption, whether you use VLANs is no longer an issue. You use whatever pNIC is required to gain the proper performance and redundancy because you are trusting the encryption to protect your traffic.

vNetworks: Simple Network

Before we get into some complex configurations of vNetworks, let us look at a simple two pNIC configuration. Several interesting configurations exist for a two-pNIC configuration. The two pNIC configuration provides the necessary performance and redundancy if each of the pNICs is a 10G pNIC even so many may find that 1G pNICs provide ample performance. Figure 7.23 depicts the simplest network.

In this use case, the Virtualization Network makes use of one pNIC, while the VM Network makes use of the other pNIC. In a failover case, both sets of networks (Virtualization and VM) use the same pNIC. Another option considered, but not possible, is depicted in Figure 7.24. It is not possible to use two vSwitches with only two pNICS and achieve redundancy, because after you assign the other pNIC to be a backup for a vSwitch, the pNIC is removed from the original vSwitch and placed on the current vSwitch.

Note that IP storage networks within a two pNIC configuration also travel over the same wires as all other traffic as needed. In this case, you will want to place the storage network on the same pNIC as the Virtualization Network.

So now we know what will work and what will not within the vNetwork for setting up redundancy.

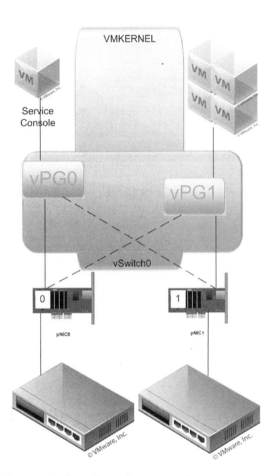

Figure 7.23 *Simple two-pNIC configuration*

vNetworks: Adding More to the Virtualization Network

As you add more elements to the Virtualization Network, you are either adding more vSwitches or portgroups, depending on the number of pNICs available and those that are already assigned to the Virtualization Network security zone. Figure 7.25 shows a classic four-pNIC combination in which all the Virtualization Network components are sharing the same set of pNICs while the VMs are using a secondary set of pNICs. In this case, I would make the Virtualization Network pNICs 10G and the VM Network pNICs either 1G or 10G. Use of this configuration will provide the necessary performance and redundancy, while maintaining the intrinsic security within the VMware vSwitch. Virtualization Networks encompass adding IP storage networks to the mix.

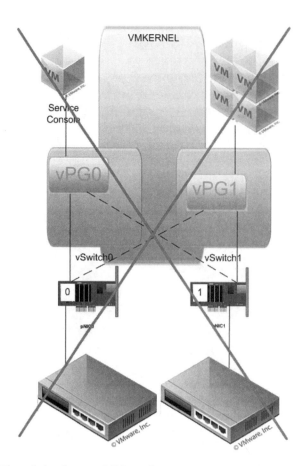

Figure 7.24 *Flawed simple two-pNIC configuration*

If you were to use the Cisco Nexus 1000V within this configuration, I would apply it to replace vSwitch1. In this way the networking team can maintain the network for the VMs as it does for other application servers. I would keep the Virtualization Network as a VMware vSwitch per the previous "vNetwork Security" discussion.

Figure 7.26 depicts a configuration using six pNICs. The additional pNICS may be needed because of physical network separation that currently exists or to gain the necessary performance for the storage networks. If 1G pNICS are in use, this configuration may be required to gain the necessary performance and redundancy for the storage networks in use. If I had a pair of 10G cards, I might switch to a four-pNIC configuration or use them purely for the storage networks.

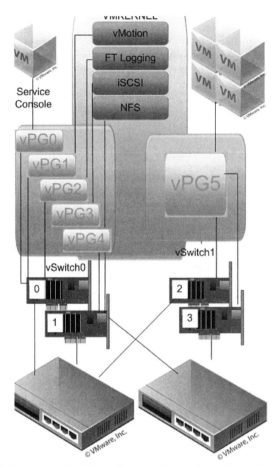

Figure 7.25 *All elements of the Virtualization Network configuration*

Regardless of the number of pNICs in use, it is very important to enable Jumbo Frames for the vmknics used for your storage networks. Enabling Jumbo Frames will be the only way to achieve the necessary storage network performance. However, the storage device must also be able to support Jumbo Frames as well as the pSwitches between the virtualization host and the storage device. To enable Jumbo Frames, use the following procedure, which is basically increasing the vmknic MTU to 9000:

```
in=`esxcfg-vmknic -l|grep -v Netmask|grep $*|awk '{print $1}'`
ipaddr=`vimsh -n -e "hostsvc/net/vnic_info $in"|grep
ipAddress|awk '{print $3}'`
netmask=`vimsh -n -e "hostsvc/net/vnic_info $in"|grep subnet-
Mask| awk '{print $3}'`
vid=`vimsh -n -e "hostsvc/net/vnic_info $in"|grep portgroup|awk
'{print $3}'|sed 1p`
esxcfg-vmknic -d -s $vid -v $in"
esxcfg-vmknic -a -i $ipaddr -n $netmask -m 9000 -s $vid -v $in"
```

The preceding script takes as an argument the vmknic portgroup name to modify. After finding the information, it then deletes the intended vmknic and then re-creates it with the proper MTU.

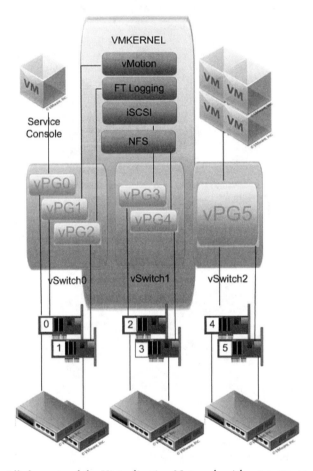

Figure 7.26 *All elements of the Virtualization Network with separate storage configuration*

vNetwork: DMZ

Many consider the introduction of a DMZ into a vNetwork as a special case, and in many ways it is. If you trust VLANs, it looks just like any other network, but you introduce another portgroup into an existing VM network configuration. However, if it uses a completely separate set of pSwitches, several configuration changes may be necessary.

The first configuration is two pNICs; it is important to realize that with only two pNICs you either have to decide on reduced redundancy or reduced physical network security and will have to use VLANs.

With four pNICs, you have some more choices, but in most cases, your only real choice is to use the pNICs you have assigned to your VM Network to your DMZ, thereby setting your virtualization hosts as DMZ-only hosts.

With six or more pNICs, you have several options, but they depend on your performance requirements. One option is seen in Figure 7.27, which places all the Virtualization Network elements on a pair of pNICs and pSwitches, the non-DMZ VMs on another pair of pNICs and pSwitches, while maintaining the DMZ on its own set of pNICs and pSwitches. It may be necessary to once more create a DMZ-only virtualization host if your network configuration is similar to that of Figure 7.26.

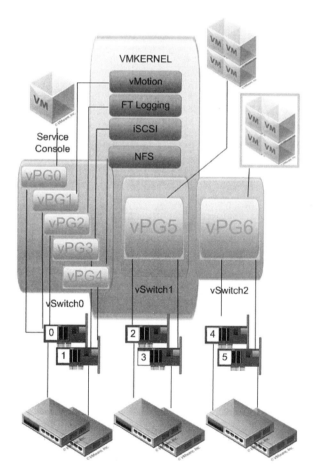

Figure 7.27 *Six pNICs with DMZ*

I will not cover cases of using more than eight pNICs, because they are doable and just extrapolations past the six pNIC example. Realize, however, that the number of pNICs, and therefore vSwitches, depends mostly on your number of pSwitches in use as well as your use of VLANs. The current vNetwork thinking on securely implementing a DMZ is to implement this as a DMZ-specific host, thereby simplifying management, configuration control, and auditing.

> ### Best Practice for Implementing a DMZ
>
> Implement a DMZ within the virtual environment by using DMZ-specific hosts. Doing so does the following:
>
> **Improves configuration control**
>
> **Improves network management**

pNIC Determination

We have been discussing vSwitches and vNICs as if they already existed, and we need to grab one and hook it up. However, these devices need to be created first, and there are a few ways to do this. The majority of vNetwork is covered in Chapter 10, but the rest of this section is a review of steps necessary before any vNetwork element is created.

The first thing to do is determine which pNIC is represented by the physical adapter list within ESX. Because there is no easy way to determine this by just looking at the hardware, it will require someone moving ethernet cables and someone watching and refreshing the physical adapter list within the management console. In many cases, it is only necessary to do this to the edge cards to determine which way the PCI bus is numbered. For example, at a recent customer site, six pNICs were involved on a Proliant DL580 G5, which did not have any onboard pNIC ports. To understand the bus ordering, someone pulled all the cables, and working together, built up a map of all pNIC ports and ESX adapter numbers by first determining which PCI addresses were associated with which adapter number on the left side of the PCI slots, and then the right side, which automatically gave us the ordering of the middle card, and incidentally told us which pNIC port was associated with the service console. Figure 7.28 shows a map and also lays out what connectivity is required for each vSwitch. In this case, there are three: vMotion, Network0, and Network1. Additional notes can be added to the map to depict which PCI slots have which cards, disks, and RAID types, as well as ILO and other necessary labels.

> **Best Practice for pNIC Determination**
>
> When trying to map pNIC port to ESX adapter numbers, work from the outside in. In addition, make a drawing of the back of the chassis and label placement of cables (and label the cables). Documenting the hardware device mapping and cabling can prove helpful later for troubleshooting.

With blades, you do not have the luxury of pulling cables to create your map, so the preferred method is to use the PCI address and refer to the vendor docs to see which slot and device corresponds to which address.

After the adapter number to the pNIC map has been determined, it is time to continue to create all the vSwitches needed by the vNetwork. There are multiple ways to do this in ESX, but there is only one supported method, and that is to use one of the management interfaces. There is nothing tricky about using a management interface to create a vSwitch; however, that is covered in the next chapter.

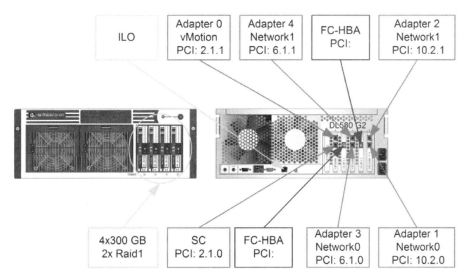

Figure 7.28 *pNIC to vSwitch sample map*

Conclusion

Creating a vNetwork is just like playing with so many tinker toys that connect everything together. This chapter has presented checklists to make help with vNetwork creation and management as well as discussions on the internals of how the vNetworks components work. Last, we have provided the basic best practices for combining the various networks. Now that we have created the vNetwork, it is possible to create VMs and install them with an appropriate OS. However, it is important to understand the underlying layers before creating any VMs. The next chapter delves into the management of ESX, where vNetworks will be created, modified, and destroyed.

Chapter 8

Configuring ESX from a Host Connection

There are many aspects of managing ESX and ESXi clusters. The key, however, is to first understand how to configure a single ESX host and from there branch out to multiple machines. Given that you can manage a host using the vSphere Client, PowerCLI, VMware Management Appliance (vMA), VMware PERL SDK, and so on, where do you start with ESX management? Should we dive directly into everyday management tasks? All our elders state to start at the beginning, so that is what we will do. In the previous chapters, the ESX or ESXi host has been chosen and installed; storage usage has been decided; and auditing has been considered, so now it is time to perform an initial configuration of ESX. The steps and tools to configure ESX or ESXi v4 differ slightly from the steps to configure ESX and ESXi v3. Given this, when we refer to ESX, we refer to both ESX and ESXi unless otherwise specified.

The goal of this chapter is to somehow logically lay out the configuration tasks that might be needed at the beginning of ESX usage and the everyday tasks necessary to continue the usage of ESX. To do this, the organization of this chapter approaches configuration from the tasks necessary to configure ESX after installation. Remember, however, that all the previous chapters, after they are read, will make management easier.

This chapter is more of a collection of how-to's with general discussion on why these work. There are plenty of references available to discuss the details of the configurations either in previous chapters or in other books. Refer to the References element at the end of this book for more details. The tasks include a Rosetta stone of sorts where they are broken down by command line, vSC, and other scripting mechanisms.

Configuration Tasks

The set of tasks to configure ESX and ESXi are finite. For ESX these steps have no particular order, but for ESXi, you need to set the password first. Most, if not all, of the tasks can be completed from the service console. For ESXi, at least the task of setting a password must be done from the management appliance, the rest of the configuration can make use of the vSC, vCLI, or CLI can be used. With large numbers of machines, however, automation is necessary and as of vSphere 4.1 there is automation for the deployment of ESXi available. Table 8.1 outlines the tasks necessary to configure ESX, whether they can be accomplished from the vSC, CLI, or vCLI. In addition, any dependency on order will be highlighted.

Table 8.1 *Configuration Tasks*

Task	vSC	vCLI	CLI	Dependency/ Notes
Administrative user	ESX(i) host only	Yes	useradd	Also within Host Profiles.
Security configuration	ESX(i) host only	No	esxcfg-firewall	Also within Host Profiles.
Network Time Protocol	Yes	No	Edit ntp.conf	Not recommended to be done by hand.
Set Management Network	Yes	No	Yes	ESXi only; ESX done during install.
Set Root Password	No	No	passwd	ESXi requires this to be the very first step.
Service console resources	Yes	Yes	Yes	Requires reboot.

Server-Specific Tasks

Modification of user rights for the host can take place only when logged in to the ESX host in question via the vSC or CLI. This task is generally not available via the VMware vCenter or any other management tools. Host Profiles can store usernames for later application within the cluster however.

The tools chosen to configure an ESX host via the command line can be used to create a configuration script that can be run over multiple hosts as needed. Some of the tasks listed in Table 8.1, specifically NTP and Security configuration settings, are also available using VMware Host Profiles. VMware Host Profiles (available with Enterprise Plus) enables you to create a well known and defined profile that can be used on multiple hosts. Unfortunately, in its current incarnation not everything can be configured within Host Profiles. A partial list of available items is depicted in Figure 8.1.

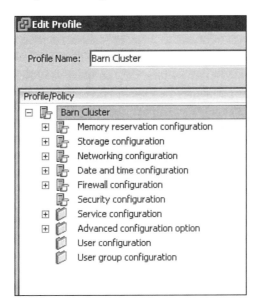

Figure 8.1 *Available Host Profiles elements*

Host Profiles applies a well-known but limited configuration to all nodes within the cluster. In addition, Host Profiles is used to determine if the limited configuration has changed in any way. The Host Profiles configuration is limited because it is not possible to manage all aspects of vSphere configuration via Host Profiles yet.

Although Figure 8.1 shows user elements as well as user and group elements, these elements are not picked up from configuration work performed on a host; instead they need to be modified after the fact. This implies that if you want to maintain the same set of administrative users on a host, you would need to edit the Host Profile and then apply the Host Profile unlike those elements that are above the Folder icons in Figure 8.1. Those elements are automatically determined from the host from which the profile was created.

At this time, Host Profiles is missing many aspects required by the VMware, CISecurity, and DISA Hardening Guidelines available for VMware ESX.

Although it is extremely useful, you must not depend on Host Profiles to maintain every configuration modification made on your hosts. In addition, Host Profiles is incomplete as a tool to verify the entire virtualization configuration. For this you need a good configuration management tool with very good VMware vSphere integration such as VMware ConfigControl, Tripwire Enterprise, or a script you can devise from this chapter as well as the book *VMware vSphere and vSphere Security: Securing the Virtual Environment* (Upper Saddle River, NJ: Prentice Hall, 2009).

Now, on to the base configuration issues.

ESXi Root Password

Unlike VMware vSphere ESX, where the root password is provided during the installation, the root password for ESXi is entered after the fact. It is extremely important to perform this step immediately after installing ESXi to allow you the necessary access to ESXi from the vSC or vCLI. Although there is CLI access to ESXi, this access is in general not necessary and should be avoided.

Setting the root password for ESXi is quite simple, yet will require console access to complete. Follow these steps:

1. When you access the console, press *F2* (you may be prompted for a password—if this is the first time, press *Enter*; otherwise, enter the password).

2. Select *Configure Password*.

3. Enter your password, as shown in Figure 8.2.

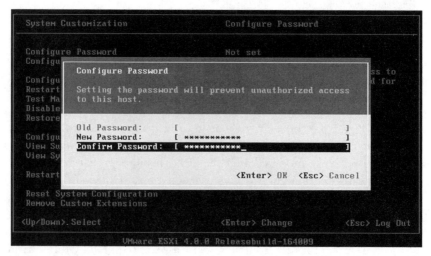

Figure 8.2 *Enter password for ESXi*

ESXi Management Network

When ESXi first boots, it attempts to use a DHCP server and this is frowned upon for virtualization hosts if the DHCP server is also to be hosted as a virtual machine. Although useful for demo labs, it becomes a chicken-and-egg problem if you are also hosting your DHCP servers within the virtualization host, so your ESX and ESXi hosts should always use a static IP address when possible. For ESX, Management Network IP address configuration is part of the installation process; for ESXi, this has to take place after installation. The steps for ESXi are simple:

1. When you access the console, press *F2* (you may be prompted for a password—if this is the first time, press *Enter*; otherwise, enter the password).

2. Select *Configure Management Network*.

3. Select *IP Configuration*.

4. Select *Static IP*, and then enter your assigned IP address, netmask, and gateway, as shown in Figure 8.3. Figure 8.3 is just an example of what to use; the values may not apply to your environment.

5. Select *DNS Configura*tion and enter your DNS IP address. Also, enter your ESXi hostname at this time, as shown in Figure 8.4, which is an example of how to configure DNS and hostnames.

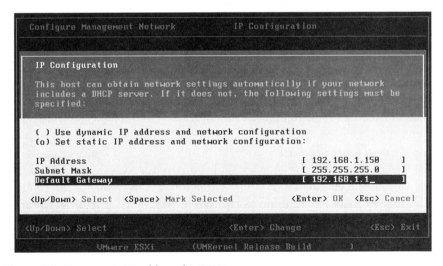

Figure 8.3 *Enter static IP address for ESXi*

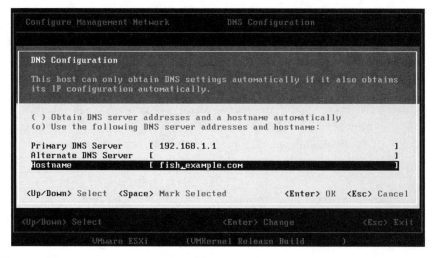

Figure 8.4 *Enter static DNS server and hostname for ESXi*

Create Administrative Users

For all versions of ESX, it is imperative that you create administrative users. Whether or not the users use local or directory service passwords depends on the network security in place. There are various ways to create an administrative user for the desired or policy directed mechanism. Unfortunately, not all these mechanisms are supported by ESXi. Specifically directory service integration is lacking from VMware ESXi until version ESXi 4.1.

The command-line methods encompass more than just one way to create users. A user can be added with a local or remote password. If using a remote password, the user can be a member of an Active Directory (AD) domain, LDAP, or part of NIS. However, when using the vSC connected directly to the host or via Host Profiles, you can create only local user accounts. The integration with a directory service is still configured by hand.

Create Local User via CLI

To create an administrative user with a local password via the command line, use the following commands. Note that adminuser is the name of the administrative user to create. In addition to creating or adding the user, it is important to set the local password for the administrative user.

```
useradd adminuser
passwd adminuser
```

In order for this user to be usable via the vSC, you will need to add the appropriate lines to the /etc/vmware/hostd/authorization.xml file as well.

Assuming no other users have been added previously, you can simply add the following lines after the first `</ACEdata>` tag. Note that for the second and subsequent users to be added, the ID number will need to be increased as new users are added. This includes changing the ACEDataID field.

```
<ACEData id="12">
  <ACEDataEntity>ha-folder-root</ACEDataEntity>
  <ACEDataID>12</ACEDataID>
  <ACEDataIsGroup>false</ACEDataIsGroup>
  <ACEDataPropagate>true</ACEDataProagate>
  <ACEDataRoleID>-1</ACEDataRoleID>
  <ACEDataUser>adminuser</ACEDataUser>
</ACEData>
```

Create Local User via vSC Direct to Host or Host Profiles

You can also connect the vSC to the ESX host in question and create a local user or use Host Profiles to enforce such a user across all your hosts. The Host Profiles approach is available only when connected to vCenter and you have an existing ESX host. However, for the first time, there may be a need to create users when the vSC is connected directly to the ESX host. A user is needed to finish the configuration of at least one host without resorting to direct logins as root (which is never recommended) and if vCenter is not available for use past its demo period.

vSC Connected Directly to ESX/ESXi Host

The steps to create a user when the vSC is connected directly to the ESX or ESXi host follow (see Figure 8.5):

1. Log in to the vSC connecting directly to the ESX or ESXi host in question.

2. Select *Inventory*.

3. Select the *User/Groups* tab.

4. Right-click and then select *Add*.

5. Enter a value in the Login field of the resulting Add New User dialog.

6. Enter the username (more of a description).

7. Enter the UID (usually 500 for the first new user), which must be unique for each user entered. There is no need to directly enter this number unless you want a specific user ID (UID) for a given user. This number is automatically generated when a user is added.

8. Enter Password (occluded) twice.

9. Check *Grant Shell Access to This User*. If you do not grant shell access for the newly created user, the user will not be able to log in directly to the host over SSH or at the console. Some organizations will have policies to not allow this type of behavior. I generally create at least one administrative user on a host to act as a surrogate in case something catastrophic happens, because direct root access is never recommended.

10. Click *OK* to accept the new user.

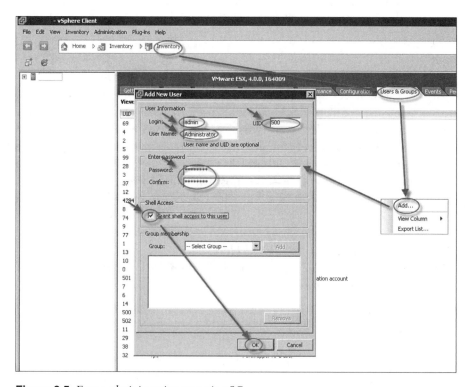

Figure 8.5 *Enter administrative user via vSC*

vSC Connected to vCenter w/Host Profiles

The steps to add a user to Host Profiles, which can then be pushed out to all hosts within the cluster, are slightly more complex but quite similar to the previous mechanisms. This method assumes you have already created a host profile. In Chapter 3, "Installation," we reviewed how to create such a host profile to aid in upgrades and installations.

1. Log in to the vSC connected to VMware vCenter using a user with appropriate privileges to modify Host Profiles.

2. Click *Home* within the Location bar, and then select Host Profiles.

3. Select the Host Profile in question.

4. Select *Edit Host Profile*.

5. Expand the Profile.

6. Right-click *User Configuration* and select *Add Profile*, as shown in Figure 8.6.

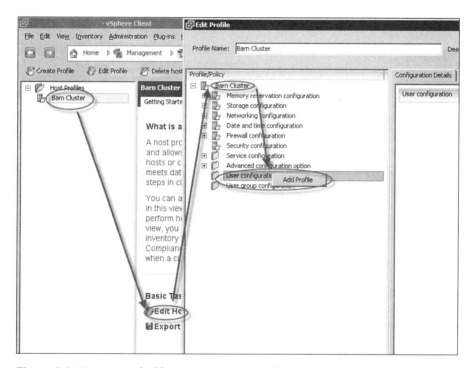

Figure 8.6 *First stage of adding user via Host Profiles*

7. Expand *User Configuration*.

8. Expand *User Profile*.

9. Select *User*.

10. Select *Assign Fixed User Configurations* policy.

11. Enter account identifier (Username).

12. Enter account password (in clear text).

13. Enter account description.

14. Enter Account Posix ID (usually 500 for the first user entered). To find which Posix IDs are already in use, you will need to either log in to the ESX or ESXi host and list out the password file, or connect to the host via the vSC and select the Users tab as if you were going to create a user via the vSC connected to a host. Posix IDs should not be lower than 500 and cannot be higher than 65356. You may want to use a policy that says to start these common IDs at 5000 or some other high number.

15. Check *Allow Shell Access*. If you do not grant shell access for the newly created user, the user will not be able to log in directly to the host over SSH or at the console. Some organizations will have policies to not allow this type of behavior. I generally create at least one administrative user on a host to act as a surrogate in case something catastrophic happens, because direct root access is never recommended.

16. Click *OK* (see Figure 8.7).

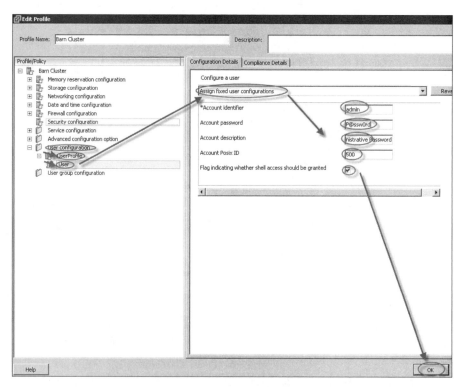

Figure 8.7 *Second stage of adding user via Host Profiles*

Non–Active Directory Network User

All versions of ESX support various forms of non-AD network users from Kerberos, NIS (Yellow Pages), and LDAP. Because most users of ESX use AD rather than the others, we'll cover AD integration in some detail; the other technologies are briefly outlined for ESX. ESX versions earlier than version 3 do not provide the necessary system tools, but all the changes can be made by hand.

A level of Linux experience is necessary to configure these subsystems for ESX. For every `enable` command that follows, there is a `disable` command, too, that does not take any of the extra arguments. In all the following examples the hash mark (#) defines the system prompt for the root user.

NIS

For NIS, all that is needed is the following command, because the service console knows to get the user information from the NIS server for a given NIS domain. In this example the NIS domain is named "domain" and the NIS server is named "server." This information is readily available from your NIS administrator.

```
# esxcfg-auth --enablenis --nisdomain=domain --nisserver=server
```

With NIS, the users are added into the NIS Server and not into the host, providing one central repository for all user authentication control.

Kerberos

For Kerberos, the user information is added using `useradd`, because the remote Kerberos server does not provide user information for the service console; it provides only a way to authenticate the user within a Kerberos realm and against a given server. In this example, the realm is named "domain" and the KDC server is named "server" and the Kerberos administrative server is named "adminServer." This information is readily available from your Kerberos Administrator.

```
# esxcfg-auth --enablekrb5 --krb5realm=domain
--krb5kdc=server --krb5adminserver=adminServer
# useradd adminUser
```

Unlike NIS, use of Kerberos requires users to exist on a given ESX host first.

LDAP

LDAP can provide authentication, and if it is being used, enable the LDAP TLS option. The LDAP TLS option provides a secure path to the LDAP server. Otherwise, credential information is passed to the server using clear text, which would invalidate LDAP as a tool for authentication. LDAP authentication is enabled as follows and requires a local user to complete it, because only the authentication details are available via LDAP:

```
# esxcfg-auth --enableldapauth --enableldaptls
--ldapserver=server --ldapbasedn=basedn
# useradd adminUser
```

Like Kerberos authentication, users must exist on the given ESX host first in order to be authenticated using LDAP.

LDAP User Information

Because the goal of many systems is to *not* store user information locally, another option is available for Kerberos and LDAP authentication, and that is to use LDAP to store the user information. User information is the username, groups, and anything unrelated to authentication credentials. To enable LDAP user information, use the following command. In this example we have provided the LDAP server name of "server" and the LDAP basedn of "basedn." This information is readily available from your LDAP server administrator.

```
# esxcfg-auth --enableldap --ldapserver=server
--ldapbasedn=basedn
```

Active Directory Domain User

There are at least three ways to integrate VMware ESX into Active Directory. For versions of ESX prior to v4.1, the first and most common method is to use only `esxcfg-auth` and then require local users to be created. The second method is to use `esxcfg-auth` but to also write a script to sync users automatically between AD and the host using LDAP queries to achieve the sync. The last method is to configure full AD integration, but that requires a few additional packages to be added to your environment. We'll discuss each of these methods in upcoming paragraphs; however, if you're using vSphere 4.0 or earlier, all these methods have been superseded by VMware's integration of the Likewise Open Active Directory integration software.

ESX Versions < v4.1

The most common integration mechanism is to use the first method listed in the previous paragraph and the next most common is the second method but only if you are heavily into automation. In either case, it is also important to increase the security posture of your ESX host to enable group policy controls often used within Active Directory integrations. Because ESX has no concept of Windows Group Policy Controls, other mechanisms must be used. The simplest way to implement group policies is to use the `pam_access` module for VMware ESX authentication and authorization. To do this, you need to follow some very basic steps.

Just using these commands will require you to create local users that match those found in AD.

1. Add the following line to /etc/pam.d/system-auth.

```
account  [default=bad  success=ok  user_unknown=ignore]  pam_
access.so
```

2. Modify the file /etc/security/access.conf to reflect your group login policy. This will limit who can log in to only those within the given group. You can simply add the appropriate lines to the end of the file. Note this file is order dependent; you would not want to deny all access as the first line. Do not copy this verbatim because it is just an example explained afterward. Only available on ESX as well as ESXi v4.1.

```
+:root:crond console
-:ALL EXCEPT root:vc/1
+:GROUPNAME: NETWORK/NETMASK
+:GROUPNAME: IP1 IP2 IP3
-:ALL:ALL
```

In this example, we are granting root access to the cron daemon, crond, as well as the console. Next, we are disallowing root access to all but virtual console 1 (vc/1), which is accessed using ALT-F1. On the next two lines, we are allowing all users in the group GROUPNAME to log in as long as they are either on the network defined by NETWORK/NETMASK or from one of the following IP addresses: IP1, IP2, or IP3. Last, we deny access to all other users and groups from all other locations. The /etc/security/access.conf file can be as complex or as simple as you desire. In general, and at a bare minimum, you will want to disallow logins unless they are coming from users within the appropriate group and from the appropriate network or IP addresses. For more detailed information use man access.conf from any Linux system or your VMware ESX service console.

Now we are ready to integrate with Active Directory with some level of group policy control also available. To enable partial integration with AD for versions of ESX prior to v4.1, use the following command.

```
# esxcfg-auth --enablead --addomain=VMWARELAB --addc=dc.
vmwarelab.com
```

Now modify /etc/pam.d/system-auth as directed previously.

The next item to do would be to write a script to sync users and groups between AD and the VMware ESX users. The last option is to fully integrate AD into ESX, which is documented within the book *VMware vSphere and Virtual Infrastructure Security*. Also in this book is a script written by Steve Beaver for syncing your users between AD and VMware ESX using LDAP queries.

For ESX >= v4.1

All methods of AD integration have been superseded with ESX and ESXi v4.1. In this latest version of ESX/i, AD integration is configurable only from within the vSphere client or the vSphere SDK. As of v4.1 AD integration is accomplished using the Likewise Open (www.likewise.com) product integrated into both ESX and ESXi. Unlike the standard Likewise installation, which includes command-line tools, Likewise Open is integrated directly into VMware's `hostd` daemon and is exposed only via an API. Note that you should add only virtualization specific users, as users with a large number of groups leads to crashes. Use as few AD groups as possible for these users. To configure AD integration with ESX/i 4.1:

1. Log in to the vSC connected to either the host or vCenter.

2. Select the *Host* to modify.

3. Select the *Configuration* tab.

4. Select the *Authentication Services* link.

5. Select the *Properties* link, as shown in Figure 8.8.

6. In the *Directory Services* Dialog, select the *Active Directory* service type.

7. Enter the Domain Name and click the *Join Domain* button.

8. Enter the appropriate credentials for the Domain Admin to use for joining the domain.

9. Click the Join Domain button, as shown in Figure 8.9.

Security Configuration

Similar to adding an administrative user, the security configuration of ESX can occur only with a direct connection to the ESX host in question or via Host Profiles. The security configuration of ESX covered herein is how to limit access the network daemons, not how to harden the ESX hosts. ESXi has no built-in mechanism to protect its daemons and should be placed behind a firewall. Unlike the user discussion mentioned previously, Host Profiles will pick up the configuration changes from the host used for the baseline. Unlike initial user configurations the ESX firewall can be modified when connected to VMware vCenter.

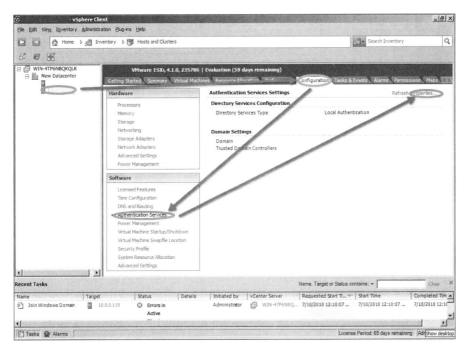

Figure 8.8 *Initiating Active Directory integration*

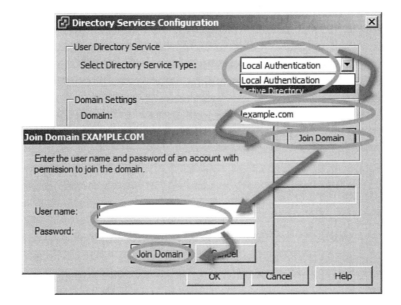

Figure 8.9 *Active Directory integration*

Command Line

ESX v4 and v3 implement a real packet-filtering firewall within the service console and have the capability to configure a defense in depth. Note that because this is not available within ESXi the vCLI does not contain the appropriate commands, yet you can make the necessary changes to ESXi using the VI SDK tools.

ESX has a single tool that controls security via the command line. The use of the esxcfg-firewall is functionally the same as using the vSC to modify the host firewall configuration, because it modifies the same local ESX host databases. By default, ESX has most services and ports disabled, but some services and ports should be enabled to allow for outbound SSH, Network Time Protocol, and the use of hardware vendor management agents. We are therefore concerned only with allowing the Network Time Protocol and outbound SSH. The following commands will do this:

```
# /usr/sbin/esxcfg-firewall -e ntpClient
# /usr/sbin/esxcfg-firewall -e sshClient
```

To determine all the possible esxcfg-firewall settings, run esxcfg-firewall –h and use the –l option to list the current firewall rules and the –s option to find a full list of protocols and ports to open or close.

vSphere Client (vSC)

The vSC, when connected directly to the ESX host, or when connected to vCenter can modify the ESX host firewall. Although many changes can be made, the equivalents to the command-line changes are outlined in the following steps:

1. After having logged in to the vSC, select the Configuration tab, and then the Security Profile software configuration element. Click the Properties link.

2. When the Security Profile dialog appears, check the SSH Client and NTP Client boxes (see Figure 8.10), and then click OK.

3. Review the changes to the security profile in the resulting configuration screen.

Network Time Protocol (NTP)

Configuring NTP is basically the same for ESX v3 and v4 systems. With vSphere, Host Profiles can be used to ensure that multiple ESX v4 hosts have an identical NTP configuration. Configuring NTP from the CLI is NOT recommended but sometimes is convenient for automated configurations.

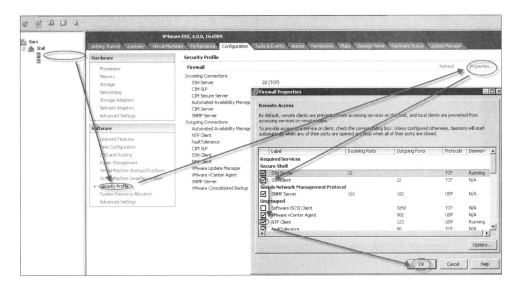

Figure 8.10 *Security profile properties*

Configuring NTP Via vSphere Client

From the vSC, use the following steps to configure NTP (as shown in Figures 8.11 and 8.12):

1. Log in to the vSC connected to either the host or vCenter.

2. Select the *Host* to modify.

3. Select the *Configuration* tab.

4. Select the *Time Configuration* link.

5. Select the *Properties* link, as shown in Figure 8.11.

6. Click the *Options* button.

7. Select *NTP Settings* and then the *Add* button.

8. Enter your NTP Server IP Address and click *OK*.

9. Check *Restart NTP Server to apply changes*.

10. Click the *OK* button.

11. Ensure *NTP Client Enabled* is checked.

12. Click the *OK* button, as shown in Figure 8.12.

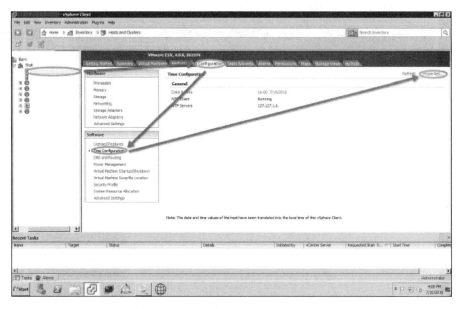

Figure 8.11 *Initial Configure NTP via the vSC*

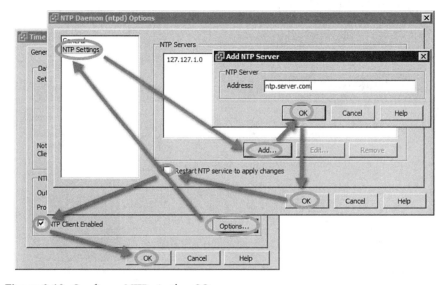

Figure 8.12 *Configure NTP via the vSC*

Note that the use of the vSC to configure NTP implies several things. First, the NTP Client firewall port will automatically be opened on ESX. Second, if the host is used as the baseline for Host Profiles, all changes to NTP and the firewall ports will automatically be picked up by Host Profiles, thereby not requiring any further modifications to the system.

It is possible to independently configure Host Profiles with the proper NTP configuration as well, thereby not requiring a baseline server. This also means it is possible to easily make sweeping NTP changes across your entire cluster just by modifying the NTP policy within Host Profiles.

Configuring NTP Via CLI

Again, configuration of NTP via the CLI is *not* recommended, because the vSC has a mechanism to configure NTP. Updating NTP via the CLI does not properly update the ESX configuration to be usable by Host Profiles. Use of the CLI method will require you to open the NTP Client firewall port by hand. From the CLI, use the following steps to configure NTP:

1. Create a script to add the IP addresses of each time source to the /etc/ ntp/step-tickers file (the a.b.c.d and e.f.g.h are the IP addresses of your time sources—do not use these values):

```
timesources="a.b.c.d e.f.g.h"
for x in $timesources
do
     echo $x >> /etc/ntp/step-tickers
done
```

Execute the created script.

2. Modify the NTP service configuration file, /etc/ntp.conf, to comment out any restrictions by running this command from the CLI.

```
/bin/sed '/^restrict/s/^/\#/' /etc/ntp.conf > /tmp/ntp.conf
/bin/mv -f /tmp/ntp.conf /etc/ntp.conf
```

3. Create a script to modify the NTP service configuration file, /etc/ntp. conf, to add in the IP address of each time source as a server (the a.b.c.d and e.f.g.h are the IP addresses of your time sources—do not use these values):

```
timesources="a.b.c.d e.f.g.h"
for x in $timesources
do
     echo "server $x" >> /etc/ntp.conf
done
Execute the created script.
```

4. Ensure the firewall allows the NTP client to work by executing the command:

```
# /usr/sbin/esxcfg-firewall -e ntpClient
```

5. Start the NTP service and use the `chkconfig` command to configure it to autostart:

```
# /sbin/service ntpd start
# /sbin/chkconfig ntpd on
```

Service Console Memory

For vSphere, there is no longer a need to modify the Service Console Memory because the service console now runs as a VM and has a default unlimited memory limit. Instead, you can set memory shares and limits for various aspects of the hypervisor command daemons. What it boils down to is that the COS is no longer responsible for a lot of the things it used to get involved with, so it doesn't need a variable RAM allocation.

In essence, this step is no longer required for vSphere but is still required for ESX v3.

The vSphere resources for the service console are set using the following mechanism. This mechanism works for both ESX and ESXi. The default settings for the system resources should be sufficient; however, if you need to change them, use the following mechanism, as shown in Figure 8.13. Use caution when making changes to the system resource pools. You can break your system and make it inoperable!

1. Select the *Host and Configuration* tab.

2. Select the *System Resource Allocation* link to show the current allocations.

3. Select the *Edit Link* to bring up the standard resource editor for setting memory and CPU resource limits.

4. Modify the custom resource values where appropriate.

5. Click *OK* to save the values.

These changes do not require a reboot of the server but will take up more resources as required for both CPU and memory resources.

You can alternatively change only those elements related to specific components of the ESX or ESXi management appliance by choosing the advanced option. This allows you to change CPU and memory resources for the specific elements using the standard resource limit editor. Unless you get advice directly from VMware or your support organization, using this advanced option is not recommended. Figure 8.14 shows all those items that can have their resources adjusted.

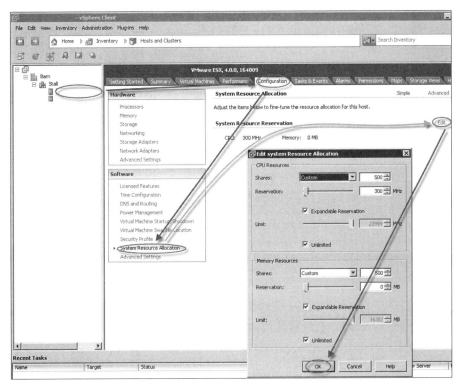

Figure 8.13 *Simple system resource limits*

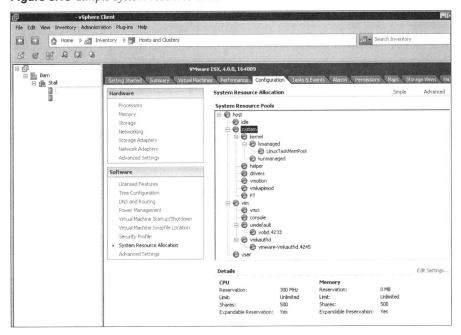

Figure 8.14 *Advanced system resource limits*

There is no CLI mechanism to change these resources. You can, however, make the necessary changes using PowerCLI or any of the other vSphere SDKs.

Command Line (ESX v3)

There is no easy way to change the amount of memory allocated to the service console from the command line.

To change the amount of memory from the command line in ESX, there are several steps. Be forewarned, however, that these steps are dangerous, and unless there is sufficient Linux experience available, they should be avoided.

1. Edit the file /etc/grub.conf.

2. Copy the first stanza in the file to the end of the file. The first line of the stanza will start with title and end the line before the next title. This copy provides a way to get back to where the system was prior to these changes.

3. Rename the new stanza by changing the title line appropriately.

4. Edit the uppermem line to reflect the total amount of allocated memory in kilobytes assigned to the service console.

5. Edit the kernel line to change the mem=XXXM parameter. XXX reflects the total amount of memory in megabytes assigned to the service console.

6. Save and exit the file.

7. Reboot the server and select the new title from the boot screen. After this works, change the default setting in /etc/grub.conf to reflect the new stanza number.

8. It now will be necessary to modify the /etc/esx.conf file to reflect the proper setting for /boot/memSize.

The previous eight steps can be scripted as follows. Note we are changing the memory size of the service console from 272 to 512MB:

```
# sed -e 's/boot\/memSize = \"272\"/boot\/memSize =
\"512\"/g'/etc/vmware/esx.conf > /tmp/esx.conf
# sed -e 's/uppermem 277504/uppermem 523264/g' -e 's/
mem=272M/mem=512M/g'
# /boot/grub/grub.conf > /tmp/grub.conf
# /bin/mv /tmp/esx.conf /etc/vmware/esx.conf
# /bin/mv /tmp/grub.conf /boot/grub/grub.conf
```

Remember that the preceding steps are extremely dangerous and should be avoided unless absolutely necessary.

vSC (ESX v3)

The vSC, when connected directly or indirectly to the ESX host, can modify the ESX service console resources.

1. After having logged in to the vSC with appropriate credentials that can modify service console memory configurations, select the *Configuration* tab and then *Memory Configuration*.

2. Click the *Properties* link to display the dialog in which to change the service console memory allocation.

3. Change the value of the allocated memory to the appropriate number, and then click *OK* and review the changes to the memory in the resulting configuration screen.

Remember this change requires a reboot.

Patching ESX and ESXi

One of the most important items to complete prior to placing an ESX or ESXi host into production is to patch your system. With vSphere, there are several ways to accomplish this. The recommended way is to use the VMware Update Manager. However, this method requires that you have an existing VMware vCenter server already available and that you can install the VMware Update Manager to work with the VMware vCenter server. If this is not possible you can use the vSphere Host Update Utility (which is being deprecated) that is bundled with the VMware vSphere client (ALL package). Either way, you need to download the patches from the VMware patch repository to a local system in order to apply them.

Patching VIA vSphere Host Update Utility

If you are installing your first host, this is the initial option to take. You really do not want to place a host that has not been properly patched into production. The steps are very simple:

1. Launch the vSphere Host Update Utility, and immediately you will be asked whether you want to download the patches. In almost all cases, you will want to click the *Yes* button, as shown in Figure 8.15.

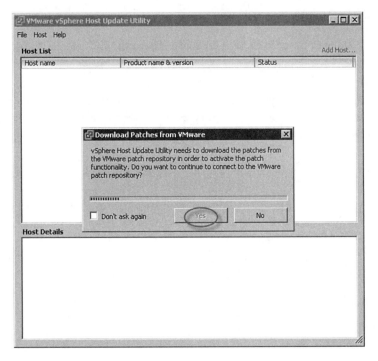

Figure 8.15 *vSphere Host Update Utility*

2. Add a host into the client by selecting the *Add Host* link in the upper right of the window.

3. Enter your hostname and then select the host.

4. Click the *Scan for Patches* button, which will also ask to download patches from VMware.

5. Enter in your Host credentials. This should be the root account because you are connecting directly to the host in question. This is also the primary reason to use VMware Update Manager instead, because the credentials for that do not need to be root or the administrator.

6. Verify whether any patches are necessary. Instead of blindly applying patches, you need to review the list of patches to determine which ones are required for your environment. For example, if there is a Fibre Channel patch but you do not use Fibre Channel, do you need to apply it? Most people apply all patches, but that is not necessary in all cases. You should know the patches you are applying.

7. Click the *Patch Host* button to display a list of patches.

8. Select the patches to apply.

9. Click the *Install* button to apply the selected patches (see Figure 8.16).

If you have hosts that are also managed by vCenter they will show up within the client as well, if you have the VUM Client also installed on the workstation from which you run the host update utility. The Host Update Utility has been deprecated as of vSphere 4.1.

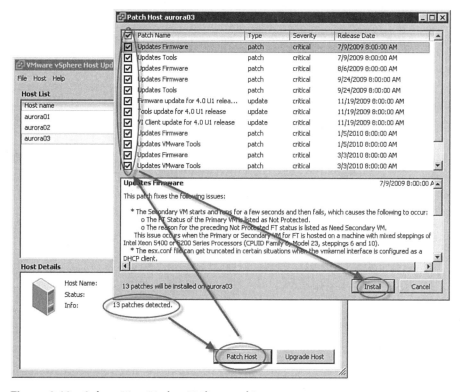

Figure 8.16 *vSphere Host Update Utility patching*

Patching VIA VMware Update Manager

After installing the VMware Update Manager (VUM),s you need to also install the VMware Update Manager Client into your vSC as a plug-in. This plug-in will enable you to manage the patch state of your ESX and ESXi hosts as well as the patch state of your VMs. We will concentrate on hosts within this discussion. VUM is a simple Microsoft installer package that most people install upon their vCenter Server host, but can be installed on another host. The vSC client is downloadable from the vCenter Server after VUM is installed and available for use. This client is installed using the vSC plug-in manager.

Before you can begin, however, you must configure VUM to download patches on a regular basis, attach your hosts, and pick out baselines to which your hosts can be compared. The most important critical component of all this is picking the appropriate time to download patches. You do not want to be downloading patches and updates when everyone else is doing so, nor when such a load could upset your Internet bandwidth. Also be aware that unless there is a security or emergency patch VMware does not often provide patches more than once a quarter.

To configure the VUM setup, do the following:

1. Click *Home* and then *Update Manager* to get to the Update Manager configuration screens. Alternatively, you could select a host, then *Update Manager*, and then the *Admin View* link.

2. Click the *Configuration* tab.

3. Make any necessary changes to the Network Connectivity screen.

4. Select the patch download settings and decide what to download. In most cases, you will need to select only one version of ESX, but if you are in a hybrid ESXv3 and ESX v4 environment, pick both. In general, I do not use VUM to patch my VMs because there are other mechanisms to do so, so I do not choose the VM options. If you want to patch VMs using VUM it is much the same as patching a host, you select the VM patches as well as the host patches.

5. If you use a proxy, now is the time to set those settings.

6. If this is the first time you have installed and used VUM, you may want to click the *Download Now* button.

7. Select the *Patch Download Settings* link to set up your download schedule. This is where you enter the information you have chosen that meets your patch requirements and network bandwidth requirements (see Figure 8.17).

8. In general, no other changes are required, but if you need to make them, now is the time.

VUM is now configured so you can switch back to the Compliance View using the appropriate link in the upper right of the Admin View windows. We can now attach baselines to the hosts in question and then run a scan and remediate as necessary. By default, two preconfigured baselines are attached to all hosts: Critical Host Patches and Non-Critical Host Patches. If these do not apply, you can create an independent baseline of any patch elements. The best practice is to use these two predefined patch baselines. To verify the patch compliance of an existing host, use the following steps (see Figure 8.18).

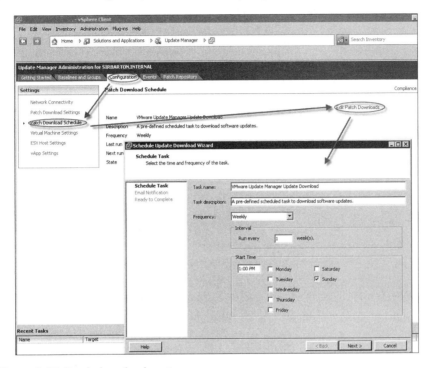

Figure 8.17 *Patch download settings*

1. Click the host to scan and then click the *Update Manager* tab. You will immediately see your current compliance shown as a big red or green circle.

2. Click the *Scan* link to scan your host against all the available patches and baselines.

3. If the host is out of compliance, click the *Remediate* button. However, this step has some gotchas!

The gotchas are related to whether you have vMotion available. To remediate an ESX or ESXi host all VMs must first be migrated from the host using vMotion or shutdown the VMs manually. If you have vMotion, this migration will take place automatically when the host is placed within Maintenance Mode. This sounds all fairly reasonable. The gotcha occurs when you also use VMware DRS in one of its partial automation modes. You will need to go to the DRS screen and okay any vMotion suggestions by hand.

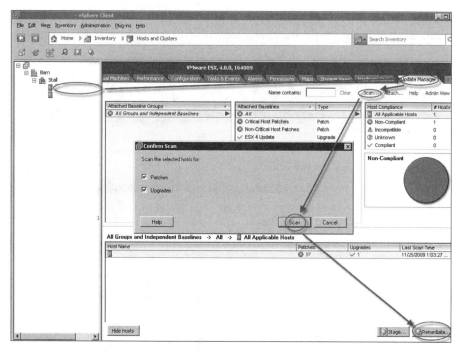

Figure 8.18 *VMware Update Manager Scan and Remediate*

> ### Best Practice
>
> When DRS is in use and you attempt to remediate a host, also check the DRS suggestions to ensure the vMotions are not waiting on approval.

If you are using VUM to patch VMs, the process is the same; but instead of applying the process to a host you are applying it directly to VMs. There are many ways to keep the Guest Operating Systems patched and up to date. VUM is the way to keep the hosts up to date and alternative for guests.

Conclusion

In this chapter, we delved into the special configuration requirements for allowing the initial connection to ESXi (setting a password and IP information) as well as how to add users by connecting the vSC directly to the host or using Host Profiles. In addition, we have covered the items that should be done first before VMs are created, such as increasing host memory and patching your system. All these items should be done prior to creating VMs on or moving VMs to this host, specifically anything related to networking and the service console, because these items require reboots. In essence, that means all the first-time tasks. The next chapter covers those tasks that can be completed either while connected to the host or via vCenter while not requiring reboots to complete.

Chapter 9

Configuring ESX from a Virtual Center or Host

This chapter is really a continuation of Chapter 8, "Configuring ESX from a Host Connection." However, this chapter makes use of the vSphere Client (vSC) connected to either the host or through the VMware vCenter Server (vCenter). This chapter continues the Rosetta stone approach to configuring the ESX host following the steps that I find most useful. Although these steps are by no means a complete list of configuration tasks, most common and some uncommon ones are discussed.

Most, if not all, the CLI methods listed within this chapter will eventually disappear as ESXi becomes more prevalent. As such, it is important to start using one of the vSphere SDK toolsets to make all your necessary changes to ESX or ESXi for use with automation. One such toolset is the vSphere PowerCLI (PowerShell), which currently runs only on a Windows machine. If you have MacOS, Linux, or some other operating system, you can check out the vGhetto Client available from SourceForge (http://vghetto.sourceforge.net). The vGhetto Client makes use of the vSphere Perl SDK and is composed of individual scripts as well as a Perl/TK graphical client that will run on all operating systems that support Perl/TK. For PowerShell scripts that do many of the items listed, check out VESI (www.thevesi.org) and Alan Renouf's site (www.virtu-al.net), among others.

Note that, throughout this chapter, I use the term ESX; unless otherwise noted, it also applies to ESXi, either directly or via the Virtual Management Appliance, vMA.

Configuration Tasks

The following list of configuration tasks (see Table 9.1) starts where the list in Chapter 8 left off. These tasks cover the intricacies of configuring the system for future virtual machines hosting.

Table 9.1 *Configuration Tasks*

Task	vSC	MUI	COS	Dependency/ Notes
Join host to vCenter	Yes	N/A	N/A	Before using the vCenter, configure servers
Licensing	Yes	Yes	Special script	Prior to HA/ DRS
Local VMFS	Yes	Yes	`vmkfstools`	Usually part of install
FC HBA VMFS	Yes	Yes	`vmkmultipa-thesxcfg-vm-hbadevsesx-cfg-rescan`	Chapters 5, "Storage with ESX," and 6, "Effects on Operations"
Virtual net-working	Yes	Yes	`esxcfg-vm-nicesxcfg-vswitchesx-cfg-route`	Chapter 7, "Networking"
iSCSI VMFS	Yes	N/A	`esxcfg-swiscis`	Chapters 5, 6, and 7
NFS	Yes	N/A	`esxcfg-nas`	Chapter 7

Join Host to vCenter

If vCenter is available, now is the time to add it into the system. The process is the same for vCenter v2 and v4. vCenter is the main tool for managing multiple ESX hosts, and vCenter v4 can manage ESX and ESXi v3 and v4 as well as read-only mode for earlier versions of ESX. It is a common interface and the only way to get access to the advanced features of ESX v4, such as VMware HA, FT, vMotion, Storage vMotion, DRS. The steps for adding a host into vCenter follow:

1. Log in to vCenter via the vSphere Client.

2. Create a datacenter (*File*, *New*, *Datacenter*) and give the new datacenter a name. All hosts within a datacenter can share templates and so on.

3. Select the datacenter, and then add a host to the datacenter (*File*, *Add Host*).

4. Make sure the hostname is resolvable by DNS. It is strongly urged that the FQDN be used; otherwise, VMware HA will have issues. It is also important that the ESX host can ping itself and other hosts by hostname; otherwise, there can be VMware HA issues.

5. Enter the username and password for the root account for the host.

6. vCenter will now contact the host in question and present some information about the host, including the machine type and VMs it has. vCenter should be on the same side of the Virtualization Management network because each of the ESX hosts itself. Access to vCenter should be via firewall, as discussed in Chapter 7.

7. Pick a location or VM folder in which to place the VMs within that host. A VM folder can be created at any time; they are independent of hosts and are covered in Chapter 10, "Virtual Machines."

8. Click *Finish* to add the host to vCenter.

Now vCenter can be used to manage the host in question and configure the advanced options of VMware vSphere. Note that the vSphere SDK can be used to add hosts into vCenter but it is not possible to do so from the CLI or vCLI directly.

Licensing

There are two licensing mechanisms to consider when discussing licensing. By two mechanisms, I mean whether we are talking about ESX v3 or ESX v4 licenses, because they are distinctly different. To manage ESX v3 from within vCenter v4, you need to point vCenter v4 to your license server used for ESX v3. The Flexera (previously FlexLM) license server is at its end of life for VMware products. This, combined with the fact that there was an increase in support calls directly related to the license server forced VMware to revert back to a key-based host license, not a server-based license.

When you purchase a license from VMware or a reseller, you receive an activation code. This code is *not* your license. You need to log in to your VMware account and register the activation code to retrieve your license file (ESX v3) or your license key (ESX v4).

ESX v4

With the advent of vSphere, VMware again radically changed its licensing. Instead of requiring a license server, VMware switched to a key-based license. The key can be entered during installation of all VMware products or by using one of the provided mechanisms. In many cases the license key in use will be entered during installation of ESX, ESXi, or vCenter. Yet, if you want to temporarily make use of such things as Host Profiles and other advanced features, you do not want to enter the license key on installation, but after you have finished upgrading, installing, and configuring your virtual environment. The temporary full Enterprise Plus demo mode provides sufficient time (30 days) to make use of these tools to aid in upgrades and configurations. When upgrading from ESX v3 to v4, the temporary availability of Host Profiles, vMotion, and Storage vMotion is quite useful.

Command Line

Because the CLI is going away, you may instead want to use a vSphere SDK tool to set the license key from a script, because the CLI methods do only half the job and are therefore incomplete.

Configuring Licensing with the vSphere Client

There are four steps to this process if you are migrating from ESX v3 to v4. The first is to enable vCenter v4 to access the license server, as shown in Figure 9.1. The second is to use evaluation licenses for vCenter v4; the third is to take advantage of the advanced features available with the evaluation licenses to affect your migration from VI3 to vSphere; and the last is to use your real licenses for ESX v4 after your migration is completed. Remember you have only 30 days to install, upgrade, and configure your ESX hosts before the evaluation licenses expire. This all assumes your real license does not have entitlement to the advanced features. If you do have entitlement, use your real licenses.

Enable vCenter v4 to Use License Manager for v3

To enable vCenter v4 to manage ESX v3 and use the VMware License Manager, you need to first tell vCenter v4 about the license manager. During migrations from ESX v3 to ESX v4, this step is paramount (see Figure 9.1).

1. Connect the vSC to vCenter v4.

2. Select the *Administration* menu and then the *vCenter Server Settings* option.

3. Select the *Licensing* link (which should be the default).

4. Check the *Reconfigure ESX 3 Hosts Using License Servers to Use This Server* setting.

5. Enter your License Server, which will be 27000@hostname, where hostname is a fully qualified domain name or IP address of the license server host.

6. Click the *OK* button.

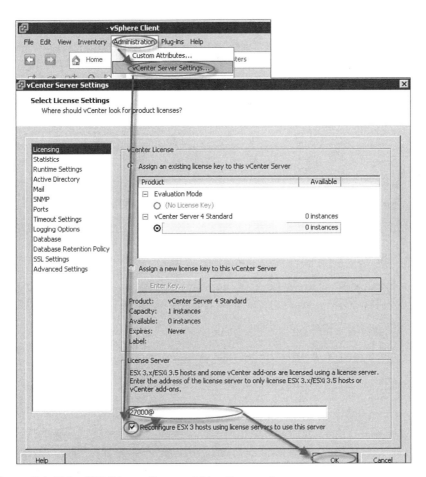

Figure 9.1 *Using VI3 License Server within vCenter v4*

vCenter v4 is now configured to use the license manager for managing ESX v3 host licenses. Even if you want to just upgrade to vCenter v4 and are not quite ready to upgrade your ESX hosts, this step is required.

> ### Best Practice
>
> Point vCenter v4 at your Virtual Infrastructure 3 (VI3) License Server during migrations.

Modify the vCenter License with a New License Key

After your migration from VI3 is complete, you can add your vCenter v4 license key into vCenter to enable those features that you have purchased. This key can be entered at any time, but if you do not have the Enterprise Plus license, you may want to use the demo licenses until your migration is completed. Remember, the activation code delivered to you is not your actual license key; for that you need to go to the VMware online store to gain access to your key. The activation code is needed to complete your registration and then to access your keys (see Figure 9.2).

1. Connect the vSC to vCenter v4.

2. Select the *Administration* menu and then the *vCenter Server Settings* option.

3. Select the *Licensing* link (which should be the default).

4. Click the *Assign a New License Key to This vCenter Server* option.

5. Click the *Enter Key* button.

6. Enter your license key for vCenter Server that you retrieved from VMware.

7. Optionally give the key a label. Labels often help with reporting.

8. Click the *OK* button in the Add License Key dialog.

9. Click the *OK* button in the vCenter Server Settings dialog.

Add/Modify the ESX Host with a New License Key

Changing or adding a license key for ESX v4 using the vSC is a somewhat more difficult process than the ones for vCenter v4, even though the dialog boxes look quite similar. The start, however, is via the configuration for the specific host involved. License keys are delivered for a set number of sockets and for up to

6 or 12 cores per socket. One key can usually be used for more than one host, because the keys can be split up among all your ESX v4 hosts (see Figure 9.3).

1. Connect the vSC to vCenter v4.

2. Select the ESX v4 host in question.

3. Select the *Configuration* tab.

4. Select the *Licensed Features* link under the Software section.

5. Click the *Edit* link.

6. Click *Assign a New License Key to This Host.*

7. Click the *Enter Key* button.

8. Enter your license key for vCenter Server that you retrieved from VMware.

9. Optionally, give the key a label; labels often help with reporting.

10. Click the *OK* button in the Add License Key dialog.

11. Click the OK button on the Assign Licenses dialog.

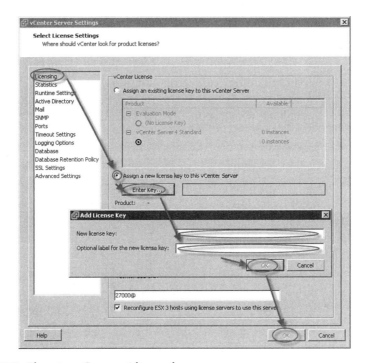

Figure 9.2 *Changing vCenter v4 license key*

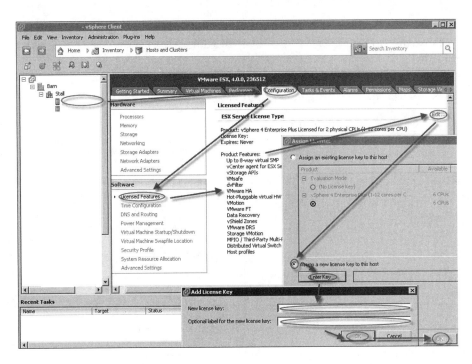

Figure 9.3 *Changing ESX v4 license key*

If you already have installed vSphere, you can make use of your existing licenses. In Figure 9.3, we see that there are still six CPUs (sockets) to assign to your hosts. If you are adding new hosts and have available CPUs on your licenses, you do not need to assign a new license key, but instead assign an existing license key to the host, which is the preferred mechanism.

Licensing for ESX v3

ESX v3 uses either a host-based license or a server license that makes use of Flex-LM from Flexera. A FlexLM server is required for any advanced ESX features such as vMotion, VMware HA, or DRS. The best practice for a License Server is to make it the same as the vCenter Server and to have both of them running as a separate physical machine and not as a VM. The reason for this may not be obvious, but it is important. If a license expires, the ESX host will cache the license key for 14 days. If the License Server is not accessible for any reason, for 14 days VMs will fail to power on, yet running VMs will continue to operate. Therefore, if there is a slip, it is possible that all the VMs will fail to boot on an ESX system reboot. FlexLM is beyond the scope of this book, but you can find FlexLM documentation on the Flexera website (www.flexerasoftware.com).

If the License Server or the vCenter Server is also running as a VM, then on an ESX host failure where these VMs are running, no form of VMware-based redundancy will take effect. The best practice, therefore, is for the vCenter and License Servers to reside on a pair of clustered physical machines or on a separate ESX cluster dedicated to management tools.

To configure ESX or ESXi 3.x, you must also install the VMware Virtual Infrastructure Client (VIC) software. Although you still access the v3.x hosts via the vSphere Client, the libraries from the VIC are required to perform configuration. In many cases, this is not an issue because most will upgrade from v3.x to v4.x of ESX or ESXi. But for the few, when you start the vSphere Client, if it says it needs to download some software to support the older version of ESX, do so and install the software.

Configuring Licensing for ESX v3 via the Command Line
There is no easy command-line mechanism available to enter ESX license keys.

If the license is for use within the License server and not for use within the host, it is possible to configure the server to see the License Server. To do this, modify the file `/etc/vmware/license.cfg` and set the MODE option to be server and the SERVER option to be 27000@licenseServerIPAddress. The hostname of the License Server can also be used. If the License Server is unreachable for more than 14 days, all licenses are revoked and no VMs can be powered up on the ESX host until such time as the problem is fixed.

Configuring Licensing for ESX v3 via the vSphere Client
To proceed with this step using the VMware vSphere Client and vCenter v4, you need to first tell vCenter about the VI3 License Server, which is covered in the "Enable vCenter v4 to Use License Manager for V3" section for ESX v4. If host-based licenses are in use, the license server is still required for advanced functionality, such as vMotion, Storage vMotion, DRS, and EVC.

The vSC, when connected directly or indirectly to the ESX host, can modify the ESX host licenses.

1. After you are logged in to the vSC, select the *Configuration* tab and then the *Licensed Feature* software configuration element (see Figure 9.4). When this is displayed, click the first blue *Edit* link.

2. Elect whether to use a host-based license or to use a License Server. When choosing a License Server, enter the FQDN or the IP address of the License Server, per Figure 9.5) and click *OK*.

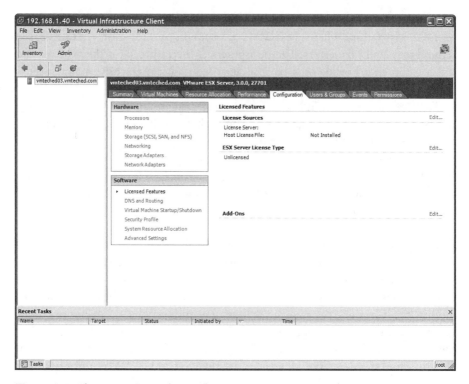

Figure 9.4 *Changing ESX v3 license key*

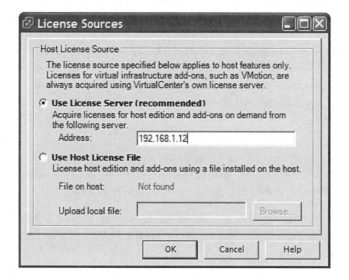

Figure 9.5 *Changing ESX v3 license key type*

3. On the Licensed Features configuration screen, click the next highlighted Edit link opposite ESX host License Type. The license type served by the License Server is selectable. If only Unlicensed is available, this indicates that the License Server has no more licenses. Select the server license, in this case ESX host Standard (see Figure 9.6), and click *OK*.

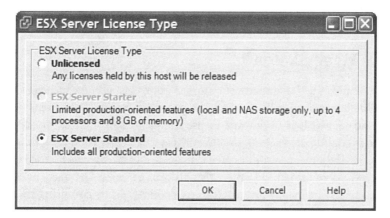

Figure 9.6 *Enable ESX v3 license key features*

4. On the Licensed Features configuration screen, click the next highlighted Edit link opposite Add-Ons. Enable those add-ons available to the license granted. The add-ons include VMware DR and HA and consolidated backups.

Virtual Swap

An important part of the vSphere memory overcommit mechanisms is the concept of virtual swap. When a virtual machine boots, a virtual swap file is created automatically and removed when a VM shuts down. However, it is possible to create VMs with memory limits and reservations so that virtual swap would never be used. We discuss this in Chapter 10.

The discussion these days is whether per VM virtual swap should live on a different datastore than the VM in question. This could either be a discussion of performance or cost. If you place the virtual swap on a unique datastore, you are incurring extra cost in disks, controllers, and so forth. If you do allow virtual swap usage, you could assign Solid State Drives (SSDs) to virtual swap because when your VMs begin to swap, this needs to be as fast as possible. Granted, you want to avoid virtual swap usage as much as possible.

This is a per-VM change that can be inherited from the cluster configuration and unrelated to the general system maintenance other than to consider the possibility of using high-speed disks for virtual swap. Please note that virtual swap should be on shared storage in order for FT and vMotion to behave appropriately. vMotion does not require virtual swap to be on shared storage, but movement of a VM will create a virtual swap on the target host and as such you may want to alleviate the extra work by keeping virtual swap on shared storage.

VMFS Manipulation

It is very important to manage your storage appropriately. As such, the following is a breakdown of tasks that may be necessary for local- and remote-based VMFS and LUNs. It is important to use unique names for each local storage device across all hosts such as the default naming convention used when adding local VMFS during install or via vSC: hostname:storage1. The reason is that the vSC, connected to vCenter, sees all storage devices at once, and having multiple names such as storage1 or datastore1 can be confusing to the end users. The best practice is to use the machine hostname as part of the local storage device name, which is the default when using the vSC to add local VMFS.

Local VMFS has many uses, not the least of which is its use as a repository for the most important VMs to protect against storage failure if a hot site is not also in use. With vSphere or any version of ESXi, the ESX operating system is installed within a VMFS. Keeping this as a local VMFS has its benefits. If you boot from SAN, the VMFS for ESX use is placed within the boot LUN presented to the host by the SAN. If you are creating Microsoft Clusters in a box, then use of local VMFS is generally a requirement for older versions of ESX and will still work within vSphere as such.

A few comments on names used by the CLI and vCLI for disk manipulations are in order because there are many names for the same device within VMware ESX, and it leads to confusion. There is the Cryptic Name and the VML name; either can be used interchangeably. However, you will most likely want to use the VML name because it is the name most of the VMware utilities want to use. The following shows the cryptic name, the device name, and the VML name. The command in ESX v4 is esxcfg-scsidevs and esxcfg-vmhbadevs in ESX v3. We will use these names in the following discussions. For ESX v4:

```
# esxcfg-scsidevs -l
mpx.vmhba0:C0:T1:L0  ← CRYPTIC NAME
    Device Type: Direct-Access
    Size: 279964 MB
    Display Name: Local VMware Disk (mpx.vmhba0:C0:T1:L0)
    Plugin: NMP
    Console Device: /dev/cciss/c0d1  ← DEVICE NAME
```

```
Devfs Path: /vmfs/devices/disks/mpx.vmhba0:C0:T1:L0
Vendor: VMware    Model: Block device    Revis: 1.0
SCSI Level: 2  Is Pseudo: false Status: on
Is RDM Capable: false Is Removable: false
Is Local: true
Other Names:
    vml.0000000000766d686261303a313a30 ← VML NAME
```

For ESX v3:

```
# esxcfg-vmhbadevs
vmhba:0:0:0 /dev/sda ← CRYPTIC NAME/DEVICE NAME
```

Rename Local VMFS via Command Line

Because the local VMFS could be the same across all hosts and is often defined as a cryptic name, `mpx.vmhbaC:T:L:P`, it is important to rename this to be something more readable and representing the host on which it resides. If the file system is to be created—that is, it is not already existent—you can use the -S option in `vmkfstools` to name the file system. However, this option works only on creation. So, there are two choices for an existing VMFS: either delete and re-create or label the volume either within the vSphere client or using the symbolic link method mentioned later in this section.

Connect to Storage Device

Before we can begin with many of these tasks, we must first connect to the storage device. In the case of NAS, these commands used within the following sections are not useful because a NAS connects using NFSv3 over TCP, and as such, it is not a block-level device but serves up individual files. For all of these tools discussed, we need to use the data found from the output of `esxcfg-info`. Therefore, we suggest you capture that output to a file for easier searching.

FC SAN

For FC SAN, there is also not much to do except to get a full list of the World Wide Port Names. There are two ways to do this on an ESX system and one that will work from both the vCLI and CLI if you already have devices mapped to the system. Use the following `esxcfg-info` command, which will return the appropriate data for just the adapters in use that you can then send on to your storage administrator, specifically the hex value of the World Wide Port Number used by FC-SAN devices for zoning and presentation. In the example, the newlines are important for the command and are preceded with a backslash. This example allows you to find the World Wide Port Numbers for a FC SAN using the CLI. In this and all following sections, the hash mark (#) represents the prompt for the root user.

```
# esxcfg-info | awk '/World Wide Port Number/{gn=1;}\
gn>0 { print $0; gn++; }\
gn>5 { gn=0; }'
            |----World Wide Port Number.......................
.....0x50014380029ab674
            |----World Wide Node Number.......................
.....0x50014380029ab675
        \==+SCSI Interface :
            |----Name.......................................
.....vmhba1
            |----
UID.............................................
fc.50014380029ab
675:50014380029ab674
            |----World Wide Port Number.......................
.....0x50014380029ab676
            |----World Wide Node Number.......................
.....0x50014380029ab677
        \==+SCSI Interface :
            |----Name.......................................
.....vmhba2
            |----
UID.............................................
fc.50014380029ab677:50014380029abs676
```

With this FC HBA information that is highlighted, the storage administrators can now present and zone LUNs to the ESX hosts. After that is completed, you can use the names in bold to rescan the SAN and then make use of the newly presented and zoned LUNs.

```
esxcfg-rescan vmhbaX
```

In the preceding command, the X in vmhbaX is the adapter number used by VMware ESX.

Software iSCSI

For iSCSI, the situation is a little different. First, you need to enable iSCSI, and then you need to scan for LUNs that have been presented to the host. The first command is easy, but then you may need to also get IQN information to determine what to give to the iSCSI Storage administrator so that they can properly present the LUNs to you for use. In the following example, the newlines are important for the command and are preceded with a backslash. This example enables iSCSI and then finds the iSCSI name and the associated vmhba device for the iSCSI device.

```
# esxcfg-swiscsi -e
# esxcfg-info | awk '/ISCSI Name/{gn=1; print $0}\
/vmhba/ {if (gn > 0) {print $0; gn=0}}'
```

```
      |----ISCSI Name.......................................
iqn.1998-01.com.vmware:xxxxxxx-4c58c00b
            |----Name.......................................
.vmhba33
```

With this iSCSI information that is highlighted, the storage administrators can now present iSCSI LUNs to the ESX hosts. After that is completed you can use the names in bold to rescan the SAN and make use of the newly presented and zoned LUNs. Use the vmhba device name found in the previous command. In many cases, this is vmhba33, but earlier versions of ESX could also be vmhba40.

```
esxcfg-rescan vmhba33
```

Alternatively, you can rescan just the software iSCSI LUNs using the following command:

```
esxcfg-swiscsi -s
```

Hardware iSCSI

Like FC-SAN, hardware iSCSI devices "just work," and you will need to use `esxcfg-info` to again find the IQN associated with the hardware iSCSI device. The major difference is that you need to find the vmhba associated with the hardware iSCSI device. You retrieve the information for your storage administrator and perform storage rescans the same as you do for software iSCSI. The major difference is that there is no need to initialize hardware iSCSI.

Renaming a VMFS

The following script can be used to rename the VMFS volume created on installation of ESX. We take advantage of the default naming convention for local storage, which is a VMFS logically named storage1:

```
# cd /vmfs/volumes
# uid=`/bin/ls -al storage1 | /bin/awk '{print $11}'`
# /bin/ln -s $uid HOSTNAME:storage1
```

Note that HOSTNAME is the first part of the fully qualified domain name (FQDN). Assuming the FQDN is vmwareyy.example.com, the HOSTNAME is vmwareyy. Logically, before we script the creation of any other VMFS, we want to deal with the name of any local VMFS. Even so, this command will work for any VMFS.

Best Practice

Do not add the hostname to the name of a shared VMFS. Instead, use some other naming convention.

Creating a VMFS

The steps to create a VMFS for all forms of media are the same. Our example, however, uses the local disk partition names, but remote partition names can also be used. Follow these steps to create a local VMFS. Our example uses HP hardware as its basis. A LUN (logical unit) in the following discussion is a generic term that implies either a single drive or a RAID array of drives. Note that these steps can wreak great havoc on a system and they require a level of expertise with Linux. In addition, the partition should be on 64MB boundaries for best performance. For these reasons, it is best to use the vSC to create a VMFS. The following does not align the VMFS on any boundaries and is used as an example:

1. Determine the controller and LUN to use. Remember that a VMFS desires to be the *only* partition on a given LUN. For example, we will be using controller 0 or the built-in RAID controller for an HP ProLiant server, and the LUN to use is the second RAID array created on the controller. That implies the device we will be using will be named `/dev/cciss/c0d1` when using older hardware, where `c0d1` refers to controller 0 and LUN 1, whereas `c0d0` is the default boot volume. Newer ProLiant hardware no longer uses this naming convention. Instead, it uses the `/dev/sdX` naming convention.

   Remember to use `esxcfg-scsidevs` (`esxcfg-vmhbadevs`) to verify that the partition you want to modify is *not* already being used as a VMFS for ESX v4 per the following:

   `# esxcfg-scsidevs —m`

   or for ESX v3

   `# esxcfg-vmhbadevs -m`

   These commands will map the cryptic or VML name to the device name to the UUID of the device and finally the name of the VMFS. You will want to manipulate *any* device not in this list, because this is the list of existing VMFS volumes.

2. Partition the new device to create one giant partition using the `fdisk` and `parted` commands. We use parted to write a new msdos disk label to the new LUN and then we use `fdisk` to delete any existing partitions and add a new one. It is possible to use `parted` for everything on ESX v4. But because ESX v3 does not contain `parted`, we provide both mechanisms for you. The following is the `parted` method:

```
# parted /dev/cciss/c0d1
GNU Parted 1.8.1
Using /dev/cciss/c0d1
Welcome to GNU Parted! Type 'help' to view a list of
commands.(parted) mklabel msdos
Warning: The existing disk label on /dev/cciss/c0d1 will be
destroyed and all
data on this disk will be lost. Do you want to continue?
Yes/No? Yes
New disk label type?  [bsd]? msdos
(parted) print

Model: Compaq Smart Array (cpqarray)
Disk /dev/cciss/c0d1: 294GB
Sector size (logical/physical): 512B/512B
Partition Table: msdos

Number  Start  End  Size  Type  File system  Flags

(parted) quit
fdisk Method
# fdisk /dev/cciss/c0d1
The number of cylinders for this disk is set to 19929.
There is nothing wrong with that, but this is larger than
1024,
and could in certain setups cause problems with:
1) software that runs at boot time (e.g., old versions of
LILO)
2) booting and partitioning software from other OSs
   (e.g., DOS FDISK, OS/2 FDISK)

Command (m for help): d
Selected partition 1

Command (m for help): n
Command action
   e   extended
   p   primary partition (1-4)
p
Partition number (1-4): 1
First cylinder (1-19929, default 1):
Using default value 1
Last cylinder or +size or +sizeM or +sizeK (1-19929, default
19929):
Using default value 19929

Command (m for help): t
Selected partition 1
Hex code (type L to list codes): fb
Changed system type of partition 1 to fb (Unknown)

Command (m for help): w
```

3. After the device is created, run the following to determine the device's cryptic name. The cryptic name is crucial to know and is sometimes extremely hard to determine. If the following commands do not get the cryptic name of the device, it might be necessary to revert to tried-and-true Linux methods by reviewing the boot log of the server and extrapolating the name of the device. The chance of not seeing a particular device within the following commands is most likely because of configuration issues with the storage subsystem; in this case, your investigation will still start with the log files.

If there is an existing local VMFS, the cryptic name is easy to extrapolate from the existing name. The controller and target values should be the same, but the LUN value should be unique, and the partition value should always be 1 because of locking considerations discussed in previous chapters.

For ESX v4, do the following:

```
# esxcfg-rescan -u vmhba0
# esxcfg-scsidevs -l
mpx.vmhba0:C0:T1:L0
    Device Type: Direct-Access
    Size: 279964 MB
    Display Name: Local VMware Disk (mpx.vmhba0:C0:T1:L0)
    Plugin: NMP
    Console Device: /dev/cciss/c0d1
    Devfs Path: /vmfs/devices/disks/mpx.vmhba0:C0:T1:L0
    Vendor: VMware      Model: Block device      Revis: 1.0
    SCSI Level: 2  Is Pseudo: false Status: on
    Is RDM Capable: false Is Removable: false
    Is Local: true
    Other Names:
        vml.0000000000766d686261303a313a30 ← Use in next step!
```

For ESX v3, do the following:

```
# esxcfg-vmhbadevs
vmhba:0:0:0 /dev/sda ← Use Cryptic name in next step.
```

4. Now use the vmkfstools command to create the VMFS on the new device. Note that XXXX is the file system human-readable name and should include the hostname of the server. For our example, vmwareyyA is a suitable name. Also, the P or partition to use will be 1 because only one partition is on the device. The cryptic name or VML name must be used until the volume is named:

```
# vmkfstools -C vmfs3 -S XXXX /vmfs/devices/disks/ vml.000000
0000766d686261303a313a30\:P
```

or for ESX v3:

```
# vmkfstools -C vmfs3 -S XXXX /vmfs/devices/disks/
vmhba\:0\:0\:0\:P
```

Note that if a Permission Denied results, the VML name used is incorrect. It is also very important to pass the partition number (P). In this case we use a partition number of 1 and then a space on the command line. Without the space, the previous ESX v4 command resulted in a Permission Denied on ESX v4.0 Update 1.

Extending a VMFS

Another useful feature of a VMFS is the capability to add an extent to an existing VMFS. An extent, as described previously, is a disk partition that is not originally part of the VMFS. The extent capability allows more partitions from separate or the same devices to be added to the VMFS so that the VMFS can cross device and partition boundaries. This is similar to the Logical Volume Manager (LVM) that is common with Linux and UNIX systems, or dynamic disks in Windows. There is the potential for performance gain as additional device queues could be used or multiple targets to service the volume. First, follow the steps in the previous section, "Creating a VMFS," targeting the new partition or device to which you would like to extend the older volume. Then you would perform the following commands:

```
# vmkfstools -Z /vmfs/volumes/newVmfsName /vmfs/
volumes/oldVmfsName
```

where newVmfsName is the freshly created VMFS and oldVmfsName is the one you want to extend.

Although this command will work with ESX v3.x for local VMFS, it fails to work on ESX v4 Update 1 with a No Such File or Directory error. So extending a local VMFS will not work on vSphere.

Deleting a VMFS or VMFS Extent

There are no CLI mechanisms to delete an extent or VMFS. If you think that there is a way using tools such as fdisk or vmkfstools, you must first ask yourself this:

Are you satisfied with your backup?

Then stop right there and do nothing via the CLI. You may be able to change the underlying disk partitions but those will *not* be reflected in any of the tools and will cause widespread confusion. When you remove an extent, you can catastrophically delete VMFS data.

Growing a VMFS

As of vSphere, it is now possible, instead of extending a VMFS, to grow a VMFS. First, the partition to grow must be re-created using the original space, and the unallocated space or a secondary partition must be created. To grow a VMFS from the command line, you need to use both fdisk and vmkfstools. Use of fdisk is considered to be extremely dangerous, so use with caution.

```
# fdisk -lu /dev/cciss/c0d0

Disk /dev/cciss/c0d0: 146.7 GB, 146778685440 bytes
255 heads, 63 sectors/track, 17844 cylinders, total 286677120 sectors
Units = sectors of 1 * 512 = 512 bytes

          Device Boot      Start         End      Blocks   Id  System
/dev/cciss/c0d0p1   *          63     2249099     1124518+  83  Linux
/dev/cciss/c0d0p2          2249100     2474009      112455  fc  VMware
VMKCORE
/dev/cciss/c0d0p3          2474010   286663859   142094925   5
Extended
/dev/cciss/c0d0p5          2474073   286663859   142094893+  fb  VMware
VMFS
```

Note the Start address of the volume to extend. In this case, the value is highlighted in bold and is 2474073. Then run the next commands using this start value for the VMFS in question. Note that you cannot grow a VMFS that is *not* added to the end of the partition space. If you attempt to grow, for example, the second partition, you would completely wipe out the third and fourth partitions listed previously. In most cases, the VMFS to grow will live on its *own* partition. Because we are trying to grow a local partition, we have others on there as well.

```
# fdisk /dev/cciss/c0d0
The number of cylinders for this disk is set to 9929.
There is nothing wrong with that, but this is larger than
1024, and could in certain setups cause problems with:
1) software that runs at boot time (e.g., old versions of
LILO)
2) booting and partitioning software from other OSs
   (e.g., DOS FDISK, OS/2 FDISK)

Command (m for help): d
Partition number (1-5): 5

Command (m for help): n
Command action
   e   extended
   p   primary partition (1-4)
p
Partition number (1-4): 4
First cylinder (1-28666359, default 1): 2474073
```

```
Using defau2lt value 1
Last cylinder or +size or +sizeM or +sizeK (1-28663859, de-
fault 28663859):
Using default value 28663859

Command (m for help): t
Partition Number (1-4): 4
Hex code (type L to list codes): fb
Changed system type of partition 1 to fb (Unknown)

Command (m for help): w
```

The above `fdisk` command syntax will re-create the last partition on the volume using the original starting address (this is very important to remember to use) and the new end address. Alternatively, you can make use of the following `vmkfstools` command to grow the VMFS after the partition has grown. Note that you use the appropriate VML or cryptic name as the `oldVmfsName` twice.

```
# vmkfstools -G /vmfs/volumes/oldVmfsName /vmfs/volumes/old-
VmfsName
```

Alternatively, instead of re-creating the partition, you can grow the volume across two partitions on the same storage device. In this case, you would first create the second partition and then use the following style of command:

```
# vmkfstools -G mpx.vmhbaC\:T\:L\:P2 /vmfs/volumes/oldVmfsName
```

Note that, in this case, the last value for the partition is different between what you want to grow (P1) and to where you want to grow the volume (P2). This is not a straight growth of the VMFS over unallocated space on the LUN. The new space must be allocated using a new partition via the `fdisk` command.

Important Note

You must first grow the LUN through your SAN device.

You must then re-create the partition using the original and unallocated space.

You must then grow the VMFS using `vmkfstools`.

Unfortunately, this does not work for local volumes as of ESX v4 Update 1, but it will work for SAN or iSCSI volumes.

Important Note

Re-creating partitions using `fdisk` is considered very dangerous and could lead to catastrophic data loss.

Back up or move *all* data from the LUN in question first.

Alternative Ways to Resize a VMFS via the Command Line

If you cannot grow the underlying LUN of a VMFS and then create a new partition, you may want to consider the following discussion. Instead of resizing, you may extend a VMFS or add an extent to VMFS as described previously. Extents do not cause performance issues, just management concerns as discussed in Chapter 5. If you do not want to use extents and cannot grow the LUN, you would ask for a new LUN of the appropriate size and then copy data from one LUN to another. This will require all your VMs to be moved from the VMFS, using Storage vMotion, or your VMs must be powered off.

If there are no existing or running VMs, by all means proceed with creating the new LUN and removing the old LUN; however, if you do have data, proceed with the following:

1. Ask yourself, *"Do you trust your backups?"* If not, then proceed to make a good backup of your VMs on the source LUN.

2. Create a new VMFS the desired size (see steps 1–4 earlier under "Creating a VMFS").

3. Shut down all the VMs currently residing on the old VMFS. The following script snippet takes as an argument the cryptic or VML name of the VMFS in question:

```
vol=`/bin/ls -al /vmfs/volumes/$1 | /usr/bin/awk '{print
$11}'`
# uncomment below for ESX versions prior to version 3
#vol=`/bin/ls -al /vmfs/$1 | /usr/bin/awk '{print $11}'`
for x in `/usr/bin/vmware-cmd -l|/usr/bin/grep $vol`
do
      state=`/usr/bin/vmware-cmd $x getstate|/usr/bin/awk
'{print $3}'`
      if [ $state -eq "on" ]
      then
            /usr/bin/vmware-cmd $x stop
      fi
done
```

4. Unregister all the VMs currently residing on the old VMFS. (This step could be considered optional, but because the names stay around inside vCenter, it is best to unregister prior to moving.) The following script snippet takes as an argument the cryptic or VML name of the VMFS in question:

```
vol=`/bin/ls -al /vmfs/volumes/$1 | /usr/bin/awk '{print
$11}'`
# uncomment below for ESX versions prior to version 3
#vol=`/bin/ls -al /vmfs/$1 | /usr/bin/awk '{print $11}'`
```

```
for x in `/usr/bin/vmware-cmd -l|/usr/bin/grep $vol`
do
    /usr/bin/vmware-cmd -s unregister $x
done
```

5. Move all the VMs from the old VMFS to the new:

```
cd /vmfs/volumes/oldVMFS; mv * /vmfs/volumes/newVMFS
```

6. Using fdisk, remove the disk partition from the old VMFS related to the extent. This is a dangerous step and requires expertise with Linux. Note that although this will remove the space allocated to the VMFS, it will *not* remove the VMFS from the LVM on ESX until you remove the primary LUN of the VMFS. Re-creating the partition as a VMFS will again show the old partition as part of an existing LVM volume or VMFS:

```
# fdisk /dev/cciss/c0d1
The number of cylinders for this disk is set to 19929.
There is nothing wrong with that, but this is larger than
1024,
and could in certain setups cause problems with:
1) software that runs at boot time (e.g., old versions of
LILO)
2) booting and partitioning software from other OSs
   (e.g., DOS FDISK, OS/2 FDISK)

Command (m for help): d
Selected partition 1

Command (m for help): w
```

7. Modify any VM configuration files left on the new VMFS so that the files all point to the proper location. Edit the files with the ending .vmdk (but not any with the word *flat* in them), .vmxf, .vmsd, and .vmx to change the location if necessary of all the VMDK (disk files) currently in use by the VM. For ESX version 3, this is not necessary, but it is for ESX versions earlier than version 3. This requires knowledge of the Linux editors nano or vi.

8. Reregister all the VMs from their current VMFS locations.

```
# /usr/bin/find /vmfs/volumes/newVMFS -name '*.vmx' -exec
 /usr/bin/vmware-cmd -s register {} \;
```

9. Verify that all VMs have been moved and registered correctly:

```
# /usr/bin/vmware-cmd -l
```

Repair a VMFS

It is possible to repair a VMFS from a catastrophic event, such as accidentally overwriting the partition table with another partition table or removing the partition table completely. However, if your VMs are running when this happens, the first thing you should do is to *not* shut them down and back them up without shutting down the VM. The steps to repair a single partition VMFS follow and require the use of `fdisk`. Using `fdisk`, however, can be dangerous and requires caution and requires expertise with Linux. These steps are a last resort and should be done extremely carefully and, if you do not have the proper expertise, under the supervision of VMware Tech Support. The basic steps are as follows:

1. Add a new primary partition number 1.

2. Take default first and last cylinders.

3. Change a partition's system ID to fb, the VMFS partition ID.

4. Move the beginning of the data in the partition to have an offset of 128 used for VMFS only if this is the *first* and only partition on the LUN; otherwise, you need to have the original start location.

5. Write the new partition table to the disk and exit.

6. Repeat for all lost VMFS partitions. This is what those instructions translated into for local device `/dev/cciss/c0d1` using `fdisk`:

```
# fdisk /dev/cciss/c0d1
Device contains neither a valid DOS partition table, nor Sun,
SGI or OSF disklabelBuilding a new DOS disklabel.
Changes will remain in memory only, until you decide to write
them. After that, of course, the previous content won't be
recoverable.
The number of cylinders for this disk is set to 39162.
There is nothing wrong with that, but this is larger than
1024,
and could, in certain setups, cause problems with two things:
software that runs at boot time (e.g., old versions of LILO)
and/or booting and partitioning software from other OSs(e.g.,
DOS FDISK, OS/2 FDISK)
Warning: invalid flag 0x0000 of partition table 4 will be
corrected by w(rite)
Command (m for help): n
Command action
e extended
```

```
p primary partition (1-4)
p
Partition number (1-4): 1
First cylinder (1-39162, default 1):
Using default value 1
Last cylinder or +size or +sizeM or +sizeK (1-39162, default
39162):
Using default value 39162
Command (m for help): t
Selected partition 1
Hex code (type L to list codes): fb
Changed system type of partition 1 to fb (Unknown)
Command (m for help): x
Expert command (m for help): b
Partition number (1-4): 1
New beginning of data (63-629137529, default 63): 128
Expert command (m for help): w
The partition table has been altered!
```

If there is more than one partition for a given VMFS volume—in other words, you had used the cross partition grow or used extents, you would need to also restore the second partition. To this end, it is often best to keep a copy of your partition tables handy using the command `fdisk -lu /dev/devName`. In the previous "Growing a VMFS" section, four partitions were in use; on restoration of that LUN, it would be extremely difficult to re-create this LUN without the partition table. You need to know the start and end location for each partition on the LUN. If you do not, there is a very good chance of data loss. Even a printed copy of this information will improve your overall ability to recover this data. Guessing the start and end locations or a partition to repair the partition table is *not* a best practice.

> ### Best Practice
>
> Keep a copy of your partition tables of all devices (including SAN devices), the output of `fdisk -lu`, for each ESX host in written form stored with your Disaster Recovery materials.
>
> When repairing a SAN device, the previous command needs to occur only once per LUN, not once per host.

VMFS Manipulation with the vSphere Client

When using the vSphere Client to manipulate a VMFS, the tasks are generally the same whether the underlying storage is local SCSI, iSCSI, or a FC device.

Connect to Storage Device

For FC SAN, there is also not much to do except to get a full list of the World Wide Port Names. The easiest way to do this is to use the following steps:

1. Log in to the vSC.

2. Select the host in question.

3. Select the *Configuration* tab for the host in question.

4. Click the *Storage Adapters* link.

5. Scroll the window until the Fibre Channel adapter is displayed with the appropriate World Wide Names, which you would then give to your storage team.

For software iSCSI, you must first enable software iSCSI and then retrieve the IQN associated with the iSCSI target which will be displayed after iSCSI is enabled. You can also find it under storage adapters as you do for FC SAN WWN.

1. Log in to the vSC.

2. Select the host in question.

3. Select the *Configuration* tab for the host in question.

4. Click the *Storage Adapters* link.

5. Scroll the window until the iSCSI Software adapter is displayed. Select the iSCSI Software Adapter and click it.

6. Click the *Properties* link.

7. When the iSCSI Initiator dialog appears click the *Configure* button.

8. Check the *Enabled* check box.

9. Click the *OK* Button.

10. IQN will now appear within the iSCSI Initiator dialog as well as within the Storage Adapters list (see Figure 9.7).

For hardware iSCSI, the actions for the FC-SAN previously mentioned will allow you to find the IQN of the hardware iSCSI HBA. This information is in place of the World Wide Name for the FC-SAN.

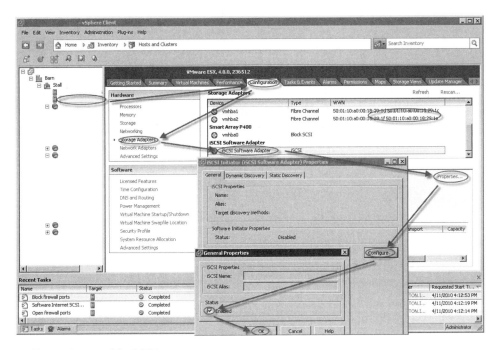

Figure 9.7 *Enable iSCSI*

Renaming a VMFS via the vSphere Client

For ESX version 3, there are two ways to rename a VMFS, as presented here. Remember, it is a good practice to name the VMFS using some form of the FQDN. The first method is to go directly to the datastore for the ESX host in question and rename the local VMFS.

1. Log in to the vSC.

2. Select the host in question.

3. Select the *Configuration* tab for the host in question.

4. Click the *Storage (SCSI, SAN, and NFS)* link.

5. Select the local storage device to rename.

6. Double-click the existing name of the local storage device to change to an entry box (or right-click the existing name and select the *Rename* option).

7. Change the name as appropriate (see Figure 9.8) and press *Enter*.

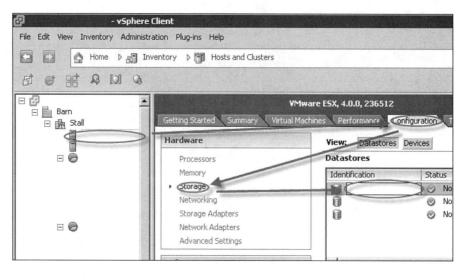

Figure 9.8 *Changing the name of datastore, first method*

The second method is to look at all the datastores and rename the datastore without knowing which ESX host is involved:

1. Log in to the vSC.

2. Click the Inventory word of the location bar, select Inventory to expand the Inventory menu, and select Datastores from the menu (see Figure 9.9).

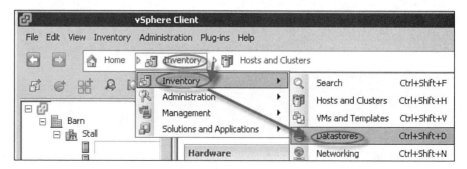

Figure 9.9 *Inventory drop-down menu*

3. Select the datastore to rename.

4. Right-click the datastore to bring up a menu and select Rename.

5. Change the name of the datastore as appropriate and press *Enter* (see Figure 9.10).

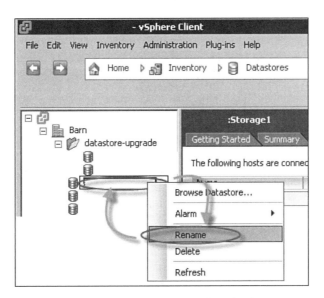

Figure 9.10 *Changing the name of datastore, second method*

Creating a VMFS via the vSphere Client

Creating a VMFS uses a wizard to answer all the questions required for adding a VMFS to the server. Remember that it is best to use one partition per SCSI device for a VMFS to alleviate locking cosncerns. Our example, however, using a default installation, does not do this because of disk space limitations:

1. Log in to the vSC.

2. Select the host in question.

3. Select the *Configuration* tab for the host in question.

4. Click the *Storage (SCSI, SAN, and NFS)* link.

5. Click the *Add Storage* link.

6. Select *Disk/LUN* from the resultant wizard and then *Next* (see Figure 9.11).

7. Select the local device using the device cryptic name `vmhbaC:T:L:P`, where `C` implies the controller, `T` implies the track or path, `L` implies the LUN, and `P` implies the partition number (see Figure 9.12). Note that it may be possible to determine which device is associated with each VM HBA because of the size of the LUN, unless you use a similar LUN size. Click Next to continue.

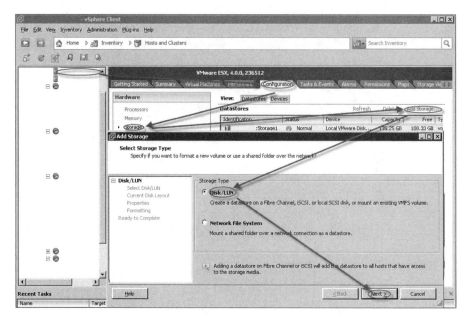

Figure 9.11 *Create VMFS*

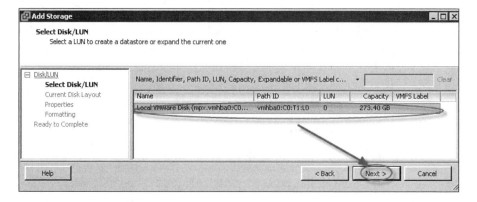

Figure 9.12 *Select local device name*

It is possible that at this juncture a screen will appear that states *Unable to Read Partition Information*. When this occurs, it implies that the disk in question has a partition table on the LUN that is somehow broken. The fix for this is to find out which device maps to the device in question. Using the cryptic name of the device, do the following:

a. Log in to the console operating system as the root user.

b. Run the command `esxcfg-vmhbadevs / esxcfg-scsidevs`.

c. Find the `/dev/sdX` device name associated with the cryptic name, where X refers to a letter or series of letters that represents the Linux SCSI disk device associated with the cryptic name.

d. Use the `fdisk /dev/sdX` command per the command-line option above to remove any partitions on the device to make room for the VMFS.

The preceding steps will remove the error from the vSC Wizard when creating a VMFS. However, do this carefully because removal of the partitions is a permanent action, and if you select the wrong volume, it will be a catastrophic mistake.

8. ESX v4 and ESXi v3: Inspect the results to ensure you have the proper local VMFS disk, and then press *Next* (see Figure 9.13). A local VMFS is required for installation of the service console within ESX v4 and is the only installation option for any version of ESXi.

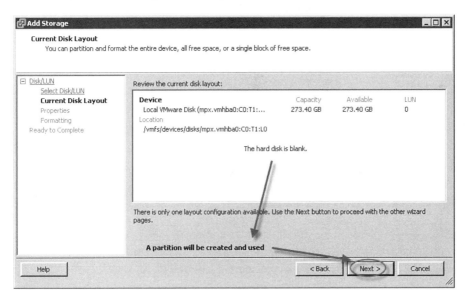

Figure 9.13 *Result inspection*

9. Provide a name to the datastore (see Figure 9.14) and click *Next*. Again, it is best to use some form of the FQDN to aid in knowing which local datastore belongs to which host.

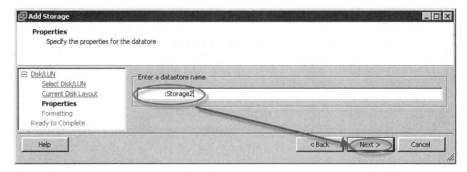

Figure 9.14 *Name Datastore*

10. Click *Next*. It is not necessary to change the LUN formatting (see Figure 9.15). In essence, the block size to be used depends on the maximum size of a VMDK to reside on the VMFS. You used to select the capacity of the LUN in step 8. This is a change, because it is now done at this step. In general, selecting the maximum capacity option is best.

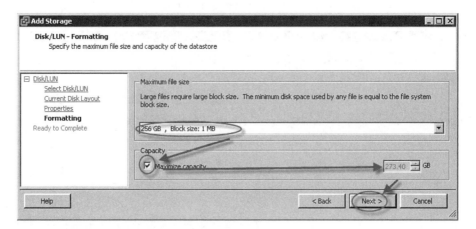

Figure 9.15 *Select block size*

11. Review all the changes (see Figure 9.16) and click *Next*.

12. Wait for the *Create VMFS Datastore* task to finish by monitoring the Recent Tasks window.

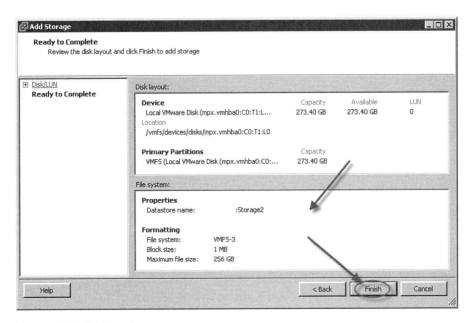

Figure 9.16 *Review changes*

Extending a VMFS

Extending a VMFS in ESX v4 and v3 is fairly straightforward because both use a Logical Volume Manager (LVM) to combine LUNs and thereby exceed the (2TB – 512 bytes) limit of a VMFS.

There have been some debates on whether to use extents. Let me set the record straight: Extents are neither inherently bad in ESX v3 or later versions, nor do they cause any performance degradations. The only issue with extents comes down to management more than anything. When you delete an extent you have to delete the entire VMFS. There is no way to remove an extent short of deleting the VMFS and re-creating it. In addition, storage teams do not always have the necessary information to determine whether the LUN presented to a system (either locally or via SAN) is actually part of an extent. Use of extents increases management but does not affect performance.

If the datastore you want to extend is using VMFS version 3.33, most of these tasks can happen only when you connect the vSphere Client (vSC) directly to the host and not via vCenter Server. The version of the VMFS is viewable under the properties for the VMFS.

> **Best Practice for Extents**
>
> Try not use to extents. To remove an extent requires the removal of the entire VMFS, not the individual extent.
>
> Storage teams cannot directly map the use of an extent to an existing VMFS; only the Virtualization Administrator can do this.
>
> VMFS is above LVM, which is above the hardware. There is a one-to-one mapping between a VMFS and a logical volume, but a one-to-many mapping of a logical volume to physical LUN. Therefore, the VMFS sees only a single large volume regardless of how many disks, RAID arrays, or SAN LUNs are involved.

To extend a VMFS, do the following:

1. Log in to the vSC connected directly to the host, not via vCenter.

2. Select the *Configuration* tab for the host in question.

3. Click the *Storage* link.

4. Select the storage identifier to manipulate.

5. Select the Properties for the identifier chosen.

6. Click the *Increase* button on the resulting dialog (see Figure 9.17).

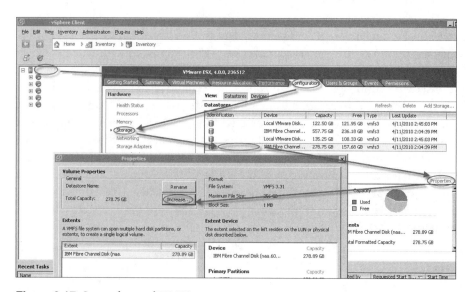

Figure 9.17 *Start of extend VMFS*

7. Select the extent to add. Note that the devices listed in the wizard are all devices not already defined as a VMFS, which will include any and all raw disk maps defined (see Figure 9.18). Click the *Next* button.

> ### *Important Note*
> Use extreme caution to ensure you have selected the correct LUN!

Note that a VMFS and any extent must minimally be 1.2GB. Given that one of the LUNs you see in the list is 100MB, we cannot use that as an extent.

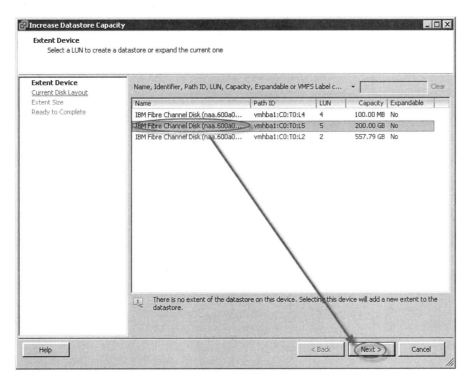

Figure 9.18 *Datastore properties*

8. Review the current disk layout of the extent to add and click *Next*. An extent is free space not already allocated to a VMFS (see Figure 9.19).

9. Decide whether to use the entire extent for VMFS or some portion and click the *Next* button as shown in Figure 9.20. The best practice is to use the entire extent.

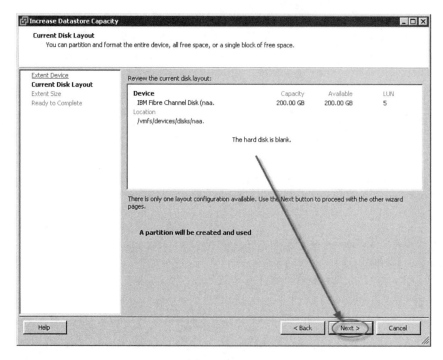

Figure 9.19 *Disk layout*

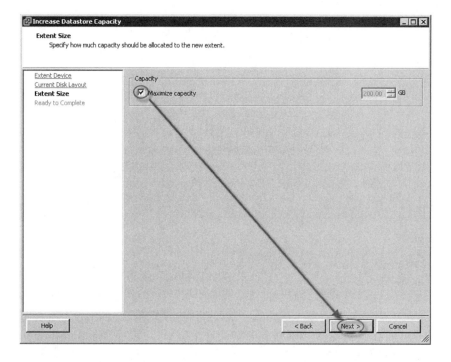

Figure 9.20 *Size the extent*

10. Review the new extent and click *Finish*.

> ### Best Practice
>
> Raw disk maps will show up as available LUNs when trying to extend. Verify which LUN to choose by looking at the primary partitions list at step 8, as in Figure 9.21.
>
> There should be no existing partitions on the LUN in question. If there are, there is a good chance this is an *in use* LUN.
>
> Pay careful attention to any errors that may display when looking at the disk layout.

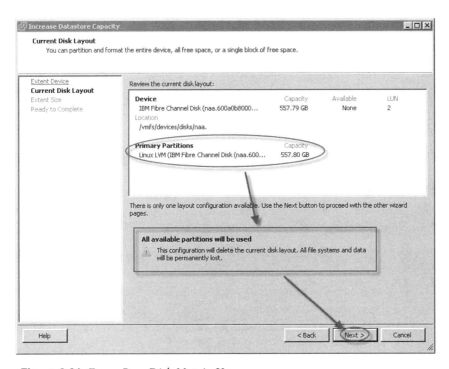

Figure 9.21 *Error: Raw Disk Map in Use*

Deleting a VMFS Extent

Deleting a VMFS extent is catastrophic. It is extremely important to shut down and migrate all existing VMs from the VMFS to be manipulated. Barring that, the only other concern is an affirmative answer to the following question:

Are you satisfied with your backup?

If there are no existing VMs, templates, ISOs, and so forth on the VMFS, by all means proceed. To delete an extent, see the following section, because it's the same for local disks.

Deleting a VMFS

Deleting a VMFS within the vSC requires some functionality that is covered two chapters from now in more detail: that is, the movement of one VM from a datastore to another. Although this is mentioned as a step, peruse Chapter 11, "Dynamic Resource Load Balancing," for further details. The steps to delete a VMFS within the vSC follow. Again, there are two methods.

The first method is to use the storage configuration of the host in question as follows:

1. Log in to the vSC.

2. Shut down and cold migrate all VMs residing on this datastore to a different datastore, or use Storage vMotion to achieve the same result. Verify that no data is left on the VMFS in question.

3. Select the host in question.

4. Select the *Configuration* tab for the host in question.

5. Click the *Storage* link.

6. Select the storage device to remove.

7. Select the *Delete* link or right-click the storage device and select *Delete* from the menu, as shown in Figure 9.22.

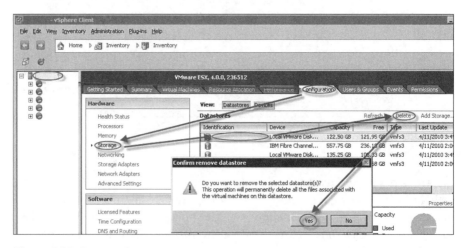

Figure 9.22 *Remove Datastore menu*

8. Answer Yes to the dialog about removing the datastore.

9. Wait for the remove request to finish.

The second method is to use the datastore inventory directly, as follows:

1. Log in to the vSC.

2. Migrate all VMs residing on this datastore to a different datastore.

3. Click the down arrow next to the Inventory button.

4. Select *Datastores* from the menu.

5. Select the datastore to remove.

6. Right-click the local storage device name and select the *Remove* menu item.

7. Answer Yes to the dialog about removing the datastore.

8. Wait for the remove request to finish.

Growing a VMFS

Growing a VMFS is not much different from extending a VMFS, but this new-to-vSphere functionality enables your storage team to extend the LUN without needing to create another LUN. The advantages are that there is now no need to have external documentation that maps the multiple "extents" that are currently in use, and it lowers the overall management requirements for after-the-fact manipulations by the storage team, because it is one heterogeneous LUN.

To grow a VMFS, you follow many of the instructions covered under extending the VMFS, mentioned previously. The key difference is that you select the same LUN on which the VMFS already exists.

1. Log in to the vSC connected to the host, not via vCenter.

2. Select the *Configuration* tab for the host in question.

3. Click the *Storage* link.

4. Select the storage identifier to manipulate.

5. Select the Properties for the identifier chosen (not shown in Figure 9.23).

6. Click the *Increase* button on the resulting dialog.

7. Select the extent to add. Note that the devices listed in the wizard are all devices not already defined as a VMFS, which will include any and all

raw disk maps defined. The device you want will match identically the existing LUN definition. In Figure 9.23 this is represented by the box. Ensure these two items in the box are identical. For local storage we use the cryptic name, but for remote storage we will use the VML name. Continue as if you were extending a VMFS as previously discussed.

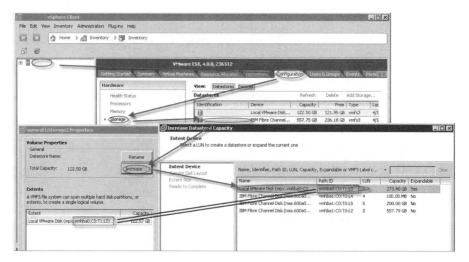

Figure 9.23 *Choosing extent device to grow*

Upgrading from VMFS v3.xx to v3.33 or v3.34

Many of the vSC VMFS manipulations will not work if the underlying VMFS is not at least at v3.33. If you are starting with new LUNs properly formatted as VMFS 3.33, there is no issue going forward, but if you are reusing LUNs created with ESX v3.x, you may decide to upgrade the version of your VMFS.

The steps for doing an upgrade are quite straightforward, yet will completely and irrevocably delete any data on the VMFS in question, so you will first want to use Storage vMotion or otherwise move the data off the VMFS to be updated. Update steps are as follows:

1. Move all VMs off the VMFS using Storage vMotion and/or Cold Migration and ensure all backups are current.

2. Delete the VMFS.

3. Create the VMFS.

The specific instructions for each of these steps have been covered in the previous sections. If you're not sure how to proceed, go back and review the sections on moving VMs, deleting VMFS volumes, and creating VMFS volumes.

Masking and Max LUN Manipulations

It is possible, and often desirable, to manipulate the presentation of LUNs to the ESX host from within the ESX host. This has the advantage that when making simple changes it is not necessary to contact the SAN management group. ESX provides advanced options to set the maximum number of LUNs from zero to the maximum number of LUNs for the ESX host version in use. On ESX v3 the default setting is 128, whereas on ESX v4.x the default setting is 256. So if there is a LUN numbered greater than the maximum number in the `Disk.MaxLUN` advanced setting, it will not be visible to the ESX host.

In addition, for ESX v3 only, there is an advanced setting that will mask off LUNs from view by the ESX host. The `Disk.MaskLUN` setting will set which LUNs the ESX host will *not* see and can be used to change the presentation LUN numbering. For example, if all ESX LUNs on the SAN were presented with LUN numbers greater than 256, it is possible to use `Disk.MaskLUN` to mask all LUNs from 1 through 256, which sets LUN 1 on the ESX host to be the real LUN 257 as presented by the SAN.

These two options on ESX v3 allow the ESX host to work around some of the SAN limitations within ESX. Without an equivalent advanced option, masking of LUNs is now a fabric zoning concern. This also implies that it is not possible to have LUN numbers greater than 256 without proper zoning in play. ESX v4 places the management of LUN presentation and zoning back in the hands of the storage team.

Command Line

There are mechanisms to manipulate LUN masks and max LUN settings from the command line.

ESX has the `esxcfg-advcfg` command to make modifications to the advanced configuration via the command line. For ESX v3 this command manipulates the contents of the files in `/proc/vmware/config`, which is *not* a direct mapping to the advanced options shown in the vSC. ESX v4 no longer modifies `/proc/vmware/config` but instead communicates with the vmkernel via a different path.

For the options we are discussing, `Disk.MaxLUN` and `Disk.MaskLUNs`, use the following commands to make the modifications. Note that although the files in the `/proc/vmware/config` file system can be manipulated directly, it is strongly recommended that this *not* happen. Use the provided command to have the changes last through a reboot.

To change the maximum LUN to a value of 16, use the following:

```
esxcfg-advcfg -s 16 /Disk/MaxLUN
```

For ESX v3, change the LUN mask to *not* allow LUN 5 to appear from either of the redundant FC HBAs in use; enter this command:

```
esxcfg-advcfg -s vmhba1:0:5\;vmhba2:0:5 /Disk/MaskLUNs
```

Now when rescanning the FC HBA for new devices and VMFS volumes, LUN 5 will not appear (as shown in the following). Any change to these configuration options requires performing a rescan.

Remember `Disk.MaskLUN` is not an option for ESX v4, only `Disk.MaxLUN`.

```
# esxcfg-rescan vmhba1
Rescanning vmhba1...done.
On scsi0, removing: 0:0 0:1 0:2 0:4 0:5.
On scsi0, adding: 0:0 0:1 0:2 0:4.
```

vSC

To set LUN advanced settings using the vSC, follow these instructions:

1. Log in to the vSC either through the vCenter Server or directly to the host.

2. Select the ESX host in question.

3. Select the *Configuration* tab.

4. Click the *Advanced Settings* link.

5. Modify the desired entries and click *OK* to commit the changes and close the dialog (see Figure 9.24).

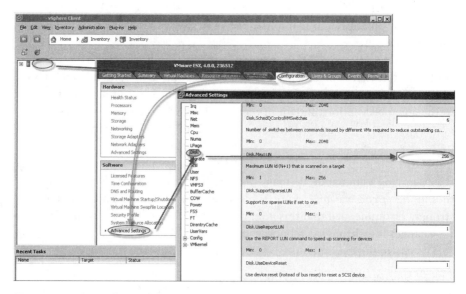

Figure 9.24 *vSC advanced settings*

Virtual Networking

The description of virtual network concepts is in the preceding chapter. What follows are the steps necessary to create and manage vSwitches and virtual distributed switches (vDS) from the command line and using the vSC. ESX requires a vSwitch to work correctly. Although this might not always appear to be necessary for an end environment, it is necessary from a management and functionality viewpoint. Without a vSwitch, there exists no way to connect the management appliance to the management tools. In fact, ESX tends not to install unless there exists at least one physical NIC, because ESX creates your first vSwitch automatically.

Because of a very old security issue (in ESX v2.x), the rule was to always create a vSwitch and if a vNIC exists within a VM, to always connect it to a vSwitch. This a good basic rule but no longer a requirement.

> ### Best Practice for Virtual Switches
>
> Always have at least one vSwitch.
>
> If a VM has a vNIC, always attach it to a vSwitch.

Configuring the Service Console or ESXi Management Appliance

The service console has its own networking configuration separate from the rest of the ESX host, as Chapter 7 outlined. The service console must be configured with its own IP address and netmask. Use of DHCP could cause serious issues with ESX if the DHCP lease expires and the DHCP server is *not* available. The consequences of this action would at a minimum be the loss of management capability.

Command Line

When using the command line to configure the service console, it is important to realize that the ESX host should use static IP, unlike potential VMs. ESXi's management appliance is connected to the network via a vmkernel device, whereas ESX uses a virtual NIC referred to as the vSwif.

The following commands can be used to create a new vSwitch for use by the service console. When installing ESX, the VM network portgroup is also created whether that is desired or not. To ensure that vSwitch0 is assigned the service console, it is desirable to remove the VM network vSwitch and assign the appropriate pNIC to the vSwitch for use by the service console. In this example, the first Broadcom adapter of the six pNICs in the server is to be assigned to the service console. In addition, for ESX v3 if you use iSCSI, which should reside on its own network, the netmask for the service console includes both the admin network and the iSCSI network. This is not a requirement for ESX v4. Finally, the default `routerIPAddress` is set for use by all the vmkernel devices used by vMotion, iSCSI, FT, and NFS:

```
# snic=`/usr/sbin/esxcfg-nics -l | /bin/grep Broadcom | /bin/
grep Up | /usr/bin/head -1 | /bin/awk '{print $1}'`
# /usr/sbin/esxcfg-vswitch -D "VM Network" vSwitch0
# /usr/sbin/esxcfg-vswitch -U vmnic0 vSwitch0
# /usr/sbin/esxcfg-vswitch -L $snic vSwitch0
# /usr/sbin/esxcfg-vswif -i esxServerIPAddress -n netMaskIn-
cludingiSCSI vswif0
# /usr/sbin/esxcfg-route defaultRouterIPAddress
```

For ESXi, the highlighted line would be dropped completely and the following used instead, with the same netmask concerns about iSCSI Storage.

```
# /usr/sbin/esxcfg-vmknic -a -i esxServerIPAddress -n netMas-
kIncludingiSCSI Management
```

For ESX v4, the highlighted line would use the netmask that only includes the esxServerIPAddress.

With ESX v3, there are three ways to include the service console or management appliance within the iSCSI network:

- Include within the same subnet via a netmask.

- Route the iSCSI authentication traffic through a router/gateway/firewall to the iSCSI device.

- Create a second vswif (vswif1) interface in the service console and place it on the iSCSI network.

Although we show the first method listed in the example, the second method is far superior from a security perspective because storage traffic should be segregated from the management tools as much as possible.

Because there are vSphere plug-ins for any storage device, such as the EMC vSphere NFS plug-in for Celerra or the Ionix Universal Infrastructure Management tool, your virtualization management network will still need to talk to the storage management network but *not* the data network (if at all possible). As more and more tools are made into plug-ins for virtualization, it is important that the storage data in transit is segregated from the virtualization administrative network. Such segregation will improve overall performance, security, and availability.

vSC

By default, the service console vSwitch will already be created when ESX is installed, and there is no need to create another vSwitch for the service console. In the future, it might be nice to add more pNICs to the service console, but the default is already there for your use, as shown in Figure 9.25 and Figure 9.27.

1. Log in to the vSC, either into the vCenter Server or directly to the host.

2. Select the ESX host in question.

3. Select the *Configuration* tab.

4. Click the *Networking* link.

5. Verify that there exists a VM Network attached to vSwitch0.

6. Click the *Properties* link to open up the properties editor, as shown in Figure 9.25.

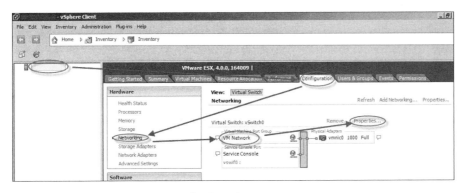

Figure 9.25 *Existing service console vSwitch*

7. Select *VM Network*.

8. Click the *Remove* button.

9. Click the *Close* button.

Note that changing the existing service console or management appliance configuration remotely will disconnect your remote tools from the ESX or ESXi host and require a reconnect with vCenter or via the tools.

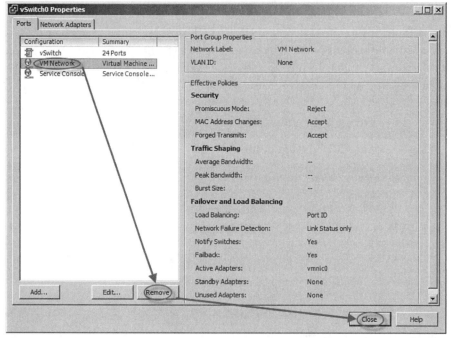

Figure 9.26 *Remove VM Network from default vSwitch*

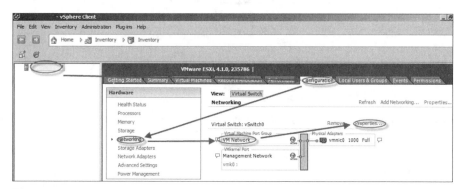

Figure 9.27 *Existing management appliance vSwitch*

Creating a VM Network vSwitch

The creation of a VM network vSwitch is required to connect a VM to the outside world or to other VMs. They could talk to the outside world using the vSwitch created for the service console, but that has several security risks unless the VM is also an Administrative VM. The following sections outline the ways to create a VM Network vSwitch. This mechanism would be used for all virtual switches to be created for use by VMs, but not for the Cisco Nexus 1000v because there is only one Cisco Nexus 1000v per host.

Command Line

In this script example, the system takes the first two Intel-based pNICs and uses them to form vSwitch1, which has a portgroup labeled as the "VM Network." This assumes you have first deleted the "VM Network" created by default and a part of vSwitch0. If you followed the steps in Chapter 8, this has already been done. After the vSwitch is added, the pNICs are then added to the vSwitch1:

```
# unic=`/usr/sbin/esxcfg-nics -l | /bin/grep Intel | /bin/
grep Up | head -2 | head -1 | /bin/awk '{print $1}'`
# vnic=`/usr/sbin/esxcfg-nics -l | /bin/grep Intel | /bin/
grep Up | head -2 | tail -1 | /bin/awk '{print $1}'`
# /usr/sbin/esxcfg-vswitch -a vSwitch1
# /usr/sbin/esxcfg-vswitch -A "VM Network" vSwitch1
# /usr/sbin/esxcfg-vswitch -L $unic vSwitch1
# /usr/sbin/esxcfg-vswitch -L $vnic vSwitch1
```

vSC

You can create a VM network vSwitch in the vSC by doing the following:

1. Log in to the vSC, either into the vCenter Server or directly to the host.

2. Select the ESX host in question.

3. Select the *Configuration* tab.

4. Click the *Networking* link.

5. Click the *Add Networking* link as shown in Figure 9.28.

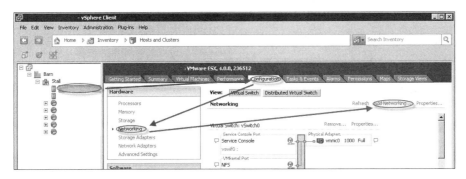

Figure 9.28 *Add Networking*

6. Select the *Virtual Machine* connection type, as shown in Figure 9.29.

7. Select at least one pNIC for the VM network vSwitch, as shown in Figure 9.30; however, two would be the best practice. More than two can be chosen, but two are needed only for redundancy.

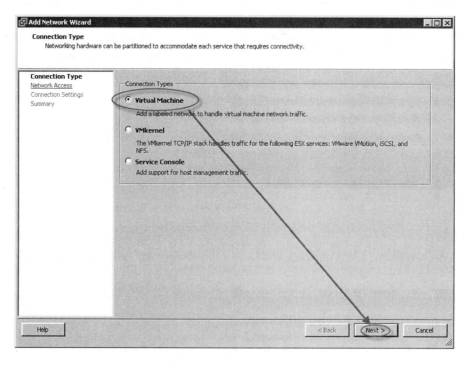

Figure 9.29 *vSwitch connection type*

8. Click Next or change the vSwitch name, and then click *Next*, as in Figure 9.31. This is also the time you can select or add a VLAN ID, which will be assigned to the portgroup created with the vSwitch.

9. Click *Finish* to complete the creation of the vSwitch.

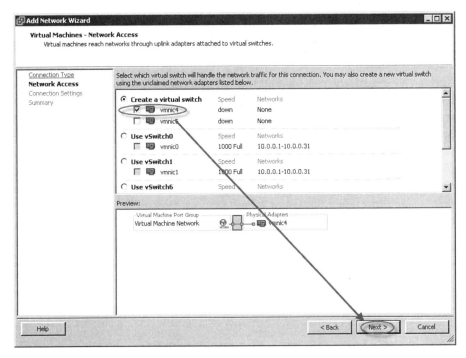

Figure 9.30 *Assign pNIC to vSwitch.*

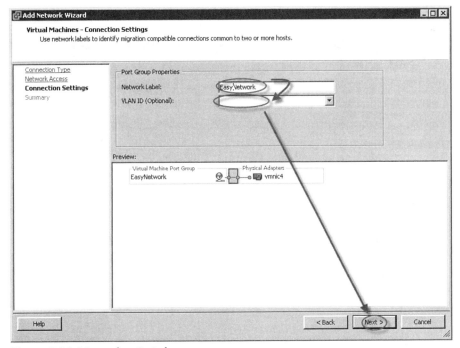

Figure 9.31 *Name the vSwitch.*

Creating a vNetwork Distributed Virtual Switch

A Virtual Distributed Switch (vDS) is used to create a single control location for a vSwitch that spans all ESX or ESXi hosts within the cluster. This control location is VMware vCenter. Note that this is not a communication path for switch data, just a control path. You will still need the appropriate network cables to effect a properly working network between your hosts because the control path is purely for administration and not for data transfer. To create a vDS is pretty straightforward now that we have created a vSwitch that can be used as a template. Because a vDS is a construct within vCenter, it is not possible to create them from the service console or management appliance. It is possible to create them using PowerShell, Perl, and other scripting mechanisms when connecting these scripts to a vCenter Server.

vSC

When using the vSC to create a vDS, there are many ways to access the same information, as shown by Figure 9.32. You can access the vDS management screens by clicking the Distributed Virtual Switch button under the vSwitch configuration screen, or you can access the Network Inventory directly.

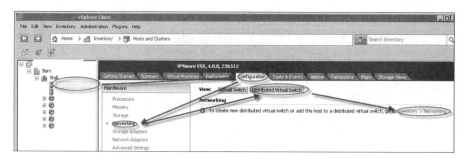

Figure 9.32 *Adding a vDS*

In either case, after you access the Network Inventory, you will need to add a dVS. You do this on the folder or datacenter in question. Unless your hosts within the VMware datacenter are different, it is often better to add dVS to the datacenter rather than a folder. However, if you have multiple clusters within the data center you may want to have a folder per cluster and arrange your networks accordingly.

> ### Best Practice
>
> When you have multiple clusters per datacenter, it is best to have a folder per cluster under networks. This gives you the capability to have per cluster vDS.

Following along with Figure 9.33, in the network inventory screen, do the following:

1. Select the datacenter (or cluster-specific folder) in which you want to create the dVS.

2. Select the *Summary* tab.

3. Select the *Add a Distributed Virtual Switch* link.

4. Give your dvSwitch a name.

5. Choose how many uplinks this dvSwitch will have on any given host.

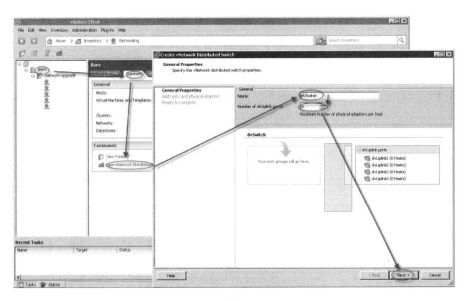

Figure 9.33 *Name the vDS and select uplinks.*

> ### Best Practice
>
> Select at least two uplinks for each dvSwitch to maintain redundancy.

6. Click the *Next* button.

7. Expand and check the hosts you want to participate within the dvSwitch.

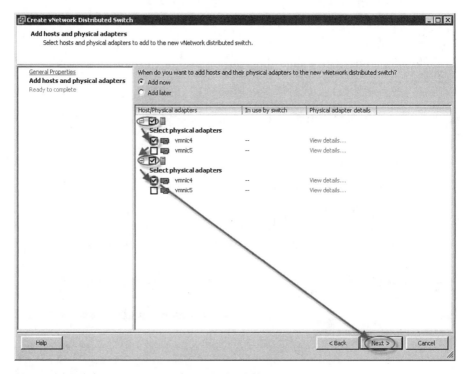

Figure 9.34 *Select participating hosts and uplinks*

8. Check the uplinks (pNICS) to assign to the dvSwitch.

9. Click the *Next* button.

10. Review and click the *Finish* button.

The result is the creation of the dvSwitch or vDS and a dvPortgroup. Now it is possible to assign VMs to the dvPortgroup just like any other portgroup. Note, however, that unless the hosts are connected somehow via the uplink, they will not communicate with each other.

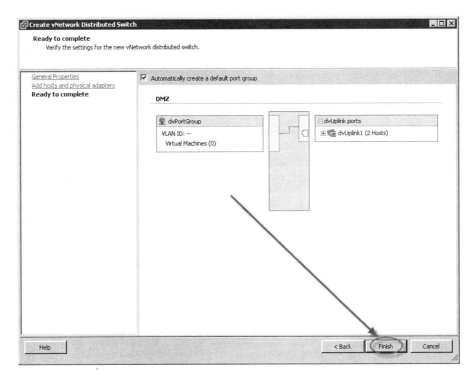

Figure 9.35 *Review and finish*

Setting Up PVLANs Within a Distributed Virtual Switch

Setting up a PVLAN (previously discussed in Chapter 7) is quite straight-forward after you have a vDS created. All we need to do is modify the vDS to ensure that Private VLANs are enabled and decide which VLAN tags to use.

This process is highlighted in Figure 9.36:

1. Select the vDS.

2. Select the *Summary* tab.

3. Click the *Edit Settings* link to bring up the Settings dialog box.

4. Select the *Private VLAN* tab.

5. Enter in the primary private VLAN.

6. Enter in the secondary private VLAN if you do not want to have a single promiscuous mode VLAN.

7. Select the type of PVLAN (isolated or community).

8. Click *OK*.

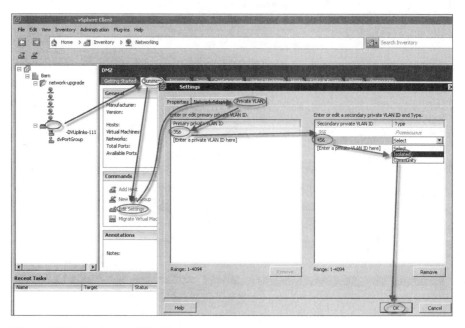

Figure 9.36 *Configure PVLANs*

Creating a vMotion vSwitch

A major feature of VMware ESX is the capability to move VMs from one machine to another machine while the VM is still running. The requirements for this are fairly simple, yet sometimes hard to meet:

- The ESX hosts must have access to some form of shared storage: NFS, iSCSI, or SAN. The VM to vMotion must reside on the shared storage.

- The ESX hosts must have vSwitches named identically.

- The ESX hosts must have the same family of processor and in most cases share the same processor instruction set.

- The VMs must not have their CD-ROM or floppy components connected. You can have the VMs connected to a client device but you will get a warning on an attempt to vMotion. This is covered in Chapter 10.

- The VMs must be connected to a nonlocal (nonprivate) vSwitch by default, but this is also possible to change.

- The appropriate vMotion license must exist and be available to the ESX host.

- vCenter is in use.

- It is strongly recommended that a dedicated gigabit or faster network be used.

If all these conditions are met, it is possible to use vMotion. vMotion requires a port on a vSwitch set up just for vMotion. Most of these conditions will be met if the host participated within an Enhanced vMotion Capability (EVC) cluster and when either a virtual distributed switch or host profiles are in use. You will still need to investigate device connectivity and location of the VM. To enable vMotion capability when private or local vSwitches are in use, vCenter has to be changed to allow this behavior. To make this change, do the following on your vCenter Server machine. Modify the file `C:\Document and Settings\ All Users\Application Data\VMware\VMware VirtualCenter\vpxd.cfg` on Windows 2003 or `C:\ProgramData\VMware\VMware VirtualCenter\ vpxd.cfg` on Windows 2008 with the following additions before the closing `</config>`. This will enable vMotion for private virtual networks not attached to a pNIC.

```
<migrate><test><CompatibleNetworks>
<VMOnVirtualIntranet>false</VMOnVirtualIntranet>
</CompatibleNetworks></test></migrate>
```

Now all your VMs will participate within vMotion, but remember that a private network is private to an ESX or ESXi host and *not* to a cluster. Therefore, if you migrate one VM on the private vSwitch, you will have to migrate them all if they need to intercommunicate, and you will have periods of no communication as the various VMs are in different states of flight between the hosts.

Command Line

This script example uses the first of the last two Intel-based pNICs of six pNICs. vSwitch2 is created, a portgroup labeled vMotion is added, and then the pNIC is assigned to the vSwitch. Finally, the pNIC assigned to the vSwitch is converted to a vmkernel pNIC and given a nonroutable IP and netmask:

```
# wnic=`/usr/sbin/esxcfg-nics -l | /bin/grep Intel | /bin/
grep Up |tail -2 | head -1 | /bin/awk '{print $1}'`
mip="192.168.1.1" # or some other non-routable IP
# /usr/sbin/esxcfg-vswitch -a vSwitch2
# /usr/sbin/esxcfg-vswitch -A "vMotion" vSwitch2
```

```
# /usr/sbin/esxcfg-vswitch -L $wnic vSwitch2
# /usr/sbin/esxcfg-vmknic -a -i $mip -n 255.255.255.0 vMotion
# vmk=`/usr/sbin/esxcfg-vmknic -l | /bin/grep vMotion |
/bin/awk '{print $1}'`
# vmware-vim-cmd hostsvc/vmotion/vnic_set $Vmk
```

vSC

Using the vSC to create a vMotion vSwitch is similar to the creation of the VM
Network vSwitch:

1. Log in to the vSC, either into the vCenter Server or directly to the host.

2. Select the ESX host in question.

3. Select the *Configuration* tab.

4. Click the *Networking* link.

5. Click the *Add Networking* link.

6. Select the vmkernel connection type that is available (see Figure 9.37).

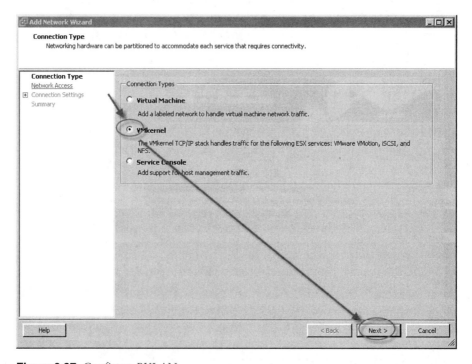

Figure 9.37 *Configure PVLANs.*

7. Select at least one pNIC for the vMotion portgroup (refer to Figure 9.30). However, two would be the best practice for redundancy. Note that this does not provide any capability to load balance because vmkernel ports do not participate in vSwitch load balancing; however, they can participate in NetIOC because that is a vSwitch egress technology across multiple pNICs.

8. Change the portgroup name to vMotion, and select *Use This Port Group for vMotion*, as shown in Figure 9.38. The best practice for the vMotion network is to use a private pSwitch or VLAN. Click *Next*.

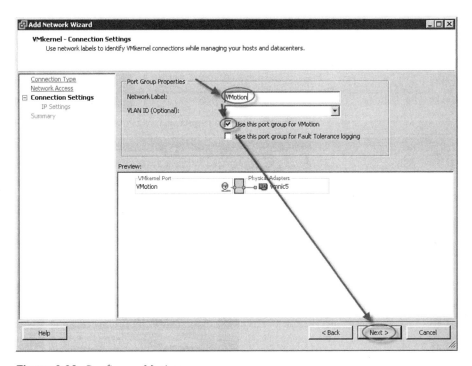

Figure 9.38 *Configure vMotion.*

Best Practice

The vMotion network should use a private pSwitch or VLAN.

9. Set the IP address and subnet mask of the vMotion network. It is also possible for the vSwitch to determine its own network address when the vMotion network already exists.

10. Click *Finish* to complete the creation of the vSwitch.

Note that now the system will ask you to specify the default gateway for all vmkernel-based portgroups on all vSwitches. There are two gateways for ESX, one for the service console that was set during installation time and one for all vmkernel devices. This split routing is because of who is actually connecting. The service console has been a virtual machine since ESX v3; as such, each VM needs a route. The vmkernel, on the other hand, is not a VM but also does routing and so needs its own default route. vMotion can be routed and is therefore able to send VMs across networks.

Creating a FT Network

A new feature of VMware vSphere is fault tolerance, where a VM with a single vCPU is running on one host, but a shadow copy is running on another host. This shadow copy is kept in vCPU Lockstep with the primary VM until there is a host or VM failure, and then the shadow copy would become the primary VM and a new shadow copy would be created on another host. The requirements for this are fairly simple, yet sometimes hard to meet:

- The ESX hosts must have shared access to some form of shared storage: NFS, iSCSI, or SAN.

- The ESX hosts must have portgroups and vSwitches named identically.

- The ESX hosts must have the same family of processor and in most cases share the same processor instruction set.

- The VM must have only one vCPU.

- vCenter must be in use.

- The hardware must support FT as described in Chapter 1, "System Considerations."

- You must have a license level that allows FT.

- It is strongly recommended that a dedicated gigabit or faster network be used.

If all these conditions are met, it is possible to use FT. FT requires a vSwitch or a port on a vSwitch set up just for FT. Many of these conditions will be met by the host participating in an Enhanced vMotion Capability (EVC) cluster and when either a virtual distributed switch or Host Profiles is also in use. However, there is no way around the need for proper physical processors because not all processors support FT.

When FT is set up, the VM is for all practical purposes vMotioned from one host to another, but the VM is not moved from the first host. Instead, a shadow copy is created that stays in lockstep with the primary VM's vCPU using VMware vLockStep technology. vLockStep uses the FT Logging network to transmit the nondeterministic data to the shadow copy VM's vCPU, thereby staying in sync. Table 9.2 shows the differences between vMotion and FT.

Table 9.2 *vMotion Compared to FT*

vMotion	FT
Quiesce the VM	Quiesce the VM
Set up VM on Second Host	Set up VM on Second Host
Transfer VM State and Configuration	Transfer VM State and Configuration
Create Memory Snapshot	Create Memory Snapshot
Transfer Memory Snapshot	Transfer Memory Snapshot
Transfer In-Use Memory	Transfer In-Use Memory
Transfer CPU State	Transfer CPU State Setting Up vLockStep
Register VM on Host B	Register Shadow Copy on Host B
Unregister VM on Host A	Transfer Nondeterministic Events to Shadow Copy on Host B, Keeping VMs in Lockstep

Command Line

This script example uses the first of the last two Intel-based pNICs. vSwitch2 is created, relabeled as FT, and then the pNIC is assigned to the vSwitch. Finally, the pNIC assigned to the FT vSwitch is converted to a vmkernel pNIC and given a nonroutable IP and netmask. This code is similar to what we used for vMotion previously. The key to note is that the final vmware-vim-cmd is quite a bit different.

```
# wnic=`/usr/sbin/esxcfg-nics -l | /bin/grep Intel | /bin/
grep Up | tail -2 | head -1 | /bin/awk '{print $1}'`
mip="192.168.1.1" # or some other non-routable IP
# /usr/sbin/esxcfg-vswitch -a vSwitch2
# /usr/sbin/esxcfg-vswitch -A "FT" vSwitch2
# /usr/sbin/esxcfg-vswitch -L $wnic vSwitch2
# /usr/sbin/esxcfg-vmknic -a -i $mip -n 255.255.255.0 FT
# vmk=`/usr/sbin/esxcfg-vmknic -l | /bin/grep FT | /bin/awk
'{print $1}'`
# vmware-vim-cmd hostsvc/advopt/update FT.Vmknic string $Vmk
```

vSC

Using the vSC to create a vMotion portgroup is similar to the creation of the VM Network vSwitch:

1. Log in to the vSC, either into the vCenter Server or directly to the host.

2. Select the ESX host in question.

3. Select the *Configuration* tab.

4. Click the *Networking* link.

5. Click the *Add Networking* link.

6. Select the vmkernel connection type that is available (refer to Figure 9.37).

7. Select at least one pNIC for the FT vSwitch (refer to Figure 9.30). However, two would be the best practice for redundancy. Note that this does not provide any capability to load balance.

8. Change the vSwitch name to FT, select *Use This Port Group for Fault Tolerance*, as shown in Figure 9.39. The best practice for the FT network is to use a private pSwitch or VLAN.

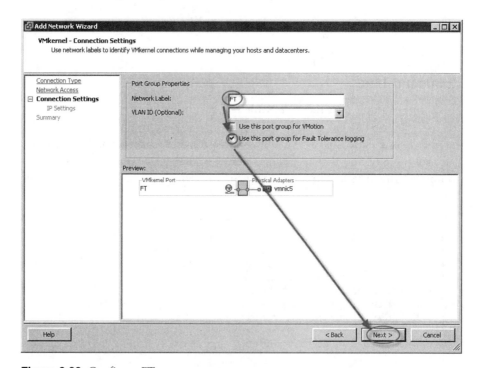

Figure 9.39 *Configure FT.*

9. Set the IP address and subnet mask of the FT network per Figure 9.40. It is important to not overlap this network with any other network because this could cause performance issues, but mainly, because CPU data is being transferred, it is possible to determine exactly what is happening within the VM if anyone is listening for this traffic. Best practice is to use a nonroutable network.

> ### Best Practice
>
> The FT network should use a private pSwitch or VLAN.

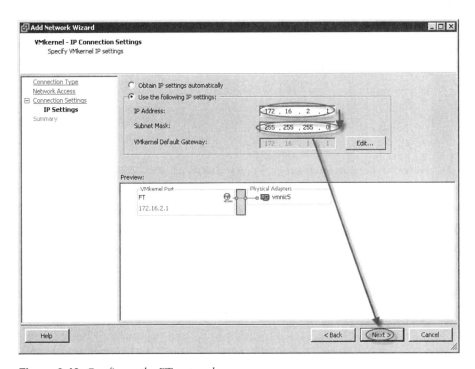

Figure 9.40 *Configure the FT network.*

10. Click *Finish* to complete the creation of the vSwitch.

Note that now the system may ask you to specify the default gateway for all vmkernel-based portgroups on all vSwitches if one has not already been specified. There are two gateways for ESX: one for the service console that was set during installation time and one for all vmkernel devices. FT can be routed and is therefore able to send VMs across networks. In general, however, this is not suggested for performance reasons because latency would then become a major issue for vLockStep.

Adding an iSCSI Network

iSCSI is available to be used by ESX directly as a datastore via hardware iSCSI initiators or the embedded software initiator. The iSCSI vSwitch portgroup must be part of the service console for ESX v3 because of the nature of the iSCSI implementation. Half of the iSCSI implementation is within the service console on ESX v3. This is no longer a requirement for ESX v4.

Command Line (ESX v4)

This code example uses the first of the last two Intel-based pNICs. vSwitch2 is created, relabeled as iSCSI, and then the pNIC is assigned to the vSwitch. Finally, the pNIC assigned to the iSCSI vSwitch is converted to a vmkernel pNIC and given the IP and netmask of the iSCSI data network.

```
# wnic=`/usr/sbin/esxcfg-nics -l | /bin/grep Intel | /bin/
grep Up | tail -2 | head -1 | /bin/awk '{print $1}'`
mip="192.168.1.1" # network used by iSCSI storage
# /usr/sbin/esxcfg-vswitch -a vSwitch2
# /usr/sbin/esxcfg-vswitch -A "iSCSI" vSwitch2
# /usr/sbin/esxcfg-vswitch -L $wnic vSwitch2
# /usr/sbin/esxcfg-vmknic -a -i $mip -n 255.255.255.0 iSCSI
```

Command Line (ESX v3)

The following code creates a new portgroup on the service console vSwitch named iSCSI. The portgroup is then converted to a vmkernel device and assigned an IP and netmask. Note that the netmask is restricted to just the iSCSI network:

```
# /usr/sbin/esxcfg-vswitch -A "iSCSI" vSwitch0
iip="10.0.1.34" # IP on iSCSI network
# /usr/sbin/esxcfg-vmknic -a -i $iip -n 255.255.255.0 iSCSI
```

vSC

The setup of the iSCSI portgroup on a vSwitch via the vSC is similar to the creation of the vMotion vSwitch because both are vmkernel devices. The differences are that instead of picking a pNIC, another vSwitch is chosen, and that the device is not assigned to be used by vMotion:

1. Log in to the vSC, either into the vCenter Server or directly to the host.

2. Select the ESX host in question.

3. Select the *Configuration* tab.

4. Click the *Networking* link.

5. Click the *Add Networking* link.

6. Select the *vmkernel* connection type (refer to Figure 9.34).

7. For ESX v4, select an unused pNIC.For ESX v3, select vSwitch0 (or the service console vSwitch) as the network access device, because this vSwitch is a portgroup off the service console vSwitch.

8. Change the vSwitch name to iSCSI, and set the IP address and subnet mask of the iSCSI network.

9. Click *Finish* to complete the creation of the vSwitch portgroup.

Adding a NAS vSwitch for Use by NFS

NFS file systems can hold VMs. NFS can also be used to hold ISO images and other bits of information necessary to create and manage VMs. ESX requires the creation of a specialized vSwitch or vSwitch portgroup for the use of NFS as a datastore. NFS file systems can be mounted directly to the service console, as well, but these types of NFS mounts cannot hold virtual machine files, just necessary management data. Note that such a mount is not possible with ESXi.

Command Line

Like the iSCSI device, NFS is its own portgroup on a vSwitch. In this code example, we take the last Intel-based pNIC and add it to a portgroup labeled NFS and convert it to a vmkernel portgroup with the appropriate IP address and netmask:

```
# znic=`/usr/sbin/esxcfg-nics -l | /bin/grep Intel | /bin/
grep Up | tail -2 | tail -1 | /bin/awk '{print $1}'`
zip="10.0.2.34" # on the NFS network
# /usr/sbin/esxcfg-vswitch -a vSwitch3
# /usr/sbin/esxcfg-vswitch -A "NFS" vSwitch3
# /usr/sbin/esxcfg-vswitch -L $znic vSwitch3
# /usr/sbin/esxcfg-vmknic -a -i $zip -n 255.255.255.0 NFS
```

vSC

The setup of the NFS portgroup via the vSC is similar to the creation of the vMotion vSwitch because both are vmkernel devices. The difference is that the device is not assigned to be used by vMotion:

1. Log in to the vSC, either into the vCenter Server or directly to the host.

2. Select the ESX host in question.

3. Select the *Configuration* tab.

4. Click the *Networking* link.

5. Click the *Add Networking* link.

6. Select the *vmkernel* connection type (refer to Figure 9.34).

7. Select the pNIC to assign to this vSwitch.

8. Change the vSwitch name to NFS, and set the IP address and subnet mask of the NFS network.

9. Click *Finish* to complete the creation of the vSwitch portgroup.

Adding a Private vSwitch

Adding a private vSwitch to an ESX host implies that any VM attached to it is local to the ESX host. This is extremely useful when duplicating network environments or placing VM-based firewalls between various subnets. A VM connected to a private vSwitch that is not also connected to a pNIC is a VM that cannot be hot migrated or used in conjunction with vMotion unless vCenter is modified to allow this behavior, which was discussed previously.

Command Line

From the ESX command line, create a private vSwitch by adding a vSwitch with the appropriate label. Our example code uses "Private Network" as the local vSwitch name:

```
/usr/sbin/esxcfg-vswitch -A "Private Network" vSwitch4
```

vSC

The setup of the private vSwitch via the vSC is similar to the creation of the VM network vSwitch. The difference is that the device is not assigned a pNIC:

1. Log in to the vSC, either into the vCenter Server or directly to the host.

2. Select the ESX host in question.

3. Select the *Configuration* tab.

4. Click the *Networking* link.

5. Click the *Add Networking* link.

6. Select the *VM Network* connection type that is available.

7. Unselect any pNIC previously selected, and do not select a pNIC.

8. Change the vSwitch name to Private Network.

9. Click *Finish* to complete the creation of the vSwitch portgroup.

Adding Additional pNICs to a vSwitch

It some cases, it would be nice to add a secondary pNIC to an existing vSwitch.

Command Line

For adding a secondary pNIC to the service console vSwitch of ESX, the following code finds the first Broadcom adapter and adds it to vSwitch0, which is the vSwitch for the service console:

```
# mnic=`/usr/sbin/esxcfg-nics -l | /bin/grep Broadcom | /bin/
grep Up | head -1 | /bin/awk '{print $1}'`
# /usr/sbin/esxcfg-vswitch -L $mnic vSwitch0
```

vSC

Within the vSC, it is possible to add a pNIC to an existing vSwitch by editing the vSwitch in question, as follows:

1. Log in to the vSC, either into the vCenter Server or directly to the host.

2. Select the ESX host in question.

3. Select the *Configuration* tab.

4. Click the *Networking* link.

5. Select the *properties* for the vSwitch to edit.

6. Select the *Network* Adapters tab.

7. Select the *Add* button.

8. Click the NIC to add to the vSwitch and then click *Next*. Review the output and click *Next* and *Finish* to complete the addition of the NIC to a vSwitch.

Adding vSwitch Portgroups

It is often important to add portgroups to a vSwitch as VLANs are added to the physical switches. Because the cabling requirements when using external switch tagging (EST) is just too high, VST will work best, and therefore vSwitches need VLANs.

Command Line

Adding a portgroup to a vSwitch from the ESX command line is done using the following command syntax:

```
esxcfg-vswitch -A portGroupName -v vlanID vSwitchName
```

vSC

Adding a vSwitch portgroup is the same as adding a vSwitch except that instead of selecting a pNIC, select the appropriate vSwitch and specify the VLAN ID. An example of this is shown earlier in the section "Adding an iSCSI Network to the Service Console vSwitch" for ESX v3.

Removing vSwitch Portgroups

When removing vSwitch portgroups, any VMs connected to that portgroup will be unable to talk to any other VM until they are attached to another portgroup. You may want to move the VMs from the portgroup to delete first.

Command Line

To delete a portgroup from a vSwitch from the ESX command line, use the following command syntax:

```
esxcfg-vswitch -D portGroupName vSwitchName
```

vSC

Deleting a portgroup from a vSwitch using the vSC goes like this:

1. Log in to the vSC, either into the vCenter Server or directly to the host.

2. Select the ESX host in question.

3. Select the *Configuration* tab.

4. Click the *Networking* link.

5. Click the *Properties* link opposite the vSwitch label to edit.

6. Select the portgroup to remove.

7. Click the *Remove* button.

8. Click *Yes* when asked, "Are you sure you want to remove this vSwitch portgroup?"

Distributed vSwitch Portgroup

Deleting a portgroup from a vDS from the vSC goes like this:

1. Log in to the vSC, either into the vCenter Server or directly to the host.

2. Press Ctrl+Shift+N to access the Network Inventory.

3. Select the dvPortgroup to delete.

4. Type Del to remove the portgroup.

5. Click *Yes* when asked, "Are you sure you want to remove this vSwitch portgroup?"

vSwitch Removal

vSwitch removal is quite straightforward and is often necessary because of networking modifications or other issues. When removing a vSwitch, any VMs connected to that vSwitch will be unable to talk to any other VM until they are attached to another portgroup. You may want to move the VMs from the vSwitch to delete first.

Command Line

Deleting vSwitches from the ESX version 3 command line is as simple as using the following, where # is the number of the vSwitch as listed using the esxcfg-vswitch –l command. This one command will remove all portgroups from the vSwitch, too:

```
esxcfg-vswitch -D vSwitch#
```

vSC

Deleting vSwitches using the vSC can be accomplished by following these steps:

1. Log in to the vSC, either into the vCenter Server or directly to the host.

2. Select the ESX host in question.

3. Select the *Configuration* tab.

4. Click the *Networking* link.

5. Click the *Remove* link opposite the vSwitch label to remove.

6. Click *Yes* when asked, "Are you sure you want to remove this vSwitch?"

Distributed vSwitch Removal

Deleting a vDS from the vSC goes like this:

1. Log in to the vSC, either into the vCenter Server or directly to the host.

2. Press Ctrl+Shift+N to access the Network Inventory.

3. Select the dvSwitch to delete.

4. Type Del to remove the dvSwitch.

5. Click *Yes* when asked, "Are you sure you want to remove this vSwitch?"

vSwitch Security

In ESX, each vSwitch and each attached portgroup has several properties that are in the realm of security. These settings provide the capability to disable VMs from forging source IP address and MAC addresses, and from entering promiscuous mode. On earlier versions of ESX, these settings are available to each VM, independent of the vSwitch or its portgroups. Moving these to the vSwitch makes much more sense because there is less to manage and it allows inheritance to take place from the vSwitch to each portgroup.

Command Line

To set the per vSwitch security settings within ESX, you must make use of the vmware-vim-cmd as we did for setting up FT and vMotion. You can configure the settings using the following:

```
# vmware-vim-cmd hostsvc/net/vswitch_setpolicy –securepolicy-
promisc=false
# vmware-vim-cmd hostsvc/net/vswitch_setpolicy –securepolicy-
macchange=false
# vmware-vim-cmd hostsvc/net/vswitch_setpolicy –securepolicy-
forgedxmit=false
```

vSC

It is possible to set the security settings on the vSwitch or the individual portgroup:

1. Log in to the vSC, either into the vCenter Server or directly to the host.

2. Select the ESX host in question.

3. Select the *Configuration* tab.

4. Click the *Networking* link.

5. Click the *Edit Properties* link opposite the vSwitch to edit.

6. Select the vSwitch from the left-side display.

7. Click the *Edit* button.

8. Select the *Security* tab.

9. Using the drop-downs, select the Accept or Reject options as appropriate (see Figure 9.41).

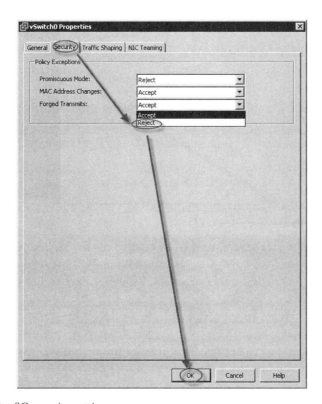

Figure 9.41 *vSC security setting*

To set the settings on the portgroup at step 6, select the portgroup to modify, select Edit, and then use the check box to override the default vSwitch settings before selecting from the drop-down (see Figure 9.42).

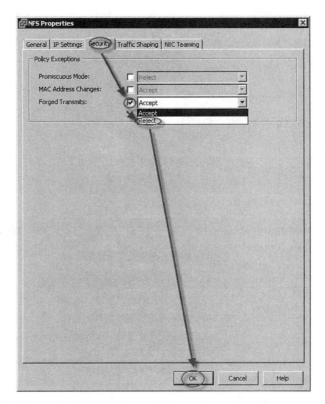

Figure 9.42 *vSC security settings*

vSwitch Properties

Each vSwitch also has several properties associated with it. Specifically, the settings are those for load balancing, failover, and pNIC state detection. For ESX version 3, there are additional properties, including the number of ports to assign to the vSwitch.

Command Line
Similar to setting security settings, it is possible to set various vSwitch properties from the command line using the same vmware-vim-cmd family of commands,

as demonstrated previously in the vSwitch Security Command Line discussion. Table 9.3 contains a list of options you can use and what they set.

Table 9.3 *vSwitch Capabilities and Policy Settings*

Setting	Option
Beacon Monitoring	`--failurecriteria-check-beacon=bool`
Traffic Shaping Policy	`--shapingpolicy-enabled=bool` `--shapingpolicy-average-bandwidth=int` `--shapingpolicy-peak-bandwidth=int` `--shapingpolicy-burst-size=int`
Active NICs in Team	`--nicorderpolicy-active=vmnic_list`
Order in which NIC Failover should occur	`--nicorderpolicy-standby=vmnic_list`
Check Failover using Speed check	`--failurecriteria-check-speed=bool`
Check Failover using link duplex check	`--failurecriteria-check-duplex=bool`
Check Failover using link error percent	`--failurecriteria-error=int`
Check Failover using Beacon Monitoring	`--failurecriteria-beacon=bool`
Whether or not to use rolling failover	`--nicteaming-rollingorder=bool`
Load Balance Policy	`--nicteaming-policy=nicteaming-policy`
Load Balance inbound Frames	`--nicteaming-reverse-policy=bool`

In the settings in the table, an int implies some integer value, and a bool implies one of the words *true* or *false*. The `vmnic_list` required is a list of vmnics derived from using either `vmware-vim-cmd` or `esxcfg-nic -l`. `nicteaming-policy` is one of `loadbalance_srcid`, `loadbalance_id`, `loadbalance_srcmac`, or `failover_explicit`.

vSC

To make the changes outlined in Table 9.3 using the vSC, follow these steps:

1. Log in to the vSC, either into the vCenter Server or directly to the host.

2. Select the ESX host in question.

3. Select the *Configuration* tab.

4. Click the *Networking* link.

5. Click the *Properties* link opposite the vSwitch to edit.

6. Select the vSwitch from the left-side display.

7. Click the *Edit* button.

8. Select the *NIC Teaming* tab.

9. Use the following actions to modify options as appropriate. Note the letters and their corresponding settings in Figure 9.43 and Figure 9.44.

    a. Select the load balancing method (1 of 4).

    b. Enable or disable beacon monitoring. Only enable if requested to by support (Yes or No).

    c. Enable or disable vSwitch notifications (Yes or No).

    d. Enable or disable Failback mode (Yes or No), which is Rolling Mode in ESX v3.

    e. Change which pNIC is the default pNIC by moving a pNIC up or down or move a pNIC to standby mode.

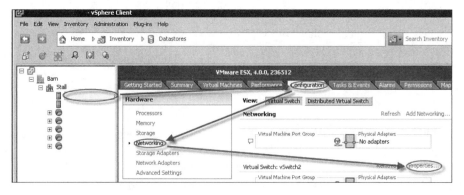

Figure 9.43 *vSC NIC team settings*

10. Select the *General* tab.

11. Using the drop-down, select the number of ports on the vSwitch. This is not the same as the number of ports per portgroup. Changing the number of ports on a vSwitch requires a reboot.

It is often a best practice to decrease the number of vSwitch ports for sensitive networks so that VMs cannot be assigned to them accidentally or on purpose because of port limitations.

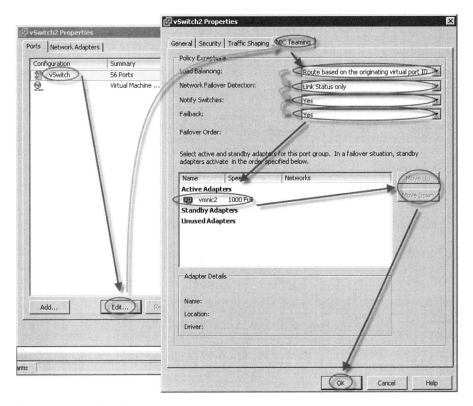

Figure 9.44 *vSC NIC team settings, part two*

Best Practice

Decrease the number of vSwitch ports for sensitive networks.

Changing vmkernel Gateways

The vmkernel gateway was introduced in ESX v3 as a way to tell what is the default vmkernel network and gateway. The default vmkernel network is the one used by vMotion by default. For ESXi, this implies that the vmkernel management appliance and vmkernel vMotion port both share the same gateway. This is often not a desired position from a security perspective but should be noted and modified.

Command Line

The vSC lets you set a generic vmkernel gateway. However, for a finer level of control, the command line offers the capability to set a per-vmkernel network gateway and netmask. For example, if you want to have a Class B network mask for one network and a Class C or some other subnet for another network, this can be easily achieved from the command line using the following commands. The dotted-decimal network format is used for each of the arguments to the command. To delete a route, use the following syntax:

```
esxcfg-route -d network netmask gateway
```

To add a route, use this syntax:

```
esxcfg-route -a network netmask gateway
```

It is also possible to specify multiple routes using these commands, just as it is possible to specify multiple routes for the service console. If the network to be modified is named default, this specifies the default route. To modify the default route, just use "default" in place of "network" in the previous examples.

vSC

The vSC network route modification only allows the modification of the default generic routes for all vmkernel devices and does not allow a per-vmkernel network granularity.

1. Log in to the vSC, either into the vCenter Server or directly to the host.

2. Select the ESX host in question.

3. Select the *Configuration* tab.

4. Click the *DNS and Routing* link.

5. Select the *Routing* tab.

6. Edit the vmkernel default gateway values (see Figure 9.45).

7. Click *OK*.

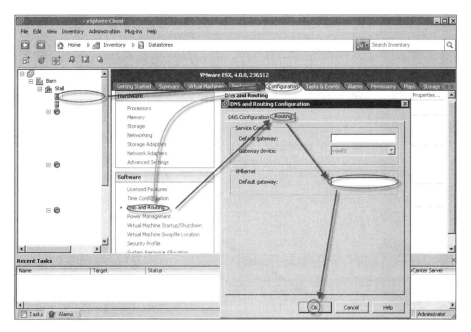

Figure 9.45 *vSC setting the default route*

Changing pNIC Settings

It may also desirable to disable autonegotiate on a pNIC. To do that, use the tools for each version of ESX outlined in the following sections. It is a VMware best practice to configure pNICS that are connected to pSwitches for autonegotiate.

Command Line

There is no real way to do this in ESX versions earlier than version 3, short of a reboot. However, the following will work for ESX:

```
esxcfg-nics -s [10|100|1000|10000] -d [full|half] vmnic#
```

vSC

Within the vSC, it is sometimes necessary to disable autonegotiation:

1. Log in to the vSC, either into the vCenter Server or directly to the host.

2. Select the ESX host in question.

3. Select the *Configuration* tab.

4. Click the *Networking* link.

5. Click the *Properties* link opposite the vSwitch to edit. This is so far the same as Figure 9.43.

6. Select the *Network Adapters* tab.

7. Select the pNIC to modify.

8. Click the *Edit* button.

9. Using the drop-down, select the speed and duplex of the pNIC (see Figure 9.46).

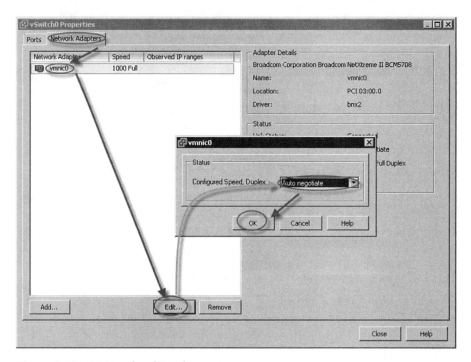

Figure 9.46 *vSC Speed and Duplex settings*

Changing Traffic-Shaping Settings

It may also be desirable to limit the amount of traffic a vSwitch or portgroup can accept. This uses the concept of traffic shaping where it is possible to limit, by the average amount of bandwidth, the peak possible bandwidth and the burst size allowed.

Command Line

For ESX, it is possible to set up traffic shaping using the vmware-vim-cmd command documented within Table 9.2 and demonstrated next. Note that the int mentioned in the following commands would be substituted for your desired values for traffic shaping.

```
# vmware-vim-cmd hostsvc/net/vswitch_setpolicy
➥--shapingpolicy-enabled=true
# vmware-vim-cmd hostsvc/net/vswitch_setpolicy
➥--shapingpolicy-average-bandwidth=int
# vmware-vim-cmd hostsvc/net/vswitch_setpolicy
➥--shapingpolicy-peak-bandwidth=int
# vmware-vim-cmd hostsvc/net/vswitch_setpolicy
➥--shapingpolicy-burst-size=int
```

vSC

Changing traffic-shaping settings can be accomplished in the vSC by doing the following:

1. Log in to the vSC, either into the vCenter Server or directly to the host.

2. Select the ESX host in question.

3. Select the *Configuration* tab.

4. Click the *Networking* link.

5. Click the *Properties* link opposite the vSwitch to edit.

6. Select the vSwitch or portgroup to modify.

7. Click the *Edit* button.

8. Select the *Traffic Shaping* tab.

9. Using the drop-down for *Status* (see Figure 9.47), select Enable Traffic Shaping, and then set the values appropriately, and finish by clicking OK.

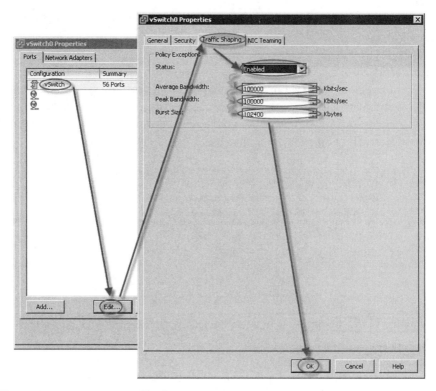

Figure 9.47 *vSC setting traffic shaping*

iSCSI VMFS

An iSCSI-based VMFS looks and acts just like a SAN-based VMFS except in the configuration of the iSCSI device. To connect to an iSCSI target, iSCSI must be enabled first and the proper portgroup on the service console vSwitch created (as discussed previously). Because there is no difference between manipulating a SAN VMFS and an iSCSI VMFS, only the enabling and configuration of an iSCSI device is covered.

Command Line

It is possible to configure iSCSI from the command line by first enabling iSCSI using the following and then determining the adapterName used (which is highlighted):

```
# esxcfg-swiscsi -e
# esxcfg-info | awk '/ISCSI Name/{gn=1; print $0}\
/vmhba/ {if (gn > 0) {print $0; gn=0}}'
     |----ISCSI Name.......................................
iqn.1998-01.com.vmware:xxxxxxx-4c58c00b
       |----Name.........................................
.vmhba33
```

Specify an iSCSI target using the following, where staticTarget is the IP address or a hostname:

```
vmkiscsi-tool -D -a staticTarget vmhba33
```

To scan an iSCSI target for VMFS or new LUNs, use the following:

```
esxcfg-swiscsi -s
```

vSC

The alternative to the command line is to use the vSC to configure an iSCSI device. To do so, follow these steps:

1. Log in to the vSC, either into the vCenter Server or directly to the host.

2. Select the ESX host in question.

3. Select the *Configuration* tab.

4. Click the *Storage Adapters* link.

5. Select the iSCSI software adapter represented by the vhba40 adapter.

6. Below the Storage Adapter window some adapter properties appear. Click the *Properties* link.

7. Click the *Configure* button.

8. Check the *Enabled* check box (see Figure 9.48), and then click *OK*. Be prepared to wait.

9. Select the *Dynamic Discovery* tab (see Figure 9.49).

10. Enter an IP address or system name in the Dynamic Discovery window in the form of ipAddress or systemName.

11. Select the iSCSI port. 3260 represents the iSCSI port to use on the server specified. Finally, click *Add*, and be prepared to wait a while.

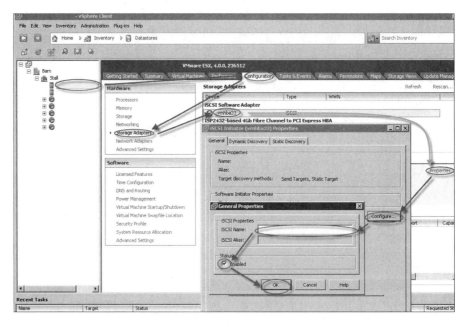

Figure 9.48 *vSC Enable iSCSI*

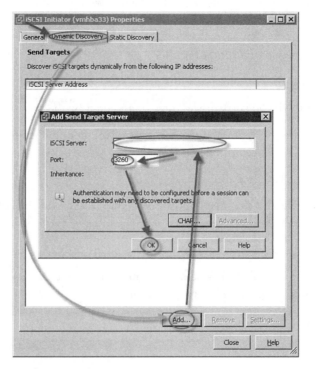

Figure 9.49 *vSC Dynamic Discovery*

When the iSCSI adapter can see the LUNs, all the standard SAN-based VMFS actions discussed earlier apply. You may first have to rescan your iSCSI device to see the LUNs.

On ESX v3, a common problem is that the iSCSI target is not available from the service console or the netmask for the iSCSI gateway is not set properly.

Network-Attached Storage

In ESX, it is possible to use NFS-based NAS as a VM datastore in addition to storing anything else the ESX host might require, such as ISO, floppy, and other image files that the ESX host could then use in the deployment of VMs. There are three approaches for accessing NFS-based shares and only one for CIFS (Windows)-based shares. These approaches are covered either by the command line or the vSC.

Command Line

All versions of ESX can mount CIFS- or NFS-based shares directly to the service console; but as of ESX v3, these service console mounted shares can be accessed only if they are under the `/vmimages` directory and then only if the `/etc/vmware/configrules` file has been modified to allow such a behavior. This is *not* recommended.

Use the following commands to mount a share to the service console for NFS. If the `mountPoint` specified is within the `/vmimages` directory umbrella, it is accessible to VMs for the purposes of using the files as ISOs or floppies in the CD-ROM and floppy virtual devices. However, for earlier versions of ESX, the `mountPoint` location is left up to the administrator:

```
mount -o nfs server:/share /mountPoint
```

To automount, add the appropriate entry into the `/etc/fstab` file, and for ESX version 3, enable the NFS client via the firewall:

```
esxcfg-firewall -e nfsClient
```

Automount of NFS volumes within the service console is not suggested because there could be host startup issues if the NFS server is unreachable. In addition, this is not available with ESXi.

For CIFS-based shares, the following command can be used to mount a CIFS share to any mount point on the system. Because the mounting of a CIFS share requires a password to be used on the command line or left in a file on the system, it is not the most secure mechanism and is not recommended.

```
# mount -t smbfs -o username=username,password=password
//server/share mountPoint
```

To automount, add the appropriate entry into the `/etc/fstab` file. If you want to hide the username and password, you can use a `credentials=/etc/.credentials` and place in `.credentials` two lines similar to the following. The credentials file can be named anything you want:

```
username=user
password=pass
```

To allow SMB-style mounts to the service console, enable the firewall for ESX version 3 using the following:

```
esxcfg-firewall -e smbClient
```

It is also possible to use the smbmount or smbclient commands to access remote shares. The `smbclient` command is used to transfer data or test connectivity. There are many ways to mount shares with the Samba tools, and they are covered in detail in other books.

This works only for ESX, not for ESXi.

Best Practice

Never mount NFS or CIFS directly to the service console.

Always use NFS-based datastores to hold deployment and other files.

ESX and ESXi can, use the vmkernel to mount a data store for VM storage directly to the ESX host using the following command. It is not possible to use this command to mount CIFS-based shares. The mounted file system would be accessible under `/vmfs/volumes/LABEL`. Each mount point in `/vmfs/volumes` also has its own UID associated with it, and ESX uses the UIDs and not the `LABEL` names internally:

```
esxcfg-nas -a -o host -s share LABEL
```

Using NFS as a datastore allows you to change volume labels without breaking everything, because the cleanup happens automatically.

vSC

When accessing an NFS datastore from the vSC, there is a handy wizard that will help:

1. Log in to the vSC, either into the vCenter Server or directly to the host.

2. Select the ESX host in question.

3. Select the *Configuration* tab.

4. Click the *Storage (SCSI, SAN, and NFS)* link.

5. Click the *Add Storage* link in the upper-right corner of the window.

6. Click the *Network File System* button.

7. Click the *Next* button.

8. Specify the server name or IP address, the share to mount, and the label for the datastore. It is also possible to mount the share read-only by checking the *Mount NFS Read-Only* check box (see Figure 9.50).

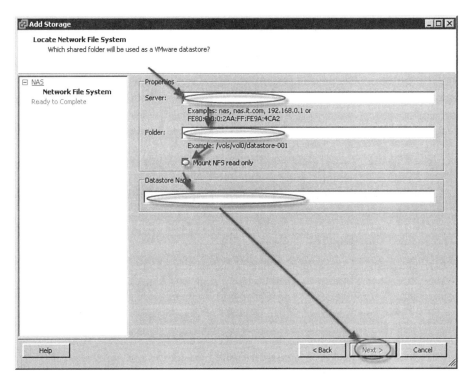

Figure 9.50 *vSC specify NFS datastore settings*

9. Click the *Next* button to review your settings, and then click *Finish*.

Mapping Information

ESX provides a feature to the vSC: the mapping feature. The maps enable an administrator to see immediately which ESX hosts or VMs are using which datastores, networks, and hosts. Not only is there the capability to map these relationships, but the elements can also be edited from the map. It is possible to see all the data at once or just a portion of the data corresponding to the host in question, VM, network, datastore, or any combination thereof. The maps provide the pictorial view of the virtual infrastructure that is extremely necessary when dealing with large-scale environments. As they say, "A picture is worth a thousand words." There is *no* command-line version of these maps available. However, Alan Renouf has a very nice script that will, if Visio is available, create a map style report. Check out www.virtu-al.net/2009/01/26/vdiagram-draw-your-vi-with-one-script/ for the vDiagram powershell script.

The mapping feature of the vSC connected to a vCenter server gives a clear understanding of which ESX hosts are connected to which datastore and network. In the past, to get a map of these connections, you had to visit each ESX host independently and then read the data and create a map by hand or use some other tool. Now it is possible to follow some simple steps to produce a handy map to tell you which ESX hosts are connected to which datastores and which networks:

1. Log in to the vSC, either into the vCenter Server or directly to the host.

2. Select the ESX datacenter, cluster, or folder in question. Selecting a single ESX host sort of defeats the purpose of creating the map for datastore connectivity.

3. Select the *Map* tab.

4. Select the map options. In the case of Figure 9.51, I selected Host to Network and Host to Datastore and whether there were any VM Fault Tolerance Relationships.

The use of maps is a great way to verify that all ESX hosts participating in a cluster or vMotion network share the proper datastores and networks. Without this information, vMotion becomes problematic. In addition, it is possible to directly interact with all the icons in the map to either manipulate a datastore, a network, or a host. This interaction opens a menu when you right-click an icon.

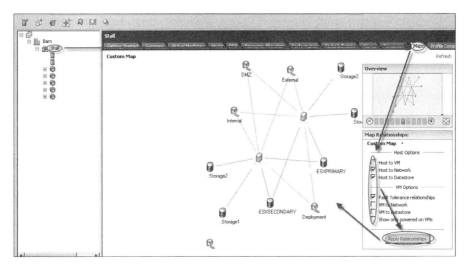

Figure 9.51 *vSC use of maps*

Secure Access to Management Interfaces

With ESX, it is possible to access the service console or management appliance or vCenter servers through a firewall using secure tunnels. SSH can produce such a tunnel and is available for all forms of client machines. For the web interfaces, a client using any operating system can be used. However, for vCenter or VMware vSphere Client (vSC) access, a .NET-enabled Windows operating system is required. The solution to the problem is to design your management network such that the following is true:

- ESX service consoles and ESXi management appliances are on the virtualization management network.

- vCenter Server is on the virtualization management network.

- All tools used by an administrator that either access ESX, ESXi, or vCenter are on the virtualization management network via Jump Machines used by the virtualization administrators. Jump Machines are VMs on which the management tools are installed, yet live within the virtualization management.

- The virtualization management network is firewalled from the rest of the network, only allowing RDP access to the administrative Jump Machines.

- For those who need less than full access, a proxy service such as Hyper9's VMM should be put into place that also talks through the firewall.

This configuration enables the best security for the management network because it is important to understand that access to the virtualization management network can provide access to everything.

Advanced Settings

The FC HBA VMFS section in this chapter touched on how to change appropriate advanced settings and provided mechanisms to do so. However, other settings are in need of manipulation occasionally. One mentioned in previous chapters is the ConflictRetries setting. The ConflictRetries setting governs how many SCSI retries to attempt before failing the SCSI command. The setting to modify is /Scsi/ConflictRetries.

```
# esxcfg-advcfg -g /Scsi/Conflictretries # View
# esxcfg-advcfg -s 80 /Scsi/Conflictretries # Set to a value
of 80
```

> **Best Practice for Advanced Settings**
>
> Do not manipulate advanced settings unless directed by a VMware support organization or you have a complete understanding of the consequences of making the change.

To set an option, use either the CLI or vSC. If it is necessary to use the command line, then for ESX, use the esxcfg-advcfg or the vmware-vim-cmd command.

Conclusion

In this chapter, we have gone through the configuration of an ESX host, and as such, you can extract a CLI-based script that does the work for you by combining all the small snippets into one script. However, this script assumes that you have a specific hardware setup—that is, that Broadcom and Intel NICs are in use and that they are in a specific order within the server. You will need to adjust the script to meet your specific needs. Such an adjustment will require Linux expertise to complete. For example, the script assumes there are two Broadcom adapters and at least four Intel pNICs and that the Broadcom adapters are listed first when you query the PCI device table, which for some onboard adapters is the way they appear.

Many of the items described herein need to be done prior to creating VMs, specifically anything related to networking and the service console, because these items can require reboots. In addition, a VMFS data store needs to be configured, and we have reviewed the mechanisms to access iSCSI-, SAN-, and NAS-based datastores, and their caveats. Now that this is completed and we have the previous chapters to back us up with necessary information, it is possible to create a VM on the host.

Chapter 10

Virtual Machines

The previous chapters dealt with the VMware ESX host, in contrast to virtual machines (VMs). They provided the information we needed to get to this stage—of being able to create and manipulate VMs, having an understanding of datastores, virtual networking, security, and the hardware required. Now we can build on our knowledge and add in some VMs.

Overview of Virtual Hardware

The next step in our progression is to understand what makes up a VM before we start to create them. In essence, what makes up the VM dictates what operating systems and devices the OS can access. For example, the wrong choice of SCSI adapter could make it very difficult to install or even run Windows XP.

With Virtual Hardware version 7, there have been some great leaps forward in functionality, such as the support for hot adding of memory, and several aspects have been made easier to manage. There is not a lot of difference between what virtual hardware is in use and how the physical hardware is actually used; the virtual hardware is emulated, paravirtualized, or fully virtualized in the physical CPU Cores (pCPUs) of the server in use. There has been some talk about which of these concepts is the best, and until now, they were not strictly necessary to understand. But they are now:

- Emulation

  Emulation is the translation of commands sent to a virtual device to what is acceptable to the physical hardware device. The implementation is in software of an exact interface to a legacy physical device so that guest OS drivers do not need to be modified. Emulation enables the out-of-the-box installation of operating systems as well as the support of legacy OSs. An example is the translation of instructions from a PCNET32 network device to a Broadcom gigabit network adapter. This translation occurs inside the hypervisor.

- Paravirtualization

  Paravirtualization is when the OS running inside the VM (guest OS) knows that it is virtualized and is using drivers specifically designed to work with the virtualization hypervisor. An example is the vmxnet network driver provided as part of the VMware Tools to most guest operating systems. Paravirtualized drivers often communicate over a per VM shared memory segment that exists in the virtual machine manager. This shared memory segment generally enables faster handling of data between the driver and hypervisor.

- Fully virtualized

  A fully virtualized guest does not have any specialized drivers, nor is there any emulation within the hypervisor. This technology pushes down into the pCPU any translation activities. Any machine that has a pCPU supporting AMD-V or Intel-VT technology has guests that can be fully virtualized.

Whether emulated, paravirtualized, or fully virtualized, each VM has a limited amount of virtual hardware that can be assigned to it when talking about VMware ESX host. Granted, although other VMware virtualization products can handle more items, such as USB and sound cards, ESX does not support those workstation-type devices unless you are using vSphere v4.x, which supports USB devices. The following list provides a breakdown of what is supported by ESX and the how the device is supported.

There are now multiple supported virtual hardware versions: Virtual Hardware version 4 (VHv4) and Virtual Hardware version 7 (VHv7). There are many differences between the two, and although vSphere supports both, it is often suggested to move to VHv7.

VMs can consist of the following devices:

- Virtual CPUs (vCPU)

  Up to four vCPUs are supported with VHv4, whereas eight are supported with VHv7. It is also possible to overcommit the number of vCPUs in relation to the number of pCPUs or cores within the system. There is one caveat: If the VM is to have X vCPUs (note that three is not a supported number prior to ESX v4), there must be at least X many threads (in the case of hyperthreaded pCPUs) or cores available to the machine. It is not possible to run a four-vCPU VM on a system with only two cores because each vCPU requires its own core or thread upon which to run.

With VHv4, it is possible to have one, two, or four vCPUs. With VHv7, it is possible to have any number of vCPUs up to eight. Although three, five, or seven vCPUs seems like odd numbers of vCPUs, it is nonetheless possible to use those numbers of vCPUs with VHv7. For certain Guest Operating Systems, it is also possible to hot add vCPUs with VHv7.

Last, VMware has taken a VMware Workstation feature and added it to VMware ESX, Multicore Virtual CPUs. In this, case it is possible to choose a single vCPU but add vCores to the vCPU, which may help with per socket licensing issues.

Note that more vCPUs does not always imply better performance. Performance depends on whether the guest OS and the application to be used on the VM use multiple CPUs. In general, if the application is threaded, it will make use of multiple CPUs. Many applications are not threaded, and adding vCPUs to a VM has an adverse performance impact.

- PCI Devices

Each VM can have up to 6 PCI devices attached at any given time for VHv4, but 15 for VHv7. For each version, there are X minus 1 PCI slots that the VM can use, because the display device takes up 1 slot. Within these X slots, it is possible to mix and match the other devices up to their maximums.

- Memory

Each VM can have up to 64GB for VHv4 or 256 GB for VHv7 of memory associated. If the physical memory is below the total used memory of the VMs, the memory for the VMs will employ one of the memory overcommit technologies within ESX (swap to disk, balloon driver, memory compression) as more is required. This causes performance issues as the used memory exceeds the available within host, and not necessarily the memory assigned to the VM. In addition, when a VM is started up, a .vswp file is created that is equal in size to the amount of memory assigned to the VM.

For 32-bit Windows VMs, the limit is 3.6GB of memory, because this is a limitation in 32-bit Windows operating systems. This limitation may not be the same for other non-Windows operating systems. Linux, for example, does not have this limitation, but to reach higher memory numbers often requires different kernels.

For certain Guest Operating Systems, it is possible to also add memory while the VM is running if you are using VHv7.

- Virtual IDE drives (vIDE)

  There is a limit of four vIDE devices. Like a standard IDE-based system, only two IDE controllers are available. But unlike them, when using VHv4 it is not possible to use IDE-based hard drives in a VM. With VHv7, this limitation has been removed, and you can now have VMs with IDE-based virtual disks. That generally makes importing IDE based systems much easier.

- Virtual floppy drives (vFloppy)

  There is a limit of two vFloppy devices. Like most PC-based systems, there is only one floppy controller available, which supports up to two devices.

- Virtual display (vDisplay, vSVGA)

  There is only one display available to a VM, which is accessible only via VMware's remote console software (more on this later). Each display can have a depth of 1, 8, 15, 16, 24, or with VHv7 32 bits. The bit depth of the display tells the virtual super VGA (vSVGA) device how many colors it can display within the remote console. Choose a bit depth that is lower than capability of the display device on which the remote console will be displayed. By default, the depth is set to 1, which lets the remote console decide how many bits to use for the vSVGA.

  As of VHv7, you can now attach up to 10 displays to the single vSVGA adapter. This addition could have uses as systems with large numbers of monitors are virtualized.

- Virtual keyboard and mouse (vKeyboard, vMouse)

  Like a normal PC-based system, there is only one vKeyboard and one vMouse device. These devices show up as standard PS/2 type devices.

- Virtual NIC (vNIC)

  There is a limit of 4 vNIC adapters with VHv4 and 10 vNIC adapters with VHv7 available to any VM. These network adapters can be of type "flexible," which implies that the driver installed within the VM chooses what vNIC type to use. This installed driver can either be a standard PC-NET32 or vlance device or VMware's vmxnet device. The PCNET32 is a simple 10Mbps-style device, whereas the vmxnet is a GbE device that knows about the virtualization layer and can reach higher speeds. The speeds reported by the vNIC with in the Guest OS are not representative of the maximum throughput achievable by the device. Even the PCNET32 (which reports 10Mbps) can push traffic at wire speeds. Admittedly, it will use a lot more CPU.

A vmxnet vNIC is a paravirtualized device per our previous definitions and is available only when VMware Tools is installed. VMware Tools is discussed later. There are three other network device types available as well: Intel E1000, vmxnet2, and vmxnet3. The E1000 not only needs to be set on the VM side, but the driver used within the VM must be an Intel E1000 driver. The same holds true for vmxnet2 and vmxnet3. The last two drivers provide performance and other improvements on the original vmxnet. vmxnet3 is available only with VHv7.

With VHv4, to select an e1000 driver, you need to edit the configuration file after the VM is created.

Available drivers:

- pcnet32—AMD Lance Device, which is a common driver across most older operating systems.

- e1000—Intel e1000 Gigabit Adapter, common in most modern operating systems. Supports TSO and Jumbo Frames.

- vmxnet—First iteration of the VMware paravirtualized driver.

- vmxnet2—Second iteration of the VMware paravirtualized driver.

- vmxnet3—Third iteration of the VMware paravirtualized driver with support for Jumbo Frames and TSO.

- Virtual SCSI controller (vSCSI controller).

Each VM can support up to four vSCSI controllers. For VHv4, each controller is either a BusLogic or LSILogic device, depending on the OS installed. Older versions of Guest OS generally support the BusLogic, whereas newer versions support the LSILogic device. VHv7 has added two new controller types to the list: LSI Logic SAS and VMware Paravirtual (PVSCSI).

The choice of which to use is important as the Guest OS will not find its disk if the wrong type of vSCSI controller is specified. Each vSCSI controller can support up to 15 virtual SCSI devices for a total 60 total SCSI devices. vSCSI controllers can have their bus sharing mode for use with shared disk clusters. Bus sharing can be set to nothing (the default), which implies there is no bus sharing, or to physical, which implies that a shared disk is shared between two or more VMs or physical machines. In the case of VMs, the VMs reside on different ESX hosts. The last mode is to set bus sharing to virtual, which is used when all the VMs participating in a shared disk cluster are on the same ESX host. We will delve into setting up clusters later.

- Virtual SCSI device (vSCSI device)

  A vSCSI device is either a VM disk file (VMDK), system LUN or raw disk map (RDM), or a SCSI pass-thru device. Because each vSCSI controller can handle up to 15 devices, there is a lot of room for disk drives. However, it should be mentioned that depending on the hardware attached and the application suite, there is often a need to put vSCSI devices on multiple controllers. A good case in point is a VMDK used as a quorum drive. Any shared-bus vSCSI controller should not host the C: or root drive for any VM and therefore should be a separate controller. In general, RDMs also use their own controller.

  Finally, it is possible to also have tape drives or tape robots be part of a VM through a SCSI pass-thru mechanism, where the ESX host passes all requests from the VM to the locally attached SCSI tape device. It is possible to attach other SCSI devices to a VM using this mechanism. The most common usage is for tape devices. An example of this type of device is provided later. Another use of these devices is to present a local SCSI LUN as if it were an RDM. These types of vSCSI devices should have their own vSCSI controller as well.

- SIO controller

  SIO is the Super I/O controller for the VM that provides I/O control for floppy disk controllers, parallel ports, serial ports, as well as keyboard and mouse interfaces.

- PCI device

  Normally, there is only one PCI Controller within any given VM, but that has changed with VHv7 and VMDirectPath, which allow a VM to directly see any PCI device within a host that supports Intel VT-d or AMD I/O Virtualization Technology (IOMMU). At the moment, only Single Root I/O virtualization is supported, which implies that if you assign a PCI card directly to a VM, that VM owns the entire PCI card. This is a useful feature for virtualization VMs that use specialized hardware. It does have the side effect of pinning a VM to a given host, however.

- Serial device

  Serial devices can be added to VMs as well using a few methods, either directly connecting to a serial port on the host, outputting to a file on a datastore as a console log, or connecting to a named pipe. We will discuss serial ports later in this chapter. In general, use of serial ports pin a VM to a host.

- Parallel device

  Parallel devices can be added to VMs as well using a few methods, either directly connecting to a parallel port on the host or outputting to a file on the host. We will discuss parallel ports later in this chapter. In general, use of parallel ports pins a VM to a host.

- VMCI device

  A VMCI device is new to VHv7 and enables you to communicate out of band between two or more VMs on the same host. In essence, you could use VMCI to bypass the virtual network. The use case for widespread VMCI use is still under development. Use of VMCI requires VMware Tools to be installed.

- USB controller

  New with VMware vSphere is the capability to connect a VM directly to any USB device in use on a given host. Like parallel and serial device connections, this would pin a VM to a specific host.

That is the complete list of all available virtual hardware. When creating a VM, each VM is automatically assigned one device of the following: vCPU, vKeyboard, vMouse, vDisplay, vNIC, vFloppy, and vIDE. The type of vNIC is up to the VM creator but defaults to the flexible vNIC. The amount of memory depends on the Guest OS to install, because 32-bit operating systems can generally access less memory than 64-bit operating systems, and the vSCSI controller does, too. By default, no vSCSI devices are attached to the controller, and that is left up to the VM creator. The vIDE device is for CD/DVD ROM access and has no virtual disks associated with it by default.

Creating VMs

There are three ways to create VMs within ESX and ESXi. The common methods are to create VMs from the command line or via the VMware vSphere Client (vSC). The alternative way is to use the vSphere SDK. In all cases, great care must be made to make sure that the files are placed in the correct locations and that the virtual hardware chosen matches up with the guest OS to use. The basic method to create a VM applies to almost all VMs. There are certain differences and considerations during the process, but the process is essentially the same regardless of the guest OS in use. In a subsequent section, we review special guest OS cases. This section is all about setting up the virtual hardware and deploying a new VM.

Normally, the process of setting up a new server and desktops requires a needs analysis, architecture review, purchase order, the wait while the hardware arrives, the time it takes to set up the hardware and configure any connections to storage and network, and then finally the installation of an OS to lead up to the installation of a specific application suite.

With ESX or ESXi, we alleviate the need for a purchase order, the wait while the hardware arrives, and the time to set up the hardware and configure any connections to storage and network. Although it would be nice to alleviate the other steps, that is not something ESX or ESXi can do. You still need to follow your process and perform the needs analysis, architecture review, and so on. Actually, these steps are by far more important in a virtual environment because it is trivially easy to create VMs and therefore impact performance of all your VMs. In addition, these reviews are necessary to determine whether you need to purchase more capacity instead of being surprised when there is not enough disk space to create the virtual disk for a VM.

> **Best Practice**
>
> Have a well-documented virtual machine life-cycle process.
>
> Impose this process as early as possible within the deployment process for a new VM.

Herein, we cover the steps necessary to create virtual hardware that can have a Guest OS installed on it. There are a few considerations before we begin. Table 10.1 lists the requirements before the virtual hardware can be created.

Table 10.1   *Considerations for Virtual Hardware*

Consideration	Comments
Number of vNICs needed	The number of vNICs depends on whether the VM will be multihomed. A vFW, vRouter, or vGateway will have at least two vNICs. Most other machines require only one vNIC. Do not add a second for failover; that is handled by the ESX host. However, you may need more for net-based backups. With ESX, there are other ways to produce backup, so you may want to use one of those methods discussed in Chapter 12, instead of a net-based backup solution.

Consideration	Comments
How the VM will be installed	If the VM will be installed via PXEboot or over the web, a network must be connected at boot time of the VM. If the installation mode is via CD-ROM, the CD-ROM must be connected at boot time.
Whether the vSCSI device be a VMDK or a system LUN	If a system LUN or RDM is to be used, is the LUN available to the ESX server? If a VMDK is to be used, what is the base size of the VMDK to use? It is wise to have a standard size in mind for at least the C: or base install drive.
Whether there will be more than one vSCSI hard disk in use	If there is more than one vSCSI device in use, what is the SCSI ID mapping? In general, it is suggested that RDMs use a different vSCSI controller than VMDKs, but it is not necessary. Also, which controller type will be used?
Will video be in use?	If so, what is the video size required? There are defaults for VMs. Larger amounts of video memory will impact memory utilization.
How much memory to assign the VM	More memory is *not* always better. How much memory does the application actually need? It is recommended to use the required memory for the application and not the stated number within vendor documentation. An application that requires only 256MB when the documentation calls for 2GB will leave the system with less memory for the creation of other VMs.
Does your Guest OS support Hot Add of CPU or Memory?	If you are using VHv7, certain guest operating systems support the Hot Add of memory or CPU, but only if VMware tools are installed.
Will you require multicore vCPUs?	Multicore Virtual CPU support is often required for licensing reasons and not as a virtual CPU general tool.

continues

Table 10.1   *(Continued)*

Consideration	Comments
Are any Pass-Thru devices required?	It is extremely important to plan out any direct connections between VMs and Serial, Parallel, or USB physical hardware via any pass-thru mechanisms such as used by these types of ports connected directly, as these devices can pin a VM to a given host and not allow for failover or the VM use of VMotion or Dynamic Resource Load Balancing.
Required number of vCPUs to install	More vCPU is *not* always better. Be sure the application suite is actually a threaded application. If not, use one vCPU. It is easy to add a second or more vCPUs, but it is difficult to go backward.
Whether any generic vSCSI devices will be used	Generic vSCSI devices include tape devices, scanners, and so on (anything that is not a hard drive of some type). In this case, you must know the SCSI LUN number in the service console for the attached device. In addition, there will be a vSCSI controller just for these types of devices.

After we answer these questions, we can begin the VM creation according to one of the three methods depending on the flavor of ESX in use. The following is a Rosetta stone very much like Chapter 8, "Configuring ESX from a Host Connection," was in terms of covering all versions of ESX. However, all the steps are similar, no matter which method is used to create a VM.

Within the vSC, VMs can be created by selecting any of the following:

- Host

  A host is a single VMware ESX or ESXi host.

- Cluster

  A cluster is a collection of VMware ESX or ESXi hosts. This concept is discussed further in Chapter 11.

- Resource pool

  A resource pool is a finite amount of a VMware ESX or ESXi host's or cluster's resources, set aside for a subset of VMs. This concept is discussed further in Chapter 11, "Dynamic Resource Load Balancing."

In addition, create a VM naming convention that does not include any special characters. Special characters do not include dashes and underlines, but do include periods, question marks, square brackets, curly braces, parenthesis, number signs, less than or greater than symbols, backward/forward slashes, @ symbols, asterisks, pipes or the vertical line, semicolons, quotes of any type, tildes, percent symbols, and ampersands, as well as spaces. Do not include any control characters or multibyte characters. Pretty much only upper- and lowercase characters, A to Z, the numerals 0 through 9, and underscores and dashes should be used to create VM names; the rest cause interaction issues when manipulating VMs from the service console or management appliance as well as within some of the vSphere SDK language bindings.

> ### Best Practice
>
> Use a VM naming convention.
>
> This naming convention should not contain special characters, including spaces.

VM Creation from vSC

When creating a VM from the vSC, it is possible to use either a direct connection to the ESX host or a connection to the vCenter Server. Yet, it is a useful interface for managing VMs remotely. The steps for creating a VM from the vSC follow:

1. Log in to the vSC.

2. Select the datacenter into which to create the VM.

3. Select the host, cluster, or resource pool into which to create the VM.

4. Select File, New, Virtual Machine, or press Ctrl+N, right-click the item, and select Virtual Machine from the menu, or click the new Virtual Machine Icon in the upper left. You will now see the New Virtual Machine Wizard (see Figures 10.1 and 10.2).

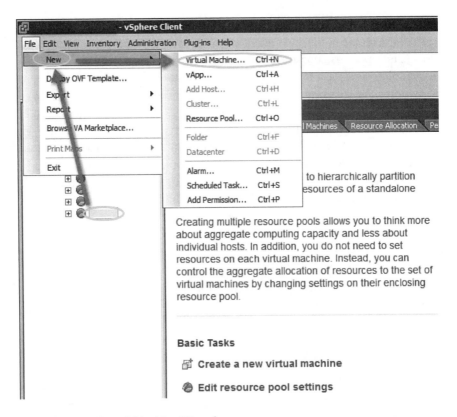

Figure 10.1 *New Virtual Machine Wizard*

5. Select *Typical* and click *Next*. Typical is also the default. For some installations, it will be necessary to use Custom. We will discuss those in another section.

6. Name the VM using a descriptive name with no spaces. Some of the tools do not like spaces or special characters in the name. Use a naming convention—perhaps Department-MachineName-Instance. After the VM is named, select the virtual machine group or folder into which it should go. Figure 10.3 illustrates naming the VM and selecting a folder. If, at this time, there are no folders, choose the default. Click *Next* to continue.

7. Choose where to store the VM and its configuration files. In general, the configuration files are usually stored with the VMDK in their own directory, named after the VM, on the datastore chosen (see Figure 10.4). Click *Next* to continue. Datastores can either be NFS, iSCSI, SAN, or local storage.

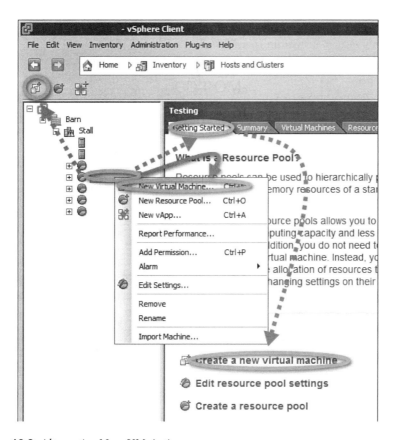

Figure 10.2 *Alternative New VM Actions*

8. Select the general type of Guest OS to install into the VM (see Figure 10.5). This stage is critical because each Guest OS has its own particular setup requirements. Using the drop-down menu, select the specific version of the operating system to use or *Other* if that option is available and the specific version is not mentioned. Use the specific version as often as possible. The *Other* options are available only for the *Other* generic type or for *Linux*. The *Other* generic type should be used only for unlisted operating systems, such as one of the BSD operating systems. Click Next to continue.

9. Select the size of the virtual disk (VMDK) to create (see Figure 10.6). It is a best practice to always make the C: or first drive of each VM a VMDK. Add RDMs to the VM for additional large drives and VMDKs

for all others. "Large" in the previous sentence is arbitrary and based on your comfort level. In general, make any drive larger than 256GBs a VM. It is also a best practice to determine a standard drive size for these initial VM disks. The system defaults to 4-40GB depending on operating system. This is often too small to install a full OS and applications.This is also the time to determine if you want to use Thin Provisioned disks, which are allocated on demand, versus allocating a fully monolithic virtual disk. For IO intensive applications, preallocating the virtual disk is recommended. This is also the time you can select to enable this VM for VMware Fault Tolerance. This is always possible to perform after allocation as well. It is also possible to make megabyte-sized drives. Small drives of this size are useful for quorum or very small operating systems. Click *Next* to continue.

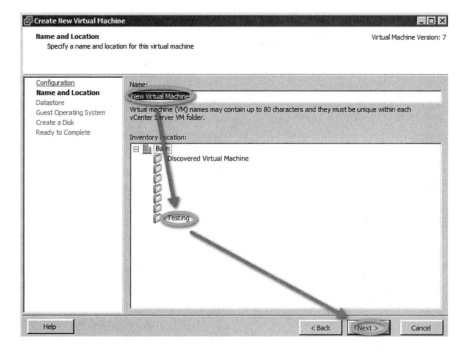

Figure 10.3 *Name and Folder*

10. Review your configuration (see Figure 10.7). If a part of the configuration is unacceptable, go back to that item using the left-side links window of the wizard. It is also possible to check the Edit the Virtual Machine

Settings Before Completion box; this is useful if you need to modify memory, CPU counts, network, and the other virtual hardware. Click *Finish* when you are satisfied with the configuration or click *Continue* if you want to edit the virtual machine settings further.

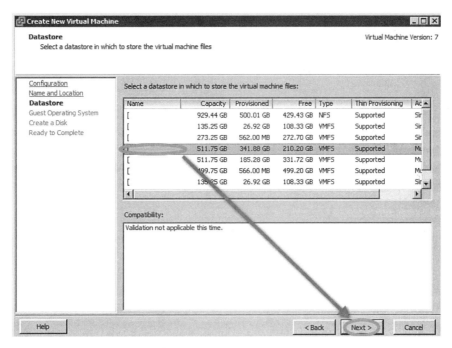

Figure 10.4 *Select a Datastore for the VM.*

If you clicked Finish, your VM is now ready to install with the guest operating system of choice. If you selected Continue and want to edit the virtual hardware before the VM is created, you will be presented with the same screen you would see if you were to edit settings on a given VM. Figure 10.8 shows this new window. Of some interest may be the Show All Devices check box. Most users will not require this to be used, but it does show all the available virtual hardware for the curious. From here, you can add new hardware or modify existing hardware. What follows is a breakdown of the options for each of the hardware types to modify or add.

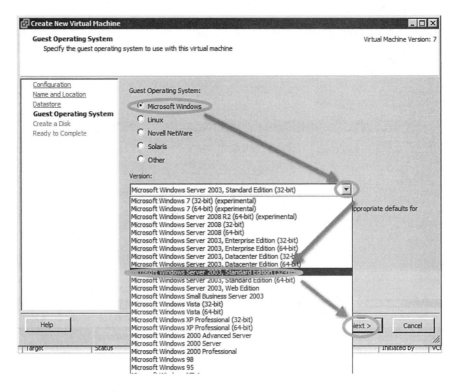

Figure 10.5 *Choose the Guest Operating System.*

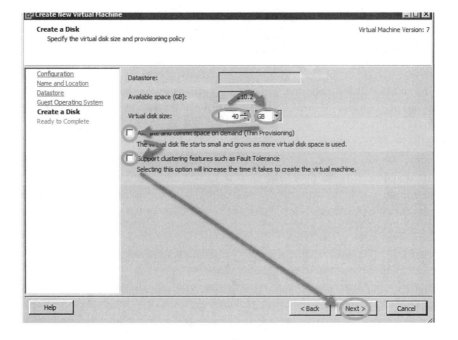

Figure 10.6 *Set the virtual disk capacity.*

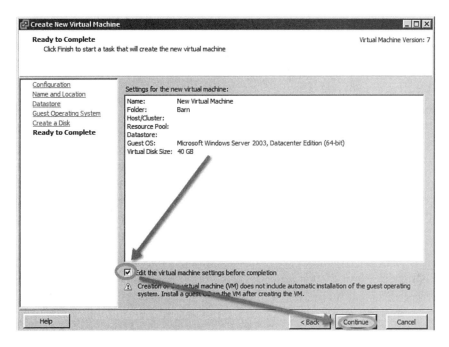

Figure 10.7 *Check your configuration over at the Ready to Complete stage.*

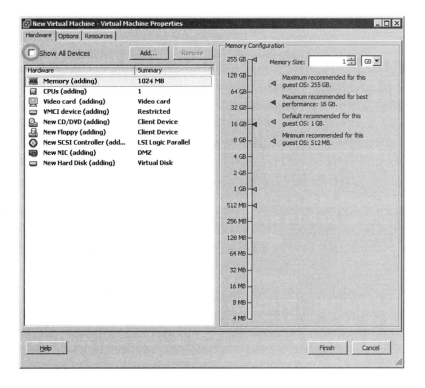

Figure 10.8 *Additional hardware dialog*

Memory

This option enables you to set the memory seen by a VM. When modifying memory, it is important to realize the minimum amount required for a given operating system and whether the selected amount would overcommit memory so that the host now needs to swap VM's memory to the virtualization host's disks. This is unrelated to the Windows pagefile.sys or other swap partitions that exist within a virtual machine. If you select more memory than is available on the VMware ESX or ESXi host, then for Windows, you will end up swapping to disk on boot and perhaps not after that; for *NIX style operating systems, this is not necessarily the case. The reason is that Windows grabs all memory assigned to it up front and scans it for errors, and so on. This act alone would start the overcommit mechanisms, such as swapping to disk.

Be aware that although you can increase the available memory to the VM, the Guest Operating System running within the VM actually controls how much memory is in use. For example, 32-bit Windows Guests, except the Enterprise Server versions, can see only a maximum of 3.6GB of memory regardless of the amount assigned to it. VHv7 has a maximum memory value of 256GB, whereas VHv4 has a maximum of 64GB of memory for any given VM.

There are two ways to change the memory of a VM. The first is to use the slider and slide the memory allocation up or down (dashed circle and lines). The recommended way is specifying the exact amount of memory desired, as shown in Figure 10.9. The steps to change memory are as follows:

1. Select the *Memory* virtual hardware element.

2. Select GB versus MB.

3. Fill in the amount of memory required.

4. Click *Finish* (only if you are finished modifying *all* hardware options).

CPUs

The number of CPUs for a given VM is a value from 1–8 for VHv7 and 1–4 for VHv4; odd-numbered CPU counts can be used if the underlying Guest Operating System supports such CPU counts. It is important to note that your CPU count cannot exceed the core count of the virtualization host on which the VM will run. So if an ESX or ESXi host has only four cores, you cannot add more than four CPUs to a VM. You will be allowed to do so, but the VM will not run. Figure 10.10 depicts how to choose the number of CPUs for the VM.

1. Select the *CPUs* virtual hardware element.

2. Select the number of CPUs for the VM.

3. Click *Finish* (only if you are finished modifying *all* hardware options).

To set up Multicore Virtual CPUs, you are required to use advanced options, which are covered later in this chapter.

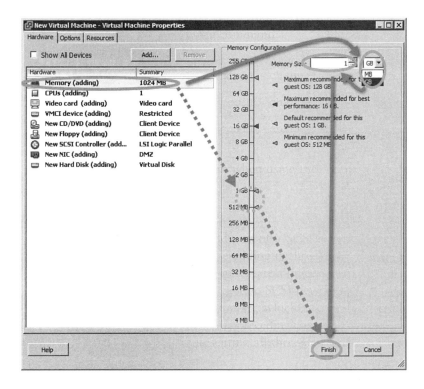

Figure 10.9 *Modify Memory*

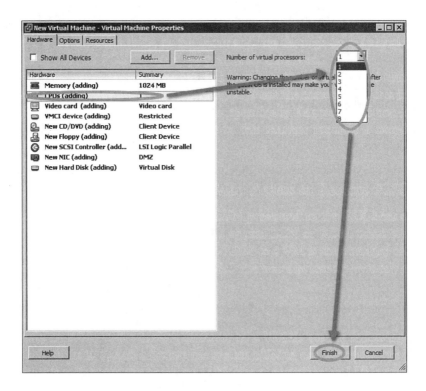

Figure 10.10 *Modify CPU count*

Video Card

It is possible to change various video hardware settings as well, including how much video RAM to set aside for each display for a given VM and the number of displays to make available to the VM (this last value is new with VHv7). Video RAM is specific memory set aside from the total memory assigned to the VM for use by the video drivers. It is possible to autodetect the memory based on where the remote console is being displayed, reserve a specific amount of memory by resolution and color depth, or enter the total available video RAM to set aside. The latter is the best practice and the default for a single display.

For more than one display, you may want to increase the assigned video RAM. More than one display would be useful for various virtual desktop scenarios where users have more than one display on their desktop. It should be noted that the memory required for multiple displays is *not* equivalent to the amount of memory for a single display multiplied by the number of displays—it can be more. Figure 10.11 shows how to change the various display settings.

1. Select the *Video card* virtual hardware element.

2. Adjust the total amount of video memory.

3. Select the number of displays for the VM.

4. Click *Finish* (only if you are finished modifying *all* hardware options).

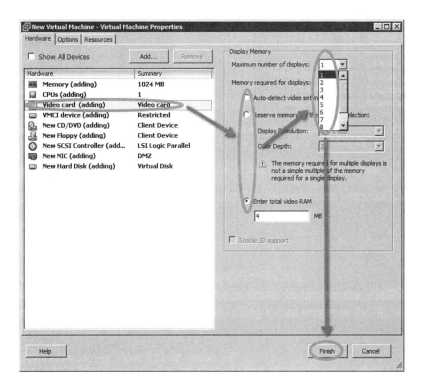

Figure 10.11 *Modify video card settings*

VMCI Device

The Virtual Machine Communication Interface (VMCI) is an out-of-band communication between one or more VMs on the same ESX or ESXi host. To make use of VMCI, it needs to be enabled on a given VM. VMCI allows data to be passed between the VMs, much like shared memory, semaphores, and other interprocess communication techniques used for multiprocess and threaded programs. Although I do not know of any VMCI-aware applications, the use case for using VMCI will increase as its benefits are realized. The best practice is to keep VMCI disabled unless absolutely required. Figure 10.12 depicts how to enable VMCI.

1. Select the *VMCI* virtual hardware element.

2. Enable VMCI.

3. Click *Finish* (only if you are finished modifying *all* hardware options).

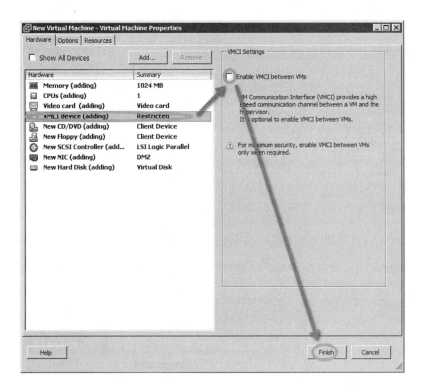

Figure 10.12 *Modify VMCI settings*

CD/DVD

It is possible to modify to what the virtual CD or DVD points as well as its IDE device node. Note that if the CD/DVD is connected to a physical device or media, even if the media is on a shared datastore, that VMotion will fail, as will FT and DRS. It also should be noted that although it is possible to use a CD/DVD as a CD/RW and DVD/RW/R+/R- device, this requires that the underlying device not be IDE but instead SCSI, which is not possible to do via the vSphere Client but is once the VM is created.

Figure 10.13 depicts how to set the CD/DVD settings. The best practice is to keep the CD/DVD as a Client Host Device, which allows a CD device to be loaded from any workstation running the vSphere Client. The Host Device selection ties the CD/DVD directly to the ESX or ESXi host's CD/DVD if one is present. You can also select a Datastore ISO file, which was the older way to use the CD/DVD device prior to the addition of the Client Device.

1. Select the *CD/DVD* virtual hardware element.

2. Choose *Device Type* (default is *Client Device*).

3. Choose the IDE device node for the CD/DVD device.

4. Click *Finish* (only if you are finished modifying *all* hardware options).

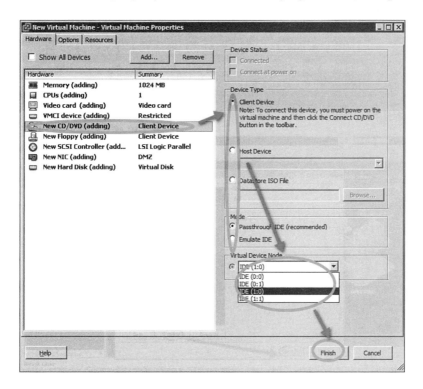

Figure 10.13 *CD/DVD settings*

Floppy

A floppy device is very similar to a CD/DVD device in that having one connected whether in use or not can cause FT, DRS, and VMotion to fail, even if the floppy image is on a shared datastore. You have the same options available as for the CD/DVD device: specifically, use of the Client Device (default and best practice), use of a floppy device, and use of the locally attached floppy device within the host, if one exists. If the floppy device does not exist on the host, the option is grayed out, as in Figure 10.14. Last, you can create a new empty floppy image within a datastore, which is useful if you want a blank floppy for writing local configuration data to from within the Guest Operating System.

1. Select the *Floppy* virtual hardware element.

2. Choose *Device Type* (default is *Client Device*).

3. Click *Finish* (only if you are finished modifying *all* hardware options).

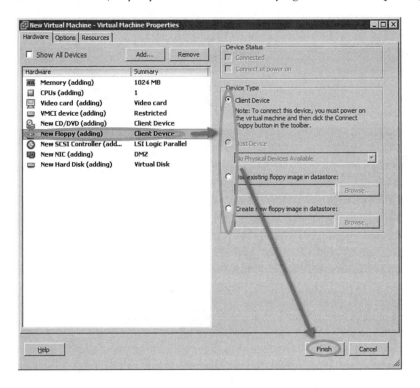

Figure 10.14 *Floppy settings*

SCSI Controller

There are two all-important SCSI controller settings: The first is the SCSI Bus Sharing and the second is the SCSI Controller Type. You use SCSI Bus Sharing when you are creating clusters of VMs, and you use the SCSI Controller Type to define the driver to use within the Guest Operating System. The SCSI controller defaults to a specific type for each Guest Operating System, and each virtual disk that contains the boot volume should use this default controller type. However, secondary virtual disks can use any of the controller types as long as it is supported by the Guest Operating System. For the VMware Paravirtual controller type, VMware Tools must be installed. Figure 10.15 depicts setting these values.

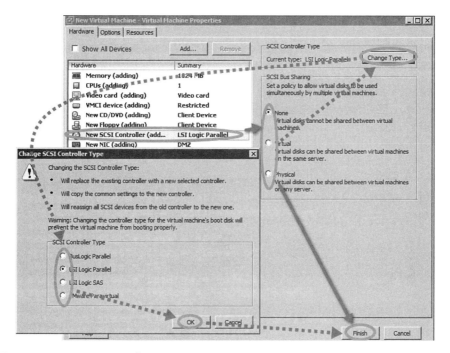

Figure 10.15 *SCSI Controller settings*

SCSI Bus Sharing has three options: None or no sharing, Virtual, where virtual disks can be shared between VMs on the same host, and Physical where virtual disks are shared between VMs on different ESX or ESXi hosts (or with a physical system). Use SCSI Bus Sharing only if you are using some form of shared disk cluster such as Microsoft Cluster Services. For the boot volume virtual disk, ensure that SCSI Bus Sharing is set to None.

Just selecting SCSI Bus Sharing does not magically allow a virtual disk to be shared—this requires a clustered file system to be used within the Guest Operating System. SCSI Controllers cannot exist within a VM without a SCSI device attached to the controller.

1. Select the *SCSI controller* virtual hardware element.

2. Choose the *SCSI Bus Sharing* for the shared disk cluster in use; *None* is the default.

3. Alternatively, click *Change Type* to bring up the SCSI Controller Type dialog.

4. Select the *SCSI Controller Type* to use and click *OK*.

5. Click *Finish* (only if you are finished modifying *all* hardware options).

NIC

There are several NIC options you can choose, but the most important is to ensure the Network Connection is selected properly and that the device status is set to Connect at Power On. It is also possible to set the MAC Address to use for this VM; however, you must set it to a valid VMware MAC Address because no other MAC is allowed at this point. If you need to change the MAC to something outside the VMware address range, you need to use a utility from within the Guest Operating System, and only if the virtual switch or portgroup is set up to allow such a change as described in Chapter 7, "Networking." Figure 10.16 depicts how to make all the necessary changes. You can add up to 10 NICs for VHv7 and 4 for VHv4.

1. Select the *NIC* virtual hardware element.

2. Check *Connect at Power On.*

3. Select *Automatic for MAC Address*; if you select *Manual*, enter the MAC address above the selection.

4. Select the network from the available networks.

5. Click *Finish* (only if you are finished modifying *all* hardware options).

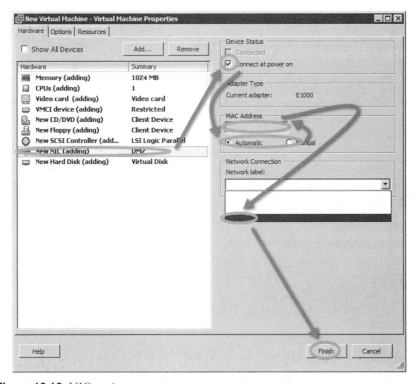

Figure 10.16 *NIC settings*

Hard Disk

Virtual Machine Disk Files, as we discuss later, can be of many types and can be of two modes. The modes tell ESX and ESXi how to handle the virtual disk created. The default mode allows snapshots to be taken of the virtual disk, and the independent mode does not allow snapshots to be taken. When in independent mode, you can choose to either allow changes to be permanently made to the virtual disk or to discard any changes when there is a power off or reset of the VM. The latter mode is useful for kiosk-style VMs that need to be reset to a baseline disk, discarding any and all changes.

It is also important to choose the correct Virtual Device Node for the given virtual disk. For SCSI-based virtual disks, there are 60 possible device nodes. After you add the first 15, in essence, you also add a new virtual SCSI controller to the virtual machine. You can also select to add a new SCSI controller at any time by ensuring the node number changes the first number; that is, 0:0 vs 1:0. If you are using raw disk maps or other types of SCSI devices, it is important to add a new SCSI controller that will be independent of boot volume within the virtual disk. This is specifically true for Shared Disk Clusters and VMware Paravirtual driver use.

Hard Disk setting changes are depicted in Figure 10.17.

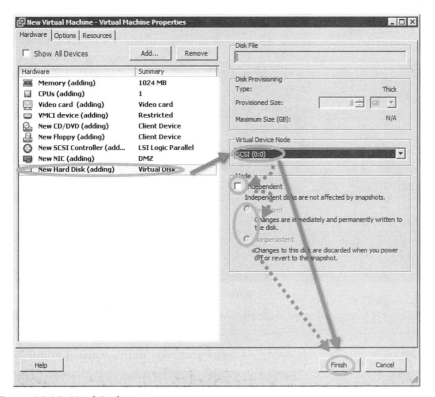

Figure 10.17 *Hard Disk settings*

1. Select the *Hard Disk* virtual hardware element.

2. Select the appropriate *Virtual Device Node*; for a single VMDK, this should be *SCSI (0:0)*.

3. Determine whether the virtual disk will be placed into Independent mode.

4. Determine whether an independent virtual disk should discard its changes.

5. Click *Finish* (only if you are finished modifying *all* hardware options).

Adding New Hardware

At this time, it is also possible to add new hardware to the VM. In many cases, new hardware will be required to properly use the VM for the intended task. Figure 10.18 shows the Add New Hardware Wizard, which is selected from the Add button within the Virtual Machine Properties window shown in Figure 10.18.

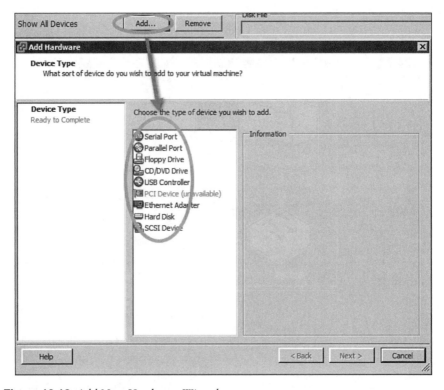

Figure 10.18 *Add New Hardware Wizard*

Serial Port

There are four types of serial ports you can add to a given VM (see Figure 10.19). The default is to have the serial port connected to a file located on a datastore the ESX host can use, as in Figure 10.20. This option allows you to log all data sent to the serial port for later review. This becomes very useful if you have set up your systems to log certain bits of data to serial ports. Linux systems, for example, can be told to log crash data to a serial port. From a security perspective, this gives you an easy way to log critical data externally to the VM, but you can also log such data using remote log servers, but only if the VM is running. In the case of a kernel crash, this log may not happen.

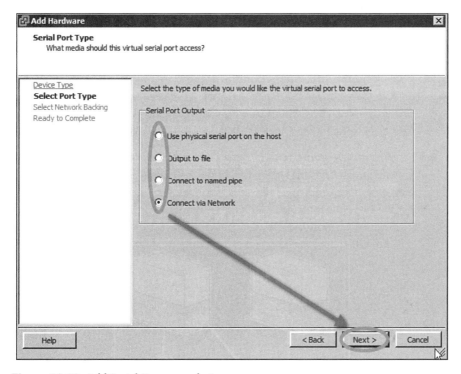

Figure 10.19 *Add Serial Port type choice*

This option is not available when running ESXi and also pins a VM to a given serial port on the ESX host as you tie a physical serial port on the ESX host to the VM per Figure 10.21. The third option allows you to pipe data from a Process or Virtual Machine of your choice, and the last option allows you to connect a serial port to the network for access via SSH (see Figure 10.23). When you set up the serial port to use a named pipe, you need to choose whether the Near End (end connected to the VM) is acting as a client or server, as in Figure 10.22. Figure 10.20 shows a box on the diagram that surrounds the Output File selection. Figures 10.21, 10.22, and 10.23 replace this box for their respective serial port types. The steps to create a serial port follow:

1. Select the *Serial Port Device*.

2. Select the appropriate *Serial Port Type* and click *Next*.

3. If using the Default or Output File serial port type, enter the name of the serial port.

4. If using the Physical Port serial port type, select the attached physical port device.

5. If using the Named Pipe Serial port type, give a name to the pipe using a naming convention similar to one you use for naming virtual machines. Select the *Near End* type of the port (Client or Server), and select the *Far End* type to be either a Process or Virtual Machine.

6. If using the Default or Network serial port type, select whether the VM will listen on its serial port or be the starting point of the serial port connection. In addition, network serial ports can be used by a virtual serial port concentrator. Like the new virtual appliance-based Avocent Cyclades ACS 6000, for virtual machine serial console management or monitoring. This type of Serial port is only available with at least ESX or ESXi v4.1.

7. Check the *Device Status* to be *Connect at Power On*.

8. Check *Yield CPU on Poll* if the serial port will be used in poll mode and not interrupt mode.

9. Click the *Next* button.

10. Click the *Finish* button after reviewing the settings.

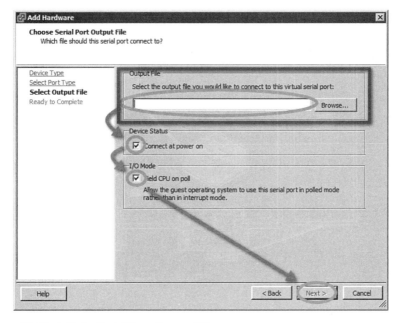

Figure 10.20 *Add the Serial Port Output File type*

Figure 10.21 *Add the Serial Port Physical type*

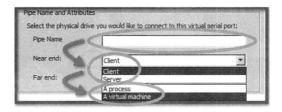

Figure 10.22 *Add the Serial Port Named Pipe type*

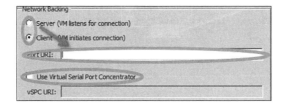

Figure 10.23 *Add the Serial Port Network type*

Parallel Port

Parallel ports work very much like serial ports. You can either specify that the port connects to an output file (default) or to a specific parallel port on the ESX host, if one exists.

1. Select the *Parallel Port Device* type.

2. Select the appropriate Parallel Port type and click *Next*.

3. If using the Default or Output File parallel port type, enter the name of the serial port.

4. If using the Physical Port parallel port type, select the attached physical port device.

5. Check the *Device Status* to be *Connect at Power On*.

6. Click the *Next* button.

7. Click the *Finish* button after reviewing the settings.

Floppy Drive

Floppy drives come in three distinct flavors. To add a new floppy drive, you follow these steps. The box in Figure 10.25 is interchangeable with the similar box in Figure 10.26.

1. Select the *Floppy Device* type.

2. Select the appropriate Floppy Type, as in Figure 10.24, and click Next.

3. If using *Physical Type*, select *Device Location* (*Client* or *Host*); if using Host, select the *Physical Device* to use, as shown in Figure 10.25.

4. If using the New or Old Image type, enter the appropriate filename that resides on a datastore the ESX or ESXi host can use, as in Figure 10.26. Note that floppy names usually end in .flp.

5. Check the *Device Status* to be *Connect at Power On*.

6. Click the *Next* button.

7. Click the *Finish* button after reviewing the settings.

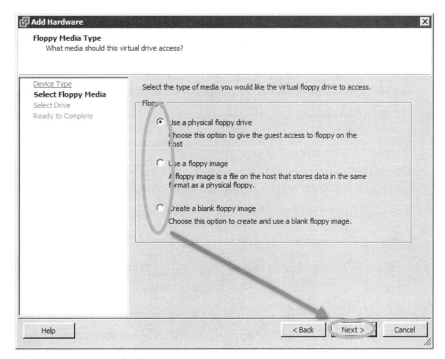

Figure 10.24 *Choose the floppy type*

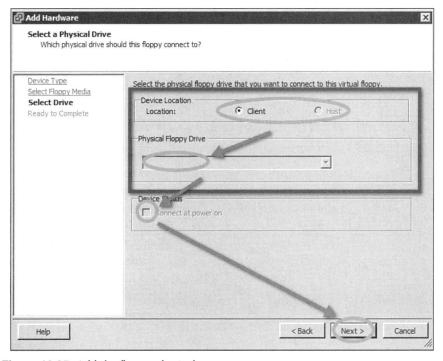

Figure 10.25 *Add the floppy physical type*

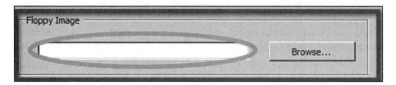

Figure 10.26 *Add the floppy new or old image type*

CD/DVD Driver

CD/DVD drives are similar to floppy drives and come in two flavors: Physical or ISO Image. To add a new CD/DVD drive, follow these steps:

1. Select the *CD/DVD Device Type*.

2. Select the appropriate CD/DVD Type, Physical or ISO Image, and click *Next*.

3. If using *Physical Type*, select *Device Location* (*Client* or *Host*); if using Host, select the *Physical Device* (see Figure 10.27).

4. If using the ISO Image type, enter the appropriate filename that resides on a datastore the ESX or ESXi host can use. Note that CD/DVD names usually end in .iso.

5. Select the *Drive mode*, either *Pass through* (recommended for Client) or *ATAPI Emulation*. When connecting to the host, ATAPI may be required.

6. Check the *Device Status* to be *Connect at Power On*.

7. Click the *Next* button.

8. Click the *Finish* button after reviewing the settings.

USB Controller

After you add a USB Controller, you can connect the VM to any USB device available to the ESX host not already in use by another VM. There are no configurable options when you add a USB Controller, so the steps are simple:

1. Select the *USB Controller Device Type*.

2. Click the *Next* button.

3. Click the *Finish* button after reviewing the settings.

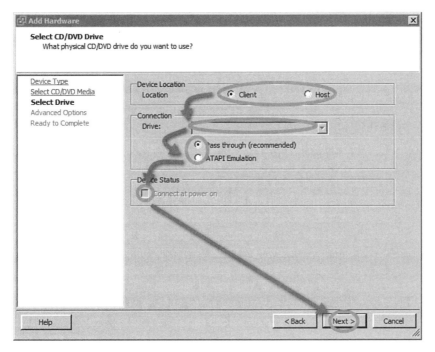

Figure 10.27 *Add the CD/DVD physical type*

PCI Device

To connect your VM to a generic PCI device, you need to have either Intel VT-d or AMD IOMMU support within the host. This allows you to enable VMDirectPath and connect the VM directly to an entire PCI Device. This is called Single Root IO Virtualization (SRIOV). Multi Root IO Virtualization (MRIOV) would pinpoint a port on a given PCI device for use by a single VM. Unfortunately, MRIOV is not yet available, so we must assign an entire PCI device to a VM via SRIOV.

1. Select the *PCI Device Type*.

2. Select the PCI Device to add as a pass-thru device.

3. Click the *Next* button.

4. Click the *Finish* button after reviewing the settings.

Ethernet Adapter

For VHv7 you can add up to 10 NICs to a given VM, whereas VHv4 can only handle up to 4. This change in VHv7 is a boon for security appliances because a single VM can now handle many more virtual network connections. The steps to add a new NIC are straightforward, as depicted in Figure 10.28:

1. Select the *NIC Device Type*.

2. Select the *Adapter Type* (Flexible, E1000, vmxnet2, or vmxnet3).

3. Select the *Network* to which to connect the NIC.

4. Check the *Device Status* to be *Connect at Power On*.

5. Click the *Next* button.

6. Click the *Finish* button after reviewing the settings.

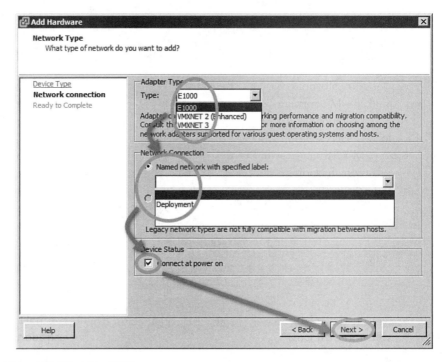

Figure 10.28 *Add a NIC*

Hard Disk

We talked about configuring a hard disk previously, and adding a hard disk is not much different. There are three types of disks you can add: New, Existing, or a Raw Disk Map (RDM), as shown in Figure 10.29. RDMs are useful for clustered file systems or disks that would be sufficiently large that treating them as a VMDK would become unwieldy, such as when trying to restore backups, which we cover within Chapter 12. It is left up to each administrator to choose the size. The process to create a new virtual disk follows and is very similar to the modification of the virtual disk mentioned previously.

1. Select the *Hard Disk Device Type*.

2. Select *Create a New Virtual Disk* and click *Next*.

3. Select units of the disk capacity: MB, GB, TB. (See Figure 10.30.)

4. Enter the size of the virtual disk per the capacity unit chosen.

5. Check whether to Thin Provision or not. For disks that experience dynamic growth, it is suggested that you do not Thin Provision because it will impact overall performance.

6. Check whether this virtual disk will participate in FT, which precludes the capability to Thin Provision.

7. Select where to store the virtual disk; the default is with the virtual machine, but for IO reasons you may want to specify a new datastore. (See Figure 10.31.)

8. Select the Virtual Device node. A virtual disk can be of either IDE or SCSI type. There are 60 SCSI virtual disks available, yet only 3 IDE disks, because one is taken by the default CD/DVD.

9. Determine whether or not the virtual disk will be independent, as described in the previous section "Overview of Virtual Hardware." If independent, choose whether the disk will be persistent or nonpersistent.

10. Click the *Next* button.

11. Click the *Finish* button after reviewing the settings.

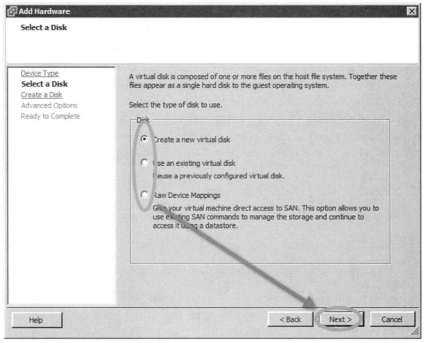

Figure 10.29 *Add the virtual disk*

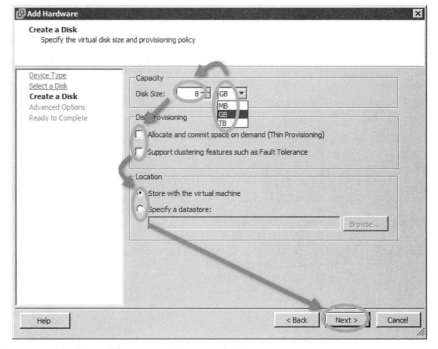

Figure 10.30 *Size and location of the virtual disk*

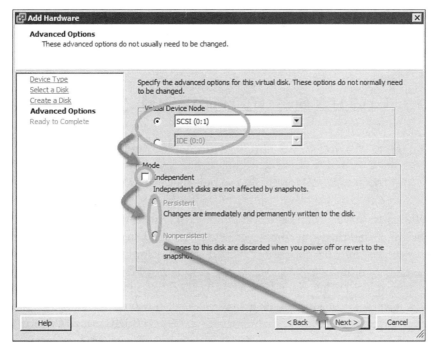

Figure 10.31 *Virtual disk advanced options*

When you add an existing virtual disk to a VM, note that if the virtual disk is already in use, the virtual disk cannot be used again *unless* the virtual disk contains a clustered file system or is a data or quorum disk for an existing cluster. In the preceding steps, steps 3–7 change to be one item: Select Existing Virtual Disk. All other steps are the same.

Best Practice

When using a virtual disk attached to another VM, ensure that the virtual disk contains a clustered file system.

A Raw Disk Map in effect allows a VM direct access to underlying storage hardware without the need for a virtual machine file system. There is negligible performance gain when you do this. In general, using an RDM requires increased management between the virtualization and storage administrators. When adding a Raw Disk Map, the preceding steps 1–4 change to the following steps:

1. Select the *RDM Type*.

2. Select the LUN to use from remote storage, as shown in Figure 10.32, and click *Next*. In the example, the LUNs shown are actually the controlling LUN of the array.

3. Select where to store the LUN mapping; in general, this is always with the VM, and click *Next*.

4. Select *Physical* versus *Virtual Mode*. Virtual Mode treats the RDM just like a virtual disk, which implies the virtual disk can have snapshots, participate in SVMotion, and so on. Click *Next*.

With a Raw Disk Map, step 9 does not exist, either; you choose your virtual device node and then you complete the wizard.

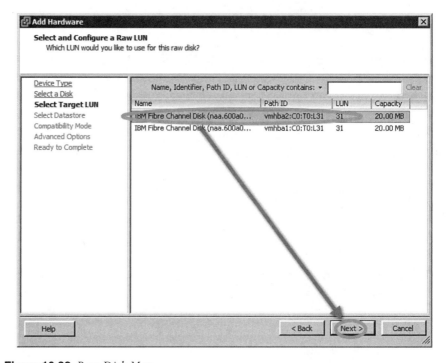

Figure 10.32 *Raw Disk Map*

SCSI Device

It is possible to add to a VM a pass-thru to a generic SCSI device that is attached to the ESX or ESXi host. This is used in effect to give a VM direct access to that device. The most common device used in this way is a SCSI Tape Library.

Adding a SCSI device is similar to adding any of the other pass-thru devices (PCI, Serial, Parallel, and RDM):

1. Select the *SCSI Device Type*.

2. Select the appropriate SCSI device, as shown in Figure 10.33.

3. Select the *Virtual Device node* to use for the SCSI Device. The caveat here is that the SCSI ID should be the same as the physical device, and the controller should be something different than that used by your virtual disks. This limits the number of SCSI IDs generically to 45 instead of 60.

4. Click the *Next* button.

5. Click the *Finish* button after reviewing the settings.

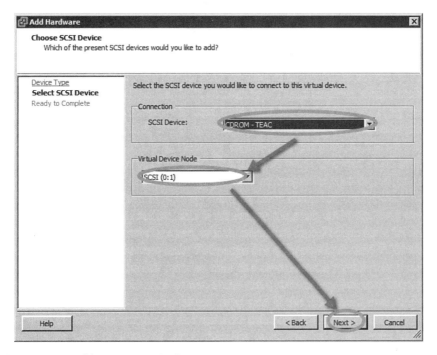

Figure 10.33 *Add a generic SCSI device*

Best Practice

The SCSI ID should match the physical device SCSI ID.

The SCSI controller should be different from any used by virtual disks.

In some cases, the device you want to add is not in the drop-down list. This could be for a number of reasons: either the device is of the wrong type, misconfigured, or unknown to ESX and ESXi. This was a more prevalent problem with ESX versions before v4.

Modify VM Options

When you create a VM, it is a best practice to visit the VM Options tab of the Virtual Machine Properties to enable a few very useful features such as Memory/CPU Hotplug, which allows you to add memory if the Guest Operating System chosen supports these features. Figure 10.34 shows many of the available options for a given VM. To enter this screen, click the Options tab; to manipulate an option, click the option. Each of these options can change the behavior of your VM and should be considered in advance of VM creation.

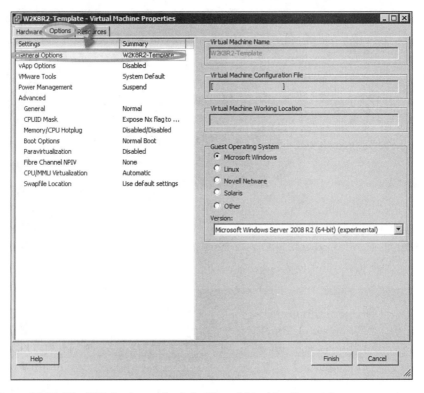

Figure 10.34 *The VM Options tab of the Virtual Machine Properties*

General Options

The best practice is to *not* modify your General Options unless you incorrectly chose the Guest Operating System when creating the virtual machine. The correct guest operating system sets up the VM to allow other advanced features.

vApp Options

vApp Options cannot be modified during VM creation time, only afterward. vApps allow you to group VMs into a single Open Virtual Format file for easy deployment. In addition, vApps act as single VM for some VM operations. We cover vApp Options in Chapter 11.

VMware Tools

The VMware Tools options define how your VM responds to various power operations that can take place from within the vSphere Client and other tools that invoke the same power controls within the VM. Figure 10.35 shows the default settings, which are the best practice settings. It is possible to modify each of the power settings to do something different. If the VM does not have VMware Tools installed, these options are moot. To change your power options, follow these steps:

1. Select the *VMware Tools* setting.

2. Select *Power Off* power control setting: *Power Off*, *Shut Down Guest*, or *System Default*, which happens to be *Shut Down Guest*. *Power Off* should be chosen if you do not desire to use VMware Tools; otherwise, you get a warning from the vSC.

3. Select *Suspend* Power Control setting: *Suspend* or *System Default*, which happens to be *Suspend*.

4. Select *Reset* Power Control setting: *Reset*, *Restart Guest*, or *System Default*, which happens to be *Reset*. *Restart Guest* should be chosen if you do not desire to use VMware Tools; otherwise, you get a warning from the vSC.

5. Then choose when to Run VMware Tools Scripts, which quiesce the virtual disks of the VM before suspending or shutting down the VM.

6. Click *Finish* (only if you are finished modifying *all* options).

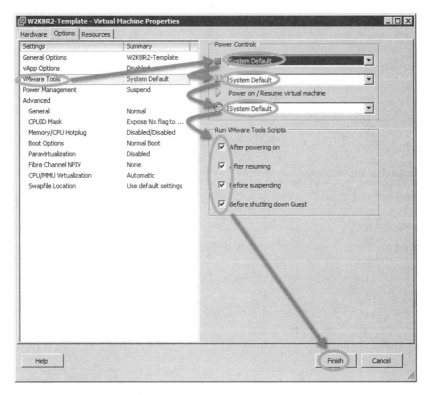

Figure 10.35 *VMware Tools settings*

Power Management

Whereas VMware Tools Options handle how VMware Tools (if installed) should respond to a power request, Power Options applies to what happens when the VM enters standby or suspend mode. Does the VM really suspend, or does the virtual hardware stay active, waiting for a wake on LAN (WoL) request? If you do use WoL, you can add a new NIC just for WoL activity. In this case, the VM is still active, but the Guest Operating System has been halted in a sleep mode versus a full suspend. To change the power management settings, use the following, as shown in Figure 10.36. WoL keeps the VM running and therefore migrations would use VMotion and Storage VMotion instead of cold migration techniques.

1. Select the *Power Management* setting.

2. Select whether the standby mode should be either *Full Suspend* or *WoL*.

3. If using WoL, you can add a new NIC on the same network as the primary NIC.

4. Click *Finish* (only if you are finished modifying *all* options).

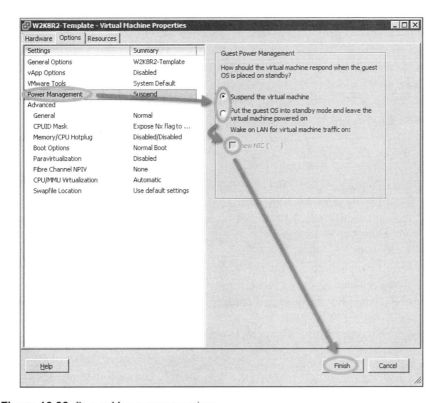

Figure 10.36 *Power Management settings*

Advanced—General

The General Advanced option allows you to control the run state of the VM. Specifically, you will be able to put the VM into various debug modes, control logging, and enter any advanced configuration settings. Note that unless absolutely necessary, and fully understood by the administrator, these general settings should not be changed. You really want the VM to *run normally* and not in any of the debug modes. However, from time to time, your VMware support representative may ask for such modes to debug your VM.

As you can see in Figure 10.37, it is possible to disable Acceleration of the VM, enable extra logging of what the VM is doing, and record debugging information. All these options are not suggested for use.

> *Best Practice*
>
> Do not enable debugging options or disable VM Acceleration.

The most likely use for the General Advanced settings is to enter VM-specific advanced options required by many of the virtualization security hardening guidelines. Advanced configuration options are entered as name-value pairs. Several of the most common advanced settings for security follow. These are all a very good idea to implement:

- Limit how much data can be sent to the VMware back door:

  ```
  tools.setinfo.sizeLimit => 1048576
  ```

- Disable the capability to set some of the information from within the VM about the VM through the VMware back door:

  ```
  isolation.tools.setInfo.disable => true
  ```

- Disable the capability for the VM to set the connection state through the VMware back door of those aspects of the virtual hardware that can be connected and disconnected (floppy, CD-ROM, network, and so on):

  ```
  isolation.tools.connectable.disable => true
  ```

- Disable the capability of the VM to call diskshrink routines through the VMware back door:

  ```
  isolation.tools.diskshrink.disable => true
  ```

- Disable the capability of the VM to call diskwiper routines through the VMware back door:

  ```
  isolation.tools.diskwiper.disable => true
  ```

- Disable Copy from remote console of a VM to the workstation:

  ```
  isolation.tools.copy.disable => true
  ```

- Disable Paste from workstation into the remote console of the VM:

  ```
  isolation.tools.paste.disable => true
  ```

- Disable changing screen resolution and depth:

  `isolation.tools.setguioptions.enable => false`

- Disable the capability for the VMware Tools to make some configuration changes:

  `isolation.tools.setinfo.disable => true`

- Disable the host/guest file system just in case this VM gets transferred to a virtualization product that supports this functionality, such as VMware Workstation, Player, or Fusion:

  `isolation.tools.hgfs.disable => true`

- Disable the capability to get version information of the virtualization host:

  `isolation.tools.getVersion.disable => true`

- Disable the capability to get memory information from the virtualization host:

  `isolation.tools.getMem.disable => true`

- Disable the capability to retrieve CPU information from the virtualization host:

  `isolation.tools.getMhz.disable => true`

- Disable the capability for VIX API to manipulate the virtual machine guest OS. If you need to use the VIX API, do not restrict the VMware back door:

  `monitor_control.restrict_backdoor => true`

- Disable the capability to retrieve virtual hardware version of the VM:

  `isolation.tools.getVersion.disable => true`

As of ESX v4.1, you can now set up multicore Virtual CPUs, which requires you to add another advanced option to the advanced settings of the VM:

`cpuid.coresPerSocket => value` must be a power of 2 so 1, 2, 4, and 8 are acceptable values.

Use of this option will disable CPU Hot Add.

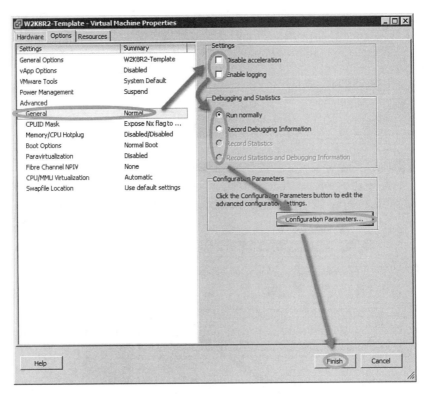

Figure 10.37 *Advanced General Settings*

Advanced—CPUID Mask

Modifying the CPUID Mask is not for the faint of heart and requires a deep level of knowledge regarding CPU functionality. VMware has implemented Enhanced vMotion Capability (EVC) to remove the need to change the CPUID Masks by hand. Even with EVC it is not possible to vMotion between hosts that have different CPU architectures; that is, AMD and Intel.

The main need for this advanced option is to decide whether to override the default setting for the NX (No eXecute)/XD (eXecute Disable) setting for this particular VM. NX/XD support is a requirement within the CPU for vSphere ESX/ESXi v4, but not for ESX v3.x. As such, it can only be exposed to VMs that have the functionality enabled within the host's BIOS.

> ### Best Practice
>
> Use EVC instead of setting CPUID Masks by hand.
>
> Use the default Expose NX/XD flag to guest.

Advanced—Memory/CPU Hotplug

If your Guest Operating System supports Memory or CPU Hotplug/Hot Add and you are using VHv7, this is one of the items you absolutely will want to change. To implement memory/CPU hotplug requires that VMware Tools be installed. Not every Guest OS supports all three functionalities that this setting suggests: Hot Add Memory into a running VM, Hot Add CPU into a running VM, and Hot Remove a CPU from a running VM. Note that no Guest OS currently supports a hot remove of a CPU. For Linux, the acpi_memhotplug.ko module is required to enable Hot Add Memory.

> ### *Best Practice*
>
> If your Guest Operating System supports hotplug for Memory or CPU, enable this feature.

The steps to enable hotplug functionality are shown in Figure 10.38 and are as follows:

1. Select the *Memory/CPU Hotplug* setting.

2. Select to enable memory hot add (if supported).

3. Select to enable CPU hot add or CPU hot add and remove (whichever is supported).

4. Click *Finish* (only if you are finished modifying *all* options).

Advanced—Boot Options

The VM Boot Options allow you to set a delay as to when the Guest Operating System will boot after the VM is started. This is a tool that could avoid a boot storm by delaying Guest OS startup, but is more likely to be set to allow the operator to enter one of the keystrokes (ESC for Boot List or F2 to Enter BIOS) to be used after the VM is booted. This is very useful when installing a VM for the first time or when you reinstall a VM using one of the CD/DVD ROM settings. The other boot option of interest will force the VM to enter the BIOS on the next startup.

In general, the VM BIOS screen may or may not appear during boot, based on the speed of the host's CPUs. When you absolutely must enter the BIOS screens or access the boot choice menu, these options can be used, as shown in Figure 10.39.

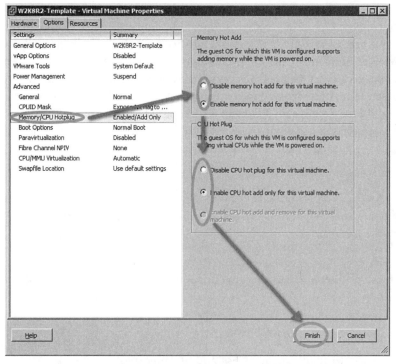

Figure 10.38 *Hotplug functionality settings*

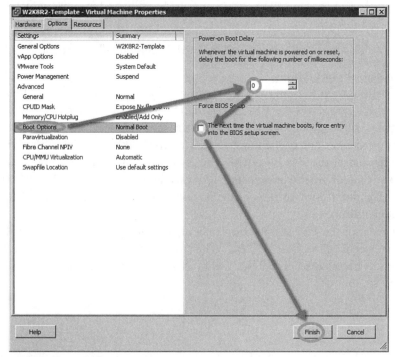

Figure 10.39 *Boot Options*

> **Best Practice**
>
> Enable these options if you are having trouble entering the BIOS from the remote console within the vSC.

Advanced—Paravirtualization

The paravirtualization setting controls whether Virtual Machine Interface (VMI) support will be enabled within the VM. VMI is a mechanism whereby the Guest Operating System's drivers can run in a paravirtualized fashion. If the Guest Operating System does not support VMI, this option should not be enabled because it can restrict vMotion to only those hosts that strictly support VMI.

> **Best Practice**
>
> Enable VMI only if the Guest Operating System supports VMI.

Advanced—Fibre Channel NPIV

VMware's implementation of NPIV is severely limited in functionality. It will only allow access to disk-based LUNs on the storage supporting N_port ID Virtualization. This limits or disallows the use of NPIV for Tape Devices, Controlling LUNs, and so on. When you enable or make use of NPIV, you also must have a Raw Disk Map in use for the VM. In essence, it is really a mechanism for a storage administrator to know more of what is going on with the LUNs than it is a mechanism for a VM to gain access to tape and other nondisk devices.

To use NPIV, you need to enable it by generating the virtual N_port IDs to use with zoning and presentation within the storage fabric, as shown in Figure 10.40.

> **Best Practice**
>
> Enable NPIV only if there are issues with storage administrators knowing which LUNs are assigned directly to VMs.

Advanced—CPU/MMU Virtualization

You can directly control how much hardware virtualization takes place by changing the value on a per-VM basis. This makes sense if you want to vMotion between disparate CPU architectures and can figure out the proper CPUID

Masks mentioned previously. In general, do not change these values unless instructed to by a support agent.

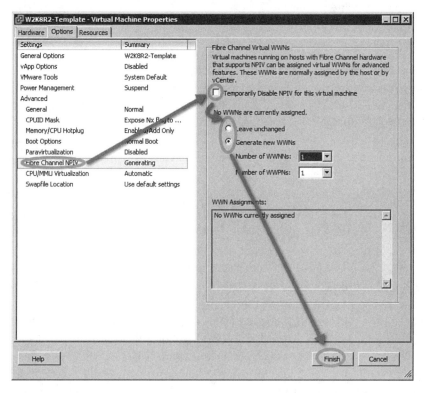

Figure 10.40 *NPIV setup*

Advanced—Swapfile Location

The last advanced option is the location of the per-VM swap file used when memory is overcommitted. You can choose the default (with the VM) or a new option for vSphere, which places the swap file on a per host datastore. This is one way to aggregate all swap files onto the fastest LUN possible, because when you start swapping your VMs, performance degrades rapidly. If this option was to change, one option is to create a LUN using SSD to increase the performance of swapping. However, there is an increased cost with using SSD, which needs to be weighed against buying more hosts, or memory for existing hosts.

> **Best Practice**
>
> Place swap files on the fastest storage possible: suggestion—perhaps affordable SSD.
>
> Ideally, set up the VM so it NEVER swaps to disk.

Modifying VM Resources

At VM creation time, it is also possible to modify VM Resources. We cover this in Chapter 11.

VM Creation from Command Line

It may seem that, with the advent of PowerShell and other such tools, understanding how to create a VM from the command line is no longer required. In fact, it is not. Many problems still require you to look through, understand, and perhaps modify one of the many configuration files for a given VM. If a VM is running, ESX and ESXi v4 lock the configuration files so that they cannot be read or otherwise manipulated from hosts not running the VM. This is not the case for ESX or ESXi v3.x. So for vSphere-based VMs, to read these files, the VM must be powered off.

This fixes a potential chicken-and-egg situation, where the file has been modified by hand, but when the VM is restarted vCenter does not pick up the changes to the VM. This was a common occurrence for ESX and ESXi v3.x and led to some confusion. However, even though the configuration files are locked, they can still be read if you use various backup tools—just not from the CLI.

Many files are associated with a VM besides the .vmx file to be discussed in this section. Table 10.2 briefly describes the files associated with a VM and their usage.

Table 10.2   *File Association via Extension*

Filename Extension	Purpose	Notes
.vmx	Main VM configuration file	Contains all the information necessary to start a VM.
.vmdk	VM disk file configuration	Is a short file describing the VM disk.
-flat.vmdk	VM disk file	A monolithic file the size of the VMDK in question containing the disk contents.

continues

Table 10.2   *(Continued)*

Filename Extension	Purpose	Notes
-rdm.vmdk	RDM VM disk file	A hard link to the LUN to which the RDM was linked. This entry takes up one slot on the VMFS metadata but is really a link to the LUN in question. Its size is the size of the LUN.
-delta.vmdk	VM disk file used by snapshots	Each delta represents a specific snapshot.
.vswp	The per-VM virtual swap file	Introduced in ESX version 3, this per-VM virtual swap file replaces the monolithic virtual swap of prior versions.
.hlog	VMotion log file	Often living long past its use, the .hlog file contains information about a VMotion.
.nvram	Nonvolatile RAM file	Each VM has its own NVRAM file containing the VM's BIOS settings.
.vmsd	VM snapshot configuration file	Introduced in ESX version 3, contains information about each snapshot.
.vmxf	VM foundry configuration file	Introduced in ESX version 3, contains information used by vCenter.
.log	VM log file	Log of all virtualization actions for the VM.
.vmsn	VM memory snapshot	Snapshot of the current memory for use when rebooting a specific snapshot.
.vmss	VM sleep state file	Used to store the state of a VM put to sleep.

It is not necessary to create every one of the preceding files when creating a VM by hand. Most of these files are created for you when a VM is used. The steps to create the VM follow:

1. Create a directory on the datastore in which the VM will reside, by using the following command:

```
cd /vmfs/volumes/dataStoreName; mkdir VMName; cd VMName;
vi VMName.vmx
```

2. Add the following lines for VHv4:

```
config.version = "8"
virtualHW.version = "4"
or for VHv7:
config.version = "8"
virtualHW.version = "7"
```

The first two lines of the configuration file define the configuration and virtual hardware versions used by ESX or ESXi. For older versions of ESX, these numbers are different. For ESX v2.5.1, for example, the config.version would be 6 and the `virtualHW.version` would be 3.

3. Define basic information about the VM. Specify the location of the nvram file and the action to take on VM power actions. The most important lines in these config file options are the `displayName` (how the VM shows up in the vSC), `memsize` (how much memory to allocate to this VM), and the `extendedConfigFile` name, which is the `vmxf` file location. Of all these lines, the `memsize` and `displayName` options are required by all versions of ESX:

```
nvram = "W2K3.nvram"
powerType.powerOff = "default"
powerType.powerOn = "default"
powerType.suspend = "default"
powerType.reset = "default"
displayName = "W2K3"
memsize = "512"
extendedConfigFile = "W2K3.vmxf"
```

4. The next chunk of the configuration file, represented in the following listing, shows the configuration of the first vSCSI disk to use. Note that the `scsi0:0.fileName` is specified using the name of the VM. Instead of `lsilogic` for the `virtualDev` type, we could specify `buslogic`. The other lines specify the shared disk cluster bus mode to use with the vSCSI controller (in this case, there is `none`) and the type of the vSCSI device, which is a `scsi-hardDisk` or VMDK:

```
scsi0.present = "true"
scsi0.sharedBus = "none"
scsi0.virtualDev = "lsilogic"
scsi0:0.present = "true"
scsi0:0.fileName = "VMName.vmdk"
scsi0:0.deviceType = "scsi-hardDisk"
```

5. The following statements define the first IDE CD-ROM-based device and its mode. Alternatively, you can specify the location of an ISO file in the `fileName` field if the filename is accessible on a datastore or in the

/vmimages folder. The clientDevice option specifies to use the CD/DVD from where the vSC is running. In addition, this IDE device does not start connected to the VM; set the startConnected option to true to have the CD-ROM available at boot:

```
ide0:0.present = "true"
ide0:0.clientDevice = "true"
ide0:0.fileName = ""
ide0:0.deviceType = "cdrom-raw"
ide0:0.startConnected = "false"
```

6. This section adds a vFloppy device to the VM, and like the vIDE CD-ROM device, this device can start connected by setting the startConnected option to true. The fileName will either be a floppy device in the clientDevice, host device, or a .flp or floppy image file that resides on an available datastore:

```
floppy0.present = "true"
floppy0.startConnected = "false"
floppy0.fileName = "/dev/fd0"
floppy0.clientDevice = "true"
```

7. As with all the other VM creation methods, it is important to have a vNIC device. The following listing defines the network name to use, which should be a defined vNetwork inside the ESX host. Note that although most premade configuration files will include a generatedAddress option, there is no need for one because the MAC address will be generated by the VM when it is registered and booted the first time. If you leave out the ethernet0.virtualDev setting, the flexible adapter will be chosen. Alternatively, you can use e1000, vmxnet2, or vmxnet3. The latter two are supported only by VHv7.

```
ethernet0.present = "true"
ethernet0.virtualDev = "e1000"
ethernet0.allowGuestConnectionControl = "false"
ethernet0.networkName = "VM Network"
ethernet0.addressType = "vpx"
```

8. The next options specify the guest OS installed using guestOS, the filename of the log file using fileName, and the shares of the CPU to give for this VMs vCPU, and the minimum size of the memory using minsize and the shares of memory allocated to the VM. The uuid.bios field should be included, but when the VM starts, it will be overwritten with a new value. The location of the log file is important and allows you to change the name of the log file from the default, including the

information on setting up CPU/Memory Hotadd. The guestOS option is extremely important because it defines some internal processing:

```
guestOS = "winnetenterprise"
uuid.bios = "50 0f 4b 4d a0 bf 71 a4-20 c5 8e 63 50 f3 b7
b7"
log.fileName = "vmware.log"
sched.cpu.min = "0"
sched.cpu.units = "mhz"
sched.cpu.shares = "normal"
sched.mem.minsize = "0"
sched.mem.shares = "normal"
mem.hotadd = "TRUE"
cpu.hotadd = "TRUE"
tools.syncTime = "FALSE"
```

Use Table 10.3 to fill out the guestOS setting. Be careful which setting you select based on the OS, because this tells the virtualization layer how to handle the VM. Table 10.3 also shows whether the Guest OS supports Memory Hotplug, CPU Hotplug, and CPU Hot remove. What if my OS is not listed, such as Fedora? Use the closest equivalent or one of the appropriate other categories. For example, Fedora Core 11 is similar to rhel5, but I would most likely use other26xlinux.

Table 10.3 *Common Guest OS Definitions*

OS	Guest OS Setting (Not Case Sensitive)	Hotplug (Mem/CPU)
Windows NT	winNT	N/A
Windows 2000 Server	win2000Serv	N/A
Windows 2000 Advanced Server	win2000AdvServ	N/A
Windows XP Professional	winXPPro	N/A
Windows 7 (experimental)	windows7	M
Windows 7 64-bit (experimental)	windows7-64	M/C
Windows 2003/2008 DataCenter Edition	winNetDatacenter	M
Windows 2003/2008 Standard Edition	winNetStandard	M
Windows 2003/2008 Enterprise Edition	winNetEnterprise	M

continues

Table 10.3   *(Continued)*

OS	Guest OS Setting (Not Case Sensitive)	Hotplug (Mem/CPU)
Windows Small Business Server 2003	winNetBusiness	M
Windows 2003/2008 Web Edition	winNetWeb	M
Windows 2008 R2 DataCenter Edition (experimental)	winNetDatacenter	M
Windows 2008 R2 Standard Edition (experimental)	winNetStandard	M
Windows 2008 R2 Enterprise Edition (experimental)	winNetEnterprise	M
Windows 2008 R2 Web Edition (experimental	winNetWeb	M
Windows Vista	longhorn	N/A
Windows XP Professional 64-bit	winXPPro-64	N/A
Windows 2003/2008 Standard Edition 64-bit	winNetStandard-64	M/C
Windows 2003/2008 Datacenter Edition 64-bit	winNetDatacenter=64	M/C
Windows 2003/2008 Enterprise Edition 64-bit	winNetEnterprise-64	M/C
Windows Vista 64-bit	longhorn-64	N/A
Novell NetWare 5.1	netware5	N/A
Novell NetWare 6.x	netware6	N/A
Sun Solaris 10	solaris10	N/A
Sun Solaris 10 64-bit	solaris10-64	N/A
Sun Solaris 9	solaris9	N/A
Sun Solaris 8	solaris8	N/A
SUSE Linux Enterprise Server (SLES 8/9/10)	sles	N/A
SUSE Linux Enterprise Server (SLES 8/9) 64-bit	sles-64	N/A
SUSE Linux Enterprise Server (SLES 10)	sles10	N/A
SUSE Linux Enterprise Server (SLES 10) 64-bit	sles10-64	M

OS	Guest OS Setting (Not Case Sensitive)	Hotplug (Mem/CPU)
SUSE Linux Enterprise Server (SLES 11)	sles11	N/A
SUSE Linux Enterprise Server (SLES 11) 64-bit	sles11-64	M
Red Hat Enterprise Linux 2	rhel2	N/A
Red Hat Enterprise Linux 3	rhel3	N/A
Red Hat Enterprise Linux 4	rhel4	N/A
Red Hat Enterprise Linux 5	rhel5	N/A
Open Enterprise Server (OES)	oes	N/A
Red Hat Enterprise Linux 3 64-bit	rhel3-64	N/A
Red Hat Enterprise Linux 4 64-bit	rhel4-64	N/A
Red Hat Enterprise Linux 5 64-bit	rhel5-64	M
Debian GNU/Linux 5	debian5	N/A
Debian GNU/Linux 5 64-bit	debian5-64	M
Debian GNU/Linux 4	debian4	N/A
Debian GNU/Linux 4 64-bit	debian4-64	M
Ubuntu Linux	ubuntu	N/A
Ubuntu Linux 64 bit	ubuntu-64	M
Other 2.6.x Linux	other26xlinux	N/A
Other 2.6.x Linux 64-bit	other26xlinux-64	M/C
Other 2.4.x Linux	otherlinux	N/A
Other 2.4.x Linux 64-bit	otherlinux-64	M/C
Other Linux	otherlinux	N/A
Other Linux 64 bit	otherlinux-64	N/A
FreeBSD	freebsd	N/A
FreeBSD 64 bit	freebsd-64	N/A
OS/2	os2	N/A

continues

Table 10.3   *(Continued)*

OS	Guest OS Setting (Not Case Sensitive)	Hotplug (Mem/CPU)
SCO OpenServer 5	openserver5	N/A
SCO Unixware 7	unixware	N/A
DOS	dos	N/A
Other	other	N/A
Other 64-bit	other-64	M/C

9. After the VM configuration file is created, it is now possible to create the VM disk file of XX gigabytes and then register the VM:

```
vmkfstools -c XXg /vmfs/volumes/dataStoreName/VMName/VM-
name.vmdk
vmware-cmd -s register /vmfs/volumes/dataStoreName/VMName/
VMName.vmx
```

It is also possible to unregister a VM, which implies that the vSC client, will no longer see the VM. To do this, substitute `unregister` for `register` in the last command above. The `register` and `unregister` functions are very useful when you move VMs by hand.

10. Enter in all your VM-specific settings, such as the security settings mentioned previously.

11. The VM is ready to install using any of the installation tools available, because on boot of the VM any missing fields would be added.

Installing Guest Operating Systems

There are various ways to install guest OSes within ESX host. The methods include using the ESX host's CD-ROM drive, an ISO image stored on the ESX host, an ISO image stored on a CD-ROM attached to the machine running the vSC, or via some network installation method such as HP Rapid Deployment Pack or Altiris' tool suite. Although the use of remote installation tools is popular, they are beyond the scope of this book, and we instead concentrate on those tools readily available to the VMware ESX host and its tools.

To install VMs, the remote console must be used, either through the vSC or the web-based tools. Just like a physical console, the remote console enables the use of removable media (CD-ROM and floppy), the capability to disconnect network cables at will, and the capability to power on and off the system. The remote console provides functionality that is not normally available in the physical world, and that is the capability to reach inside the VM and disconnect the CD-ROM and floppy devices while the VM is running.

Using Local to the ESX Host CD-ROMs

The first type of DVD/CD-ROM installation is the type that uses the local ESX host DVD/CD-ROM device. This option often requires that the installation happen within the datacenter because the DVD/CD-ROM must be placed in the tray. Exceptions to this generalization are the use of remote console tools, such as the HP Remote Insight Lights Out Edition II or newer cards, which have a virtual CD-ROM capability. These devices create a secondary CD-ROM device that can be used in place of the default device, which is /dev/cdrom.

Command Line

The following are the changes necessary to the VMX configuration file to use the local CD-ROM device. Note that you will need to unregister the VM, make the changes, and then reregister the VM for these changes to take effect after the VM has been created.

```
ide0:0.present = "true"
ide0:0.clientDevice = "false"
ide0:0.fileName = "/dev/cdrom"
ide0:0.deviceType = "atapi-cdrom"
ide0:0.startConnected = "true"
```

vSC

Unlike the preceding functions, using the remote console or vSC tools is slightly easier; for one thing, you do not need to memorize paths to locations of devices or ISO images, because it is possible to use a file dialog to find everything.

1. Log in to the vSC.

2. Select the VM in question to modify.

3. Click the Edit Settings link in the middle pane.

4. Select the DVD/CD-ROM virtual device to display the settings for the device

5. Check the *Connected* and *Connect at Power On* check boxes.

6. Ensure the *Host Device* option button is selected and that the proper host device is in use.

7. Click *OK* to continue.

Using a Local or Shared ESX Host ISO Image

This option is available to every version of ESX. However, as of ESX v3, all shares or files must reside in the /vmimages directory or any remote datastore seen by the host. The best practice is to use a datastore.

> *Best Practice*
>
> Use a datastore for storage of your installation ISO images, such as an NFS datastore.
>
> Be sure to place the ISOs within a directory on the datastore—perhaps one named "ISOs."

Command Line

The following are the changes necessary to the VMX configuration file to use the local ISO image. You will need to unregister the VM, make the changes, and then reregister the VM for these changes to take effect after the VM has been created:

```
ide0:0.present = "true"
ide0:0.clientDevice = "false"
ide0:0.fileName = "/vmfs/volumes/DataStoreName/ISOs/nam-
eOfISOImage"
ide0:0.deviceType = "cdrom-image"
ide0:0.startConnected = "true"
```

vSC

Again, using the remote console or vSC tools is slightly easier than using the functions just covered; you do not need to memorize paths to locations of devices or ISO images, because it is possible to use a file dialog to find everything.

1. Log in to the vSC.

2. Select the VM in question to modify.

3. Click the *Edit Settings* link in the middle pane.

4. Select the DVD/CD-ROM virtual device to display the settings for the device.

5. Check the *Connected* and *Connect at Power On* check boxes.

6. Ensure the *Datastore ISO file* option button is selected and that the proper file is specified.

7. Click *OK* to continue.

It is possible to specify the name of the ISO file instead of browsing to the file using the Browse button. However, it is a best practice to browse to the file in question because not every vSC client version will properly pick up the file if it is typed into the dialog box.

Using Client Device or ISO

This option has been available since ESX v3. This powerful option enables installation media that reside on the vSC client device to be used during installation of a VM. This option alleviates the need to have enough disk space on the ESX host for local ISO images, shares mounted on the ESX host, or even entering the server lab. Everything can be done from any machine that can run the vSC. The downside to using this approach is that all the I/O against the installation media must traverse the network from the vSC to the host, which may have a significant impact on the amount of time required for the installation.

Command Line

If the client is not in use, these settings are effectively ignored. Note that the new clientDevice option specifies using the filename of the client device. To install from the client, use the following commands. You will need to unregister the VM, make the changes, and then reregister the VM for these changes to take effect after the VM has been created:

```
ide0:0.present = "true"
ide0:0.clientDevice = "true"
ide0:0.fileName = "path\to\deviceoriso\on\client\system"
ide0:0.deviceType = "cdrom-raw"
ide0:0.startConnected = "false"
```

vSC

The vSC is the only client that can be used to invoke a clientDevice connection, and it can do so only if the remote console is actually in use. These security precautions prevent arbitrary access to a client device from a server, and vice versa. The steps to install from the vSC are as follows:

1. Log in to the vSC.

2. Select the VM in question to modify.

3. Click the *Edit Settings* link in the middle pane.

4. Select the *DVD/CD-ROM* virtual device to display the settings for the device.

5. Ensure the *Client Device* option button is selected.

6. Click *OK* to continue.

7. Click *OK* to close the *Edit Settings* window.

8. Select the *CD-ROM Tool* that appears in the icon bar of the vSC.

9. Select *CD/DVD Drive 1*.

10. Select the appropriate Connect To options, as shown in Figure 10.41.

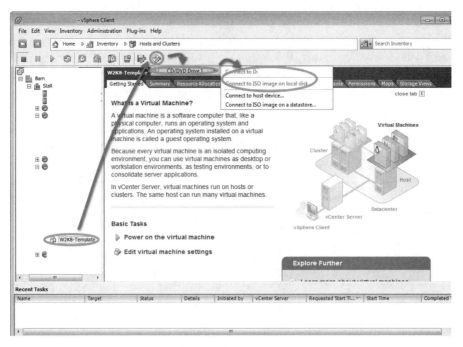

Figure 10.41 *Virtual CD-ROM*

This is an extremely powerful feature of the vSC because it is no longer necessary to enter the datacenter to access a CD-ROM or even make ISO files. ISO files residing on VMFS or in /vmimages are by far a faster device to use than virtual devices. As previously mentioned, it is the best practice to use a datastore for your ISO images. Note that the Client Device requires the VM to be booted in order to make use of it, so you may end up with a chicken-and-egg situation.

The solution to this was discussed previously in the "Advanced—Boot Options" section. Using boot delay gives you enough time to mount the CD/DVD-ROM via the Client Device.

Importance of DVD/CD-ROM Devices

DVD/CD-ROM devices and ISO images are important because they allow a much easier installation of many servers without having to physically be in the datacenter. It is possible to restrict access to these features to a limited set of people using roles and permissions. It is also important to note that if a VM is connected to a CD-ROM, it is not possible to use vMotion to move the VM from machine to machine. Therefore, it is wise to disconnect the device when you are finished using it.

Other Installation Options

Each VM can be installed over the network because the base networking device for the virtual hardware has the capability to use PXE (Preboot eXecution Environment) boot commands. If there is a DHCP server and a PXEboot server, it is possible to use a network-based installation. A best practice for network-based installs is to install them within their own vNetwork with no outside access. In this fashion, it is possible to apply patches before the VM is placed out in the wild and offer some protection from zero-day hacks.

Some of the options for a PXEboot environment include Altiris, HP's Rapid Deployment Pack, the Ultimate Deployment Appliance (www.ultimatedeployment.org/), and a Linux system using a PXEboot setup. These tools are beyond the scope of this book, but they provide an alternative for installing VMs.

Special Situations

Special situations arise when putting together the virtual hardware for a VM and when installing a VM with a guest OS. Here are some issues that have occurred when I have discussed this with customers.

Using CD/RW and DVD/RW/R+/R- Devices

The easiest way to use the CD/DVD device as a CD/RW or DVD/RW/R+/R- is to use a SCSI device that is also a CD/RW or DVD/RW/R+/R- device. An example of this is in Figure 10.32 within the SCSI Device section previously discussed. It is not possible to use the client device as a read/write device, only the local device on the host. It is far easier to write an ISO within the VM and then transfer it to a specialized VM or machine that has access to a writer of the appropriate sort.

Virtual Guest Tagging Driver

When we discussed virtual networking in Chapter 7, we discussed the concept of virtual guest tagging (VGT) as a VLAN tagging option for a guest OS. At that time, we mentioned that there needs to be a special driver to allow this behavior. There is no VMware-provided driver to enable VGT; this is a driver that will come from the OS vendor or a third party. In general, this requires access to the networking hardware, and be sure that your vendor-supplied driver understands the Intel e1000, PCNET32, or vmxnet family of devices. The alternative is to use VMDirectPath, which can be used to map a NIC directly to the host and in this way gain direct access to physical hardware.

Virtual Hardware for Non-Disk SCSI Devices

Although connecting a tape device or some other form of nondisk SCSI device (SCSI tape, SCSI scanner, and so on) directly to an ESX host is never a best practice, there is often a need to do just that. ESX supports a SCSI pass-thru mode that allows a VM to directly access any SCSI device, and this tie between physical and virtual hardware adds quite a bit of power to the VMware ESX host VMs. To access a nondisk-based SCSI device from a VM is straightforward, but there is a giant caveat: Only one VM can access the device at any time, and this includes the ESX host. The nature of SCSI locking is not a shared locking system between multiple systems. To handle SCSI locking between shared systems, there needs to be code in each system to handle this behavior. For nondisk SCSI devices, this code does not exist. For disk systems, this is where clustering software comes into play.

Before assigning a physical nondisk SCSI device to a VM, first be sure that the proper hardware is in use on the ESX host. We discussed this in Chapter 1, "System Considerations." Then, to assign a physical non-disk SCSI device to a VM, there are just a few steps. The first step is to determine the SCSI IDs of the device in question, which are available to the ESX host by using the following command:

```
# cat /proc/scsi/scsi
Attached devices:
Host: scsi1 Channel: 00 Id: 01 Lun: 00
  Vendor: HP       Model: C7200            Rev: 162D
  Type:   Medium Changer                   ANSI SCSI
  revision: 03
Host: scsi1 Channel: 00 Id: 02 Lun: 00
  Vendor: QUANTUM  Model: SuperDLT1        Rev: 4949
```

```
    Type:   Sequential-Access                ANSI SCSI
    revision: 02
Host: scsi1 Channel: 00 Id: 03 Lun: 00
    Vendor: QUANTUM  Model: SuperDLT1         Rev: 4949
    Type:   Sequential-Access                ANSI SCSI
    revision: 02
```

The results will give the SCSI ID for each device in question. These IDs are extremely important when initializing SCSI pass-thru mode. The SCSI ID is the field after the Id: label in the output. Also, note that the output has the vendor and model name of the device. These are also necessary when using the graphical interfaces to choose the appropriate device. When adding the virtual hardware for these devices to a VM, select any unused SCSI adapter number and the same SCSI ID number when selecting the virtual SCSI device. To map the SCSI ID to a device name, use the following command:

```
# dmesg | grep sg
Attached scsi generic sg1 at scsi1, channel 0, id 1, lun 0,
type 8
Attached scsi generic sg2 at scsi1, channel 0, id 2, lun 0,
type 1
Attached scsi generic sg3 at scsi1, channel 0, id 3, lun 0,
type 1
```

The generic device name is important when using the command line to configure the VM.

Command Line

When using the command line, the addition of a SCSI generic device is fairly straightforward. In this example, we are adding in three devices representing a tape changer and two tape drives. First we create a unique virtual SCSI adapter, present it to the VM, and then link a generic SCSI device via its device name (fileName) to a specific SCSI node number, which is composed of the SCSI adapter number and the SCSI ID from the preceding command. In this example, we have nodes 2:1 through 2:3 representing all three devices. Note that deviceType is set to scsi-passthru:

```
scsi2.present = "TRUE"
scsi2:1.present = "TRUE"
scsi2:1.deviceType = "scsi-passthru"
scsi2:1.fileName = "/dev/sg1"
scsi2:2.present = "TRUE"
scsi2:2.deviceType = "scsi-passthru"
scsi2:2.fileName = "/dev/sg2"
scsi2:3.present = "TRUE"
scsi2:3.deviceType = "scsi-passthru"
scsi2:3.fileName = "/dev/sg3"
```

vSC

The vSC does the same thing as the command line through its graphical interface, using the Add SCSI Device steps previously discussed.

If the SCSI device is not in the list, you may have to add the device using the command line or your SCSI Host Bus Adapter is not the correct type. It is important to only the supported SCSI adapters, specifically Adaptec SCSI non-RAID Host Bus Adapters. Adding tape drives in this manner requires a non-RAID SCSI Host Bus Adapter.

Virtual Hardware for Raw Disk Map Access to Remote SCSI

Access to a raw disk map (RDM) of a LUN presented to the ESX host shows up as a SCSI device that can be used as a system LUN or RDM when creating virtual drives for a VM. Adding a remote RDM to a VM is the standard form of a RDM for VMware ESX host. For the vSC this was discussed previously under the "Add Disk" section.

Command Line

To create an RDM in the current directory of a VMFS, use the following command where the X, Y, and Z dictate the system LUN to use. Note that the partition value is 0, implying the complete LUN. Use of partitions on LUNs presented to ESX is never recommended:

```
vmkfstools -r /vmfs/devices/disks/vmhbaX:Y:Z:0 foo-rdm.vmdk
```

After the RDM has been created, add it to the VM configuration file by using the following lines. Note that this maps the RDM to SCSI adapter 0, which is the default adapter. Many times, it is better to use a different adapter for performance reasons:

```
scsi0:0.present = "true"
scsi0:0.fileName = "foo-rdm.vmdk"
scsi0:0.redo = "true"
scsi0:0.deviceType = "scsi-hardDisk"
```

Virtual Hardware for RDM-Like Access to Local SCSI

A local hard drive can be mapped as an RDM in quite a different fashion when using ESX v3. This method is not supported on ESX v4. Instead of treating the local LUN you want to map to a VM as an RDM, you need to treat it like a raw disk type. Raw from a Local SCSI is no longer a supported option with ESX v4, however. The steps for ESX v3 follow.

Run fdisk -l to find the LUN.

```
# fdisk -l
Disk /dev/cciss/c0d0: 146.8 GB, 146807930880 bytes 255 heads, 63
 sectors/track, 17848 cylinders Units = cylinders of 16065 * 512
 = 8225280 bytes
Device Boot     Start      End    Blocks    Id   System
 /dev/cciss/c0d0p1    *       1       13     104391    83   Linux
 /dev/cciss/c0d0p2           14      650    5116702+   83   Linux
 /dev/cciss/c0d0p3          651     1287    5116702+   83   Linux
 /dev/cciss/c0d0p4         1288    17848  133026232+    f   Win95
                                                      Ext'd (LBA)
/dev/cciss/c0d0p5          1288     1924    5116671    83   Linux
 /dev/cciss/c0d0p6         1925     2561    5116671    83   Linux
 /dev/cciss/c0d0p7         2562     3198    5116671    83   Linux
 /dev/cciss/c0d0p8         3199     3453    2048256    82   Linux swap
/dev/cciss/c0d0p9          3454    17835  115523383+   fb   Unknown
known /dev/cciss/c0d0p10  17836    17848     104391    fc   Unknown

Disk /dev/cciss/c0d1: 440.4 GB, 440430842880 bytes 255 heads, 63
 sectors/track, 53546 cylinders Units = cylinders of 16065 * 512
 = 8225280 bytes
Disk /dev/cciss/c0d1 doesn't contain a valid partition table
```

Run esxcfg-vmhbadevs to find the vmhba device associated with the LUN.

```
# esxcfg-vmhbadevs
vmhba0:0:0      /dev/cciss/c0d0
vmhba0:1:0      /dev/cciss/c0d1
```

Create the VM with a standard virtual disk (VMDK).

Use vmkfstools from the command-line interface to import the VMDK into the vmhba device associated with the LUN using a disk target of RAW. Kill the import after you hit 1%.

```
# vmkfstools -i OpenFiler.vmdk -d
 raw:/vmfs/devices/disks/vmhba0:1:0:0 OpenFiler_1.vmdk
Destination disk format: raw disk out of '/vmfs/devices/
disks/vmhba0:1:0:0' Cloning disk 'OpenFiler.vmdk'...
Clone: 1% done.<ctrl-C>
```

Review the resultant VMDK metadata file. Note that the size of the LUN it references. For size, use 860216490. This number is derived by dividing 440430842880 (highlighted previously) by 512.

```
# cat OpenFiler_1.vmdk
# Disk DescriptorFile
version=1
CID=c0699ec2
parentCID=ffffffff
createType="vmfsRaw"
# Extent description RW 860216490 VMFSRAW "/vmfs/devices/
disks/vmhba0:1:0:0"
# The Disk Data Base #DDB
ddb.virtualHWVersion = "4"
```

```
ddb.uuid = "60 00 C2 97 5c a6 e9 59-f3 de ba f6 83 ed 15 73"
ddb.geometry.cylinders = "1044"
ddb.geometry.heads = "255"
ddb.geometry.sectors = "63" ddb.adapterType = "lsilogic"
```

Using the vSC add an existing disk into the VM or add the following lines to the VMX file. In this case, we have named the disk OpenFiler_1.vmdk.

```
scsi1.present = "true"
scsi1.sharedBus = "none"
scsi1.virtualDev = "lsilogic"
scsi1:0.present = "true"
scsi1:0.fileName = "OpenFiler_1.vmdk"
scsi1:0.deviceType = "scsi-hardDisk"
```

Although all the devices previously listed are for an HP server, it is important to realize that every supported server has its own method for naming a local device, and it is important to have a clear understanding of how your hardware appears within a Linux environment.

VM Disk Modes and Snapshots

The old ESX disk modes exist for versions of ESX, and they can be enabled at any time. Unfortunately, enabling these modes will disable the capability to take disk snapshots. Before we discuss the disk modes, snapshots need to be expanded on.

Snapshots first appeared in Workstation version 5. A snapshot creates delta disk, memory, and configuration files that are used to keep all the changes since the previous delta of the original VM. In this way, it is possible to create multiple starting points for a single VM. It is also possible to create a tree of snapshots from a single VM. An example of its use is for testing new patches. It might be necessary to layer multiple patches and, by using snapshots, each patch applied could have what appears to be its own VM image on which to work. After a patch is accepted, it is possible to merge the snapshot into the main disk image or even remove the snapshot with no change to the parent disk image, whether that is another snapshot or the default VMDK. As of ESX v3, snapshots only contain a list of changed blocks from the previous snapshot in the tree or the master disk, whichever is appropriate. As such, snapshots can only grow to the size of the actual virtual disk and no bigger. If a block is changed more than once, that block is the only thing that changes within a snapshot.

There is a little confusion about the control of the snapshot, because deleting a snapshot commits the snapshot to the previous snapshot delta or the parent VMDK, depending on its location in the tree.

So we must reiterate: *Deleting a snapshot commits the snapshot, which takes the changed blocks within the snapshot and moves them to the previous virtual disk or snapshot within the snapshot tree.*

To take a snapshot, select the VM, and press the snapshot icon within the icon bar of the vSC (the dashed circle within the box of Figure 10.42). There is also the capability to revert to the previous snapshot and to go to a specific snapshot in the tree (see Figure 10.42). The Revert to Snapshot (the circle with a thin line within the box) option goes to the snapshot immediately to the left of your current position within the snapshot tree, and the Go to Snapshot (available within the snapshot manager, which is accessed using the steps in Figure 10.42) option moves anywhere within the tree. Judicious use of the Revert to Snapshot and the Go to Snapshot will allow the creation of multiple branches of snapshots. However, use of too many snapshots will slow down a VM considerably. Figure 10.42 lays out the steps to delete a snapshot.

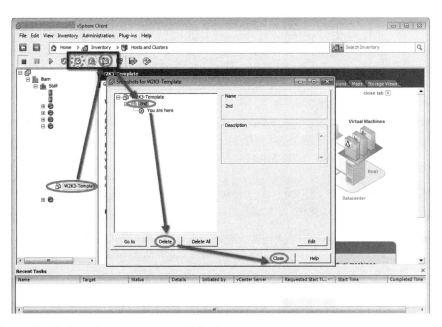

Figure 10.42 *Snapshot management (delete)*

Backup software designed for ESX makes quite a bit of use of snapshot functionality because the snapshot will quiesce a VMDK before the delta is created. After the delta is created, the original VMDK is backed up using your standard backup software. See Chapter 12 for more information about backups. However, it is possible to place a VM into a mode where snapshots do not work.

Snapshots of raw disks, RDMs in physical mode, and independent disks are not supported. Independent mode VMDKs allow the VMDK to be persistent (changes are committed when the VM is powered off) or nonpersistent (changes are discarded when the VM is powered off). Earlier versions of ESX throw in two more disk modes: undoable (asks whether changes should be applied when VM is powered off) and append (changes are appended to the disk on power off). Because undoable and append modes are similar to the nonpersistent and persistent modes, they are no longer available.

The best practice for ESX is to use VMDKs in the standard mode and not independent mode so that all tools such as snapshots and backups work normally.

> **Best Practice**
>
> Keep VMDKs in standard, not independent, disk modes.

Previously in this section, we mentioned that it is possible to remove a snapshot. Delete in the snapshot interface (refer to Figure 10.42) will commit all changes to the previous snapshot or original VMDK. To remove the snapshot, you must edit the configuration files by hand and make the necessary edits to remove all references from the deleted VMDK. Here are the steps to do so when you are in the directory that houses the VM in question. The common location is /vmfs/volumes/VMHBANAME/VMName. For brevity, all reference to the vmware.log files have been removed because they are unimportant to the task:

1. Back up the VM without powering the VM on. Then make sure the VM in question is powered off.

2. Back up everything using a mechanism that allows you to SCP all the VM files from the VMFS on which the VM files reside, because these changes can be catastrophic. Standard backup tools for ESX may not be sufficient.

3. Get a listing of the directory, because the snapshot VMDK delta file will show up here. In this case, there are at least three snapshots available. Knowing which one to remove depends on how they are labeled:

```
# ls
C1I1-000001-delta.vmdk    C1I1-2cab5a66.vswp    C1I1.vmdk
C1I1-000001.vmdk          C1I1-flat.vmdk        C1I1.vmsd
C1I1-000002-delta.vmdk    C1I1.nvram            C1I1.vmx
C1I1-000002.vmdk          C1I1-Snapshot1.vmsn   C1I1.vmxf
C1I1-000003-delta.vmdk    C1I1-Snapshot2.vmsn
C1I1-000003.vmdk          C1I1-Snapshot3.vmsn
```

4. The snapshot label is held with the .vmsd file and will equate the snapshot name to delta file. For example, if we want to remove the snapshot labeled 02 but leave the rest, we can find the label within the .vmsd file and thus the files associated with the snapshot. Note that the current snapshot is set to `snapshot?.uid="3"`:

```
# cat C1I1.vmsd
snapshot.lastUID = "3"
snapshot.numSnapshots = "3"
snapshot.current = "3"
...

snapshot1.uid = "2"
snapshot1.filename = "C1I1-Snapshot2.vmsn"
snapshot1.parent = "1"
snapshot1.displayName = "02"
snapshot1.description = "Level 02"
snapshot1.type = "1"
snapshot1.createTimeHigh = "274520"
snapshot1.createTimeLow = "-1301417629"
snapshot1.numDisks = "1"
snapshot1.disk0.fileName = "C1I1-000001.vmdk"
snapshot1.disk0.node = "scsi0:0"
...
```

Removing snapshots that are not at the end of the snapshot stream is basically impossible because the running of a VM depends on its disk, and the delta.vmdk file of the right snapshot depends on the previous snapshot's delta file, and so forth. Everything is interconnected, and removing a snapshot from the middle of the snapshot levels will make all the levels afterward have a corrupted disk. So, make sure that the snapshot is a leaf node of the snapshot tree. To determine whether this is in the middle of a snapshot branch, look at the `snapshot?.parent` values, and determine whether any snapshot has as its `snapshot?.parent` value the UID of the snapshot you plan to remove. If the snapshot is a leaf node, by all means proceed.

5. Note that the `snapshot?.disk0.fileName` in the snapshot stanza of the .vmsd represents the delta file on which this snapshot depends and not the currently used snapshot. The currently used snapshot disk file is the one listed in the .vmx file. Because the snapshot disk0 node is `scsi0:0`, look up the `scsi0:0.fileName` line in the .vmx file to determine the currently used VMDK file.

6. Shut down the VM if it is running. It is impossible to remove a snapshot while a VM is running. You can use the command `vmware-cmd full-PathToVMXFile stop` to shut down a VM. Often, I use the following from the command line. Be sure to use a unique machine name, however:

```
vmware-cmd `vmware-cmd -l|grep machineName` stop
```

7. Revert the snapshot to the snapshot to the left. Run this command twice:

```
vmware-cmd fullPathToVMXFile revertsnapshot
```

8. Remove the files associated with the original snapshot, the delta-vmdk, and the .vmsn file.

9. Power on the VM.

Command Line

It is also possible to use the command line to manipulate snapshots.

To create a snapshot, use the following:

```
vmware-cmd fullPathToVMXFile createsnapshot name description
quiesce memory
```

To remove *all* snapshots, use the following. Note that the last line empties the vmsd file for the VM in question. If the vmsd file is not emptied, snapshot numbers will continue where the file last left off:

```
vmware-cmd fullPathToVMXFile removesnapshots


echo "" > VM.vmsd
```

To move around the snapshot tree, use the following command:

```
vmware-cmd fullPathToVMXFile revertsnapshot
```

When using ESX v3 and v4, some aspects of `vmware-cmd` do not behave properly, such as get and set options; however, the ones we have listed work as expected. CLI-based tools are being replaced with PowerShell and other vSphere SDK-based tools.

OS Installation Peculiarities

When installing a particular OS into an ESX VM, certain hardware and software are required to make it work. In general, the main issues with operating systems is the choice of vSCSI adapter in use. In most cases, a BUSLogic adapter will work for most older versions of operating systems, such as Windows XP and Debian Linux/3. The exception has been Fedora Core and Fedora Linux guest operating systems. These require the LSIlogic vSCSI adapter.

It is best to fully understand what drivers are available at installation time of the guest OS you want to use, as well as what is available after installation. These continue to change as new versions of operating systems are developed.

> **Best Practice**
>
> For all Guest Operating Systems, pay close attention to the SCSI adapter required for installation.

Cloning, Templates, and Deploying VMs

A lot of literature already exists on cloning and deploying VMs, as well as on the fresh installation of a VM. This book will not regurgitate existing sources of information. However, we will discuss the use of the sysprep and the open source Linux tools to customize deployments when using templates.

Templates are fully installed VMs that are used as the basis for the creation of other VMs. This method is faster than reinstalling a VM because a template is generally fully patched and has the applicable application preinstalled and either just waiting for configuration or already configured. Templates can be deployed as if they were being cloned to create a VM within any host, cluster, or resource pool in the vCenter datacenter. Clusters and resource pools are covered in Chapter 11 and were introduced in ESX v3.

The cloning of a VM or deployment of a template will invoke a customization phase during which a predefined customization can be chosen or a new one defined. The customization scripts for Windows invoke sysprep, whereas for Linux they invoke an open source tool that can be used to configure the Linux network and not much else. The storage of predefined customization scripts within vCenter aids in making customizations saved as XML files.

Even so, the best practice is to create a Resource Pool and Folder structure that contains all your templates so that you can update and maintain them as part of your guest operating system life-cycle process.

> **Best Practice**
>
> When making templates, place them within their own Resource Pool and Folder.
>
> Maintain patches within your templates.

VM Solutions

We discuss a number of solutions in this book, and most of them require some form of specific VM hardware. Although we will not discuss the installation of the OS in this section, we do discuss the necessary VM and ESX virtual hardware and where some of it should exist. In addition, we also discuss the downloadable virtual appliances and how they fit into the realm of ESX.

Private Lab

A private lab environment does not require much in the way of new virtual hardware. To create a virtual private lab, first create within ESX a vSwitch that is not connected to an external pNIC. After that is done and the vSwitch is properly labeled, to create the private lab environment connect each appropriate VM to the vSwitch using its label. This is as easy as editing the settings for the VM and setting the vNIC network label appropriately.

- Additional virtual hardware required:

    An additional vSwitch, per Figure 10.43, right side not connected to an external pNIC

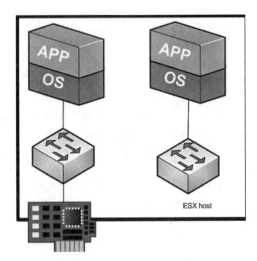

Figure 10.43 *Private lab*

Firewalled Private Lab

A firewall private lab is slightly different in that there now needs to be a vFW between the virtual lab vSwitch and another vSwitch where the VMs on the second vSwitch need access to the first vSwitch. The second vSwitch could be another virtual private lab or even represent an external connection. This vFW is a specialized VM with two vNICs associated with it. The first vNIC points to the virtual private lab vSwitch, and the second points to the external vSwitch. The vFW can be an existing virtual appliance firewall, Linux, or Windows using ICS. However, the best practice is to use specialized firewall software. In many cases, SmoothWall (www.smoothwall.org) is a good choice, but so is VMware vShield Edge as of ESX v4.1. I have also used m0n0wall, IPCop, vYatta, Fedora, SLES, RHEL, and various other Linux flavors as firewalls acting as both a vFW and DHCP server.

In some cases, VMware vShield Zones and VMsafe (such as vShield App) style firewalls can also be used, but this depends on your requirements. If your firewall private lab requires NAT or Port Redirection in order to work, such as you get from an edge firewall, then vShield Zones and VMsafe style firewalls will not work for you. If, however, all you need is a zone-to-zone firewall with no edge firewall functionality, VMware vShield Zones and VMsafe based firewalls are ideal. In the case of using VMsafe, the private lab would in most cases need its own DHCP and DNS services unless you also pass those through the firewall (which is not recommended).

- New virtual hardware required for vFW appliance:

  An additional vSwitch for the protected (green) side of the vFW

  An additional vNIC for the vFW appliance, as shown in Figure 10.44

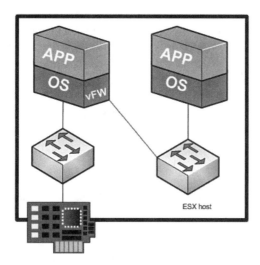

Figure 10.44 *Firewalled private lab with vFW*

- New virtual hardware required for VMsafe firewall:

  VMsafe rules applied to the vNICs of the protected VMs (see Figure 10.45)

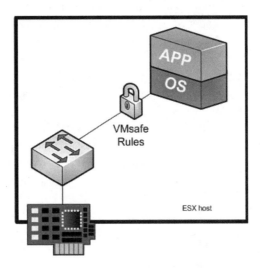

Figure 10.45 *Firewalled private lab with VMsafe*

Firewalled Lab Bench

A firewalled lab bench is one of our examples from Chapter 7, where the firewall was a VM or a vFW. Just as in the previous notes, the vFW requires two vNICs. The first is connected to a vSwitch *not* connected to the lab bench and a vSwitch that represents the lab bench. This often requires more pNICs on a system to create it, and the lab bench will need its own pSwitch or VLAN with a single external connection to the ESX host hosting the vFW. There might be more cabling needed, depending on how many ESX hosts may need to access the lab bench. You could use VMsafe with this configuration, but you would still need a VM with two vNICs to access the external pNIC for the lab bench.

- New virtual hardware required for vFW method:

  An additional vSwitch for the pNIC attached to the lab bench (see Figure 10.46)

  An additional vNIC for the vFW

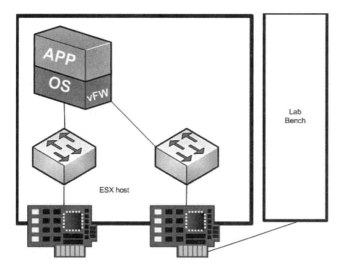

Figure 10.46 *Firewalled lab bench with vFW*

* New virtual hardware required for VMsafe method:

  An additional vSwitch for the pNIC attached to the lab bench

  An additional vNIC for the vGateway or vRouter (vGW in Figure 10.47)

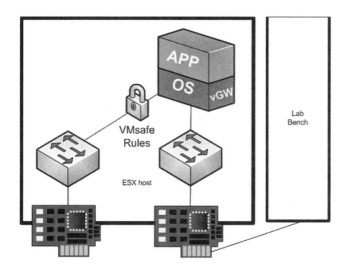

Figure 10.47 *Firewalled lab bench with VMsafe*

Cluster in a Box

Cluster in a Box refers to a shared disk cluster, such as Microsoft Cluster Services. Although we will not discuss how to install Microsoft Cluster, we do delve into the virtual hardware necessary. First, create a VM into which you plan to install Microsoft Windows, preferably a form of Enterprise Edition, because it has an easier Cluster Services setup than Microsoft Windows 2000 Advanced Server. However, either will work. After the VM has been created, add a heartbeat vNIC connected to any existing vSwitch, or even a private one just for the heartbeat (recommended). With Cluster in a Box, the VMDK for the C: drives can live on a shared datastore or a local datastore, preferably local storage. The same goes for any quorum or shared drives. With ESX v4 it is now possible to use boot from SAN and cluster in a box together, which was not possible with ESX v3.

After the first node has been created, it is now possible to create the other nodes. Be sure to place the primary VMDK onto local storage and not a SAN or iSCSI LUN, and then hook up the heartbeat vNIC to the same vSwitch as the first node, and attach to the existing shared VMDKs to the VM.

ESX supports Cluster in a Box for up to two nodes only.

- New virtual hardware required:

  An additional vNIC for the heartbeat network

  A local VMFS to store the node boot drives

  An additional RDM or VMDK for each shared cluster disk, including the small quorum drive

Cluster Between ESX Hosts

The only difference between this option and the Cluster in a Box is that the RDMs must live on SAN or iSCSI LUNs. The boot drive for all cluster nodes must be on a local VMFS and not a SAN or iSCSI LUN for ESX v3, but this restriction has been relaxed for ESX v4.

ESX v3 supported up to 8 nodes within a cluster between ESX hosts, but ESX v4 supports up to 16 nodes.

- New virtual hardware required:

  An additional vNIC for the heartbeat network

  A local VMFS to store the node boot drives (ESX v3 requirement)

  An additional RDM for each shared drive, including the small quorum drive

Cluster Between Virtual and Physical Servers

This is a neat possibility, and because we are using RDMs or LUNs for the preceding options, it is extremely simple to have a physical machine access the same LUNs for its shared drives. The vNIC for the VM will need to be able to reach the physical machine.

- New virtual hardware required:

  An additional vNIC for the heartbeat network. (Be sure this vNIC is attached to a pNIC that can reach the physical server.)

  A local VMFS to store the node boot drives (ESX v3 requirement).

  An additional RDM for each shared drive, including the small quorum drive.

vCenter as a VM

vCenter can be within a VM. If you find yourself in this situation, management of the vCenter Server becomes difficult. If the ESX host hosting the vCenter Server dies, there is no capability for managing VMware HA (but existing VMware HA configurations will still work), nor is there any capability for VMotion or any other vCenter feature to be of use. To solve this problem, use some form of monitor tool such as VMware HA, to move the VM from server to server and reboot the VM on the new host, or even employ VMware FT if your vCenter server can be limited to one vCPU. Downtime is limited to the time it takes to register the VM on a new host and boot up. A number of tools can do this for you. vCenter and the license manager for ESX v3 are critical to the success of an ESX cluster and therefore should either be run on their own host or have the ESX host failure case considered. For ESX v4, the license manager is no longer a concern, but maintaining vCenter is.

VMware has realized this and there are other options for vCenter HA, such as the VMware vCenter Server Heartbeat product, which keeps two vCenters in sync with each other. In either case, increased auditing is required when vCenter and other ESX or ESXi management tools are virtualized. I have them virtualized, but also have an out-of-normal management path to reboot this all-important VM if possible, such as contacting the ESX host on which it lives directly via the vCLI, CLI, vSphere SDK, and so on.

- New virtual hardware required:

  None

Virtual Appliances

Not all virtual appliances and vApps (collection of virtual appliances managed as one) are created equal. Most virtual appliances were created in VMware Workstation, so importing them into ESX requires the use of the VMware Converter software or the Deploy OVF Template from within the vSC if the vApp is already in OVF form. However, not all systems behave properly once imported into ESX or ESXi, such as Windows XP Professional SP0 VMs with the workstation VMware Tools installed. In this case, it is important to fully remove the VMware Workstation tools or import the VM without updating VMware Tools until you can upgrade the VM to at least SP1. The problem occurs because of a known issue with LSASS, which crashes the machine if VMware Tools is updated. This has been fixed with Windows XP Professional SP1.

It is important to investigate and test the functionality of a virtual appliance and make the necessary adjustments. Because ESX and ESXi v4 can now use IDE-based disk drives, many more of the vApps made with VMware workstation can be imported into ESX or ESXi v4 with less hassle.

- New virtual hardware required:

  Depends on the type of virtual appliance

vApps also have their own intrinsics within the vSC, as we discussed previously. They can be enabled only on import of a vApp made by exporting a VM using VMware Converter or using VMware Studio to create one. vApps are not just single VMs but can contain multiple VMs. The Open Virtual Machine Format (OVF) for vApps is just one aspect that composes a vApp. OVF allows you to ship VMs with all their state information from site to site or even use OVF as a part of your deployment process.

The vSC can import OVFs natively or browse the VA (Virtual Appliance) marketplace directly. This is a handy method to import well-known virtual appliances directly from the VMware website. Although this can be done directly, the best practice is to first download the vApp to import and verify that its checksums match and that there are no known differences. You would not want to import a virtual appliance or vApp that has a virus within it. Verification is required. I like to do this by hand, but the Browse VA Marketplace import does this as well.

VMware Tools

After a VM is installed, it is imperative that some form of VMware Tools be installed. VMware Tools provides drivers for the VM that understand virtualization and will make things perform better. Some VMs can live without VMware Tools installed, such as most Linux systems. However, this is not always the case.

The worst offender is NetWare. It is imperative for NetWare that VMware Tools be installed because the NetWare kernel uses a spin loop when there is no processing going on within the VM and not a sleep loop. Because it is a spin loop, it will quietly appear to eat through all the ESX resources assigned to it.

Installing VMware Tools for Windows is completely mouse driven, but for other operating systems you need to understand the various packaging technologies for installation or products. After VMware Tools has been installed, it displays some instructions for changing the screen update speed to have full hardware acceleration. The change is for any Windows VM, and it keeps the mouse from appearing slow when using the remote console, which is a common complaint for many users. To change the hardware acceleration setting, simply follow these steps:

1. Right-click the desktop.

2. Select the *Settings* tab.

3. Click the *Advanced* button.

4. Select the *Troubleshoot* tab.

5. Change the hardware acceleration to Full.

6. Click *OK* to save the settings.

However, mouse performance for VMs when you access a VMware remote console from within another VM does suffer somewhat. This behavior occurs whether it is via VMware Workstation, Server, or ESX.

For some versions of Linux kernels, VMware does not provide working VMware Tools drivers. However, the VMware Tools OS-Specific Packaging provides the most up-to-date packaging for Linux Systems by using the Open Source VM-Tools sponsored by VMware (www.vmware.com/pdf/osp_install_guide.pdf).

For security reasons, you may not want to install the entire VMware Tools drivers, because many of the Escape-the-VM attacks are actually attacking the paravirtualized drivers within the VMs. The svga driver for Windows is the current attack vector for Escape-the-VM attacks. Although these types of attacks generally work within hosted environments (VMware Workstation, Fusion, or Server), they fail within the ESX or ESXi environment; at worse, they crash the VM. If you go the route of not installing all the VMware Tools, remember that for VMware View based VMs, the VMware Tools svga driver is required to be installed; otherwise, desktop usability will suffer due to performance issues. In addition, VMs without the tools installed will be poor tenants of the virtual environment because they will not necessarily share in memory ballooning and other overcommit technologies that save on memory and CPU.

It is important to document why you are not using VMware Tools within ESX or ESXi. The risk of Escape-the-VM from VMware Tools is currently very small.

VMX Changes

Every now and then, it will be necessary to modify the VMX file to add new options to solve various issues with the VM. Since ESX v3, there is no need to make these changes from the service console, because the vSC has this capability. However, to make the changes from the service console, all you need do is edit the VMX configuration file for the VM in question. Most changes to the configuration file should happen only when a VM is powered off.

When the VM configuration file is modified from the service console or management appliance it is very important to realize that the VM must first be powered down (for ESX v4) because the VMX file is locked so you cannot read or write to it, and that the VM should be unregistered from vCenter, then re-registered after the VMX changes are completed. Otherwise, the changes may not be picked up. One way to do this follows:

```
cd /vmfs/volumes/<DATASTORE>/<VMNAME>
#vmware-cmd -s unregister `pwd`/*.vmx
# modify VMX file using your favorite editor
# vmware-cmd -s register `pwd`/*.vmx
```

Here are some more popular settings to add to the advanced options of the VM per our previous discussion under the Advanced—General section. There are literally hundreds of other advanced settings undefined by this book. The short list in Table 10.4 is provided to solve specific problems that have been encountered. Any other settings could impact behavior or performance adversely. The full list of VM configuration parameters are at http://sanbarrow.com/vmx.html. Please note that the sanbarrow site contains a full list of options, because VMware Workstation 4 and many of the options do not apply to VMware ESX or ESXi.

Table 10.4 *Configuration Parameters*

Parameter	Value	Notes
keyboard.typematicMinDelay	200000	For Linux machines, it slows down the auto-repeat within X. Often, I disable auto-repeat entirely using the command `xset r off` in a configuration file. Be sure to place this line at the bottom of the file.
mks.ipc.maxBufferedPackets	0	Prevents the remote console from suddenly going black.
mks.ipc.maxBufferedBytes	0	Prevents the remote console from suddenly going black.
svga.maxWidth	Some integer	Maximum width of the monitor: 640, 800, 1024, 1280, 1920, and so on.
svga.maxHeight	Some integer	Maximum height of the monitor: 480, 600, 768, 1024, 1200, and so on.
svga.vramSize	Some integer	svga.maxWidth * svga.maxHeight * 4
gui.maxconnection	Some integer	Sets the maximum number of console connections allowed.

However, for those Guest Operating Systems that have the support, it is possible to hot plug new or existing hard disks, ethernet adapters, and SCSI devices for all versions of VMs supported by vCenter. For VHv7-based VMs, it is possible to hot plug memory, CPUs, and USB controllers. The hot plug functionality makes it extremely easy to keep VMs running while adding new hardware. But if you want to change advanced options, that requires that you reboot the VM.

Conclusion

This chapter covered many aspects of a VM and how the virtual hardware all fits together. We did not discuss any specific OS. That I leave to you, but we do discuss those things you need to understand to really work with virtual hardware. In the next chapter, we delve into the concept of dynamic resources and the load balancing of VMs across VMware ESX hosts. Until you understand the way virtual hardware works, it is impossible to discuss how resources can be balanced.

Chapter 11

Dynamic Resource Load Balancing

Dynamic Resource Load Balancing (DRLB) is the automatic balancing of resource usage across multiple ESX hosts. DRLB ranges from simply scripting of vMotion to moving a VM from host to host through the automatic assignment of more resources on-the-fly, while the VM is running. DRLB is more than VMware Dynamic Resource Scheduling encompassing this technology and others from VMware. DRLB is the front line of any disaster prevention and recovery process and the basis for forming an ESX host cluster. Although DRLB covers a wide range of functionality, it can be broken down into various business continuity processes, some of which require creative scripting to accomplish and others of which exist in various VMware and third-party tools.

In this chapter, there is no difference between ESX and ESXi functionality for DRLB, just the method of implementation. Given this, we use the term ESX throughout the chapter to imply both products unless explicitly stated otherwise.

Defining DRLB

Let's break down DRLB into various processes, with the first one being the simple clustering of ESX hosts. Without the concept of a cluster of ESX hosts, there is no real possibility of pursuing DRLB. Minimally, clusters of ESX hosts share the same datastores; the more advanced definition is those hosts that reside within the VMware vCenter cluster object.

The second component of DRLB is the capability to monitor ESX hosts and VMs then based on resource utilization, make changes to where VMs live (host and datastore) or to the currently assigned resources (increasing/decreasing memory, adding vCPU, and so on). The changes to the currently assigned resources are to either give more resources or take some away as necessary.

The third component of DRLB is the capability to specify secondary locations for a VM to start up if the VM fails or the ESX host fails for some reasons. This ends up being a form of disaster recovery (DR), but only one step on the road to DR. The next chapter covers DR and backup in detail. In essence, this is a major aspect of clustering and is easily applied to ESX either using provided tools or a poor man's approach.

The Basics

The basic premise behind DRLB is monitoring and the interpretation of what is being monitored. Without some form of understanding about what can be monitored, DRLB cannot be pursued with any chance of success. Although the concept of monitoring is not new and is discussed in other chapters of this book, it is important enough to mention again more in detail. The first thing to cover with monitoring is VMware vCenter Server as seen through the vSphere Client (vSC).

vCenter viewed through the vSC provides wonderful graphs by VM and ESX host for CPU, memory, disk, and network utilization and will store this data for trend analysis of resources. Trend analysis will enable the careful consideration of existing data to determine whether it is necessary to permanently rebalance the cluster nodes or change some of the resources allocated to VMs on a permanent basis. DRLB is not a permanent solution, but is just the automation of resource load balancing to prevent catastrophic failures or to quickly bring up backup VMs if an unexpected failure occurs. Performing an analysis over time and fairly often is the best tool for keeping a well-balanced ESX cluster.

DRLB uses this data to account for sudden and unexpected behaviors to maintain the peak performance of the datacenter when issues arise. Even so, intelligent decisions must be made in some automated fashion. For example, let's assume that the CPU utilization of a VM goes off the scale and at the same time the ESX host also goes above the defined threshold. It could be that the DRLB tool automatically moves the problem VM to a named host, but then that host hits a high in utilization and the VM is again moved. This cycle could go on forever, with the VM never really finding a home and caught in an endless loop of movements. There needs to be intelligence in the movement of a VM from host to host so that the target host chosen is not or will not also be overloaded. In other words, its thresholds for automatic movement are not met by moving the VM in question. In essence, DRLB must be adaptive and able to make the necessary decisions as a human would. If this cannot be done, DRLB is extremely limited in functionality. It boils down to the tools used for monitoring and how hard it is to get that data into an adaptive tool to prevent such infinite loops of migrations.

The first step in understanding how to apply DRLB is to set some utilization goals for each member of the ESX datacenter. Most, if not all, of my customers look at the utilization goals as no more than 80% utilized at any given time. Most opt for a lot less than this number, but 80% is a nice number because it provides headroom for subsequent changes in resource allocation and provides a base number to realize when more ESX hosts are necessary for the entire datacenter. Specifically, 80% CPU utilization is often the target when determining that a new ESX host is necessary for a virtual environment. The other three items on the hit parade—memory, network, and disk utilization—are becoming important as utilization goals, and they need to be understood, too.

Memory utilization is how much memory is in use during prime time and is not related to how much is actually assigned to a VM. Memory is generally 100% assigned either to VMs or to a pool of memory waiting for VMs in case of vMotion from another host. The 80% goal really does not apply to memory. However, memory is a finite resource, and in some cases, 80% memory utilization could be realized with only four VMs that use 1GB of memory but with 4GB assigned to each. This implies that on an ESX host with 16GB of memory, the memory above 5GB is unused and therefore a wasted resource. But there are only four VMs—how do we get to 5GB of used memory? The service console and vmkernel can take the other 1GB of memory. Trend analysis would assist in determining how much memory is used over time for each VM, enabling better utilization of memory. Such trend analysis should take into account such things as content-based page sharing, memory ballooning, memory compression, as well as VM memory swapped to disk. The last you want to avoid at all cost.

Network utilization is generally in packets or megabits transferred per second, and although it used to be very hard to have sustained traffic that fills a gigabit pipe with virtualization, this is no longer the case. At most, only seven-tenths of a network is actually used, which translates into 7Mbps for a 10Mbps link, 70Mbps for a 100Mbps link, 700Mbps for a gigabit link, and 7000Mbps for a 10Gb link. Full duplex implies that the seven-tenths number is possible when going in both directions at the same time, which implies that transmits and receives both have a seven-tenths rate, and if the ESX host ever hits this limit with all its VMs combined and sustains this rate, it's possible that network performance will be a major issue. Because seven-tenths is the most we can expect, we should look at an 80% limit on networking as well, which places the bandwidth limit at slightly higher than one-half the stated rate. Nor is network utilization limited to just the raw bandwidth numbers of the hardware, but the simultaneous requirements of VMs on the same or multiple vSwitches.

Disk utilization is a number like networking that depends on the datastore in use. Fibre uses at least 4Gbps, iSCSI provides bandwidth at least 1Gbps but up to 10Gbs, whereas NAS is generally 1Gbps, and direct attached SCSI is 320MBps (roughly 2.6Gbps). Each of these has separate sustained rate limits, just like networking speeds, and NAS responds to the same limits as network utilization discussed previously. Although in general SAN currently can handle more data transfer than NAS, there is still a finite limit. Again, the 80% limit can be applied, but this is the sum of all disk accesses, reads, and writes per second over all VMs. That is at least 3.2Gpbs for Fibre, one-half the network rates for NAS and iSCSI, and 250MBps for direct attached SCSI. In addition, the number of SCSI locks involved increases for the number of hosts attached to a particular device, and that will add delays. For information on SCSI locking, see Chapter 5, "Storage with ESX." With the advent of 10Gbps networking, storage IO is becoming a major issue and VMware has added Storage IO Control (SIOC) to set some per virtual disk IO constraints.

However, does that mean an ESX host or cluster can push these limits without suffering a performance issue? The answer is no. In rare cases, these upper limits can be hit with no impact on performance of ESX, but the utilization goals need to be adjusted for the type of work the VM is performing. Perhaps an ESX host can burst to these limits, but sustained utilization of these limits would be hard to maintain. The key to determining utilization goals is to understand that the addition of a single VM to the environment will change the overall environment in sometimes radical ways. It is not necessarily possible to assume that adding a 5% utilized VM to the existing VM mix will increase everything by 5%. It could increase by more because the vmkernel now has more work to do, and each VM could now have less physical resources, so the impact could be greater overall.

> **Best Practice**
>
> Understand that the addition of a single VM to the environment will change the overall environment in sometimes radical ways.
>
> Each VM impacts the performance of every other VM.

Creating a baseline will help you understand the utilization of the whole cluster or host. Assume our baseline has 20 VMs and shows only 40% utilized for CPU, 1Mbps for network utilization, a few kilobits per second utilization for disk, with an overall memory consumption of 20GB. The assumption will help you realize what is overloaded; we could have a single VM and push this server out of balance with a CPU utilization of 80% while maintaining all else at low-utilization numbers; the packets per second transfer rate is actually fairly high, yet the transfer rate is low. This implies that the vmkernel has to work harder to handle the small size of the packets, thereby increasing the overall utilization.

Hundreds, if not thousands, of examples display drastic changes in utilization after the behavior of any VM changes. In all these cases, balancing of the VMs should occur. Automating DRLB is a step toward balancing VMs across ESX hosts.

There are now third-party tools to help you understand overall utilization or capacity. Such tools from Akorri, Vkernel, and Hyper9 even have mechanisms to automatically, or upon approval, make the necessary changes to your virtual environment to improve overall utilization and the balance across all your nodes. Unlike the third-party tools, the VMware tools DRS, SIOC, and NetIOC look at the resource contention to determine whether something should be done. If there is no contention among the memory, CPU, network, or disk resources, the VMware tools will not do anything. They will maintain the status quo and not perform any DRLB.

The Advanced Features

DRLB within a virtual environment consists of many components. In essence, many of the advanced options within VMware vSphere and the Virtual Environment provide the functionality required to implement full DRLB. Even so, most of the functionality is not yet automated or widely integrated into the automation process. For this, we have to rely on either third-party tools, such as VKernel and Hyper9 or, by hand, PowerShell and other vSphere SDK scripts. Table 11.1 lists the DRLB tools within VMware and the resources they impact, and in some cases, how they impact those resources.

Table 11.1 *DRLB Tools/Resource Impacts*

Tool	CPU	Memory	Network	Disk
DRS	Contention	Contention	N/A	N/A
Resource Pools	Yes	Yes	N/A	N/A
vDS	N/A	N/A	Yes	N/A
DPM	Yes	Yes	Yes	Yes
Storage DRS[1]	N/A	N/A	N/A	Contention
FT (ESX v4)	Yes	Yes	N/A	N/A
HA	Yes	Yes	Yes	Yes
SIOC (ESX v4.1)	N/A	N/A	N/A	Egress FC-HBA Traffic Shaping by VM

continues

Table 11.1   *(Continued)*

NetIOC (ESX v4.1)	N/A	N/A	Egress pNIC Traffic Shaping	N/A
Load Balanc- ing	N/A	N/A	vSwitch pNIC vNIC assign- ment	N/A
LBT (ESX v4.1)	N/A	N/A	Modify pNIC- vNIC assign- ment	Modify pNIC- vmknic assign- ment
vSwitch Traf- fic Shaping	N/A	N/A	Ingress vNIC Traffic Shap- ing by port- group	Ingress vmknic traffic shaping by portgroup
vMotion	N/A[2]	N/A	N/A	N/A
Storage vMo- tion	N/A[3]	N/A	N/A	N/A
Hotplug Mem- ory (ESX v4)	N/A	Yes	N/A	N/A
Hotplug CPU (ESXv4)	Yes	N/A	N/A	N/A
Hotremove CPU (ESX v4)	Yes	N/A	N/A	N/A
Hotplug Disk	N/A	N/A	N/A	Yes
Hotplug vNIC	N/A	N/A	Yes	N/A
vTeleport[4]	N/A	N/A	Yes	Yes

[1] Demoed at VMworld 2009.

[2] vMotion is an underlying technology for DRS.

[3] Storage vMotion is an underlying technology for Storage DRS.

[4] vTeleport requires stretch Layer-2 network and EMC VPLEX.

One of the most important features of DRLB is the concept of resource pools. A resource pool is a way of limiting the host CPU and memory utilization of a group of VMs. For an ESX host or cluster of ESX hosts, there is a single limit for the maximum amount of resources available to the host or cluster. In the case of clusters, the maximum amount of resources available is based on adding up the maximum amount of resources available for all the hosts. Granted, the only resources a resource pool will manage are CPU and memory. Resource pools can be layered and thereby further subdivide the maximum amount of resources available to a group or even a single VM. Resource pools, if used properly, will keep a single group of VMs from using all available resources.

The best way to explain this is to look at how resource pools are configured. They can be configured to give a strict limit on the amount of resources or to allow the pool to borrow from a parent pool. A resource pool is very similar to a pool of water. There is a finite amount of water, and if all the water is gone, there is no more. If we further subdivide the pool of water into buckets of water and hand them out, when the bucket of water is gone, there is no more water for the holder of the bucket. However, if the holder of the bucket is allowed to ask for more water, the parent or original pool of water can give more water to the holder of the bucket. If there is no more water in the pool, there is no more water to loan out.

Resource pools are created with the vSC client connected to vCenter. Use of clusters requires vCenter, and we cover clusters in detail later in this chapter. The important part of creating a resource pool is to determine how many resources are allowed for the group of VMs running within a pool and the behaviors that take place when resources exceed the amount within the pool. To create a resource pool, follow these steps:

1. Log in to vCenter using the vSC.

2. Select the host or cluster into which a resource pool will be created. A host within a cluster cannot have a separate resource pool.

3. Select the *Create Resource Pool* icon or right-click the object and select *Create New Resource Pool*, as shown in Figure 11.1.

4. Give the resource pool a name.

5. Set the shares for CPU and memory resources.

6. Set the reserved amount of CPU and memory specific for this pool; this is the memory that is always available to the pool.

7. Check if this is an expandable reservation—one that can borrow from the pool above.

8. Check if this is an unlimited resource limit. This is not recommended except for the topmost resources (see Figure 11.2).

9. Click *OK* to set the resource pool.

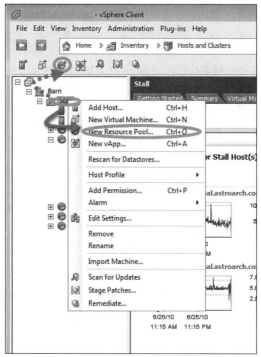

Figure 11.1 *Creating New Resource Pool*

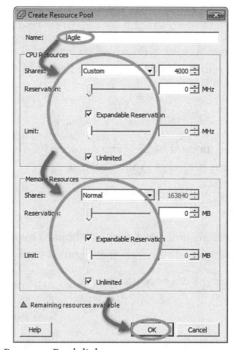

Figure 11.2 *Create Resource Pool dialog*

The next advanced concept is the ESX cluster. An ESX cluster is a combination of hosts that will all share a group of resource pools and within which a set of VMs will work. An ESX cluster increases the amount of resources that are available within a resource pool. A cluster is required for VMware DRS.

Resource pools within clusters are used to provide the necessary information so that DRS can judge whether contention exists within a host with respect to CPU and memory. If there is contention with CPU and memory, DRS can automatically move a VM from one host to another within the same cluster. How aggressive the determination of CPU and memory contention is based on a setting when you configure DRS within the cluster. Even if you do not define additional resources pools, there always exists one pool that comprises all hosts within an ESX cluster, and that is ultimately used to determine CPU and memory contention.

Creation of a cluster is as easy as creating a resource pool. A cluster needs at least two ESX hosts and is created by following these steps:

1. Log in to vCenter using the vSC.

2. Select the datacenter into which to create the cluster.

3. Select the *Create Cluster* icon or right-click the datacenter object and select *New Cluster*, as in Figure 11.3.

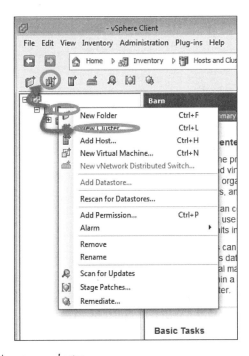

Figure 11.3 *Creating a new cluster*

4. Give the cluster a name and select the options for the cluster. You need the appropriate licenses for VMware HA and VMware DRS. Select the appropriate check boxes (see Figure 11.4).

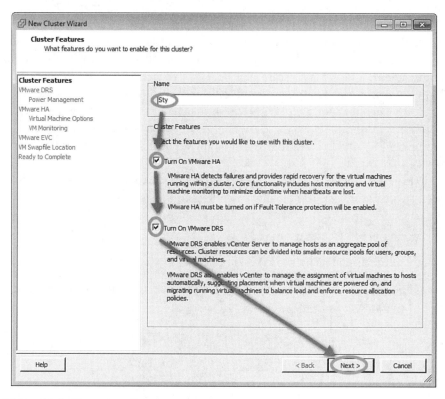

Figure 11.4 *Cluster creation*

5. When you selected VMware DRS, you will be asked to configure it. The options for VMware DRS include the following, as in Figure 11.5:

Manual—This option will allow vCenter to warn you that balancing should take place but leaves the actual balancing of the VMs across the cluster hosts in your hands.

Partially Automated—This option will, on a VM power on, move the VM to a recommended host. In all other cases, it is like Manual.

Fully Automated—This option will automatically move VMs from overutilized ESX hosts to underutilized ESX hosts. There is a slide bar to set the automated mode from Conservative to Aggressive. Conservative will not move a VM until the server utilization has stayed above the threshold for quite a bit, whereas Aggressive will move the VM when the utilization has gone over a threshold.

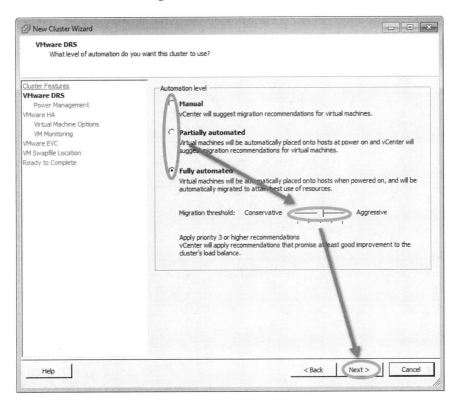

Figure 11.5 *DRS Configuration*

6. When you select VMware DRS, you will be asked to configure it. The options for VMware DRS include the following, as shown in Figure 11.6:

    Off—vCenter will not provide power management recommendations.

    Manual—vCenter will make recommendations for you to approve for evacuating hosts and powering them off.

    Automatic—This option will automatically evacuate VMs from underutilized ESX hosts to the other ESX hosts within the cluster and power down the underutilized hosts. There is a slide bar to set the automated mode from Conservative to Aggressive. All modes will power on hosts to meet VMware HA capacity requirements. How aggressive the power on of a host is depends of the resource utilization (memory and CPU) required by the target utilization range; while power off depends on how far below the target utilization range the cluster goes.

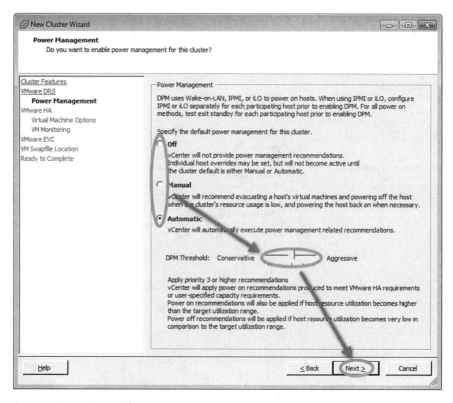

Figure 11.6 *DPM Configuration*

7. When VMware HA is selected, you are presented with a screen that allows you to configure HA (see Figure 11.7):

   You will need to choose whether to enable Host Monitoring Status, which verifies the heartbeat between the hosts. This is a simple way of disabling heartbeat monitoring if you plan a network outage that would keep the service console or management appliances from talking to each other.

   Choose the HA admission control settings. For small clusters, you want to allow VMs to be powered on even if they violate availability constraints, whereas for larger clusters you may not want this. If you have many hosts going into maintenance, you may want to allow violation of availability constraints.

You will need to choose the number of ESX host failures the cluster can withstand. The default is one host. If you have more than two hosts, you can change the number, and what you change it to truly depends on the amount of spare capacity in your cluster. If your hosts are only half utilized and you have six hosts, you might be able to handle three host failures. VMware HA will restart VMs on underutilized hosts. It is also possible per VM to set the host on which it and any dependencies will restart. We talk more about this in Chapter 12, "Disaster Recovery, Business Continuity, and Backup."

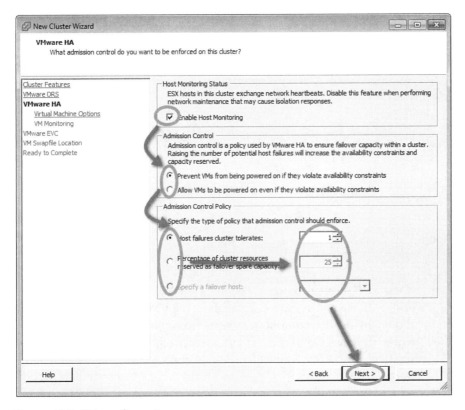

Figure 11.7 *HA configuration*

8. Set the default VM Isolation response settings for all VMs within the VMware HA cluster: restart priority and Host Isolation Response. In general, if a host is isolated you want to shut down the VMs so that they can be booted on another host (see Figure 11.8).

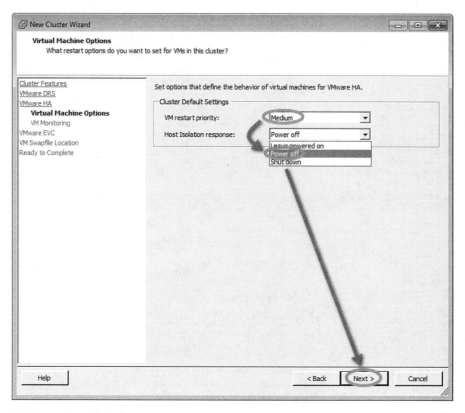

Figure 11.8 *Default VM Response*

9. VMware HA can also detect whether a VM has prematurely died, yet the host is still up and available. In this case, the VM would then reboot. This is done by the detection of heartbeats from the VMware Tools installed within the guest OS. If these fail to be received, the VM is restarted. How sensitive this is by default depends on the sensitivity settings. High is recommended.

10. Select the supported EVC mode for ESX v3 and v4. There are two modes, one for AMD Hosts (w/3Dnow! support) and one for Intel Hosts. With the advent of ESX v4.1, there is now a third option: AMD Hosts without 3Dnow! support, because 3Dnow! support has disappeared from some

AMD chipsets. Only one EVC mode is supported per cluster. To best use EVC, which enhances vMotion capability, you should not mix CPU families within a single cluster.

Within each EVC mode are different selectable subfamilies of chipsets and CPU types from which to choose. More are added for each release.

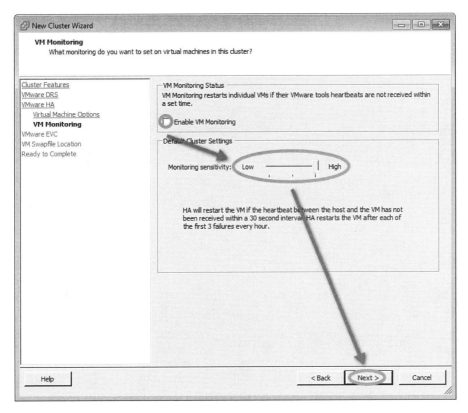

Figure 11.9 *VM Monitoring*

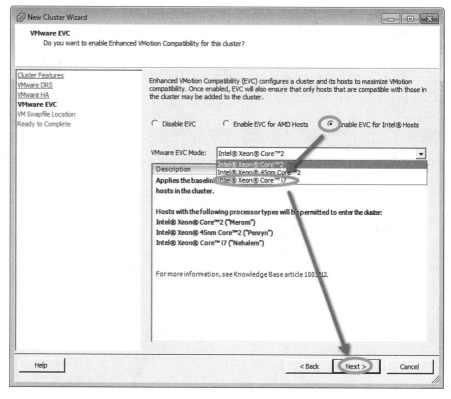

Figure 11.10 *EVC configuration*

11. Finally, choose where to store your per VM swap files. We discuss this later, but if you need to swap based on memory overcommit, you should swap to the fastest spindle-based storage available (see Figure 11.11). If you do overcommit memory, the default will suffice.

12. Select Finish to create the cluster.

13. Select a host and drag it into the cluster to add a host into a cluster. At that time, any existing resource pools can be included, or you can restart with the cluster. I believe that restarting resource pool allocation is the better way to go because the old pools do not apply with more hosts.

14. Be sure to drag the rest of the hosts into the cluster. Each time you drag a host into the cluster, the cluster services will be started.

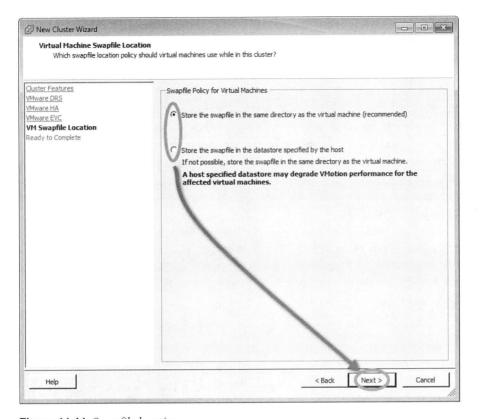

Figure 11.11 *Swapfile location*

Clusters provide for an ever-increasing need of having more resources available for VMs than a single host can provide and the capability to perform DRS or the inclusive capability of DRLB. However, to understand how the scheduling happens and more about scheduling, we need to first understand how the system monitors itself.

Tied to ESX clusters are many of the DRLB tools available to ESX. Part of those clusters are virtual distributed switched (vDS) that provide the capability to maintain a common switching network across all members of an ESX cluster, as well as providing a common framework for more advanced functionality such as NetIOC and LBT. These two features were introduced with ESX v4.1, require vDS, and improve overall networking. NetIOC provides traffic shaping of portgroups on a given pNIC, and LBT enables the host to decide whether the assignment of vNIC to pNIC should be modified to improve overall throughput. LBT works only if there is contention within the vDS tied to the pNICs in question.

The final concept required by DRLB is the capability to hot plug and hot remove memory, CPU, network, and disk resources from a VM at any time based on a set of given rules. Although this functionality is not fully automated yet within a VMware provided tool, third parties are working on this. VKernel and Hyper9 have such tools that rely on using the vSphere SDK to provide automation. You can also build your own scripts to perform these actions to fit your specific needs. Even though we can hot plug resources, we cannot take away resources as easily. Hot removal of memory and CPU does not yet exist, because these require changes to the guest operating system kernels to make them a reality. Hot plug exists, yet hot removal of CPU and memory does not. Even though hot removal is mentioned within the vSphere client, I have yet to find a guest OS that supports this functionality.

The basic building blocks for DRLB are present within ESX and whether we can make use of them depends on the tool and resource in question. Now let's discuss Table 11.1 in more detail by resource. However, before we do this, we need to discuss the concept of shares. Shares are a key component of the current ESX DRLB tools.

Shares

How much of a host a VM can use is determined by the number of resource shares assigned to a VM by the host. This is the last piece of the puzzle concerning DRLB. There is no set number of shares assigned to a host, because the full number of shares depends upon the quantity of assigned vCPUs, memory, vNetworks, and vDisk to all VMs.

Shares are broken down as follows:

- There are 2,000 vCPU shares assigned to the service console (this does not exist on ESXi).

- For every vCPU on a host, there are 1,000 vCPU shares by default.

- For every megabyte of memory assigned to a VM, there is one vMemory share.

- For every vDisk on a host, there are 1,000 vDisk shares.

- There are no shares associated with a vNIC.

Given the preceding rules, consider an example of eight VMs on a single host with two dual-core 3.1GHz CPUs and 16GB of memory. Although the speed and memory of the system is relatively unimportant to the conversation, it will help to point out an important feature. Four of the VMs have a single vCPU, a single vDisk, and 1GB of memory assigned to each; one has four vCPUs, two vDisks, and 2GB of memory assigned; the last three have two vCPUs, 512MB of memory, and one vDisk each. In addition, the service console is using 384MB of memory. Using the previously defined rules, the host has how many shares?

CPU shares: (4 * 1 vCPU + 4 vCPU + 3 * 2 vCPU + 2 SC) * 1,000 = 16,000

Memory shares: (4 * 1024MB + 2048MB + 3 * 512MB + 1 SC * 384) = 8,064

Disk shares: (4 * 1 vDisk + 1 * 2 vDisk + 3 * 1 vDisk + 2 * 1 vDisk) * 1,000 = 11,000

Therefore, the answer is

16,000 CPU shares, 8,064 memory shares, and 11,000 disk shares

How are these shares applied to how the vmkernel manages each VM? In the preceding example, the four-vCPU machine is the most interesting because it uses the most resources when it runs. It uses the resources outlined in Table 11.2.

Table 11.2 *Sample Resource Utilization*

VM	CPU Shares	Memory Shares	Disk Shares
Single vCPU VMs	1,000 / 16,000	1,024 / 8,064	1,000 / 11,000
4 vCPU VMs	4,000 / 16,000	2,048 / 8,064	2,000 / 11,000
2 vCPU VMs	2,000 / 16,000	512 / 8,064	1,000 / 11,000

These numbers define how much CPU, memory, and disk each VM gets when that VM runs only when there is host resource contention. So, a four-vCPU machine would get four times the CPU of a single vCPU machine. In addition, a four-vCPU machine can only run on a host with at least four cores, thereby possibly limiting where the VM can be moved with VMware DRS. This is a very important concept. Just as important to performance is the amount of disk and memory used by each VM. However, in many cases these are overlooked because CPU usage is the main telling point for performance. But let's say that the four-vCPU machine is also a database server with quite a lot of disk IO. Would it not be prudent to increase its disk shares so that it can get more disk IO done when it runs? Suppose we want to increase its disk shares by 1,000 shares per disk, giving it a total of 4,000 shares. If that is the case, the total number of disk shares also increases by 2,000.

Disk shares: (4 * 1 vDisk + 2 * 2 vDisk + 3 * 1 vDisk + 2 * 1 vDisk) * 1,000 = 13,000

4 vCPU VM disk shares: 4,000 / 13,000

All other (7) VM disk shares: 1,000 / 13,000

As you can see from continuing the discussion of shares, while the number of disk shares for the VM has doubled, there is a subsequent increase in the total number of shares available to the host or cluster. This increase in shares is the basic design of ESX resources. The more VMs you run, the fewer resources per VM the system grants. However, the number of resource shares available increase as VMs are added or when resources are modified by hand. Also remember that the service console also has resources associated with it in the realm of two times the normal resources, except for memory.

In addition to the capability to change resources at will, it is possible to set limits on resources and reservations. Limits are the maximum amount of resources a VM can use, and reservations are the amount of resources reserved just for this VM. If the reserved amount of resources is not available, a VM will not start.

The changes to resources, whether CPU, disk, or memory, affect the performance of a VM and may not always trigger a VMware DRS vMotion to occur. If a VM is IO bound, it would use less CPU but wait longer to finish its disk I/O, and therefore have an overall lower chance of being moved to a less-utilized server. However, if a VM is CPU bound, it would definitely be a candidate for ESX to suggest it be moved, or automatically move it, to a less-used host using VMware DRS.

With the introduction of NetIOC and SIOC with ESX v4.1, there are now new shares to consider. For SIOC, the shares are set per VMDK for a VMDK that lives on a FC-HBA presented datastore. For NetIOC, the shares are set on the portgroup associated with a vDS. Both of these IO Controls are used to shape traffic on egress, in other words how the pipe from the host to the network or storage device is divided between all the VMs. The rules for these shares are the same as other shares within the system.

Resource Pool Addendum

With the explanation of shares, we can further enhance the usage of resource pools. A resource pool takes the total available CPU and memory resources and allows them to be divided up into groups or smaller chunks of available resources. The split in resources for resource pools can be used to ensure that the selected VMs only use, at maximum, the resources that are available in the pool. Each resource pool can be further subdivided to grant even fewer resources to each group. This advancement in resource management can guarantee that a VM cannot take over all the resources of an ESX host. Just like a VM, a resource pool can have a reservation and a hard limit on the amount of resources it can use. But, unlike a VM, it can also borrow resources from the parent resource pool as necessary.

Because resources are the monetary unit in a virtual environment, it is possible to reduce resources based on how much a VM owner is willing to pay for the use of the VM. This can translate into something billable to the VMware ESX host VM owners. Because this is the monetary unit of a virtualization host, it might not be wise, unless a customer pays for the resources, to allow a resource pool to borrow from a parent pool. But again, it depends on the billing. However, this still does not explain how to split up network and disk usage.

Network Resources

Network resources are handled differently in ESX v4 than in earlier versions. In ESX v2, each VM could have its own traffic shaping controls, which could lead to quite a bit of illogical setups where each VM was assigned more resources than was physically possible. As of ESX v3, each vSwitch can have traffic shaping applied and then from the amount of traffic available, you can further apply traffic shaping to each port group off a vSwitch. With ESX v4, however, VMware introduced the virtual distributed vSwitch, which enables more interesting network controls. It was not until the introduction of ESX v4.1 that the vDS had more capabilities not found in traditional VMware vSwitches. NetIOC and LBT add quite a bit of necessary and automated functionality to the vNetwork. Traffic shaping is still the major way to control traffic being received from the network, but with ESX v4.1 we can shape the traffic going out of the host—in other words, on egress.

Traffic shaping is discussed in Chapter 7, "Networking." However, let's reiterate: Traffic shaping enables the administrator to set the average bandwidth a vSwitch or port group can attain, its peak bandwidth, and quantity of burst transmission packets. These numbers will, like resources, allow the vSwitch to control how much of the network a VM can use. If traffic shaping is enabled, like resource shares, the VM can be limited on the bandwidth it could use, and this could lead to a VM being I/O bound while it waits on the network. I/O bound does not necessarily translate to CPU usage for a VM, but because traffic shaping happens in the vSwitch, the overall system CPU usage can increase as this is handled. vSwitch utilization has a direct impact on the amount of CPU the vmkernel will use.

When a VM loads and has a vNIC that is connected to a vDS that is connected to a pNIC, there is a mapping from vNIC to pNIC created. This mapping does not change until the VM is powered off and powered back on. From a DRLB and uptime perspective this is a bad idea. So VMware introduced LBT, which modifies the vNIC-to-pNIC mapping that takes place within the vDS. Every 30 seconds LBT looks at the vDS for contention, and if it finds some contention it can change the vNIC to pNIC mapping for any number of VMs until the contention goes away. This happens on data moving out of the host (referred to as southbound by some, or egress by others).

NetIOC is also an important concept for a vDS because it enables you to divide up the pNICs' bandwidth among all the VMs connected to the vDS. There is minimal traffic shaping available with NetIOC. The first element is to set a maximum, and the other is handled by using shares. Each vNIC on the pNIC has a default and even set of shares that can be modified to give a VM more outbound bandwidth than other VMs.

Disk Resources

The disk shares we discussed previously apply to a single ESX host. However, when you employ Storage IO Control (SIOC), the disk shares specified apply to the entire cluster as well as to the host and come into play when the overall latency for a given FC-HBA LUN is too high. SIOC uses the same disk share setting that already existed per virtual disk for Disk IO share application within the ESX host to apply to the entire cluster.

A component of SIOC writes latency and other metadata to metadata of a VMFS formatted LUN. SIOC uses the latency data to determine whether there is contention (latency) of this LUN within the entire ESX cluster, and if there is contention, the shares set up for disk IO are also used to shape the disk traffic headed toward the storage processors on the FC array. SIOC does egress-based traffic shaping across the cluster. The latency and other metadata updates once every 30 seconds and contention is assumed to occur across the cluster when the latency exceeds 20ms.

Use cases for this include applying more shares to a database LUN to ensure that, within a single host, the database LUN has the required throughput. This also ensures that when there is contention (latency) within the cluster, the database LUN gets more of the overall traffic going out of the ESX host to the FC array. SIOC is controlled solely through the disk shares settings.

CPU Resources

As we discussed in Chapter 10, "Virtual Machines," if you employ virtual hardware v7 (VHv7) within your VMs, you now have the capability to hot plug and remove CPUs. However, whether this is possible depends entirely on the Guest OS in use. In addition, it is also possible to use any number of vCPUs up to eight, including odd numbers. There is no automated DRLB functionality that will add or remove vCPUs at need, but there are components of the vSphere SDK that will enable you to do so without rebooting a host. Automation of this aspect of DRLB has been missing from ESX v3, yet now exists in ESX v4. It should be noted that no Guest OS enables the hot removal of a vCPU at this time.

In our previous discussion of shares, we discussed CPU shares and how they impact how long a VM lives on any given CPU in a CPU overcommit situation. If the total number of vCPUs exceeds the total number of cores on host, CPU shares come into play because now contention exists within the environment. As well as shares, CPU limits and reservations are settable in MHz for each VM. Reservations will guarantee that when the vCPUs for a given VM run they will be guaranteed that many CPU resources, while a limit sets an upper bound for CPU utilization. Last, are the concepts of CPU affinity or anti-affinity, which have very specific use cases generally related to high-performance technical computing.

vCPU shares and limits per VM have been settable since ESX started. Resource pools are the only real DRLB mechanism in play now for CPU contention, and Resource Pools control how DRS vMotions VMs from host to host. It would be very useful to modify the shares, limits, and possibly the number of vCPUs on-the-fly to ensure well-balanced nodes of a cluster.

Memory Resources

If you use VHv7 as discussed in Chapter 10, it is now possible to hot plug memory into a VM as needed. Included with this is the capability to set memory shares, reservations, and limits, just like you can for vCPUs, and they apply in much the same way. However, the memory hot plug enables a VM that needs more memory to be given more memory if any is available. Memory resources also have several additional automated mechanisms to protect against slow paging of memory to disk when more memory is used than is available within the system. The order in which these mechanisms are used is as follows:

1. Content-Based Page Sharing (CBPS)—Also known as Transparent Based Page Sharing, it collapses 4K pages of memory to a single page if they are identical. CBPS takes place when the CPU/Core assigned to the vmkernel is idle.

2. Memory ballooning—Allows one VM to borrow unused memory from another VM, but only if the memory ballooning device driver is available for the guest OS in use within the VMs.

3. Memory compression—Compresses memory in use within the VM and decompresses it on access.

4. Swapping to the per VM memory swap file—This is the slowest by far and the most understood component of any modern operating system. One way to increase the speed of this type of swapping is to use solid-state drives for all swapping.

The performance of all these mechanisms also decreases as you go through each one. CBPS is faster than ballooning, which is faster than compression, which is faster than swapping. But all these mechanisms allow a host's memory to be overcommitted and are automatic. The controls that are in place are related to how much memory to allow to be ballooned. This should be kept low so that compression takes over.

DRLB would employ all these mechanisms—shares, limits, reservations, and memory hot plug—to better balance VM memory utilization across all the hosts in question. DRS is the automated tool to balance VMs across nodes by moving the VM using vMotion when CPU or memory is in contention only. However, the other mechanisms can be automated via the vSphere SDK to produce well-balanced nodes.

vApps

vApps are not strictly a DRLB construct, but they can be used as one to ensure that a group of VMs behave properly according to a set number of rules. vApps provide a mechanism to group multiple VMs as a single virtual application. Whereas resource pools apply to nodes within a cluster, vApps provide the same functionality for groupings of VMs. In fact, they have many of the same controls as resource pools. To create a vApp, follow these steps:

1. Log in to vCenter using the vSC.

2. Select the cluster into which the vApp will be created.

3. Select the *Create vApp* icon or right-click the object and select *Create New vApp*, as shown in Figure 11.12.

4. Give the vApp a name.

5. Set the shares for CPU and memory resources.

6. Set the reserved amount of CPU and memory specific for this pool; this is the memory that is always available to the vApp.

7. Check if this is an expandable reservation—one that can borrow from the pool above.

8. Check if this is an unlimited resource limit. This is not recommended except for the topmost resources (see Figure 11.13).

9. Select *OK* to add the vApp.

10. Add VMs to the vApp using drag and drop.

Figure 11.12 *Creating new resource pool*

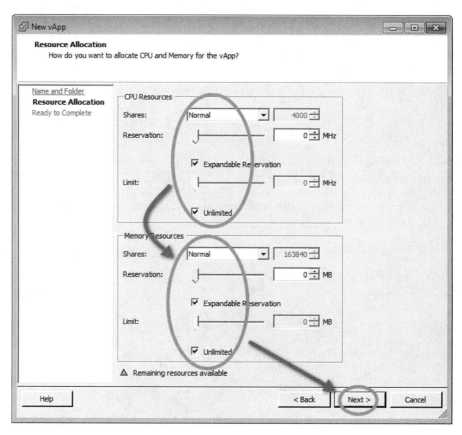

Figure 11.13 *New Resource Pool dialog*

vApps get manipulated like VMs in many ways, sort of a team of VMs with set resources per cluster. You can apply power operations to all VMs within a vApp by manipulating the vApp, but you cannot vMotion or migrate a vApp because it lives at the cluster level, not the host level, and as such encompasses all the hosts. vApps enable the segregation of power controls to a subset of VMs so that the order of the power on within the vApp is well defined. Whereas you may have thousands of VMs spread over hundreds of Resource Pools, vApps are composed of smaller numbers of VMs that cover an entire application from front end, to middleware, to back end, for example.

Monitoring

There are a myriad of ways to monitor an ESX host, but few monitoring tools feed into the capability to perform DRLB or have this capability built in. The first is the vCenter Server (vCenter). vCenter will allow scripts to be called when certain thresholds or actions occur. Others include Akorri Balancepoint, vKernel, and Hyper9. Each presents, in a different way, the capability to monitor resources. Each has one thing in common, and that is the capability to vMotion a VM to another host if this is allowed within your license level for ESX and vCenter. Choosing the new host, however, can be as easy as having the +1 server of an N+1 configuration be used as an offload location, or more complex as determining which host has the least amount of utilization and moving a VM there. The first thing to review is the alarm functionality and what can be accomplished with these tools. Then we will look at performance monitoring tools and finally resource shares or how much of a resource a specific VM can use. All these present the background that is ultimately used by DRS, which is a subset of DRLB.

DPM is also another aspect of DRS and could enable this +1 server to be used as a hot spare in case it is needed as VMs are added and moved around. DPM enables an ESX host to be powered on and off as required, which not only could improve overall utilization but also provide for extra capacity as required. And then when not required, it could be powered back off to save on power and cooling costs. Use of DPM does require quite a bit of planning, such as a hot spare not being used for other tasks just because it can be.

Alarms

Alarms are thrown when a VM or ESX host has issues; they show up as different colored triangles on a VM or host on the left-side panel of the vSC. Alarms can also be accessed on the Alarm tab of the right-side panel. These alarms can be used to trigger DRLB actions. Besides the default alarms, quite a few other alarms are available. The alarms can have actions associated with them, such as the capability to send email, run a script on the vCenter server, send an SNMP trap, or perform a power operation on a VM. Given these options, alarms have an incredible power. The alarms trigger when VMs or hosts change state. All changes in state act as triggers and are defined by the administrator except for some predefined basics. The basic alarms trigger when a host loses connectivity to the vCenter Server, the CPU utilization of a VM or host is greater than 75%, or memory utilization of a VM or host is greater than 75%. The basic alarms would need to be duplicated to trigger any action besides the default, which is to show the alarm in vCenter.

Some useful state changes are when vMotion is started or completed; the VM power state changes; a VM is created or destroyed; and CPU, disk, memory, or network usage goes above a certain percentage or specific amount. It is also possible to set a warning (yellow), all clear (green), or problem (red) alarm within vCenter. In addition, you can set a tolerance range in which an alarm will not trigger unless it goes above or below the specified range. It is also possible to set the frequency of an alarm. For example, you can set things so that the system does not report a new alarm of this type until a specified time limit has expired.

Virtual Center Alarms have increased in functionality from early generations of vCenter. Unfortunately, much more tuning needs to be done to the alarm subsystem to make it useful and practical. vCenter alarms have a weakness. They lack the capability to configure specific time periods when alarms should and should not be armed. For instance, VM and host resource usage tends to skyrocket after hours when virus scans and network backups are performed. This causes CPU, disk IO, and network utilization thresholds to be crossed for an extended period of time after hours. The result is that excessive alarms are generated, typically resulting in an overage of nuisance email alerts.

There is, however, one caveat. If network issues exist between the vCenter Server and the ESX hosts or VMs, it is possible to get false positives on some alarms, specifically those dealing with host availability or power settings. Setting alarms within the vCenter is fairly straightforward and is a great way to monitor the utilization of VMs and ESX hosts. Here are the steps to set up CPU and memory utilization alarms. The default setups are to warn when the utilization goes above 75% and to notify that a problem exists when the utilization is above 90%. Because the default alarms cannot be modified, here is how you create alarms that can perform other actions:

1. Log in to the vSC.

2. Select the host or VM on which to set the alarm.

3. Select the *Alarm* tab.

4. Select the *Definitions* button.

5. Right-click in the blank space in the right-side frame and select the *New Alarm* menu option (see Figure 11.14).

6. Give the alarm a name (see Figure 11.15) and a description, and choose whether to monitor a VM or a host. If you select a VM on which to add an alarm, it will automatically set it to monitor a VM, and the same holds true for a host. To get the choice, choose a cluster, datacenter, or so forth.

7. Enter the trigger priority of Red or Green. Red triggers an alarm by default, but you can set this alarm to trigger when it changes to green.

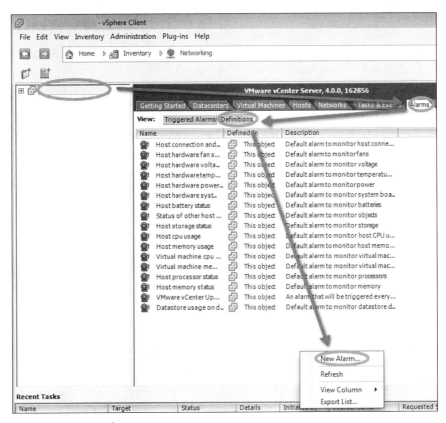

Figure 11.14 *New alarm*

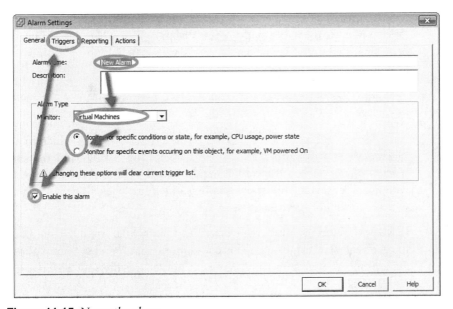

Figure 11.15 *Name the alarm*

8. Enable the alarm.

9. Select the Triggers tab and add a trigger. Add as many triggers as necessary (see Figure 11.16). The following triggers are supported:

(VM) VM CPU Usage (%)—Provides an alarm based on the % of CPU Usage used by the VM.

(VM) VM CPU Ready Time (ms)—Provides an alarm based on the CPU Ready Time in ms for each VM. A high CPU Ready Time often implies an overloaded host.

(VM) VM Disk Aborts—Provides an alarm on the count of disk IO aborts, which could be useful in determining if the VM's virtual disk has gone read-only. These values also climb when the disk subsystem is overloaded.

(VM) VM Disk Resets—Provides an alarm on the count of disk IO resets, which could be useful in determining if the VM's virtual disk has gone read-only. These values also climb when the disk subsystem is overloaded.

(VM) VM Disk Usage (KBps)—Provides a per-VM alarm when the disk usage exceeds a certain KBps setting, which could imply the VM is writing to disk more than expected, such as when error logs are written.

(VM) VM Fault Tolerance Latency—Provides a per-VM alarm to determine when the FT latency increases past an acceptable point, which could imply issues with the FT Logging network.

(VM) VM Heartbeat—Provides a per-VM alarm for when the VM heartbeat fails. If the VM heartbeat fails, VMware HA may trigger an isolation event if VM Monitoring is enabled.

(VM) VM Memory Usage (%)—Provides a per-VM alarm if the memory usage of a host increases by a given %. This is useful for knowing whether an application is using more memory than normal.

(VM) VM Network Usage (KBps)—Provides a per-VM alarm if the network usage exceeds the specified bandwidth. This is useful for knowing whether a VM suddenly starts sending out more packets than normal, which could imply a virus or malware.

(VM) VM Snapshot Size (GB)—Provides a per-VM alarm if the snapshot file grows past a certain size. This could imply that someone forgot about a snapshot or that something has radically changed many blocks on a virtual disk.

(VM) VM State—Provides an alarm for when a VM changes power state, which is useful for determining if a VM prematurely powers off or crashes.

(VM) VM Total Disk Latency (ms)—Provides an alarm for when the disk latency for a given VM exceeds a specified value of ms. Disk latency often implies an overloaded storage subsystem.

(VM) VM Total Size on Disk (GB)—Provides an alarm if a virtual disk grows past a certain size. For thin provisioned disks this type of alarm is crucial.

(Host) Host Connection State—Provides a per-host alarm on the connection state of the host as seen from vCenter.

(Host) Host Console SwapIn Rate (KBps)—Provides an alarm based on the amount of memory swapped in from disk for a host console VM.

(Host) Host Console SwapOut Rate (KBps)—Provides an alarm based on the amount of memory swapped out to disk for a host console VM.

(Host) Host CPU Usage (%)—Provides a per Host alarm for CPU utilization in % available. Above 80% usually implies a need for a new host.

(Host) Host Disk Usage (KBps)—Provides a per-host alarm for disk utilization in KBps. If this is elevated on one host versus another, it could imply an unbalanced cluster.

(Host) Host Memory Usage (%)—Provides a per-host alarm for memory utilization.

(Host) Host Network Usage (kbps)—Provides a per-host alarm for network utilization.

(Host) Host Power State—Provides a per-host alarm for the power state of the host with respect to DPM.

(Host) Host Swap Pages Write (KBps)—Provides a per-host alarm for the amount of VM swap pages written to disk in KBps. This number should be as close to zero as possible.

(Clusters) All HA Hosts Isolated—Provides a per-cluster alarm on when a host is isolated by HA.

(Datacenters) Added License—Provides a per-datacenter alarm for when a new license is added.

(Datastore) Datastore Capacity Increased—Provides a per-datastore alarm for when a datastore has grown.

(Networks) Distributed Virtual Port Group Created—Provides a per-network alarm for when a vDS portgroup has been created.

(vDS) Host Left Distributed Virtual Switch—Provides a per-vDS alarm for when a host leaves a vDS.

After the trigger type is decided, you decide on the condition: Warning level, Warning Condition Length (time period), Alert level, and Alert Condition length (time period). Condition will be Greater Than, Less Than, Is Equal To, or Is Not Equal To, and so on. The warning and alert levels will depend on each trigger. The condition lengths are in 0 or 30 seconds, then minutes afterward.

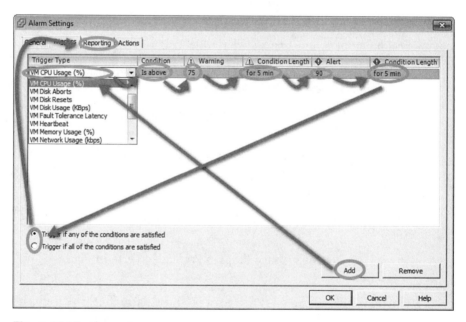

Figure 11.16 *Alarm triggers*

10. Select the Reporting tab.

11. Choose the tolerance (or how many percentage points above and below the limit until the alarm triggers). For example, you could use the default and set the tolerance to 5%, which means the alarm will not trigger yellow until the VM CPU usage is > 80%.

12. Choose the frequency in minutes. In other words, do not report any change to this alarm for the time limit set. You could, for example, set this to 10 minutes, which implies that if the VM CPU usage drops below and raises once more above 80% (75% + 5% tolerance) within 10 minutes, there will not be a report. This allows a single report, and, assuming there is a spike, it may just go away and not go off again. This is a good way to tell whether the alarm you have is really vital. If the frequency is low enough, you could see whether there is a trend over a set time limit.

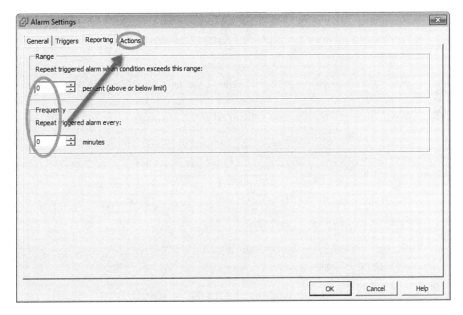

Figure 11.17 *Alarm reporting*

13. Select the Actions tab, and then add an action. You can have more than one action for each alarm. You could set up a series of alarms that, depending on the alarm, perform increasingly serious actions.

14. Select an action:

Send a notification email—This sends an email to the value entered. An email can be sent to a pager, cell phone, email list, logging server, and so on. The first trigger could send to an email list, the second trigger could be sent to a pager, and a third trigger could page. However, this implies three different alarms and not all within the same definition.

Send a notification trap—Send a trap to a management server that understands vCenter SNMPD MIBS.

Run a command—Run a command or program specified by the value. The script or program must exist on the vCenter host.Power on a VM— Power on a VM, which is useful when an alarm triggers that the VM has powered off for some reason.

Power off a VM—Power off a VM, which is useful when a VM that perhaps competes for resources powers on.

Suspend a VM—Suspends a VM, which is useful if utilization jumps too high and you need a temporary reprieve. This type of trigger can free up resources temporarily.

Reset a VM—Reboots the VM and thereby cleans up memory utilization. This could be a useful action if an application has a known memory leak and you want to reboot the VM automatically before there is a catastrophic failure.

Migrate a VM—Migrate a VM, which is useful if you want to automatically load balance your nodes.

Reboot guest on VM—Reboot a Guest is useful if you detect a VM heartbeat or other Guest OS failure.

Shutdown guest on VM—Shut down a VM is useful if you detect a VM heartbeat or other Guest OS failure.

15. Select a direction and whether to repeat the action:

    From green to yellow—Alarm triggered as a warning.

    From yellow to red—Alarm triggered as a problem.

    From red to yellow—Alarm notifies that the problem is no longer vital but there is still a warning.

    From yellow to green—The all-clear alarm.

16. If the action is a repeating action, set the repeat duration for the action.

17. Select OK to set the alarm.

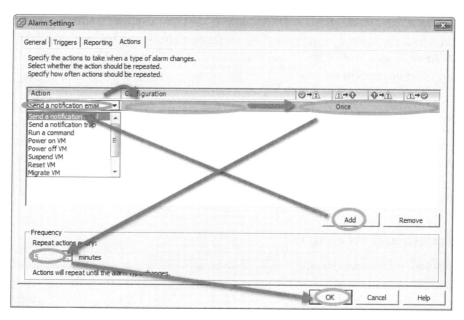

Figure 11.18 *Alarm action*

Useful alarms include the default, but there are some others that would be nice to have. If VMware DRS is in automated mode, or perhaps more than one person can perform vMotions, it is possible to trigger alarms for every vMotion completed or started. At the very least, you can get an email that tells you when the vMotion happened, and you can then investigate why it happened to better understand how VMware DRS triggers itself.

Another extremely useful alarm is one that is triggered when the VM network usage goes above a certain percent. This alarm will help pinpoint VMs that are overusing network resources. The default alarms do not handle network utilization, but this type of alarm can be created. I set up this alarm to let me know when a VM or even a network is overloaded. If it remains consistently overloaded, there is need for more network bandwidth for the ESX host. However, this type of alarm may not be practical when network backups are running because of the number of alarms that can be generated.

The last useful alarm is VM or host disk usage. If the disk usage consistently goes above the alarm state, it may be necessary to increase the amount of storage. Perhaps you can solve the problem by adding a new LUN, perhaps from a different SAN, to offset the load. Again, these are not default alarms or actions, but they are extremely useful for determining when more resources are required for your ESX host or cluster.

Alarms can also tie into another auditing tool that can then audit all actions on which the alarms can trigger. This could be a check and balance over other auditing modes and be able to at least pinpoint key time frames to investigate for other changes to the cluster.

Alarms are powerful, and they give you trigger points to let you know when a system is overloaded or an unexpected action occurs. If you never expect a VM to power down or crash, it would be useful to set an alarm. Perhaps set up one per VM. This way you get a timestamp as to when the problem occurred, which gives you a leg up on analysis of the issue. Time is the one thing you need to know when reviewing log files and performance. When something happened is just as important as what happened, as you will see in the next section.

Performance Analysis

Another tool for monitoring is to review the performance of the ESX host hosts, clusters, resource pools, and VMs by using the Performance tab on the right-side panel of the vSC. There are also tools such as Akorri Balancepoint, vFoglight from Vizioncore, vKernel, and other third parties. All these tools provide quite a bit of useful information when there is a need to look at performance. Some people constantly review the performance graphs from these tools, and others wait for an alarm to trigger a problem.

Performance analysis inside ESX in many ways is an art form, but there are simple rules to understand before beginning:

- The performance within a VM does not always map to the real perform-ance for the VM inside ESX. The only time that there is a legitimate map-ping of what the VM states to the real performance is when there is a one-to-one mapping between vCPUs to pCPUs. In most cases, this almost never happens. Tools that gather performance data from within a VM are useful for determining whether there was a change, but not the exact val-ues. Tools such as Windows Task Manager's Performance tab, HP Open-View, and so forth are great for seeing what has changed within a VM but not the exact value of a change. I have seen situations within a VM where the vCPU utilization was around 80%, yet the real utilization using ESX-based tools was only 15% for the VM. If the descheduler VMware Tool is in use, there is a closer mapping between what ESX shows and what the VM will show. ESX is the final arbiter of performance values, not the VM. Descheduler is no longer available for ESX v4.

A common question concerns why a VM does not internally show the proper performance numbers. The answer is that it is mainly because of the use of a vCPU rather than a pCPU. A vCPU uses only a part of the pCPU, the time slice allotted for the VM. Because the program counters used by the performance tools look at the total speed of a full CPU and the number of cycles of the CPU, the calculations are based on a pCPU and not the reduced cycles and speed allocated as a vCPU. So, the numbers can be off by quite a bit. For example, a pCPU of 2.4GHz may give only 32MHz for the vCPU time slice for a VM. Although on a full 2.4GHz the pCPU utilization could be 15%, but with a 32MHz vCPU, the performance is 80% because there are reduced cycles and speed available to the vCPU. Is there a formula for determining the difference? Not that I have found. After you have a baseline of performance, the internal measurements become a gauge telling you whether things are better or worse.

- The addition of a new VM to a virtualization host will affect the performance of every VM. I have seen customers who look only at the performance of the single VM that has an issue instead of the performance of the whole ESX host. The two are not unrelated.

- Addition of a VM to a cluster of ESX hosts will affect the performance of the entire cluster, which is why tools like SIOC exist. The latency values per LUN can be reviewed.

- The addition of vSwitches (Cisco and vDS) to a VMware ESX host will also affect the performance of every VM. Increasing network paths will increase the amount of pCPU and memory that the vmkernel uses and allow for a new balancing act across physical networks.

- Because most multicore pCPUs share the same L2 Cache, it is wise to look at the number of cores as one less than the actual number.

- After one of the memory overcommit mechanisms (CBPS, Ballooning, Compression, Swapping) is employed, per VM performance will suffer and perhaps impact all VMs because of increased pCPU and Disk IO loads.

- The use of mixed operating systems within an ESX host affects performance. ESX caches common blocks of code for a VM using CBPS; in this way, the memory needed for the code segments of a guest operating system is shared between multiple VMs using the same guest (see Figure 11.19).

This allows less memory to be shared for like VMs. Consider this an advanced form of shared libraries. In a shared library, the nonvolatile code or instructions to issue for a given function are shared, but the volatile and private memory of the same function used by multiple applications is not shared.

However, when there are disparate guest operating systems, the code sharing does not happen as often.

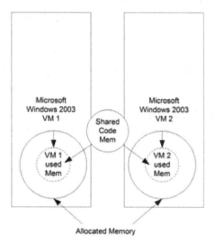

Figure 11.19 *Multiple Guest OS caching, CBPS*

- Mixing VMs with different vCPUs on a host can cause performance problems. When there are VMs with mixed vCPU counts on the same ESX host, the scheduler has to work quite a bit harder than it does if all the VMs have the same number of vCPUs. Because a vCPU is mapped to a pCPU when the VM is running, consider the following example. The example shown in Figure 11.20 takes a four-core host, and we will try to fit into those four cores all the vCPUs to run three VMs with single vCPUs, two VMs with dual vCPUs, and one VM with a quad vCPU. Each set of lines represents when a vCPU will run. The first time the solid lines will run; the next time the dashed lines of the dual vCPU VM and a single vCPU VM will run, and one of the existing single vCPU VMs is not swapped out. Last, the dotted lines of the quad vCPU VM will run.

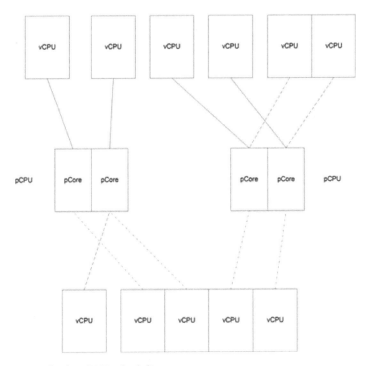

Figure 11.20 *Multiple vCPU scheduling*

- Use of RDMs for large file shares will change performance, and there is one less layer to go through the share. However, this could also impact performance adversely because more storage network bandwidth could be used.

- Use of per VMDirectPath could improve overall performance for some resources because the hypervisor is completely bypassed. However, this could increase vCPU and other requirements within the VM.

- After deploying any VMs, always get a new baseline to assist with future performance analysis, either from within the VM or without.

Now that we have the basics of what will affect performance, how do we monitor performance to determine the cause of any problem? Table 11.3 outlines the available tools and some notes about them. Also note that the items listed previously are not the end all and be all of performance, but merely some considerations when looking at performance.

Table 11.3 *Performance-Monitoring Tools*

Tool	ESX v3.x	ESX v4.x	Notes
Virtual Center	V2.x	V4.x	vCenter has a resolution of up to 5 minutes, but is only displayed every half hour.
vFoglight from Vizioncore	Yes	Yes	Provides a single pane to see all utilizations for a server or VM. The resolution is once a minute. In addition, it provides a graphical way to manage all VM processes.
Akorri Balance-point	Yes	Yes	Performance optimization tool.
Zenoss	Yes	Yes	More of a monitoring package with ESX functionality available.
vKernel	Yes	Yes	Provides free/for charge tools to look at storage performance and per-VM performance over time.
esxtop	Yes	Yes	Used when a problem occurs as its resolution is as low as 10 seconds.

Each tool has its own uses and many more tools also are available. However, we shall discuss mainly esxtop and vCenter analysis. vFoglight and vKernel are useful tools for looking at a finer resolution without having to resort to the CLI and esxtop. To view performance in vCenter, select the host, cluster, or VM to review, and then select the Performance tab. In the following discussion, we have the normal alarms and noticed that we got a yellow or warning alarm, and want to know what gave the alarm and why. It is easier to explain performance analysis by looking at a real problem.

Figure 11.21 shows a change in performance of the VM, which occurred at 9:35 PM on June 25, 2010. The system went from around 12.5% CPU usage to 25% and finally to an average value below 12.5%. So the question to ask is, what happened at 9:35 PM? When we look at the logs for the application on the VM, we notice an increase in socket connections and related CPU processing, which explains the CPU utilization and then the steady state. However, this is not the only performance chart to look at. We should also look at the chart for the complete system. Isolating just a single VM does not show the complete performance implication. However, this overview also shows that we used more memory at the 9:35 PM time, which also implies more processing was occurring.

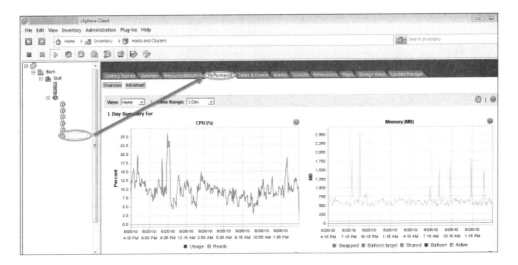

Figure 11.21 *VM performance overview*

If we next look at the host performance graphs, we see that the CPU and memory utilization is well below normal levels. Actually, we show that this host, from memory and CPU perspectives, is fairly well underutilized. Yet this does not give us any hints as to exactly what happened at 9:35 PM on 6/25/2010 (see Figure 11.22).

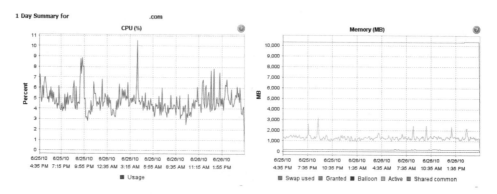

Figure 11.22 *Host performance overview*

Understanding performance is not just about the graphs. You need to understand how your applications work, how tools work inside ESX, and how they interact with each other. The application in question is Apache, which can have spikes in utilization based on incoming packets, which says we need to really look at network graphs. If we look at Figure 11.23, we notice that there was a very large increase in disk traffic, which would imply more processing happened with only a modest increase in network traffic.

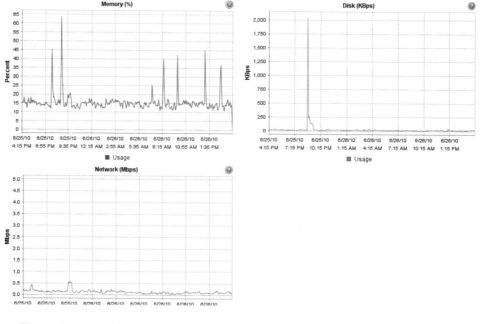

Figure 11.23 *Disk/network performance overview*

> *Best Practice for Performance Monitoring*
>
> Keep the vCenter Server and ESX hosts synchronized using an NTP or external clock service.

Putting It All Together

Because resources and utilization govern DRLB and its subset encompassed within VMware DRS, it is first important to realize how the resource and utilization tools within ESX interact. The preceding description now allows us to visit how to automate the load balancing of VMs across hosts. But, first we need to expand our rules for load balancing and how they relate to CPU utilization.

- CPU-bound VMs will impact overall CPU usage and trigger vCenter CPU alarms, and possibly VMware DRS migration.

- Disk IO-bound VMs may not impact overall CPU usage, may not trigger vCenter CPU alarms, and most likely will not trigger a VMware DRS migration. However, if you are using FC storage, SIOC may help with this (requires ESX v4.1).

- Network IO-bound VMs will impact overall CPU usage of the vmkernel, may not trigger vCenter alarms, and most likely will not trigger a VMware DRS migration. However, if you are using vDS, NetIOC could assist with this as well as LBT (requires ESX v4.1).

- High overall network usage will impact overall CPU usage, may trigger a vCenter CPU alarm, and most likely will trigger a VMware DRS migration.

- High overall disk usage will impact overall CPU usage, may trigger a vCenter CPU alarm, and most likely will trigger a VMware DRS migration.

- High overall memory usage may not impact overall CPU usage, may trigger a vCenter memory alarm, and most likely will not trigger a VMware DRS migration.

As you can see, CPU usage is the main trigger for a VMware DRS migration. The use of vMotion is only one tool in the toolbox for load balancing the virtual environment. vCenter Alarms can trigger scripts when CPU and other usage of a VM hits a certain level, too, but that is still only one piece of the puzzle.

The other pieces of the puzzle are the capability to change CPU, disk, and memory shares on-the-fly and adjust traffic shaping to reduce network utilization of VMs. All these adjustments can happen on-the-fly. Changes to the resource shares and traffic-shaping settings take place at once. These changes, plus the capability to vMotion, can better balance VM utilization across the host, cluster, and datacenter. Currently implemented as a product is the capability to migrate running machines on-the-fly (VMware DRS or other automated vMotion). All other methods of resource management are purely a by-hand mechanism. Resource pools and vApps are a step toward automation of this behavior by limiting a group of VMs to a certain amount of resources, as are the capabilities to hotplug memory and CPU.

Now, how do you manipulate the other settings? Unfortunately, there is no automated way to do this yet and no easy answer. You can use the VMware SDK, VI Perl Toolkit, to read the options, but to set them requires a bit more logic than what is available. There is some hope in using alarms within vCenter to call Powershell and other vSphere SDK scripts to implement some, if not all, of these options. In addition, high usage and other alarms could force a migration of the VMs from host to host, thereby complementing the existing VMware DRS CPU usage constraints with increased capabilities.

Conclusion

Although VMware DRS uses CPU and memory contention to determine which VMs to move from host to host, there is more to the balancing act besides this simple yet vital approach. This is one reason why VMware DRS is only a small part of DRLB, which encompasses all the available resources and would do more than just move VMs from host to host. After we add in Load-Based Teaming, NetIOC, and SIOC, then DRLB has grown to include network and storage. Unfortunately, to realize full DRLB requires much scripting and knowledge of your hardware environment and requires changing not just the host on which the VM resides but the amount of a host a VM can use by integrating in hotplug/remove mechanisms. vSphere adds many more tools to our DRLB toolbox that we can automate using the vSphere SDK.

The last aspect of DRLB is disaster recovery and business continuity, and that is discussed in Chapter 12.

Chapter 12

Disaster Recovery, Business Continuity, and Backup

Disaster Recovery (DR) takes many forms, and the preceding chapter on DRLB covers a small part of DR. Actually, DRLB is more a preventative measure than a prelude to DR. However, although being able to prevent the need for DR is a great goal, too many disasters happen to rely on any one mechanism. In this chapter, we categorize disasters and provide solutions for each one. You will see that the backup tool to use will not dictate how to perform DR, but it's the other way around. In addition to DR, there is the concept of Business Continuity (BC) or the need to keep things running even if a disaster happens. Some of what we discuss in this chapter is BC and not truly DR. However, the two go hand in hand because BC plans are often tied to DR plans and handle a subset of the disasters.

> ### What Is the Goal of Disaster Recovery?
>
> The goal of DR is to either prevent or recovery quickly from downtime caused by either man or nature.

> ### What Is the Goal of Business Continuity or Disaster Avoidance?
>
> The goal of BC is to maintain the business functions in the face of possible downtime caused by man or nature.

As you can see, DR and BC are interrelated: DR is intended to prevent or recover from downtime while BC attempts to maintain business function.

Virtualization provides us the tools to do each of these. In the following discussion, unless otherwise stated, ESX and ESXi can be used interchangeably.

Disaster Types

There are various forms of well-defined disasters and ways to prevent or work around these to meet the defined goal. There is no one way to get around disasters, but knowing they exist is the first step in planning for them. Having a DR or BC plan is the first step toward prevention, implementation, and reduction in downtime. At a conference presentation, I asked a room of 200 customers if any of them had a DR or BC plan. Only two people stated they had a DR or BC plan, which was disconcerting but by no means unexpected.

> ### Best Practice for DR and BC
> Create a written DR and BC plan.

Writing the DR and BC plan will help immensely, in the case that it is needed, because there will be absolutely no confusion about it in an emergency situation. For one customer, the author was requested to make a DR plan to cover all possible disasters. Never in the customer's wildest dreams did they think it would need to be used. Unfortunately, the "wildest dream" scenario occurred, and the written DR plan enabled the customer to restore the environment in an orderly fashion extremely quickly. It is in your best interest to have a written DR plan that covers all possible disasters to minimize confusion and reduce downtime when, and not if, a disaster occurs.

> ### Best Practice for DR and BC
> Plan for failure; do not fail to plan.

Yes, this last best practice sounds like so many other truisms in life, but it is definitely worth considering around DR and BC, because failures will occur with surprising frequency, and it is better to have a plan than everyone running around trying to do everything at once. So what should be in a DR and BC plan? First, we should understand the types of disasters possible and use these as a basis for a DR and BC plan template. Granted, some of the following examples are scary and unthinkable, but they are not improbable. It is suggested that you use the following list and add to it items that are common to your region of the world as a first step to understanding what you may face when you start a DR or BC plan. A customer I consulted for asked for a DR plan, and we did one considering all the following possibilities. When finished, we were told that a regional disaster was not possible and that it did not need to be considered. Unfortunately, Katrina happened, which goes to show that if we can think it up, it is possible. Perhaps a disaster is improbable, but nature is surprising.

Disasters take many forms. The following list is undoubtedly not exhaustive, but it includes many different types of potential disasters.

- Application failure

  An application failure is the sudden death of a necessary application, which can be caused by poorly coded applications and are exploited by denial-of-service (DoS) attacks that force an application to crash.

- VM failure

  A VM failure could be man-made, by nature, or both. Consider the man-made possibilities such as where a security patch needs to be applied or software is to be added to the VM. By nature could be the failure of the VM due to an OS bug, an unimplemented procedure within the virtualization layer, or an application issue that used up enough resources to cause the VM to crash. In general, VM failures are unrelated to hardware because the virtualization layer removes the hardware from the equation. But it does not remove OS bugs from the equation.

- ESX host failure

  A machine failure can be man-made, by nature, or even both. For example, a man-made failure could be the planned outage to upgrade firmware, hardware, the ESX OS, or the possible occurrence of a hardware failure of some sort that causes a crash. Another example is if power is inadvertently shut off to the server.

- Communication failure

  A communication failure is unrelated to ESX, but will affect ESX nonetheless. Communication can be via Fibre Channel, Ethernet, or for such items as VMCI, VMsafe, VIX, and so on via some out-of-band mechanism. The errors could be related to a communication card, cable, switch, or a device at the non-ESX side of the communication. An example of this type of failure is a Fibre or network cable being pulled from the box or a switch is powered off or rebooted.

- Chassis failure

  Chassis failures can cause either a single host to fail or multiple hosts to fail. As datacenters become denser, more and more blade and other shared hardware chassis come into play. This could simply be a failure of a single fan to the back or mid plane components failing outright. This type of failure could cause many ESX hosts to fail or have a communication failure that could affect more than one host.

- Rack disaster

  Rack failures are extremely bad and are often caused by the rack being moved around or even toppling over. Not only will such an incident cause failures to the systems or communications, but it could cause physical injury to someone caught by the rack when it topples. Another rack failure could be the removal of power to fans of and around the whole rack, causing a massive overheat situation where all the servers in the rack fail simultaneously.

- Datacenter disaster

  Datacenter disasters include air conditioning failures that cause overheating, power spikes, lack of power, earthquakes, floods, fire, and anything else imaginable that could render the datacenter unavailable. An example of this type of disaster is the inadvertent triggering of a sprinkler system or a sprinkler tank bursting and flooding the datacenter below. It may seem odd, but some datacenters still use water and no other flame prevention system. Use of halon and other gasses can be dangerous to human life and, therefore, these gasses may not be used.

- Building disaster

  Like datacenter disasters, these disasters cause the building to become untenable. These include loss of power or some form of massive physical destruction. An example of this type of disaster is what happened to the World Trade Center.

- Campus disaster

  Campus disasters include a host of natural and man-made disasters where destruction is total. An example of this type of disaster is tornadoes, which may strike one place and skip another but can render to rubble anything in its path.

- Citywide disaster

  Citywide disasters are campus disasters on a much larger scale. In some cases, the town is the campus (as is the case for larger universities). Examples range from earthquakes, to hurricanes, to atomic bombs.

- Regional disaster

  Regional disasters include massive power outages similar to the blackout in the New England area in 2003 and hurricanes such as Katrina that cover well over 200 miles of coastline.

- National disasters

  For small countries, such as Singapore or Luxembourg, a national disaster is equivalent to a citywide disaster and could equate to a regional disaster. National disasters in larger countries may be unthinkable, but it is not impossible.

- Multinational disaster

  Again, because most countries touch other countries and there are myriad small countries all connected, this must be a consideration for planning. Tsunamis, earthquakes, and other massive natural disasters are occurring around us. Another option is a massive planned terrorist attack on a single multinational company.

- World disaster

  This sort of disaster is unthinkable and way out of scope!

Recovery Methods

Now that the different levels of disasters are defined, a set of tools and skills necessary to recover from each one can be determined. The tools and skills will be specific to ESX and will outline physical, operational, and backup methodologies that will reduce downtime or prevent a disaster:

- Application failure

  The recovery mechanism for a failed application is to have some form of watchdog that will launch the application anew if it was detected to be down. Multiple VMs running the same application connected to a network load balancer will also help in this situation by reducing the traffic to any one VM, and hence the application, and will remove application from the list of possible targets if it is down. Many of these types of clusters also come with ways of restarting applications if they are down. Use of shared data disk clustering à la Microsoft clusters is also a possible solution.

- VM failure

Recovery from a VM failure can be as simple as rebooting the VM in question via some form of watchdog such as VMware HA VM Monitoring or VMware FT. However, if the VM dies, it is often necessary to determine why the problem occurred, and therefore this type of failure often needs debugging. In this case, the setup of VMware FT or some form of shared data disk cluster à la Microsoft clusters will allow a secondary VM to take over the duties of the failed VM. Any VM failure should be investigated to determine the cause. Another mechanism is to have a secondary VM ready and waiting to take over duties if necessary. If the data of the primary VM is necessary to continue, consider placing the data on a second VMDK and have both VMs pointing to the second disk. Just make sure that only one is booted at the same time. Use DRLB tools to automatically launch this secondary VM if necessary.

With VMware FT, this last suggestion may seem unnecessary, but if there is a Guest OS or application failure the shadow VM created by FT may also fail as the primary VM and shadow VM are in vLockStep.

- Machine failure

Hardware often has issues. To alleviate machine failures have a second machine running and ready to take on the load of the first machine. Use VMware HA or other high-availability tools to automatically specify a host on which to launch the VMs if a host fails. In addition, if you know the host will fail due to a software or hardware upgrade, first vMotion all the VMs to the secondary host. VMware HA can be set up when you create a VMware cluster or even after the fact. We discussed the creation of VMware clusters in Chapter 11, "Dynamic Resource Load Balancing." VMware HA makes use of the Legato Automated Availability Management (Legato AAM) suite to manage the ESX host cluster failover. There is more on HA later in this chapter in the section "Business Continuity."

VMware DPM, used in conjunction with VMware HA and VMware DRS, would enable another machine to act as a hot spare. This would of course require one node (usually the +1 node) to be in a rack, installed, kept updated, and otherwise ready to be used as dictated by VMware DRS.

- Communication failure

  Everyone knows that Fibre and network connections fail, so ensure that multiple switches and paths are available for the communications to and from the ESX host. In addition, make local copies of the most important VMs so that they can be launched using a local disk in the case of a SAN failure. This often requires more local disk for the host and the avoidance of booting from SAN.

- Chassis disaster

  To avoid devastating chassis disasters, it is best to divide your most important VMs between multiple chassis but also maintaining enough headroom on all blades within a chassis so that if VMware HA needs to be used, the VMs have a home on a new chassis. In large datacenters, it may be useful to have a hot spare chassis with blades in it waiting to be used via VMware DRS and DPM or one that is ready to accept blades.

- Rack disaster

  To avoid a rack disaster, make sure racks are on earthquake-proof stands, are locked in place, and perhaps have stabilizers deployed. But also be sure that your ESX hosts and switches are divided and placed into separate racks in different locations on the datacenter floor, so that there is no catastrophic failure and that if a rack does fail, everything can be brought back up on the other rack.

- Datacenter disaster

  To avoid datacenter disasters, add more hosts to a secondary datacenter either in the same building or elsewhere on the campus. Often this is referred to as a hot site and requires an investment in new SAN and ESX hosts. Also ensure there are adequate backups to tape secured in a vault. In addition, it is possible with ESX version 3 to vMotion VMs across subnets via routers. In this way, if a datacenter was planned to go down, it would be possible to move running VMs to another datacenter where other hosts reside.

  VMware Site Recovery Manager (SRM) is one tool that can be used to maintain a hot site as could Veeam Backup or Vizioncore vReplicator.

  EMC's VPLEX technology could also be used to maintain consistent writes between two different datacenters no more than 60km away. VPLEX offers the capability to maintain a complete synchronous backup of data on two different and distinct storage subsystems. EMC VPLEX with vTeleport could even move VMs from datacenter to datacenter as needed. Granted, as we discussed in Chapter 5, "Storage with ESX," use of vTeleport (long distance vMotion) requires a stretched Layer-2 network between the datacenters.

- Building disaster

The use of a hot site and offsite tape backups will get around building disasters. Just be sure the hot site is not located in the same building.

EMC VPLEX and vTeleport would also allow for a solid BC by maintaining both datacenters in a synchronous model.

- Campus disaster

Just like a building disaster, just be sure the other location is off the campus.

- Citywide disaster

Similar to campus disasters, just be sure the hot site or backup location is outside the city.

- Regional disaster

Similar to campus disasters, just be sure the hot site or backup location is outside the region.

- National disasters

Similar to campus disasters, just be sure the hot site or backup location is outside the country, or if the countries are small, in another country far away.

- Multinational disasters

Because this could be considered a regional disaster in many cases, see the national DR strategy.

- World disasters

We can dream some here and place a datacenter on another astronomical body or space station.

The major tools to use for DR and BC follow:

- Application Monitoring
- VMware Fault Tolerance or VMware HA VM Monitoring

- VMware HA, DRS, and DPM all working together with the use of hot spare systems or chassis

- VMware SRM, Veeam Backup, PhD Virtual Backup, or Vizioncore vReplicator

- EMC VPLEX with vTeleport

Best Practices

Now that the actions to take for each disaster are outlined, a list of best practices can be developed to define a DR or BC plan to use. The following list considers an ESX host, from a single host to enterprisewide, with DR and BC in mind. The list covers mainly ESX, not all the other parts to creating a successful and highly redundant network. The list is divided between local practices and remote practices. This way the growth of an implementation can be seen. The idea behind these best practices is to look at our list of possible failures and to have a response to each one and to know that many eggs are being placed into one basket. On average for larger machines, ESX hosts can house 20+ VMs. That is a lot of service that could go down if a disaster happens.

First, we need to consider the local practices around DR:

- Implement ESX using N+1 hosts where N is the necessary number of hosts to run the VMs required. The extra host is used for DR.

- When racking the hosts, ensure that hosts are stored in different racks in different parts of the datacenter.

- Be sure there are at least two Fibre Channel (FC) cards, if employing FC SAN, using different PCI buses if possible.

- Be sure there are at least two NIC ports for each network to be attached to the host using different PCI buses if possible.

- When cabling the hosts, ensure that redundant cables go to different switches and that no redundant path uses the same PCI card.

- Be sure that all racks are stabilized.

- Be sure that there is enough cable available so that machines can be fully extended from the rack as necessary.

- Ensure there is enough local disk space to store exported versions of the VMs and to run the most important VMs if necessary.

- Ensure HA is configured so that VMs running on a failed host are automatically started on another host.

- Use storage replication (VPLEX, SRM, and the like) to ensure SANs are redundant, either within the same datacenter or across datacenters.

- Create DRLB scripts to start VMs locally if SAN connectivity is lost.

- Create DRLB scripts or enable VMware DRS to move VMs when all resources loads are too high on a single host.

Second, we need to consider the remote practices around DR:

- When creating DR backups, ensure there is safe storage for tapes onsite and offsite.

- Follow all the local items, listed previously, at any remote sites.

- Create a list of tasks necessary to be completed if there is a massive site failure. This list should include who does what and the necessary dependencies for each task.

The suggestions translate into more physical hardware to create a redundant and safe installation of ESX. It also translates into more software and licenses, too. Before going down the path of hot sites and offsite tape storage, the local DR plan needs to be fully understood from a software perspective, specifically the methods for producing backups, and there are plenty of methods. Some methods adversely impact performance; others do not. Some methods and security controls lend themselves to expansion to hot sites, and others will take sneaker nets and other mechanisms to get the data from one site to the other.

Backup and Business Continuity

The simplest approach to DR is to make a good backup of everything so that restoration is simplified when the time comes, but backups can happen in two distinctly different ways with ESX. In some cases, some of these suggestions do not make sense because the application in use can govern how things go. As an example, we were asked to look at DR backup for an application with its own built-in DR capabilities with a DR plan that the machine be reinstalled on new hardware if an issue occurred. The time to redeploy in their current environment was approximately an hour, and it took the same amount of time for a full DR backup through ESX. Because of this, the customer decided not to go with full DR backups.

Backup

What is a full DR backup? As stated previously, there are two major backup styles. The first, in terms of ESX, is referred to as a backup for individual file restoration or a backup made from within the VM. The second is a DR-level backup of the full VM disk image and configuration file. The difference is the restoration method. A standard backup, using agents running within the VM, usually follows these steps for restoration:

1. Install OS onto machine.

2. Install restoration tools.

3. Test restoration tools.

4. Restore system.

5. Test restoration.

A full DR-level backup has the following restoration process:

1. Restore VMDK and configuration file.

2. Register VM into ESX.

3. Boot VM.

As you can see, the restoration process for a full DR backup is much faster than the normal method, which in many cases makes a DR backup more acceptable, but it generally requires more hardware. But what hardware is really the question, and one that needs to be considered for ESX. A standard ESX standalone ESX host consists of lots of memory and as much disk as can be placed into the server. A standard remote datastore–attached ESX host consists of lots of memory and very little local disk space, and a boot from SAN (BFS) ESX host usually has no local disk space, which is not a best practice, as outlined in Chapter 3, "Installation." Our best practice for installing ESX outlines a need for local storage on which safe backups and ready-to-use backups could be placed.

There are few ways to create backups, and the methods are similar no matter where the data will eventually reside. DR backups can be made many ways using an equally different number of tools: VMware Data Recovery (VDR), VMware Consolidated Backup (VCB), and one of the other third-party tools. The goal is to eventually place the data on a tape device, local storage, remote storage, or a remote hot site for restoration of full VMDKs, bringing up VMs at a hot site or even file level restore. File restore backups can be made using VDR, VCB, and other third-party backup agents.

Backup Paths
The choice of which tool to use depends entirely on the backup patch you choose to use. Some paths, as we shall see, are product specific whereas others span multiple products.

Path 1
Path 1, featured in Figure 12.1, represents a common backup approach for all versions of ESX but not ESXi. This approach still provides a level of redundancy that protects a system from catastrophic SAN or NAS failures. This is a full DR-level backup:

- VMs are exported from the remote VMFS to the backup storage location, which can be anything the ESX host Service Console can see: CIFS, NFS, FTP, SCP, and so on. If the backup storage location is on another network use of a secure copy mechanism is recommended.

- The most important VMs are copied to a local VMFS (usually the tool in use would first copy from the remote VMFS to the local VMFS and then out to the backup storage).

- A remote backup server can then send the data to tape storage or anywhere else within the public or private cloud.

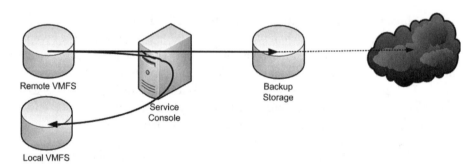

Remote VMFS

Local VMFS

Service Console

Backup Storage

Figure 12.1 *Path 1*

Path 2
Path 2, featured in Figure 12.2, represents the Path 1 approach for all versions of VMware ESXi. This approach like Path 1 provides a level of redundancy that protects a system from catastrophic SAN or NAS failures.

- VMs are exported from the remote VMFS to the backup storage location, using the `vifs --get` command.

- VMs can then be imported to a local VMFS from the backup storage location using the `vifs --put` command.

- A remote backup server can then send the data to tape storage or anywhere else within the public or private cloud.

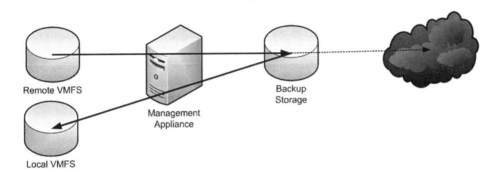

Figure 12.2 *Path 2*

Path 3

Path 3, featured in Figure 12.3, represents the use of the vStorage API either a VCB or VDR proxy server. VCB installs on Windows 2003 or 2008. When using VCB, this can also be a full file level backup if the file system of the Guest OS is understood by the Windows 2003 or 2008 proxy server, which can also be a VM. With VDR, which is already a VM, the same holds true:

- The remote storage datastores are mounted onto the proxy server either directly from the SAN or NAS device or via a network link (dashed line in Figure 12.3), which implies the backup travels through the service console or management appliance.

- When the VMDK is exported or the per-file backup is finished, the proxy server unmounts the VMDKs of the VM.

- The data is then sent to tape or a tape server or anywhere else within the public or private cloud from the proxy server.

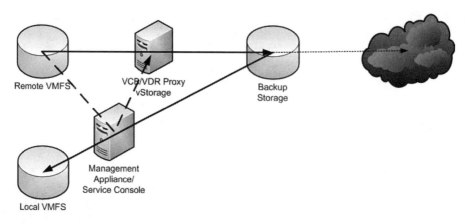

Figure 12.3 *Path 3*

Path 4

Path 4, featured in Figure 12.4, is a LUN-to-LUN mirror handled entirely within the storage components of the virtual environment. LUN-to-LUN mirrors often require increased license levels for the storage components as well as at least the same family of storage products. In many cases, the storage components need to be identical make and models. Standard LUN-to-LUN mirrors are crash consistent copies of the LUN and the VMs residing upon the LUN. Because of this, VMware introduced VMware Site Recovery Manager (SRM), which aids the LUN-to-LUN mirroring technology by providing a control path through vCenter to inform the VMs (via VMware Tools) to quiesce their disks and create snapshots, to allow the LUN to LUN mirroring to create effective backups.

- The remote storage NAS or SAN device sends the data to a secondary LUN either on the same array or a different array.

- The backup storage device can then be sent to a tape device or library or anywhere else within the public or private cloud.

Here is an alternative using SRM:

- A LUN-to-LUN request is made within the storage fabric. The storage fabric communicates with SRM.

- SRM communicate with vCenter to get a list of VMs on the LUN to be mirrored.

- SRM communicates with vCenter to have it inform the VMs on the LUN to quiesce their disks and create snapshots (hopefully on separate LUNs).

- SRM informs the array to perform the LUN-to-LUN mirror. SRM then informs vCenter after the mirror is complete to commit the snapshots to the VMs.

- The backup storage device can then be sent to a tape device or library or anywhere else within the public or private cloud.

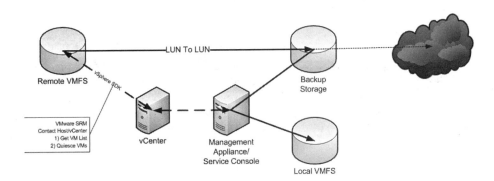

Figure 12.4 *Path 4*

Additional Hot Site Backup Paths

Figure 12.4 also demonstrates one method to create a hot site from the original ESX environment. A hot site is limited in distance by the technology used to copy data from one location to another. There are three methods to copy data from site to site: via Fibre, via network, and via sneaker. In addition to the four existing paths, we can now add the paths covered in this section. In addition to the LUN-to-LUN mirror or copy, we can add the following paths.

Path 5

Path 5, featured in Figure 12.5, represents the use of EMC VPLEX to maintain synchronous storage cache between two distinct datacenters (or storage arrays) no more than 100 miles (60 km) apart. In essence, writes on one VPLEX are transmitted to the VPLEX paired with it. The distance apart will depend entirely on the network latency between the two VPLEX devices: more latency may imply shorter distances.

The storage that sits behind a VPLEX does not need to be alike storage; they could be different makes and models, unlike LUN mirroring. Because of this, it is theoretically possible to put a VPLEX behind a VPLEX and either chain

VPLEX pairs from one end of a country to another or to create trees where pairs of VPLEX devices go off in all sorts of directions. Each pair of VPLEX devices, in these cases, would maintain a synchronous cache across no more than one pair.

Tying VPLEX to vTeleport and a stretch Layer-2 network and you have a mechanism to quickly move all VMs from one datacenter to another datacenter with zero downtime. This provides an unparalleled level of disaster avoidance and backup capability.

Any of the existing backup paths could then be used within each datacenter for a redundant backup.

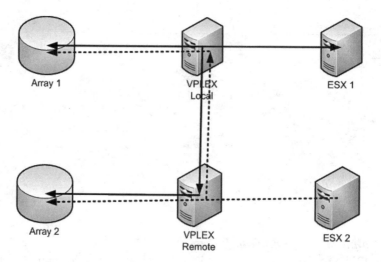

Figure 12.5 *Path 5*

Path 6

Path 6, featured in Figure 12.6, provides for an external mechanism to replicate data from one site to another or between disparate storage makes and models.

- A backup/replication proxy device copies the LUN from one array to another.

- The data is also replicated to a local VMFS.

- The data is also replicated to backup storage.

- The backup storage device can then be sent to a tape device or library or anywhere else within the public or private cloud.

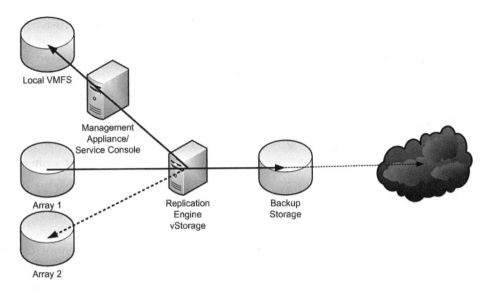

Figure 12.6 *Path 6*

Summary of Backup

No matter how the data gets from the primary site to the hot site, the key is to get it there quickly, safely, and in a state that will run a VM. If all these paths fail, however, remember your tapes sitting offsite in a vault and the combination to get access to them quickly. Above all, always test your backups and paths whether local or using a hot site. Always remember, backup and DR go hand in hand.

Testing your backups is a very important aspect of any DR plan. These tests could just be to see whether the tapes restore properly or could be as lavish as starting up the VMs and verifying your applications are running properly. Veeam SureBackup does the latter for you for certain applications. It provides a mechanism to automate backup restoration testing. It is also very important to periodically test that your hot site or remote datacenter can run all the VMs migrated to it.

Best Practice

Test your backups and hot sites frequently.

Business Continuity

BC with ESX can be accomplished in several fashions. Just like backups, BC has multiple paths that it can take. Some of these paths are automated, whereas others require human intervention. One of the ideas behind BC is to provide a way for the business to continue uninterrupted and the VMware cluster technology provides a part of this by the implementation of VMware DRS, VMware FT, and VMware HA. Where DR-level backups are generally geared toward the re-creation of the environment, BC is the application of clustering technology to prevent the need for such time-consuming restoration. This is achieved using VMware HA, DRS, FT, and vTeleport using stretch Layer-2 networks and EMC VPLEX but also through the use of preconfigured hot sites that can come online in a fraction of the full restoration time. These concepts are discussed within Chapter 11.

Our methods discussed at the beginning of this chapter implement hot sites by using replication and synchronous storage cache. However, hot servers or servers in the datacenter that do not do anything until they are needed are other options, which are ready to power on using VMware DPM. VMware DRS with DPM covers this latter case. VMware HA is a high-availability-based solution that will, when an ESX host crashes, boot the VMs running there onto other ESX hosts either randomly (according to VMware DRS rules) or by using defined placement and boot order rules. VMware FT allows a shadow VM to be running alongside the parent VM. If the parent VM fails or the host on which it lives fails, the shadow VM takes over. These technologies cover the needs of BC.

Outside of VMware DRS, HA, and FT a myriad of other BC options are available. These include having as many redundant components as possible in different places within the datacenter, building, or campus, and there are multiple paths to all these devices from the ESX hosts. This leads to a much higher cost in and availability of hardware, but it will be the difference between a short service interruption and an absolute disaster. Consider the case of an ESX host crashing with smoke pouring out of a vent. If you had invested in VMware HA, the software would automatically boot the VMs on another system while VMware DRS would load balance the VMs if there is CPU or memory contention. If DPM is available a hot-spare host could take over some the load without the need for human intervention. Or if the VMs were limited sufficiently to use VMware FT, the shadow VMs would automatically take over without the delay of rebooting. On the other hand if you purchased a HP C-class blade in a RAID blade configuration the ESX host would fail over using a complete hardware solution. This leads to the question of which is better: hardware or software solutions? And the answer is, as always, it depends on the cost benefit. This same HP C-class blade has one limitation, the designated RAID blade must be in the same chassis of the failing node, and they must both share disks on a disk blade. This limits the amount of processing power to the blade chassis; and what happens if the chassis itself fails?

Many sites keep identical preinstalled hardware locked in a closet to solve some of these problems. However, it is your disaster to recover from, so think of all the solutions and draft the plan for both DR and BC appropriate for your environment. Any plan should include all aspects of BC, including

- How long it takes for a hot site to boot

- What steps to take to bring up a hot site

- The steps to take if a natural disaster is heading in your direction (such as a hurricane)

In essence, you need a run-book that covers all contingency plans with respect to DR and BC.

The Tools

Now that the theory is explained, what tools are available for performing the tasks? Although each family of enterprise class remote storage has its own names for the capability to make LUN-to-LUN copies, refer to the VMware SAN compatibility documentation to determine what is and is not supported, because it might turn out that the hot-copy mechanism for your SAN is not supported by any version of ESX. If VMware SRM is supported with your storage device, this is the recommended way to go.

> ### Best Practice
> When choosing to use LUN-to-LUN copies, ensure that your SAN or NAS is supported by SRM.

Beyond the remote storage-to-remote storage copies, many other tools are available from VMware and various vendors. All these tools must first take a snapshot of a VM, which changes the file to which disk writes occur so that the backup software can make a copy of the parent VMDK. Figure 12.7 shows the process by which a snapshot is used to make a backup:

1. At this stage, the VM is running normally, writing to the proper VMDK.

2. A snapshot has been requested, the VMDK is quiesced, and the snapshot is created. The existing write traffic to the VMDK is redirected to the snapshot, which records only changed blocks from the VMDK. Read actions read through the snapshot to the VMDK as needed (the dotted line).

3. The backup of the VMDK is taken while all new or changed data is written to the snapshot.

4. The original read/write path to the VMDK is once more established and the changes stored within the snapshot are committed to the VMDK, and the snapshot is once more deleted.

5. We are back with a normally running VM.

A snapshot contains only the changed blocks from the primary VMDK, so a snapshot can never grow larger than the parent VMDK. As such it maintains a list or map of changed blocks. Change Block Tracking (CBT) makes use of this map to determine exactly what blocks have changed from the parent VMDK. CBT is available via the vStorage API. CBT is also used within backup tools when creating incremental backups to reduce the overall transfer of data. It is far more efficient to use the existing CBT map than to try and create a list of blocks that changed during the backup procedure. Some of the backup tools go one step further and use Active Block Management (ABM) that combines CBT with the capability to inquire of the actual filesystem what blocks represent deleted data or whitespace so that the list of blocks to back up is further reduced. Even within the CBT capability, ABM will make a huge difference in backup times by removing those blocks of data that do not require backups.

When the backup is made of the VMDK or Virtual RDM in step 3, the disk is usually hot-added to a backup appliance so that the backup appliance (which runs as a VM in many cases) can bypass any network mechanism to access the virtual disk's data. This increases overall performance. However, backups are disk intensive and if your storage device already has issues, adding a backup device to it would not be a good idea. This is where specialized scripts that can use Storage vMotion to move a VMDK to a lesser-used LUN would come in handy. Unfortunately, Storage DRS has been demoed, but has not been made available.

Another useful tool in the backup/replication toolbox is the use of deduplication. Deduplication is used on SAN and NAS arrays to combine blocks of disk that are identical into a single block with a reference to that block within the chain of blocks associated with a file. Deduplication within a backup/replication tool is designed to limit not only what gets written to disk but what is transferred over the network links in use.

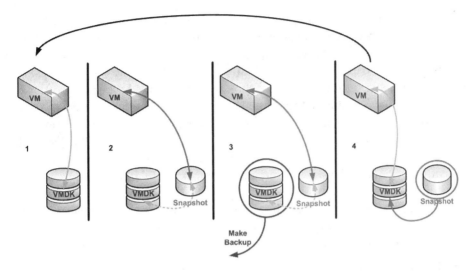

Figure 12.7 *Snapshot processing*

Each SCSI disk associated with a VMDK should be backed up separately to reduce the overall time spent with a snapshot in use. Now, because we discussed snapshots in Chapter 8, "Configuring ESX from a Host Connection," it is possible to have a tree of snapshots for every VM. In this case, most tools will not work, including VCB and VDR products. They require all snapshots to be deleted (committed) first. These situations may require a specialized backup script to be used. The VDR and VCB tools will not back up templates, and those also require a specialized backup script.

Before the snapshot is created, if the disk was not quiesced, a crash-consistent backup is created, which implies that a boot of a restored VMDK will boot as if the VM had crashed. Quiescing disks becomes paramount, because it ensures that all changes to the VMDK have been made before a backup is taken. Nearly all forms of VMDKs can be queiesced if the Guest OS that writes to those disks can support some form of queisce functionality. In Windows this functionality is VSS, whereas in Linux it could just be judicious use of the sync command. Non-SRM enabled LUN-to-LUN or remote storage-to-remote storage copies also produce crash-consistent backups, which is why VMware SRM should be used if at all possible.

A backup should not be restored to anything other than a VMFS because the default VMDK formats are sparse files or monolithic files that have a beginning marker, some data, and an end marker and not much else. Restoration of such files to non-VMFS can result in loss of data. However, if the VM is first exported, resides on an NFS datastore, or is in 2Gb sparse disk format, it can be restored to any file system and imported back into ESX with no possibility of data loss. With SAN or NAS connections, it is not even necessary for the host that creates the VM snapshot to be the host that actually does the backup. This generally requires extra scripting, but it is possible for a host that is running the VM to create the VM snapshot and then signal a backup host that the backup can be made. When the backup is completed, another signal is made to the running host to commit the snapshot. In this way, the backup host offloads the work from the running ESX host. The signals could even be reversed so that the backup host does all the work and calls the running host only as necessary.

Modern virtual disk backup tools from Veeam, Vizioncore, PHD Virtual, and VMware have removed the need for "by hand" scripting from the requirements since ESX v3 days. However, many companies still have backup scripts in use that tie into these other products to drop the backed-up data to tape. Tapes can be accessed from VMs, which would pin the VM to a given host, making BC difficult to achieve for the pinned VM.

Local Tape Devices

Local tape devices and libraries require two things: a specific Adaptec SCSI HBA and software to control the robot or tape, ansd a VM to which to connect the tape via SCSI pass-thru mode. When there is a problem with the local tape or tape library device, the ESX host often has to be rebooted, and although it is possible to remove and reload the appropriate kernel module, some devices are not fully reconfigured unless they are seen at boot time. Using tape devices and libraries attached to remote archive servers is the recommended choice if possible.

> ### Best Practices for Local Tape Devices
>
> Do not use local tape devices; if it becomes absolutely necessary, be sure to understand the impact on the local ESX host and plan VM deployments accordingly.

VMware Data Recovery

VMware Data Recovery is a follow on to VMware Consolidated Backup. Unlike VCB, VDR does not require a Windows host or VM on which to run. It is a self-contained virtual appliance with a Data Recovery Client plug-in to the vSphere Client to aid in management and use of VDR. VDR is actually Linux based, which simplifies licensing concerns. The VDR appliance ships as an ISO image as of v1.2 that contains both the OVF formatted appliance and the Data Recovery Client Plug-in. Import of the OVF is as described in Chapter 10,

"Virtual Machines." The Data Recovery Client plug-in installs like any other Windows application and should be installed on the server on which you are running the vSphere Client that must be a windows machine.

There is, however, a Restoration module that will run on Linux or Windows for your use, so be sure to install this tool as well where appropriate.

VDR has a few limits:

- Will back up only if the appropriate ESX license level is in use.

- Maximum of eight VMs can be backed up at the same time.

- Each appliance can back up only 100 VMs. If more than 100 VMs are specified, those over 100 will be omitted.

The limitations are fairly minor as the license levels currently supported are Essentials, Essentials Plus, Advanced, Enterprise, and Enterprise Plus, which just leaves out Standard. In addition, you can run more than one VDR appliance to handle the extra number of VMs. However, VDR protects folders of VMs, and as such if you have two appliances protecting the same folder there is a good chance that each VDR will back up the same VM and some would still be missed, as the VDR appliances do not communicate with each other. Therefore, if you do need to protect more than 100 VMs in a single folder, subdivide the folder into folders with 100 VMs each and then protect the subfolders with individual VDR appliances.

VDR not only backs up the VMs, it will deduplicate the backup before storing it to a backup storage device. A backup storage device must be seen by the VDR appliance and can be implemented either via a network share, such as NFS or CIFS, or as a block-level device mounted via Raw Disk Map or VMDK. When planning your backup usage of VDR, you must realize that this is a VM and can see only the backup storage devices presented to it, not all the datastores on the host. The best solution is to use a RDM or network device and not to use a VMDK. How these devices are added to the VDR appliance is also critical; because of the way VDR performs hot-add of virtual disks it is required that any RDMs added to the appliance be added as the zeroeth device of a SCSI controller. In Figure 12.8, we add a 500GB RDM to the VDR appliance and select the next available zeroeth (:0) device. This device can be used for data deduplication.

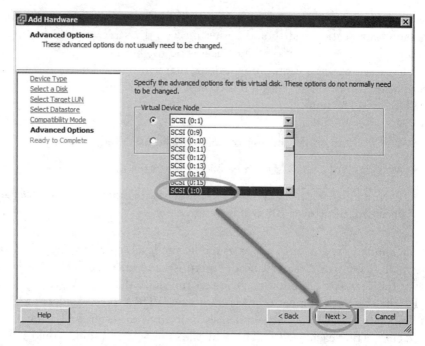

Figure 12.8 *Adding a zeroeth SCSI device*

However, if you want your backups to be seen by a tape, replication, or other backup server, you will want to use some form of network-based backup storage. Unfortunately, even though the underlying layer is Linux, NFS-based storage cannot be directly presented to VDR; instead, you can present only a VMDK that lives on an NFS datastore within the ESX host. That means to get data to another VM connected to a remote tape server would require more capability.

From a security perspective, you never want your backup tools to directly access your vCenter or ESX hosts as the root or administrative user. Instead, create a Backup Agent user (any username you desire) with the appropriate roles and permissions. Minimally, this user will require the following roles and permissions on each VM to be backed up:

- VirtualMachine, Configuration, Disk change tracking

- VirtualMachine, Provisioning, Allow read-only disk access

- VirtualMachine, Provisioning, Allow VM download

- VirtualMachine, State, Create snapshot

- VirtualMachine, State, Remove snapshot

Whereas on the VDR appliance, the following roles are required:

- Datastore, Allocate space

- VirtualMachine, Configuration, Add new disk

- VirtualMachine, Configuration, Change resource

- VirtualMachine, Configuration, Remove disk

- VirtualMachine, Configuration, Settings

Finally, the user needs read access to the Global License role so that it can check to see whether you are allowed to use VDR properly. In addition, these same privileges are generally needed by all backup tools.

> ### Best Practice
> When using VDR, ensure your protected folders contain, at most, 100 VMs.
>
> Use a Backup Agent user instead of Administrator when accessing vCenter.
>
> Use the next zeroeth (:0) SCSI device for all backup storage media added to the VDR appliance.
>
> Use CIFS storage to allow backups to be seen by tape servers.

VDR is configured via the vSphere Client after the Data Recovery Client is installed and made available. To access the client after it is installed, go to the Homes, Solutions and Applications, VMware Data Recovery. The process to create a backup is as follows:

1. Connect vCenter to VDR.

2. Add a destination file share or disk to the appliance.

3. Create a backup job.

4. Schedule/run the backup job.

After the job is run, the backup could be copied to a tape server restored to a hot site or local VMFS in keeping with our backup paths discussed previously.

Third-Party Tools

There are three major third-party tools for creating full disk backups and performing replication. Each of these works similarly to the VMware counterparts. To distinguish themselves they incorporate different approaches and functions. Veeam, Vizioncore, and PhD Virtual are the three main tools in this space with Symantec and HP Data Protector close seconds. For those with large legacy backup systems, Pancetera provides a tool to bridge the gap to the virtual environment.

Conclusion

It is imperative when using ESX that you create a DR and BC plan that results in successful backups and hot sites. The goal of this chapter was to present what is available to the users of ESX and the advanced capabilities of VMware clusters in terms of BC. Just be sure that a good DR and BC plan exists that covers all the possible disasters and that the plan is implemented and tested as often as necessary. Testing of backups and hot sites should be done as often as defined by your DR and BC policy.

Epilogue

The Future of the Virtual Environment

Closing a book of this type is nearly impossible because the nature of virtualization is changing daily—and sometimes hourly. This makes tracking the future of virtualization difficult at best. More and more of the peripheral functions of the hypervisor are moving into hardware:

> Intel-VT/AMD RVI both push many of the long and repetitive virtualization instruction streams down into the hardware so that only one instruction needs be called from the hypervisor to implement hundreds of repetitive instructions in the areas of VM to VM context switching, and for other similar tasks such as zeroing memory.

> VMware AAI will do the same thing for the storage subsystem by reducing the number of storage calls to make for repetitive storage-related items, such as zeroing blocks of storage.

> Cisco Palo Adapters and HP Virtual Connect seem to be moving the virtual network into hardware as well by providing, in effect, adapters that on one side have a set number of physical ports but on the other side can have hundreds of virtual NIC ports (physical virtual NIC or pvNIC ports). This capability with VMDirectPath and other "hypervisor" bypass technologies could enable a VM to go directly to the pvNIC ports and would also increase network performance. To get to this point we are still waiting for Multi-Root IO Virtualization.

> TPM/TXT pushes some aspects of security policies into the hardware.

EMC VPLEX, and its follow-on technologies, expand the datacenter from one location to many, removing the need for complex, difficult to manage site replication tools, as well as the need for long distance storage of vMotions, because the data resides at two locations at the same time. If we move this forward to asynchronous behavior, an entire datacenter could be stretched across the globe. This implies the networks within one data center will stretch to others as well. Cisco OTV and other tools are designed to solve the networking problem.

In the past, the issue has always been the number of resources we can bring to the host to consolidate our servers as virtual machines. With ESX v2.x, the issue was mostly an issue of CPU capability. The solution was multicore CPUs, and in the future expect many, many more cores per socket. Memory became a problem as VM load increased, but this is solved by dense memory and systems that can hold a TB or more. Networking and bandwidth issues cropped up, and 10G as well as VMDirectPath are the solutions. Storage has always been an issue, but VAAI is designed to combat this, and stretched storage networks will help as well.

Resources are no longer an issue. You can virtualize nearly every server in your datacenter, including those with specialized PCI cards via VMDirectPath PassThru. The amount of resources we can apply to any one virtualization problem will continue to grow, so if resources are not the future, what is?

We will start to see more and more automation products so that we can finally achieve full Dynamic Resource Load Balancing as well as self-healing capabilities that remove the administrator from the day-to-day tedium of managing a wide-ranging virtual infrastructure. The management tools will allow companies to, in effect, sell IT as a self-service.

VMware and third parties are rolling out new management products. Even other hypervisor vendors are creating management tools that work with VMware products. Management products are growing to fill the gap in areas of CMDB and security that were easy to handle within the physical environment but difficult until now in the virtual environment. In essence, virtualization is mainstream; companies are creating products to fit the needs of the business.

Secure Multi-Tenancy is being discussed, and now that memory compression exists, I expect memory encryption to occur. The biggest threat with Secure Multi-Tenancy is the ability of administrators to see, manipulate, and retrieve data they have no rights to and no need to see. With memory encryption, encryption within the VM is now safe, and this is the only way to protect your data from administrators. Secure Multi-Tenancy is all about protecting the data.

Virtualization has been driving technology over the last decade, and this will not change into the next decade. Although it may not be about resources, it will be about utilization and increased capacity, as well as how to manage and provide even more efficiencies that make the IT administrator's life easier.

Go Forward!

If there is anything to take from this book, take away the following: With planning and understanding of all the different subsystems that affect virtualization, it is easy to be successful with virtualization within the datacenter. Plan ahead, run the appropriate tests, and go forward and virtualize!

References

Benvenuti, Christian. *Understanding LINUX Network Internals*. Sebastopol, CA.: O'Reilly Media, Inc., 2006.

Boche.net: www.boche.net.

Bovet, David, and Marco Cesati. *Understanding the LINUX Kernel*. Sebastopol, CA: O'Reilly Media, 2001.

Eric Sloof's Blog: www.ntpro.nl/blog

Kroah-Hartman, Greg. *Linux Kernel in a Nutshell*. Sebastopol, CA: O'Reilly Media, 2007.

Massed VMware links: www.vSphere-land.com.

Preston, W. Curtis. *UNIX Backup and Recovery*. Sebastopol, CA: O'Reilly Media, 2007.

Processor information: www.sandpile.org.

Purdy, Gregor N. *Linux iptables Pocket Reference*. Sebastopol, CA: O'Reilly Media, 2004.

Siever, Ellen et al. *LINUX in a Nutshell, 5th Edition*. Sebastopol, CA.: O'Reilly Media, 2005.

The Virtualization Practice: www.virtualizationpractice.com/blog/.

VMware community forums: communities.vmware.com/index.jspa.

VMware Documentation: www.vmware.com/support/pubs/ and www.vmware.com/support/pubs/vs_pages/vsp_pubs_esx41_vc41.html.

VMware Virtual Infrastructure HCL: www.vmware.com/resources/compatibility/search.php.

Index

Symbols and Numbers

%post section option (kickstart file), 120-121
%vmlicense_text section option (kick-start file), 120
1U server systems, 20-21
2U server systems, 21-22
10Gb Ethernet, 16
802.1Q VLANs, 215

A

accepteula option (kickstart file), 120
access control lists (ACLs), 356
Active Directory, 276
administrative users, 270-280
advanced settings
  best practices, 380
  ConflictRetries setting, 380
aic... module
  ESX v3.0, 42
  ESX v3.5, 42
aic79xx module
  ESX v3.5, 41
  ESX v4, 41
aic7xxx module
  ESX 2.5.x, 41
  ESX v3.0, 41
  ESX v3.5, 41
Akorri Balancepoint, 137, 507
Alan Renouf's Web site, 293, 378
alarms, 495-504
Altor Networks via Juniper, 137
Application (APP), 39
application failure
  defined, 515
  recovery methods, 517-518
application monitoring, 116, 137, 520
arbitrated loop topology, 152-153

architecture
  ESX, 38-39
  ESXi, 38-39
  VMware vSphere™ environment, 1
Assured Computing Environment, 2.4
ata_piix module
  ESX v3.0, 41
  ESX v3.5, 41
  ESX v4, 41
auditing
  auditing recipes, 124-134
  common auditing conclusions, 128
  compliance regulations, 124
  ESX system, 138-141
  forensic analysis, 141-142
  search tools, 127-128
auth or authconfig option (kickstart file), 120
authentication, 125-126
authorization, 125-126
auto tiering, 155
automated dashboard search queries, 127-128
automating installation, 118-121
availability constructs, 60
average bandwidth, 220

B

backup network, 246
backups
  break-ins, 141-142
  business continuity (BC), 522-531
  functional comparison, 65-66
  local tape devices, 534
  LUN Mirroring, 66
  Path 1, 524
  Path 2, 524
  Path 3, 525
  Path 4, 526
  Path 5, 527
  Path 6, 528

PRENTICE HALL

REGISTER

THIS PRODUCT

informit.com/register

Register the Addison-Wesley, Exam Cram, Prentice Hall, Que, and Sams products you own to unlock great benefits.

To begin the registration process, simply go to **informit.com/register** to sign in or create an account. You will then be prompted to enter the 10- or 13-digit ISBN that appears on the back cover of your product.

Registering your products can unlock the following benefits:

- Access to supplemental content, including bonus chapters, source code, or project files.
- A coupon to be used on your next purchase.

Registration benefits vary by product. Benefits will be listed on your Account page under Registered Products.

About InformIT — THE TRUSTED TECHNOLOGY LEARNING SOURCE

INFORMIT IS HOME TO THE LEADING TECHNOLOGY PUBLISHING IMPRINTS Addison-Wesley Professional, Cisco Press, Exam Cram, IBM Press, Prentice Hall Professional, Que, and Sams. Here you will gain access to quality and trusted content and resources from the authors, creators, innovators, and leaders of technology. Whether you're looking for a book on a new technology, a helpful article, timely newsletters, or access to the Safari Books Online digital library, InformIT has a solution for you.

THE TRUSTED TECHNOLOGY LEARNING SOURCE

Addison-Wesley | Cisco Press | Exam Cram
IBM Press | Que | Prentice Hall | Sams

SAFARI BOOKS ONLINE

FREE Online Edition

Your purchase of **VMware ESX and ESXi in the Enterprise** includes access to a free online edition for 45 days through the Safari Books Online subscription service. Nearly every Prentice Hall book is available online through Safari Books Online, along with more than 5,000 other technical books and videos from publishers such as Addison-Wesley Professional, Cisco Press, Exam Cram, IBM Press, O'Reilly, Que, and Sams.

SAFARI BOOKS ONLINE allows you to search for a specific answer, cut and paste code, download chapters, and stay current with emerging technologies.

Activate your FREE Online Edition at www.informit.com/safarifree

> **STEP 1:** Enter the coupon code: ELPHQVH.

> **STEP 2:** New Safari users, complete the brief registration form.
> Safari subscribers, just log in.

If you have difficulty registering on Safari or accessing the online edition, please e-mail customer-service@safaribooksonline.com